MUSIC GROOVES

MUSIC GROOVES

Charles Keil

&

Steven Feld

THE UNIVERSITY OF CHICAGO PRESS
CHICAGO AND LONDON

THE UNIVERSITY OF CHICAGO PRESS, CHICAGO 60637
THE UNIVERSITY OF CHICAGO PRESS, LTD., LONDON
© 1994 by The University of Chicago
All rights reserved. Published 1994
Printed in the United States of America
03   02   01   00   99   98   97   2   3   4   5

ISBN: 0-226-42956-3 (cloth)
        0-226-42957-1 (paper)

Library of Congress Cataloging-in-Publication Data

Keil, Charles.
   Music grooves : essays and dialogues / Charles Keil & Steven
Feld.
        p.   cm.
   Includes bibliographical references (p.   ) and index.
   1. Ethnomusicology.   2. Music—Philosophy and aesthetics.
3. Music and society.   4. Music and anthropology.   5. Popular
culture.   I. Feld, Steven.
   ML60.K26   1994
   780′.89—dc20   94–8226
                                                          CIP
                                                          MN

⊗The paper used in this publication meets the minimum
requirements of the American National Standard for Information
Sciences—Permanence of Paper for Printed Library Materials,
ANSI Z39.48-1984.

Contents

Preface

Music Grooves is an adventure in scholarly and personal dialogue. Starting with ways our essays of the last ten or so years speak to each other, we've crafted the book to link two thematic preoccupations that we take to be central to the study of music, one concerning the experience of musical participation, another concerning the experience of musical mediation. The essays are thus divided into two sections, and for each of these we've juxtaposed the pieces chronologically so that their dialogic qualities and potentials might emerge and reframe their individual and historical specificity.

To more personally and vocally unite the essay materials, we spent a week in June 1991 doing what we like to do best, gabbing about music and playing and listening to it together. We structured some of the conversation by interviewing each other about our essays. These dialogues were tape recorded, then edited to give broader context for the two thematic sections and to re-create older linkages while exploring new ones. To encourage our readers to explore these issues further, we have added detailed comments to each.

The introductory dialogue, "Getting into the Dialogic Groove," introduces the whole project and locates our concerns and hopes for the book in our own interrelated personal and professional biographies. Each of the other dialogues, "Grooving on Participation" and "Commodified Grooves," follows the essay section on which it comments. These dialogues reopen themes from the essays that precede them, reinvigorating those more polished prose pronouncements with some of the rambling, ambivalence, digression, disagreement, and puzzlement that animated and followed their original publication. We find ourselves talking through differences and acknowledging the pleasure of just sounding out ideas with someone who shares similar quests and struggles.

Rewrapping the emergent, dialogic quality of the essays with the essaistic quality of the dialogues is meant to signal our desire for a more reflexive discourse on music and society, as well as for more experimentally crafted forms of inscribing it. We hope you'll connect with our main concern—participatory practice—by getting into the dialogic groove and joining our ongoing conversations.

While we took off for a year to work on other projects in Greece, Australia, and Papua New Guinea, friends kept the idea and practical realities of the book in motion. The encouragement of T. David Brent and Rob Walser, and the technical skills of Tom Porcello and Frances Terry have been much appreciated. Many heads are not just better than two but have filled us up with everything we are talking about. To the family, friends, neighbors, colleagues, students, musician pals, and people in the communities that have so graciously hosted us over the years, we hope you will get a kick out of hearing your thoughts and feelings reverberating through these pages. All knowledge is acknowledge. And to Angeliki Keil and Alison Leitch, the next dance, please.

GETTING INTO
THE DIALOGIC GROOVE

SF: Let's start with what we're creating here . . . a book of juxtaposed essays and dialogues, pieces that are layered, blended, reacting, interacting, an interplay of ideas, agendas, and arguments that emerged for us over the last ten years or so, springboards for more dialogues, like the ones readers can have with this . . .

CK: And it's roughly in the sequence in which they were written, a historical sequence, and an intellectual one as well but one that can be read in many ways, in various orders . . .

SF: . . . a representation in one concrete way of lots of other dialogues that we were having verbally, informally, vaguely, emergently . . . ideas flowing out of discussions about how to study music . . .

CK: . . . and how to merge those studies with more participation, with more musical practices and meanings in our own lives . . . but in little bits and pieces, that's what's so amazing about it, that we would get on the phone, and one little spark . . .

SF: . . . tunes sent back and forth, postcards from China or New Guinea, wherever we were doing fieldwork, fragments of articles, whatever, a little germ of a thing . . . an overlapping of intellectual biographies that lead to the decision to do a dialogic book rather than separate collections of our essays . . .

CK: . . . and it's so much better to do it this way, because this is the way it keeps evolving . . .

SF: . . . out of conversations, particularly ones focused on the connections between musical participation and mediation, world musics and popular musics, scholarly perspectives and critical perspectives . . .

CK: For me, and I think for you too, so much of this scholarly and musical dialogue is rooted in similar biography, one that begins in a white-black dialogue, growing up white in a world of black music . . .

SF: . . . white male bonding through black music, listening to those tunes, learning to play them, escaping the suburbs in a room with a record player, trying to play along with John Coltrane or hang with friends . . .

Charlie's drumming debut, age 8

CK: The accent on male bonding is really important; it happened for me right around eleven, twelve, thirteen; I'd been hearing my mother's Fats Waller, Duke Ellington, and Woody Herman records as a kid, their music coming out of the box. And then all of a sudden around twelve or thirteen I could get together with other people and make this music.

SF: Were there other guys at your age who were . . .

CK: Oh yeah, Pat Williams, my basic buddy, who's now a Hollywood movie composer, does themes for TV shows and so forth.

Steve with his first record player, age 3

SF: You guys were playing music together?

CK: Yeah, in sixth grade we played "The World Is Waiting for the Sunrise" and "Harbor Lights," a trumpet and drums duet for the sixth-grade graduation ceremony. I took some four-bar breaks on the snare drum.

SF: It was the same thing for me—white suburb, my around-the-corner neighbor was Mike Brecker, who's now a great jazz saxophone player. He was playing alto in the junior high school orchestra, and I was playing trombone, and I think we were crazed by too much of Wagner's overture to "Die Meistersinger" or some such. Mike taught me "When the Saints Go Marching In," then moved on to Cannonball Adderley and Bobby Timmons blues tunes, like "Moanin'." But our listening was well in advance of our playing 'cause I remember that this was also the period when we flipped over John Coltrane *Live at Birdland.* We must have listened to that thing a hundred times.

Coltrane Live at Birdland, cover and inside cover, 1963. MCA Records, Inc.

CK: We listened to "Sing, Sing, Sing" and pounded out the Gene Krupa solos on the cafeteria tables, that's how hip we were in the early fifties! The 1939 Carnegie Hall swing concert is where we jumped in, the Firehouse Five Plus Two; Dixieland and early swing era were the things that got us galvanized at eleven and twelve.

SF: I hit that age around '62, and there was Coltrane; the next five years kept me listening to *Live at Birdland, A Love Supreme, Ascension* and relating that to all this great music that came before it. There was something about that music that was so immediate, so captivating, so powerful, so angry, and so much about people being together in the music. Jumping back and forth between listening to that stuff and to the Jimmy Smith blues grooves on the local radio, or listening to the Motown hits on AM and at dance parties, things about black and white were everywhere.

CK: Isn't it astounding? When I'm hearing you speak about all these things, I'm thinking *range,* what an incredible range of music. Because it's the Eddie Condon and Wild Bill Davison thing for me, and the 1939 Goodman concert where Lester Young and Count Basie sit in, and all those magical soloists. In my head those are as live to me as if I was there in the band. And then to have it all go through hard bop to Ornette Coleman and John Coltrane. When you think about it, it's such a profusion, a cornucopia of thousands of grooves.

Was there any black musician who you latched onto early? We found this guy, Harold "Ducky" Edwards, in Stamford, Connecticut, who had played tenor with Hot Lips Page's sextet and had done two European tours. He was in the sax section of Benny Carter's big band, and he was a veteran, a wonderful, sweet person who took us under his wing and showed us how to swing by modeling it, by being there and playing on our gigs. He was like an uncle to us.

SF: For me, it really was all through the recordings. My dad played the piano and was into standards and Broadway tunes. He listened to a lot of other stuff—Oscar Peterson, Art Tatum—those records were around the house when I was a kid. But at the same time there was all this more showy music, Sammy Davis live at the Copa, Sinatra, Mel Tormé. So I heard a whole range of music at home. But Michael was the first person who turned me on to serious jazz listening, in eighth grade or so. And that went on all the way through high school. There were sessions at Mike's house, and I guess that's where I actually met black musicians for the first time.

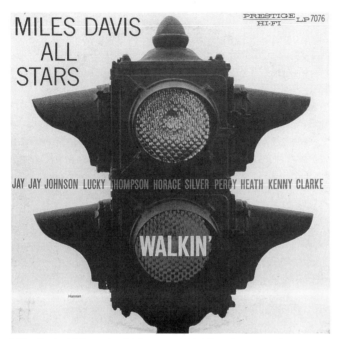

Miles Davis All Stars, *Walkin'*, cover, 1954. Prestige Records.

CK: When you're sitting down and listening to the records, it seems
to me real important to understand *how* people listen together,
how guys bond around music. Around the time we were getting
out of high school there was that Miles Davis *Walkin'* album, and
we would sit there listening to particular phrases by J. J. Johnson,
putting the needle back to hear how he phrased each part, or we'd
listen to little moments, a little four-bar break by Wild Bill Davison,
maybe fifty times together and just shake our heads and marvel
over the control, the power, the perfection of it. Phrase by phrase,
gesture by gesture, figuring out together what's that move, what's
that gesture about? Picking the needle up and putting it back
down in the groove to find *that* moment. Did you guys do that
kind of stuff?

SF: Yeah, but not with Coltrane, because the music had an incredibly
powerful temporal dimension . . . and the solos were so long . . .

CK: . . . so it was more about hearing the flow together . . .

SF: . . . being in the whole thing, finding each of those moments in
this large flow . . .

CK: . . . sheets of sound. You don't pick the needle up on that!

SF: Runs, articulations, fingers moving really fast. Dense. So for me it was more like learning to get into these massive stretches of sonic density and to constantly shift perspective, from Elvin's ride cymbal to McCoy's left hand to the upper register of Coltrane's sound to . . .

CK: Where's mom? Where are the women when we're doing all of that?

SF: Far away. This was a real private experience for me, separate from the whole family . . .

CK: You locked yourself in your room?

SF: I remember when I discovered headphones—the ultimate way to tune out my parents and the world was with headphones, what an incredible invention! They got me through high school! School was such a drag, but around tenth grade there was a time that we actually convinced a teacher that in order to write a research paper, we had to go down to the library and sit with headphones on and listen to these records for hours. That's how I even got time in high school to listen to *A Love Supreme.*

CK: Headphones were never a thing for me, never. It always feels funny for me to put on headphones when I'm working at the radio station and have to wear them. They feel like an imposition. I never have gotten into listening to music on headphones. Fifty years on the planet and I feel like they remove me from the world . . .

SF: Music was *both* the ultimate private thing and the ultimate public thing for me. Private because the headphones really took the rest of the house, family, and suburbs and erased them. Public because it was the most social of all the things that I could do with my friends . . .

CK: I guess I ask about mom and the rest of the family—as you say, it's a way to get away—because I'm always surprised at how taken for granted it is that the guys, be it the boys or the father, will dominate the use of the recording equipment and the sound equipment in most households in America. It's a men's preserve.

SF: My dad dominated the public space of the house more with his Steinway grand than with a stereo. When he came home from work there was dinner, then he was gone for a while at the Steinway, just working it out. That was his therapy. He was a professional musician turned builder. He projected a lot of ambivalence, you know: he was into making a good living, doing the business thing, but I only remember him being relaxed when he could sit down and play. If I had anything serious to ask I always waited until he

Charlie's uncle Hop Rudd at the drum set, late 1950s. Photo courtesy of Priscilla Wolf.

had played for a while. My mom recently reminded me that when I was really little I'd only go to sleep under the piano.

CK: That's an interesting difference. My father sang in the chorus of Gilbert and Sullivan a couple of times and did a little bit of musicking here and there, but it really wasn't an identity thing for him.

SF: Your house wasn't filled with music?

CK: Well, my mother was the stride piano player, and she played trap set in college in the twenties. And my uncle Hop Rudd, her older brother, used to come by. It made a huge impression on me that this uncle of mine was a youth. In his forties, fifties, sixties, and

Steve's cousin David Goodis, with Lauren Bacall and Humphrey Bogart. Warner Brothers
publicity for *Dark Passage,* 1947. Photo courtesy of Anita Feld.

seventies, he was behind a drum set; he'd carry his drum set to
parties and play with records. He was like an irrepressible force,
just getting out the kit and banging, getting that groove to happen, anywhere, anytime.

SF: I had one great family influence completely apart from this home
scene. My cousin David Goodis was a novelist. He wrote *Shoot the
Piano Player,* which Truffaut made into a famous film, and *Dark
Passage,* which became a Humphrey Bogart–Lauren Bacall film,
and several other wonderful B-noir novels and screen pieces, some
for Hitchcock. David was the out-cat in the family—blue suede

shoes, bachelor cousin—the one who was up or out all night and slept during the day. We had this extensive network of cousins who would gather for events, particularly around the Jewish holidays, and David would always make those times full of stories and exotic ideas for me. It was David who turned me on to Charlie Parker when I was thirteen years old with a record of "Cool Blues." I think "Laird Baird" was on the B side. And David played the kazoo, bebop kazoo, muted by a whiskey shot glass. He could mimic Bird's solos perfectly on kazoo . . .

CK: I thought that ended with Red McKenzie and the Mound City Blue Blowers!

SF: . . . so when I was thirteen or so David gave me a kazoo and encouraged me to play along with records. Of course that was perfect; I was just starting with trombone, but with a kazoo, you're *there* almost as soon as you can hear it; you're off, doing it.

CK: Every kid should have a cousin David, an uncle Hop, or a Harold Edwards in the next town over. How are we going to get that to happen? Every child in America should have one of those magic moments where somebody older, wiser, and crazier says, You can do it. A huge number of children, I think, have been pacified by canned music and never get cousin David coming by saying, Jam on the kazoo, it can happen for you! And it's extremely important that they do . . .

SF: It was pretty amazing to me to have someone in my family who stayed up all night and wrote books, who listened to Bird and Stravinsky, who could do perfect imitations of all the Marx Brothers routines, knew every Lenny Bruce bit, spent his time in parts of town that my parents called dangerous, someone in the family who lived on the edge . . .

CK: . . . an alternative path to follow and still be a Feld . . .

SF: . . . in the suburbs in the early sixties . . .

CK: . . . that was serious!

SF: When you went to college was there a scholarly or intellectual parallel to this kind of musical socialization and bonding we've been talking about?

CK: After my first two years of study in the Yale Western Civ trip I took every course I could find that had anything to do with Afro-America or Africa. My very last few months as a senior I had some all-night sessions with Bob Thompson that made a big impact on me. Until that moment I really felt like I was on this quest to understand what was going on in the black world all by myself and that, while there were legitimizing forces at work in anthropology, I had to seek out Malcolm X by myself. Coming across Bob Thompson at the end kind of confirmed what I was doing. He hadn't gone to Africa yet. I had come back from a summer in Nigeria where my mind was completely blown by the incredible diversity of music in Iboland. These seven villages were all called Eha Amufu on the map, and every single one of those villages had a different set of xylophones and musical styles and scales, and I'm saying to myself, "Holy smoke! If this one little pinpoint on the map has got all this happening, what in the hell is going on in the rest of this emergent state with two hundred languages, and subdivisions of those, where every clan has its own style?" And Bob was just about to go to Yorubaland to do his first fieldwork, so he was aching to hear all the things that I had to say. We had dialogues about things like Jahn's *Muntu;* we could sense that this was an overgeneralization about all of Africa, put together from bits and pieces of Maya Deren and Father Tempels's *Bantu Philosophy* and so forth. We were grooving on *Muntu* and trying to figure out how you could further specify what it addressed, how you could make it real and do fieldwork around it. That was my main academic parallel to drumming to keep the rhythm section going for eight fifty-minute sets, 8 P.M. to 4 A.M., six nights a week for the month of August 1958 at the Star Bar in Frankfurt, Germany—that was intellectually formative! The following summer at the Jazz Cellar in Frankfurt, Steve Swallow, my bass-playing buddy, took it as divine revelation when the Brit trumpet player said, "it's the sounds, mate, not the notes"; that was probably decisive.

SF: And graduate school, what happened there? Compared to making music, was it a much more monologic universe?

CK: Anthropology seemed to me the closest thing I could find in an academic discipline to my particular vision quest to discover *where the music comes from.* I went and took the course with Leonard Meyer after I passed all the big hurdles; that provoked not so much a dialogue as a kind of angry reaction, over the first five or six weeks of his course, to hearing Lenny spin out his theories of syntax and style and meaning and music having to earn itself by deferred gratification. It was driving me nuts . . .

SF: You mean his stuff in *Emotion and Meaning in Music?*

CK: I was deeply angry about this version of what music was about because it didn't explain John Coltrane *at all.* It didn't explain the honking, the repeated one-note R & B saxophone solo. Stuff that was dull syntactically was absolutely the greatest processually. So I was pushed by that course to define what another way of evaluating music might be. It doesn't get any more dialogic than that, I suppose, but I felt like I had to write it out and prove it in a countertext, and that became "Motion and Feeling through Music." I had the same kind of rebellious response to Alan Merriam during my year at Indiana before the course with Meyer. I couldn't get with the program of giving up musical participation for supposedly greater scholarly objectivity—more time for footnotes. You had the same tension with him in the seventies, right?

SF: Wasn't Alan a spectacularly serious academic? I admired his commitment to African music and to ethnomusicology and his energy for beating the walls down to tell anthropologists how important music and the arts should be to the anthropology curriculum. He fought good fights with the musicologists too, flag-waving for anthropology. But when I got to Indiana it was clear there would be some major differences between us over politics and music. This was 1971, and I was just coming out of four turbulent college years. I organized a Vietnam teach-in in the spring of my freshman year at Hofstra, on what turned out to be the very day that Martin Luther King was shot. That put imperialism and racism together for me in such a powerful way. That's when I found anthropology and from there, eventually, ethnomusicology. During my last year in college I sat in on Stanley Diamond's political anthropology lectures and took Edmund Carpenter's media classes at the New School. And the music I was hearing was all angry, Coltrane and beyond. Coming to Indiana from that New York lefty scene there was bound to be some friction. Anthropology made great sense to me as a way of intellectually engaging with both music and politics, but I just couldn't get with the apolitical, unaesthetic scholarly grad school resocialization program.

CK: I think that an important commonality between us is that we both sought out anthropology as an oasis that was still holistic. Alan's agenda of trying to bridge the gap between the humanities and the social sciences was noble. I think he felt so committed to it that

"The Academic Cats," Northwestern University faculty jazz group of the late 1940s and early 1950s. Alan P. Merriam with clarinet in rear; Richard Waterman, bass; Raymond Mack, drums; William Bascom, clarinet (at microphone). Photo courtesy of Patricia Waterman and Chris Waterman.

the experiential dynamic of being involved in the music, of learning to play gamelan or whatever, seemed flaky to him, not the way to meet the intellectual challenge.

SF: For me, the most important aspect of my entire undergraduate experience from '67 to '71 was studying in an anthropology department where there was a very explicit connection between scholarship and a personal and political commitment to things like community and fighting racism and imperialism. Gerry Rosenfeld taught an incredible course on poverty, and Alexander Lesser did one on race, taking us right back to the materials he read in courses on race with Franz Boas, telling us about Boas's first race course, co-taught with W. E. B. Du Bois. And Colin Turnbull did one on contemporary Africa, explaining the dynamics of colonialism, independence,

and "development." Gitel Steed did one on community, and Sam
Leff did one on the anthropology of countercultures and rapid cultural change. In a couple of years with those teachers I was exposed to an incredible integration of research and commitment.

CK: That was an exceptional department for giving you a sense of the
continuity of the struggles over those issues. It's only recently that I
realized that Boas was Jewish, Herskovits was Jewish. These guys
were coming up with relativism and a whole world view and a position on the race thing with such energy and such conviction. It's
some measure of our social amnesia and our ahistoricalness, even
in academic life in the United States today, that we don't hold that
tradition up as a kind of torch, that we don't know how the torch
was passed from person to person, what kept it going. It sounds
like your department helped sort it out for you very nicely early on.

SF: I didn't feel any disjuncture between academia and commitment.
But there was a disjuncture between these things and the music,
the artistic side of things. And in graduate school there was even
more rupture, more split, more alienation. My way of rebelling
against it was choosing a completely different kind of art form,
going to film school for a year. And the final way I rebelled against
it was that when I got out of graduate school, I stopped reading,
established the New Mexico Jazz Workshop with some friends, and
played trombone for a year to get my head remusicalized enough
to be excited about a fieldwork adventure in Papua New Guinea.

CK: I'm thinking that it's probably a good thing that the music, the
real music, doesn't get academicized, that there's not a course in
invite-Malcolm-X-to-Yale or whatever. Now that was a dialogue,
talking to Malcolm! Going down to the Temple Restaurant and
being escorted in by Brother Joseph, the bodyguard, to sit with
Malcolm for an hour, hour and a half, two hours at a clip to just
talk with him. Those were dialogues that sure as hell shaped my life
at the same time that Coltrane's music was getting my whole head
to think differently. The talks at Yale were Malcolm's first to white
audiences, I think—fall 1960, spring '61. I thought, this guy has
got to be heard. It was an apolitical, amusical world, the university,
Yale and the University of Chicago. The academic discipline is to
shield you from groovy experiences in music or in political activism.

SF: I guess we met up through Alan Merriam's African humanities
seminar at Indiana. You came out there to give talks in 1972 and

'73, presenting early versions of material from *Tiv Song* and your stuff on urban Yoruba music. There were parties and we discovered that we already knew each other through the world of Monk's music. I remember hanging in a bar, pounding out a few rhythms, singing some Tiv songs, and the way your talks on the Nigerian scene deeply mixed the personal and the political with this thing called scholarship. You reminded me of the New York politics-scholarship-music world I came from like nobody else; god, it was comforting . . .

CK: I am so glad that those messages came through, because when I look back at that time now, I think I was in a kind of intellectual and emotional daze, a ball of confusion, from 1968, when I came back from Nigeria, until the mid-seventies, after those visits to Indiana. I was emotionally traumatized by the massacres in Nigeria, the whole two-year Biafra war, and the Vietnam war. All my high idealism and total commitment to understanding the roots of black music came apart at the seams on the banks of the Benue River with those dead Ibo bodies. At the time I was coming to Indiana, there was no choice about the political-moral dimension of scholarship. That was *all* I was thinking about. The music was just a survival mechanism.

SF: I was in shock in Indiana because I had been cut off from a lot of the music and politics that made sense to me. You were the first speaker in that series who made it clear that it was always going to be a struggle. You started talking about the smell of death that you will never get out of your head and the rhythms of drummers that you'll also never get out of your head. I felt like the real world was back: the music of anthropology and the politics of anthropology.

CK: That's good to hear, glad I helped you keep the faith. Graduate school requires the learning of abstractions and theories and ideas, and now I value that, like we both valued our encounters with Robert P. Armstrong, Mr. Metaphysical, Mr. Idealist, around that time. We valued him for the abstract formulations that he did that no one else had done. And I think that's the best graduate school can do for you, asking you to momentarily disconnect politically and musically and think "concepts."

SF: Robert P.'s aesthetics course was what got me through my last year at Indiana. He was so happily free from academic culture in certain ways. He'd call up and say it would be great to have dinner, then insist on bringing the food and the wine (*fine* wine) and doing

Robert Plant Armstrong, in front of a Yoruba bead painting he commissioned from Jimoh Buraimoh. Photo © Peter Robbins. Photo courtesy of John Buxton.

all the cooking. Here was this guy, in those elegant suits, cooking in your grubby grad student kitchen, talking dense continental phenomenology with the utmost enthusiasm. He was so warm and so genuine . . .

CK: . . . I think it's because he stayed out of departments for twenty-five years, directing Northwestern University Press . . .

SF: . . . and he wasn't bothered by being called an art collector. Bob could talk lovingly about every piece in his collection, about living with them and being with them all the time, and that completely cut through my deeper political fears about the objectification of these pieces behind glass or on walls. I think he provided us with a way of engaging those problems . . .

CK: . . . the belief, the dynamic, the reverse missionary zeal of insisting these things be included in our world of experience . . .

SF: I think Bob Armstrong is extremely important to this book. These essays and dialogues are about a profound ambivalence and concern that we both feel about participation and commodification. Bob was so committed to art *objects,* but at the same time he was committed to living with them and saying these are *not* objects, they are presences. He would say, we're not looking at them, we're witnessing living, breathing stuff, so let's live and breath with it and let's dig its livingness and breathingness. The tension between what we're calling the participatory and the commodified is embodied dialectically in all of Armstrong's work and in the problems and delights that both of us have had with it.

CK: It models how a white, Western male, in full charge of his phenomenological, theoretical faculties, can push through to mystical participation, can push through to iconicizing a Yoruba *ibeji,* not crossing himself in front of that shrine but saying here's what you do, in effect, to make that *ibeji* part of you. Because he pushed through to participation in his own way.

SF: Armstrong's way of dealing with sculpture gave me a whole new way of thinking about records, a way of thinking about how the physicality and commodity of grooves is related to the experience of grooves, an understanding of the unity of materiality and pleasure.

CK: So are you going to handle those CDs like little *ibejis?* No grooves on them, but they shine!

SF: They do shine, and I delight in the idea of these little things going into the cabinet where I can't see what they're doing! It is wonderfully mystified; Bob would have loved CDs.

CK: Maybe not. He might have wanted the scratch, the patina. That's what's missing in CDs—the patina, the use. See what I mean? After you've played an LP for a while, or even a tape, you begin to get the hiss and the scratch, the little skip. Can't get that on a CD.

SF: True, but I don't think Bob would have been too uptight about patina, because Bob didn't fetishize authenticity. He was writing about Amos Tutuola and about Twins Seven Seven as the same essence, cream of Yorubaness, as *ibejis.*

CK: Isn't it interesting that a totally mad idealist like Bob Armstrong can send you back to the material, physical world with a vengeance? I got high as a kite, an adrenaline rush, reading the hundred pages of theory in Armstrong's *The Affecting Presence.* That elegant theory of how things must fit together in a culture solved the problem that I came to Indiana with: what the last chapter of *Tiv Song* was going to be about. A little light went on. I wanted to

turn Bob Armstrong right side up, like Marx turned Hegel right side
up, put his feet on the ground . . .

—————

SF: So five years went by. I went to Papua New Guinea, then wrote
a dissertation, finishing just around the time that *Tiv Song* was
published. We hooked back up once I moved back to the east coast
and started teaching at the Annenberg School in 1980.

CK: And that's really what prompted our discussions of commodification and mediation, you doing media work around all those communications folks, me running through Marxist theory for ten years
trying to figure out how to make that work for ethnomusicology.
There was again a meeting of the minds, on very different planes this
time, with both of us trying to deal with media commodification.

SF: You came down and gave "People's Music Comparatively" at
Annenberg in about 1983, somewhere around the time I went to
Buffalo and gave a version of a paper on Kaluli drumming. You were
looking at things more and more comparatively, and I was living
in the intense density of this experience of Kaluli ethnography. I
couldn't see a way of resolving your urge to compare blues, polka,
Cuban, Japanese, Chinese, and Greek musics and my interest in
thick, in-depth ethnographic description.

CK: I was trying to figure out a generally Marxist paradigm, a crass,
vulgar—in the sense of people-serving—evolutionary schema that
would make sense of things in my mind . . .

SF: That's how the issue of Tiv and Kaluli classlessness opened up a lot
of dialogues, leading to our symposium on the comparative sociomusicology of classless societies at the ethnomusicology meetings
in '83 in Tallahassee. I guess that's when our dialogues became
more frequent . . .

CK: To me the crucial question in the discussions was, How did we
lose classlessness? How did the inequalities, which I take to be
pretty much patriarchal—men moving up over women and
nature—how did that happen? That was what I wanted to get out
of that comparative thing but didn't.

SF: But it did bring us together in a new way of talking about the participation issue, forcing me to reconsider the social distribution of
expressive resources among Kaluli men and women. You really
pushed me toward understanding participation as the key to the

emergence and crystallization of style. That opened up a lot of windows onto how Kaluli are grooving in and on their world.

CK: Participation is a good sum-up term, or global term, for all these different ongoing processes that keep them, in effect, classless. You were starting to report the drum throb and the waterfall imagery exactly at a moment when I was coming to see participation as absolutely crucial, but it was still very abstract to me. Lévy-Bruhl is reporting "pre-logic" and getting into trouble, Lévi-Strauss is reporting that the Bororo think they're birds. Barfield is telling me that the rainbow is totally in our minds and has to be configured. I'm reading my Barfield and my Lévy-Bruhl and Leenhardt's *Do Kamo* and all these French and British theorists of participation, and it's all remote, all written thirty, fifty, seventy years ago. And you come along with this fresh Kaluli material that relates to these very issues, the issues of participatory consciousness and how we might reenergize and restore it, power it, bring it back, and cut down alienation. I'm seeing my way out of Marxism as a negating, mediating, Frankfurt school nightmare, into participatory theory, and you're the guy. You're coming back with "They think waterfalls, they think birds, their lives are wrapped up in the natural world." *Sound and Sentiment* provided the specifics of that, the boy who becomes a *muni* bird, the myth, the story, the song, and the weeping. You were able to do that not just because of the meticulousness of your collaborative work with Buck and Bambi Schieffelin— you were so into that world that it couldn't help but emerge—but also because that was a moment in the overall intellectual history of the West where people allowed themselves to hear what the natives, the indiginees, were saying about their localities and about their participation in nature. In a way, Native Americans have probably been telling that to anthropologists since the 1880s—"Hey, this music is about the earth, and the spirit, and the connections to the spiritual world and the natural world"—but nobody could quite take it down as such until the 1980s, when we're losing even the remnants of those kinds of connections. I think that's why Marina Roseman hears it so clearly among the Temiar. Now we can hear it; people go out listening. We're asking them the questions, finally, that are all about participatory consciousness.

SF: The mid-1980s was when I realized that, in our discussions, you were supplying the tension on my tonearm. You were always thinking of more comparisons, thinking more historically, and always had more to throw at me as I got further into Kaluli ethnography. That forced my thinking to come out of the microgroove, helped me recognize that symbolic analyses and Geertzian interpretation weren't incompatible with more materialist, ecological, political, global, transnational perspectives.

CK: And conversely, one of the really creative tensions between the two of us throughout the eighties has been my ever more aggressively simple-minded focus on participation here and now, rather than on comparison and criticism. Somehow we have to increase belief and imagination and the capacity for prophecy and poetry in each person. Music is our last and best source of participatory consciousness, and it has this capacity not just to model but maybe to enact some ideal communities. I want to get the kids moving. I want everybody playing, grooving, jamming. That's why Bill Blake immersion suits me more than all that pop-crit metatheory stuff. Marxism and feminism accept alienation as axiomatic, even revel in it, and have long been missing the First Force—Blakean Joy, eternal delight, the "songs of innocence" that are sure as hell not songs of ignorance. I want more participatory immersion, more cultured creations, fewer mediated substitutions, even less civilized criticism. But you, to your credit, are looking for what we can hold onto from linguistics and symbolic anthropology. You are insisting that music still needs every good head on the planet to help us figure out how these things cohere. What is that larger configuration about? What are we really tapping into? What's so groovy about a groove? Why are we doing this? You persist in holding the whole academic world at gunpoint and saying, You've got to be good for something . . .

SF: Yeah, that's a very creative tension to me. But ethnography is the main hope I see for holding all the theory at gunpoint in the postmodern academic world. I don't think academics can fully understand the power of the participation idea without ethnography, without dealing with the grounded realities that are the social life of those "codes" and "texts" everyone wants to "read." That's why so much cultural studies and pop culture theory is ungroovy to me; it just reads like the idea police sniping from blinds and lookouts on the outskirts of town, far from real life in action, just declaring "meanings" rather than fully investigating their genesis and lived lives.

I think the last two articles in our first section, the ones on participatory discrepancies and Kaluli "lift-up-over sounding" are the culmination of dialogues dialectically bringing together, as best as we could, theory and ethnography. In "Participatory Discrepancies and the Power of Music" you synthesize twenty years of thinking about musical experience, process, and texture that begins in "Motion and Feeling through Music" as a response to Lenny Meyer. Then in the "lift-up-over sounding" paper I'm responding to you responding to Meyer, and at the same time responding to the Kaluli spin on all of this theorizing. Those two pieces also show how thinking about musical mediation becomes essential to understanding the participatory power of music. But they are just beginnings in what could be big ethnographic studies acknowledging the rich intellectual tradition of the phenomenology of the senses and the social world.

———

CK: I think one of the things we have in common is that we both take the obsolescence of high culture, or its irrelevance to these participation-mediation issues, as a springboard. Written music? Art museums? Quaint, residues. Yet popular music, participation, all these positive things, come up against the mediated form taking over jazz, taking over rock, taking over anything which seems critical, revolutionary, or consciousness-changing. The revolutionary spirit got stuck in scores in Beethoven's day, and now it gets commodified over and over again. In my own thinking, the big transformation from taking a purely Luddite stance against mediation, to being all for participation but thinking mediation was a *more* powerful thing, came when I traced out the relationship between blues and polka in "People's Music Comparatively." I concluded that if there hadn't been mediation, if there hadn't been radio and records in the 1920s, there wouldn't be any blues or polka "tradition." People's music wouldn't exist without the media suction that forces people to identify themselves with a particular form, to say, "We're Polish-Americans; we do polkas, waltzes, and obereks." Or, "Minstrelsy and vaudeville are giving us something called the blues craze on records; we can deal with that, we'll be blues people." The dialectic begins in some way with mediation, not with participation. It begins with a media suction that says, "We need something." If you want to sell furniture, tombstones, or washers on the Polish-American hour, what's going to fill out the show? Polkas.

SF: Is your concern the particular forces of ownership that technology imposes? Or the way people can only get music through cash transactions in the marketplace?

CK: I used to see all that as only the enemy. Still do, but now part of me sees this mediation as having a potential to plant seeds in places that would never get planted, to move music around in ways which at least have the potential for hybridization and cross-fertilization, and to keep people in touch with an emerging planetary culture while they, hopefully, hold onto their own.

SF: There are two aspects historically to the way your thoughts on mediation have influenced mine. One goes back to talking about male bonding around music and how the experience of playing along with records, picking up the grooves and learning the phrases, says that you can talk back to the mediation process, can create spaces to participate in it. The other dimension is that your work really separates the technology per se from the larger issues. It wasn't until you started talking about polka and blues from a class perspective that I started to think about the ownership of music. I got to thinking about world beat, about the ways musicians around the world participate in activities that become more and more commodified, about how smaller and smaller groups of people own larger and larger amounts of music. As more musical heterogeneity moves into the commodified world of music, more homogeneous ownership dominates large-scale musical practices. It's the homogenizers who want more musical diversity, more variety, in this world beat mix. You showed me how a resistance-accommodation dialectic is always working in blues and polka. It started to seem equally true to me for the world music arena. We're living with an *image* of a world of musical diversity and empowerment, but I've come to see that as a world of less and less diversity in terms of ownership, control, and who profits.

SF: *Music Grooves.* We've got a duality, maybe a double duality, in the title. What's it about to you?

CK: The clear duality is the word "grooves." As a verb, music pulls and draws you, through participatory discrepancies, into itself, and gives you that participation consciousness. It's one of the few things that gives you that . . .

SF: OK, the present verb. It's the music that grooves. To groove, to cycle, to draw you in and work on you, to repeat with variation . . .

CK: . . . and to me, that repetition and redundancy, which to most people is a bore, is music's glory. That's where a groove comes from . . .

SF: . . . and when we say, "It's the music that grooves," we're drawing attention to the ephemerality of the music, to our participation in and experience of it. When we say, "It grooves," we're also saying there's something that's regular and somewhat sustainable, identifiable and repetitive. "Grooves" are a process, and it's the music that grooves. But part of the duality is that as music grooves, there is always something new *and* something familiar.

CK: Amiri Baraka's "changing same." The minute I read that phrase I said, "That's it!" It's some deep philosophical principle about how we are, as humans on this planet, that we groove. We groove on reality, and I think that's how our brains got built and shaped. We've got this developed cortex from watching the leaves flutter, tracking the animals, from grooving on reality and reveling in the repetition and redundancy of information with minor but frequent variations. *Slight* variations. Slight variations become magical, hypnotizing, mesmerizing. They give you deep identification or participatory consciousness. You flow into repetition. Again, it's a kind of Western fetish that novelty is progress and newness is what it's about, while repetition and redundancy both have a bad connotation. "Repetitious," "redundant," "ritualistic"—there are a whole bunch of words that I would like to free of their negative connotations so that we could get deeper into immanence, into potentiality.

SF: So what about "grooves" as a noun? It also has a dual meaning. The grooves are the feeling and the participatory experience of music, but also the physical recesses on the disc, the sound patterns and cycles as held, as commodified, as physically engrained forms. And the grooves are also the discs themselves. The music grooves are the vinyl products—"I want to check out your grooves."

CK: I'm thinking also of the sexual metaphor, the phallic needle that drops into the vaginal groove. There's something very male, sexual, and appropriative about having the records, pulling them out of their sleeves, and commanding that sound.

SF: The connotations of "groove" reach every aspect of the sexual, the social, all the ultimate things people can do together, and the duality of the physical form and the ephemeral experience.

CK: When I try to think of what the groove represents, or of what's behind the groove, I don't think there is anything behind it. I think it is what it is, that the groove is the ultimate thing.

SF: I like the way the title puts the emphasis on the grooves, rather than on the music. I think it draws attention to the way that music is many things, some nominal, some verbal, at the same or different times, in the same or different places.

CK: And we both want to see that, in its own hegemonic way, extended, to see that the grooving of two tennis players or fencers is similar to the interplay of a jazz rhythm section at some level. That kind of physical grooving, being together and tuning up to somebody else's sense of time is what we're here on the planet for . . .

SF: . . . that's why the sexual union notion of grooves is an apposite and powerful parallel . . .

CK: . . . because of the way science and rationalism and empiricism have tended to squeeze the participatory out from everybody's lives, it's all the more important that we treasure the musical experience for keeping it there. Plus music doesn't put more people on the planet the way the sexual thing tends to. The one other place where you can think of people being lost in their context is fear, anxiety, panic. Both sexuality and anxiety have their problems as ways to resolve alienation, as ways to get out of yourself. So getting out musically is, I think, the most important thing happening on the planet. I agree with that rap from James Brown you just came across . . .

SF: . . . yeah, in Gene Santoro's article in the *Nation* (3 June 1991) here's James talking: "Y'know, one thing about music: It's the key to *every*thing, the universal language of man's commitment to be together. Yeah, a baby can *feel* before it can *see*, so the feeling is far beyond sight, sound is far beyond sight, um-hmm. So that we ought to have music *every*where, in the churches, in the political meetings, in the hospitals and dentists' offices. 'Cause, see what the music is doing? It's so *vast*, so *beyond* our thinking, because it reaches your soul and you can feel before you can see, that it's mind over matter. You say "ouch" and you don't even know where the pain is coming from, but the *feeling* is *real*."

Ain't that a groove! What better spokesperson than James Brown for the linkage between the experiential and the mediated dimensions of the groove?

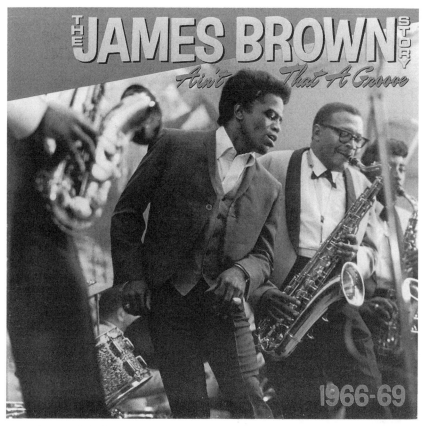

James Brown, *Ain't That a Groove,* cover, 1984. Polydor Records, Polygram.

CK: Isn't James a wonder? He does these incredible trenchant lyrics, like "We don't need no masterpiece, mo' peas," that come out of a complete innocence about criticism. I don't think he knows about critics or has anything looking over his shoulder.

SF: But he's so perfectly caught in every one of the contradictions. Here he is talking up Nixon and Bush and Hubert Humphrey as his heroes, yet he's constantly issuing a kind of vernacular poetry which is totally critical of the world that those people come from and the world that they're trying to maintain.

CK: Let's face it, James encompasses opposites. Probably nobody has encompassed opposites better since Walt Whitman . . .

SF: . . . except possibly Aretha. "Sock it to me" gives James a good run for his money in dialectics!

CK: I think James has inspired a lot of people to have the courage of their convictions to get out there and do it. If James can do it, I can do it. That's what I say to myself a lot of the time. If he can make up a song on the spot, I can make up a song. "We don't need no masterpiece, mo' peas."

SF: So much of his stuff comes out of a process of recording in the studio which is live jamming, with a tremendous amount of spontaneity. Proto-rapping, verbal riffs like "mo' peas," "get on the good foot," "popcorn," just like horn riffs. Funk is layered riffing. Mediation of participation.

CK: And because he's going from the sound to the sense—"mother popcorn," "mama come here quick, bring me that lickin' stick"— it's the pops and clicks, the /p/s, the /k/s, the sounds of the words, not that they mean anything particular to James, either when he utters them, or later. It's the sound of those words together.

SF: That's what's so compelling about each "Ow!"—those exclamatory vocal interjections where his mouth is articulating with the horn section, punching, riffing. Just like Aretha's "O"s, bending and dipping to hang in, over, take you right to the groove. I think we should dedicate the book to James and Aretha.

CK: OK, let's do it! Who else would you nominate? Who are the other heavy groovesters? I think immediately of Kenny Clarke, Elvin Jones. My whole list of drummers comes to mind. Art Blakey. Then the bassists: Al McKibbon, Wilbur Ware. Then Horace Silver. How does it go in your head?

SF: Vocalists: Louis Armstrong, Ray Charles, Johnny Hartman . . . Sarah Vaughn, Betty Carter, most of all Billie Holiday . . .

CK: . . . again, a textural thing, her sound. Her attack, where she places the notes, is not as important as the contour . . .

SF: . . . the grain, the inflection. Like Ulahi in Bosavi. I have it in my diary from 1976: The very first time I listened to Ulahi sing at a creek, I thought, this is the Billie Holiday of Bosavi. That liquid sound, that low voice. When you listen to her on *Voices of the Rainforest* it's the same thing, whether she's singing at the waterfall or beating sago or cutting weeds with a machete. Her timing, her phrasing when she sings "ni dikidiyabo," it's just special, has an impeccable feel for micromoments, for placing accents. Just like Billie Holiday: "I need that *person* . . . much *worse than* just bad." "Person," "worse than"—taking these linguistic elements, from different universes of syntax and semantics, uniting them in sound and

Billie Holiday, *The Unforgettable Lady Day,* cover, 1957. Polydor Records, Polygram.

in flow with her voice, reorganizes language and music in that moment. Just like Louis Armstrong when he sings, "Birds *do it, bees
do* it, even educated *fleas* do *it,* let's do *it*"—that's a special league
where vocal texture and timbre come together as the total sensuality of sound.

CK: It feels good to be talking music as experience. We've got a whole
other worldview here, more of a world-hear, a world-sense. A bind
that we have doing this in book form is that we're trying to break
free of an essentializing, objectifying, text-obsessed university for
which all books and knowledge are about putting things in rows
and sequences and segmenting the continuum, chopping things
apart—all those things that we are gut-opposed to. And yet we're
doing it in a book . . .

Ulahi, holding her infant Bage, and singing with cicadas; Bosavi, Papua New Guinea, 1976. Photo Steven Feld.

Ulahi, listening to playback of *Voices of the Rainforest;* Bosavi, Papua New Guinea, 1990. Photo Steven Feld.

Louis Armstrong and Billie Holiday. Publicity still from the film *New Orleans,* 1947. Photo courtesy of Ole Brask.

SF: . . . but see the irony here. What did we do this morning? You got up and took out your cornet and started playing as soon as I put on a CD, and we had trouble turning off Jerry Gonzalez's *Rumba Para Monk* to move into another room and turn on *this* tape recorder. If the bonding is primarily through and in the grooves, what kind of groove is this book?

CK: It's a book to tell people about an apprehensible reality that is in your hands, fingers, feet, butt, hips, gut, and unified mind-body in social context, in your sound-context relationship to the world! Olavo Alén Rodriguez in Cuba, whom I've only visited a couple of times but who always has something important to give me, told me that it's not just better to give than to receive, but that in music it is absolutely essential. You have to give music to other people, and you must do it physically. In order to understand what any musician is doing, you have to have done some of it yourself. I used to think you could do it just through listening, but that alone won't let you connect to the music or to other people. All the listening in the

world does not condition your mind-body to *be* musical and therefore to take the next step in listening. I thought listening was part
of the solution: the more you listened, the better you would get at
it. I think, though, that Olavo was right. Unless you physically do
it, it's not really apprehensible, and you're not hearing all there is
to hear inside the music. You're not entering it. Participation is crucial. That's why it's really important to me that you're a trombone
player, participating in making those grooves, too, and keeping
that in a creative tension with your scholarship. That commitment
to keeping up your musical life and keeping your participatory
mode going is what keeps us on the same wavelength, keeps us
in the same groove.

Further Comments

p. 1 . . . *springboards for more dialogues* . . . The notion that another voice, an interlocutor, is essential to both the structure of language and the performance of speech genres is widely associated with the writings of Mikhail M. Bakhtin. Key texts for understanding the influence, in the poststructuralist intellectual milieu of the last twenty years, of Bakhtin's notions of dialogue, heteroglossia, and multivocality include Mikhail Bakhtin, *Problems of Dostoevsky's Poetics* (Ann Arbor: Ardis, 1973), *The Dialogic Imagination* (Austin: University of Texas Press, 1981), *Rabelais and His World* (Bloomington: Indiana University press, 1984), and *Speech Genres and Other Late Essays* (Austin: University of Texas Press, 1986). Also V. N. Voloshinov, *Marxism and the Philosophy of Language* (Cambridge: Harvard University Press, 1986).

The secondary literature includes a number of excellent reviews placing Bakhtin's dialogism in the broad intellectual context of linguistics, literature, and philosophy; for example, Michael Holquist, *Dialogism: Bakhtin and His World* (London: Routledge, 1990); Michael Holquist and Katerina Clark, *Mikhail Bakhtin* (Cambridge: Harvard University Press, 1984); Tzvetan Todorov, *Mikhail Bakhtin: The Dialogical Principle* (Minneapolis: University of Minnesota Press, 1984). Also helpful is the glossary prepared by Michael Holquist for his translation of *The Dialogic Imagination* (Bakhtin 1981:423–34). For additional literary critical perspectives see Gary Saul Morson and Caryl Emerson, eds., *Rethinking Bakhtin: Extensions and Challenges* (Evanston: Northwestern University Press, 1989), and Susan Stewart, "Shouts on the Street: Bakhtin's Anti-Linguistics," *Critical Inquiry* 10 (1983):265–81. For a creative reading of popular music along these lines see George Lipsitz, "Against the Wind: Dialogic Aspects of Rock and Roll," in *Time Passages: Collective Memory and American Popular Culture,* 99–132 (Minneapolis: University of Minnesota Press, 1990).

Among anthropological commentators, Dennis Tedlock's work links the linguistic and ethnographic dimensions of dialogism forcefully; see "The Analogical Tradition and the Emergence of a Dialogical Anthropology," *Journal of Anthropological Research* 35, no. 4 (1979):387–400, "Questions Concerning Dialogical Anthropology," *Journal of Anthropological Research* 43, no. 4 (1987):325–37, and *The Spoken Word and the Work of Interpretation* (Philadelphia: University of Pennsylvania Press, 1983). See also the papers in Tulio Maranhão, ed., *The Interpretation of Dialogue* (Chicago: University of Chicago Press, 1990). [SF]

p. 1 . . . *a representation . . . of lots of other dialogues* . . . These dialogues, tape-recorded during a week spent together in June 1991, have been edited a number of times, first by Tom Porcello, who cleaned up the hemming, the hawing, the sputtering and profanity, the "you know"s and "man, like"s, and the obvious repetitions of words and phrases as he meticulously transcribed the tapes. Steve Feld edited the transcript into sections, then we each made cuts, comparing our separate edits and agreeing on what could go. We also added a word here, a phrase there—"massaging" and "tweaking" are the verbs used these days. Readers Charlie Weigl, Tony Grajeda, Larry Chisolm, Mike Frisch, and Angeliki Keil in Buffalo and Tom Porcello and Aaron Fox in Austin helped us decide what to cut and what to keep. An additional round of phone dialogues, in February 1992, transcribed by Michelle Smith, was edited and added into the third dialogue. All three dialogues, along with other parts of the manuscript, were polished further thanks to the critical comments from press readers and T. David Brent. In short, these dialogues have been shaped a lot for easier and more pleasurable reading; while we have labored to keep the spirit and details of the original interchanges, this editing also tends to make us appear "smarter" or at least more lucid than we actually sound when we talk in front of a tape recorder. Crafting transcripts of oral expression for greater clarity on the page feels good to us. Because we would like people to follow our example of talking to one another and editing their statements for publication, we are eager to debunk any notion that "only professors or experts could do this." Given an interesting question or topic and varied experiential bases for dialogues about it, anyone and everyone can do this (see, for example, Susan Crafts, Daniel Cavicchi, and Charles Keil, eds., *My Music* [Middletown: Wesleyan University Press, 1993]). Nor do we want to understate the amount of hard work it takes to edit, distill, massage, and punch up taped dialogue for a book. Hence this long footnote and an invitation to call us and talk about any similar project you may have in mind. [CK]

p. 1 . . . *wherever we were doing fieldwork* . . . Various experiences have submerged me into fieldworklike liminality, culture shock, or heightened awareness of self, otherness, and difference—studying in France (1974), living in northern New Mexico (since 1972), working one-to-one on American Indian languages (early 1970s), and hanging out, observing, and participating in music bar scenes (since I was a teenager). Nonetheless, the ethnographic, linguistic, and ethnomusicological research I've always called "my fieldwork" involved living with the Kaluli people of the Sululeb and Bolekini longhouse communities in Bosavi, Papua New Guinea, 1976–77, 1982, 1984, 1990, and 1992. [SF]

I began thinking of myself as a fieldworker during a two-week study cruise in the West Indies, in the spring of 1960, and a summer work-study experience in Nigeria that same year. Since then I have studied Nation of Islam (1960–62), African-American blues (1962–65), Tiv music and culture (1965–67) Yoruba jùjú (1967), Greek popular music (1972), Polish-American polkas (1973–77), Chinese popular music (1980), American music in daily life (1984–1990), Greek *zurna* and *dauli* (various times from the 1960s to the present), and, in recent years, Afro-Cuban drumming. [CK]

p. 2 . . . *growing up white in a world of black music* . . . My new Afterword to *Urban Blues* (1966; Chicago: University of Chicago Press, 1991) explores white responses to black music and culture from a variety of angles. [CK]

p. 3 . . . *listened to that thing a hundred times.* I have fond memories of all sorts of early records I played as a youngster, from Mickey Katz's klezmer bands to Tubby the Tuba, "light classics," my dad's Art Tatum collection, and the recordings we made in the living room using an early home model disc-cutting recorder and later a reel-to-reel tape recorder; these included recordings of me singing, talking, and performing from age two and recordings of all of my family making music and clowning together. By junior high school my favorite listening was blues and soul-gospel-based jazz, especially the organ trios and quartets of Jimmy Smith, Jimmy McGriff, Brother Jack McDuff, and Richard "Groove" Holmes, and the Cannonball Adderley Riverside sextet sessions, with Nat Adderley and either Yusef Lateef or Charles Lloyd. By high school my strongest musical influences were the John Coltrane Quartet of the early 1960s and the Miles Davis quintets of the mid-60s, with Herbie Hancock on piano, Ron Carter on bass, Tony Williams on drums, and either George Coleman or Wayne Shorter on tenor saxophone. During these years I also listened to a lot of Stevie Wonder, the Temptations, the Supremes, and James Brown. Through high school and college I also began seriously listening to trombone players; my early favorites were Kid Ory, Jack Teagarden, J. J. Johnson, Curtis Fuller, Vic Dickenson, Grachan Moncur III, and Roswell Rudd. [SF]

p. 5 . . . *galvanized at eleven and twelve.* My earliest childhood musical memories are of Duke Ellington and Fats Waller 78s, my mother's stride piano playing, and the groove of "When he jammed with bass and guitar/They hollered, 'Beat me daddy, eight to the bar!'" by Woody Herman. When LPs first came along I got a lot of mileage out of the Fire House Five Plus Two; *Jazz Concert at Eddie Condon's; Jam Session Coast to Coast;* and Benny Goodman's *Carnegie Hall Jazz Concert Volume 1.* By the end of high school I was a Horace Silver devotee and had memorized everything on the Miles Davis All Stars album, *Walkin'.*

Thanks again to Pat Williams, Doug "Digger" MacLaughlin, Gail Anderson Kilburne, Paul Rockwell, Bruce Taylor, Stan Snyder, Phil Fields, Tony Chirco, Russell Spang, Gus Helmecke, Luther Thompson, and all the people I musicked with growing up. [CK]

p. 7 . . . *to McCoy's left hand to the upper register of Coltrane's sound* . . . The John Coltrane Quartet (Coltrane, tenor and soprano saxophone; McCoy Tyner, piano; Jimmy Garrison, bass; Elvin Jones, drums) essential discography covers roughly 1959 to 1965. The early recordings, on the Atlantic label, include *Giant Steps, Coltrane Jazz,* and *My Favorite Things.* The later recordings, on Impulse, include *Africa/Brass, Live at the Village Vanguard, Ballads, Impressions, Live at Birdland, Crescent,* and *A Love Supreme.* [SF]

p. 9 *My cousin David Goodis was a novelist.* David Goodis, 1917–1967, wrote seventeen novels in twenty-one years, as well as many screen and radio plays and magazine pieces. Many lapsed into obscurity but have recently been republished. Among the best known are *Black Friday* (1954; New York: Vintage, 1990); *Burglar* (1953; New York: Creative Arts, 1989), made into a film in 1957; *Cassidy's Girl* (1951; New York: Creative Arts, 1988); *Night Fall* (1947; New York: Creative Arts, 1987); *Night Squad* (1960; New York: Creative Arts, 1989); and *Street of No Return* (1955; New York: Creative Arts, 1988). Of books that became films the best known are *Dark Passage* (New York: Messner, 1946), which Goodis adapted in 1947 for the Warner Brothers movie starring Humphrey Bogart and Lauren Bacall, and *Down There* (New York: Gold Medal, 1956), adapted by François Truffaut in 1961 as *Tirez sur le pianiste* ("Shoot the Piano Player") and reissued as *Shoot the Piano Player* (New York: Grove, 1962; New York: Vintage, 1990). Truffaut's New Wave classic led to critical acclaim for Goodis in France, including a literary biography by Philippe Garnier, *Goodis: La vie en noir et blanc* (Paris: Seuil, 1984). [SF]

p. 10 *... some all-night sessions with Bob Thompson ...* The basic Robert Farris Thompson books are *Black Gods and Kings: Yoruba Art at UCLA* (Los Angeles: University of California, Museum and Laboratories of Ethnic Arts and Technology, 1971), *African Art in Motion: Icon and Act* (Los Angeles: University of California Press, 1974), and *Flash of the Spirit: African and Afro-American Art and Philosophy* (New York: Random House, 1983). [CK]

p. 11 *We were grooving on* Muntu ... Janheinz Jahn, *Muntu: An Outline of the New African Culture* (New York: Grove Press, 1961), was built upon the works of Reverend Placide Tempels, *Bantu Philosophy* (Elizabethville, Congo: Lovania, 1945; Paris: Collection Présence Africaine, 1959), and Maya Deren, *Divine Horsemen: Living Gods of Haiti* (New York: Thames and Hudson, 1953). Using Bantu grammar categories as philosophical principles, Jahn takes the Sapir-Whorf hypothesis that language embodies worldview about as far out as it can go. [CK]

p. 11 *... "it's the sounds, mate ..."* While I may have felt that the search for jazz origins was a personal quest, I learned a lot from roommate David Z. Levin, from arguments with Jonathan Weiss over the devolution of jazz after Oliver, Armstrong, and Morton, and from fellow musicians Dan Hunt, Steve Swallow, Ian Underwood, Chuck Folds, Roz Rudd, Brad Terry, Tony Greenwald, Craig Llewellyn, and Dave Melhorn. The money from Yale fraternities and Yale alumni days enabled me to play in Dixie and swing bands that featured great stylists like Rex Stewart, Buddy Tate, Buck Clayton, Ahmed Abdul Malik, and Herbie Nichols. [CK]

p. 12 . . . *his stuff in* Emotion and Meaning in Music . . . Leonard Meyer's books constitute a rigorous and seminal body of theory on musical style in the Western European art music tradition; see his *Emotion and Meaning in Music* (Chicago: University of Chicago Press, 1956), *Music, the Arts, and Ideas* (Chicago: University of Chicago Press, 1967), *Explaining Music* (Chicago: University of Chicago Press, 1973), and *Style and Music* (Philadelphia: University of Pennsylvania Press, 1989). [SF]

p. 12 . . . *a spectacularly serious academic.* Alan P. Merriam, 1923–1980, co-founder of the Society for Ethnomusicology, served as its president and editor of its journal and played many other roles in its intellectual life. He taught at Indiana University, where he was active in the anthropology department and African studies program from 1962 to 1980. His B.M. (Montana) and M.M. (Northwestern) focused on small- and large-band jazz, arranging, and clarinet. At Northwestern he took a Ph.D. in anthropology under Melville Herskovits and Richard Waterman. His fieldwork, with the Flathead Indians of Montana (1950) and in central Africa (a survey in 1951–52, a year with the Basongye in 1959–60, and a brief return visit in 1973), was the basis for many publications including *Ethnomusicology of the Flathead Indians* (Chicago: Aldine, 1967), *Congo: Background to Conflict* (Evanston: Northwestern University Press, 1960), and *An African World* (Bloomington: Indiana University Press, 1974). Merriam was also a serious bibliographer (with volumes on jazz and ethnomusicological writings) and discographer, with publications including *African Music on LP* (Evanston: Northwestern University Press, 1970). In addition to his *The Anthropology of Music* (Evanston: Northwestern University Press, 1964), he set out his anthropological agenda and vision for the field of ethnomusicology in "Ethnomusicology: Discussion and Definition of the Field," *Ethnomusicology* 4 (1960):107–14; "The Purposes of Ethnomusicology: An Anthropological View," *Ethnomusicology* 7 (1963):206–13; "Ethnomusicology," in *International Encyclopedia of the Social Sciences,* ed. David Sills, 10:562–66 (New York: Macmillan, 1968); "Ethnomusicology Revisited," *Ethnomusicology* 13, no. 2 (1969):213–29; "Ethnomusicology Today," *Current Musicology,* no. 20 (1975), 50–66; and "Definitions of 'Comparative Musicology' and 'Ethnomusicology': An Historical-Theoretical Perspective," *Ethnomusicology* 21, no. 2 (1977):189–204.

For other assessments of Merriam's work, see Frank Gillis, "Alan P. Merriam, 1923–1980," *Ethnomusicology* 24, no. 3 (1980):v–vii; Stephen Wild, "Alan P. Merriam: Professor," *Ethnomusicology* 26 (1):91–98, 1982; Bruno Nettl, "Alan P. Merriam: Scholar and Leader," *Ethnomusicology* 26, no. 1 (1982):99–105; and Caroline Card and Carl Rahkonen, "Alan P. Merriam: Bibliography and Discography," *Ethnomusicology* 26, no. 1 (1982):107–20. [SF]

Merriam's 1964 compilation of ethnomusicological wisdom, *the Anthropology of Music,* has yet to be replaced as the survey text in the field. Tim

Rice's paper, "Toward the Remodeling of Ethnomusicology" and responses to it from Kay Shelemay, Anthony Seeger, Ellen Koskoff, Dane Harwood, and Richard Crawford, in *Ethnomusicology* 31, no. 3 (1987), serve to update Merriam's functionalist model (How do concepts shape the behaviors which shape musical products? in the simpler, idealist, top-down version; How do culture, society, and music interact? in the more cybernetic versions) with a more interpretive approach and the accent on "formative processes." "How do people historically construct, socially maintain, and individually create and experience music?" asks Rice (1987: 473), putting "history," the "individual," and "experience" squarely into the model. As a single question summarizing a field of inquiry, Rice's formulation is a big improvement on the interpretive model of Geertz (1973: 363–64). Yet both models and the commentators on them ignore the key issues of participatory consciousness and mediation/commodification, assuming instead some sort of postparticipatory, precommodified world in which normal social science would account for normal people rationally shaping their musical destinies. Such a world does not exist. [CK]

p. 12 . . . *Edmund Carpenter's media classes* . . . Edmund Carpenter trained as an ethnographer with Frank Speck at the University of Pennsylvania, receiving his Ph.D. in 1950. His field research was in northern Canada with Inuit people. With Marshall McLuhan he codirected the University of Toronto's Center for Culture and Technology and coedited its journal, *Explorations,* from 1953 to 1959. Selections from the journal (including his own famous essay "Acoustic Space") appeared in a book coedited with McLuhan, *Explorations in Communication* (Boston: Beacon, 1960); other selections appeared in a book edited by McLuhan, *Verbi-Voco-Visual Explorations* (New York: Something Else Press, 1967). In the 1960s Carpenter, along with McLuhan and Tony Schwartz, taught media and communications at Fordham; Carpenter later taught at the New School and Adelphi. His books include, with D. Varley and R. Flaherty, *Eskimo* (Toronto: University of Toronto Press, 1959); with Ken Heyman, *They Became What They Beheld* (New York: Weidenfeld, 1970); *Oh, What a Blow That Phantom Gave Me!* (New York: Holt, Rinehart Winston, 1972); and *Eskimo Realities* (New York: Holt, Rinehart Winston, 1973). Among his best known articles are: "The Eskimo Artist," in *Anthropology and Art: Readings in Cross-Cultural Aesthetics,* ed. Charlotte Otten (Garden City: Natural History Press, 1971); "If Wittgenstein Had Been an Eskimo," *Varsity Graduate* (University of Toronto), 12, no. 3 (1969):50–66 (a brief version appeared under the same title in *Natural History* 89, no. 2 [February 1980]: 72–77); and "Comments," in *Tradition and Creativity in Tribal Art,* ed. Daniel Biebuyck, 203–13 (Berkeley: University of California Press, 1969); other articles were published in popular magazines (*Natural History, TV Guide*) as well as ethnological journals.

As a teacher Carpenter was extraordinarily witty, irreverent, and acerbic. Although I've come to recognize problems inherent in his tendency to overtheorize an oral-literate great divide (see my "Orality and Consciousness," in *The Oral and Literate in Music,* ed. Y. Tokumaru and O. Yamaguti, 18–28, [Tokyo: Academia Music, 1986]), his work remains a seminal and artistically vibrant call for what has more recently developed into a more mainstream anthropology of the senses; see, for example, David Howes, ed., *The Varieties of Sensory Experience: A Reader in the Anthropology of the Senses* (Toronto: University of Toronto Press, 1991). [SF]

p. 14 . . . *integration of research and commitment.* My undergraduate teachers were students of Franz Boas, Ruth Benedict, Conrad Arensberg, Solon Kimball, E. E. Evans-Pritchard, George Peter Murdock, and Margaret Mead. In graduate school, my teachers were students of Melville Herskovits, Alfred Kroeber, and Edward Sapir. I was thus provided with an extraordinary set of linkages to the formative periods of American and British anthropological theory. [SF]

p. 14 . . . *we don't know how the torch was passed* . . . It saddens me to see a deterioration in the historically powerful civil rights alliance between African-Americans and Jewish-Americans, specifically, and in communications between blacks and whites generally in the U.S. Hopefully the destructive spiral of white racism, black anger and threats, then more white racism and blaming the victim, can be broken. Recent manifestations of African-American nationalism—more confrontational, polemical, and fantastic than ever before—put more pressure on white people to be "bad parents" in relation to "children" having temper tantrums. Should rap death threats against cops, the governor of Arizona, and white people in general (one song, for example, advocated an annual "killing week") be (*a*) ignored, (*b*) minimized, as artistic expression, profitable pop culture, just words, free speech, signifying, blowing off steam, or (*c*) taken seriously, as shouts of Fire! in crowded theaters where the vast majority of those crushed at the exits are likely to be black? Whenever the symbolism of violence is acted out it has been, is, and will probably be a disaster for African-American communities. In contrast, even the symbolism of autonomy—slogans and bumper stickers *about* buying black, buying land, building the factory and owning the jobs, opening shops, controlling neighborhood schools—is not very visible recently, so I assume the reality, the substance of community building, is even further away. Vaudeville violence, murderous minstrelsy, vengeance symbolism on MTV, and the scapegoating in real life of other minorities—Jews, Koreans, Arabs—are all pathetic responses to a deepening class struggle between rich and poor that requires long-term planning and imaginative strategies for stopping the violence, empowering the children, and building communities. [CK]

p. 14 . . . *going to film school for a year.* Visual anthropology, in the sense of the study of visual manifestations of culture and the making of photographic representations of it, has been around since the emergence of anthropology as a discipline. To me this area has always seemed fertile ground, both for the integration of artistic practices within ethnography and for meditation on the uses of the visual. Some of the basic orientations toward image making in social research and ethnomusicology are stated in Gregory Bateson and Margaret Mead, *Balinese Character* (New York: New York Academy of Sciences, 1942); Howard Becker, "Photography and Sociology," *Studies in the Anthropology of Visual Communication* 1, no. 1 (1974):3–26; "Do Photographs Tell the Truth?" *Afterimage,* 5 February 1978, 9–13; Paul Byers, "Cameras Don't Take Pictures," *Columbia University Forum* 9, no. 1 (1966):28–32; John Collier, *Visual Anthropology: Photography as a Research Method* (New York: Holt, Rinehart, Winston, 1967); Peter Crawford and David Turton, eds., *Film as Ethnography* (Manchester: Manchester University Press, 1992); A. M. Dauer, "Research Films in Ethnomusicology," *Yearbook of the International Folk Music Council* 1 (1969):226–31; Luc de Heusch, *Cinema and Social Science* (Paris: UNESCO, 1960), reprinted in *Visual Anthropology* 1, no. 2 (1988):99–156; Paul Hockings, ed., *Principles of Visual Anthropology* (The Hague: Mouton, 1975); Paul Hockings and Yasuhiro Omori, eds., *Cinematographic Theory and New Dimensions in Ethnographic Film,* Senri Ethnological Studies, no. 24 (Osaka: National Museum of Ethnology, 1988); Alan Lomax, "Choreometrics and Ethnographic Filmmaking," *Filmmaker's Newsletter* 4, no. 4 (1971):22–30, and "Audio-visual tools for the Analysis of Culture Style," in *Principles of Visual Anthropology,* ed. Paul Hockings; Jack Rollwagen, ed., *Anthropological Filmmaking* (New York: Harwood, 1988); Jay Ruby, "Ethnography as Trompe l'Oeil: Film and Anthropology," in *A Crack in the Mirror: Reflexive Perspectives in Anthropology,* ed. Jay Ruby and Barbara Myerhoff, 121–31 (Philadelphia: University of Pennsylvania Press, 1982); Allen Grimshaw, ed., *Sociological Methods and Research* (special issue on sound-image records in social-interaction research) 11, no. 2 (1982); Ruth Stone and Verlon Stone, "Event, Feedback, and Analysis: Research Media in the Study of Music Events," *Ethnomusicology* 25, no. 2 (1981):215–25; Jon Wagner, ed., *Images of Information: Still Photography in the Social Sciences* (Beverly Hills: Sage, 1979); Sol Worth, *Studying Visual Communication* (Philadelphia: University of Pennsylvania Press, 1981); and Hugo Zemp, "Filming Music and Looking at Music Films," *Ethnomusicology* 32, no. 3 (1988):393–427.

Some of my own early perspectives on visual anthropology and ethnomusicology can be found in Steven Feld and Carroll Williams, "Toward a Researchable Film Language," *Studies in the Anthropology of Visual Communication* 2, no. 1 (1974):25–32; Steven Feld, "Ethnomusicology and Visual Communication," *Ethnomusicology* 20, no. 2 (1976):293–325.

For many in the visual anthropology field, Jean Rouch's work represents a particularly intense integration of the arts of ethnography and film. For introductions to Rouch's cinema and ethnography see my "Themes in the Cinema of Jean Rouch," *Visual Anthropology* 2 (1989):223–47, and Paul Stoller, *The Cinematic Griot* (Chicago: University of Chicago Press, 1992). My translations of Rouch's major writings are of *Le caméra et les hommes,* as

"The camera and man," *Studies in the Anthropology of Visual Communication* 1, no. 1 (1974): 37–44; *La situation et tendances du cinéma en Afrique,* as "The Situation and Tendencies of the Cinema in Africa," *Studies in the Anthropology of Visual Communication* 2, no. 1 (1975): 51–58, and 2, no. 2 (1975): 112–21; with Shari Robertson, *Essai sur les avatars de la personne du possedé, du magicien, du sorcier, du cinéaste et de l'ethnographe,* as "On the Vicissitudes of the Self: The Possessed Dancer, the Magician, the Sorcerer, the Filmmaker and the Ethnographer," *Studies in the Anthropology of Visual Communication* 5, no. 1 (1978): 2–8; with Anny Ewing, *Chronique d'un été* (by Rouch and Edgar Morin), as "Chronicle of a Summer," *Studies in Visual Communication* 11, no. 1 (1985): 2–78; and, with Anny Ewing, *Entretien de Jean Rouch avec le Professeur Enrico Fulchignoni,* as "Conversation between Jean Rouch and Enrico Fulchignoni," *Visual Anthropology* 2 (1989): 265–300. [SF]

In conducting and presenting our polka research my wife, Angie, and I worked closely with photographer Dick Blau to juxtapose text and pictures in *Polka Happiness* (Philadelphia: Temple University Press, 1992) and *Polka Perspectives* (Chicago: University of Chicago Press, forthcoming). I know that I am very naive about taking pictures, snapping at the obvious, trying to capture the energy, the high points of an event, and that my friend Dick is much more aware of the specific contexts (from store fronts and street corners to backyards and alleys), the interactive (selling and taking of tickets, giving and receiving of autographs), the before and after (musicians setting up; dancers standing or sitting, exhausted but happy) that would never catch my attention. While we share a general, cumulative sense of satisfaction that the images add up and complement the narrative, we know how tricky it is to capture polka dancers in motion in a way that says "polka" and not simply generic dancing joy and how difficult it was to select one picture for the cover that would sum things up. The whole process of taking and selecting pictures seems more mysterious, arbitrary, intuitive, and fortuitous the more I do it; the faith we have that a picture will save the day, illustrating our main concept or summing up our argument, is sometimes misplaced. [CK]

p. 15 . . . *the world of Monk's music.* Thelonious Monk's important earlier recordings on the Blue Note label have been reissued in sets by both Blue Note and Mosaic. Later important recordings, including *Monk and Coltrane, Live at Town Hall, Brilliant Corners, Monk's Music, Live at the Five Spot,* and *Alone in San Francisco* appeared on Riverside and have all been reissued singly and in sets. The last segment of Monk's recording career was with Columbia; some of the important recordings are *Monk's Dream, Criss-Cross, Monk's Time, Solo Monk,* and *Misterioso.* Of the European volumes that have been reissued, the Mosaic compilation of the Vogue and Black Lion sessions is a standout.

In the late 1970s I formed a quartet in Santa Fe, modeled on the Steve Lacy–Roswell Rudd–Henry Grimes–Dennis Charles 1962–65 Monk study band (their only recording is *School Days,* a live 1963 session, released by Emanem in 1975), to work through a number of Monk charts. Writing arrangements and learning the tunes with Jay Peck, David Moir, and Pete Amahl humbled me as I came to appreciate how much Monk contributed to the use of whole-tone scales, ♭5 and ♭9 harmonies, and swing, stride, and shuffle grooves. Only later was I able to approach the ballads and Monk's maze of seeming harmonic dead ends that quickly turn into familiar cycles. "Ruby My Dear" and "Pannonica" still have the capacity to amaze me almost daily. In the ten years since Monk's death, his music has flourished and been widely recorded. Of that voluminous output some of the most imaginative melodic and rhythmic rehearings for me have come from Jerry Gonzalez's re-grooving of Monk to the clavé, on his 1989 *Rumba Para Monk* CD on Sunnyside. I find myself returning regularly to Monk's Riverside volumes, but also to Steve Lacy's many renditions of Monk tunes. No Monkologist has been more dedicated than Lacy; his recordings of the Monk songbook in solo and small group settings represent a thirty-five-year labor of love. Of the earlier volumes my favorite is still *Reflections,* a 1958 Prestige date with Mal Waldron, Buell Neidlinger, and Elvin Jones; the solos on "Four in One," "Skippy," and "Ask Me Now" are a remarkable textbook on Monk's harmonic theories. Of the more recent recordings, the solo *Only Monk,* recorded in 1985 on Soul Note, offers a compelling "Work," a mysterious "Misterioso," and wild versions of two of the less often recorded pieces, "Humph" and "Who Knows." And the reunion volume with Roswell Rudd, *Regeneration,* also on Soul Note (1983), is full of Monkish energy, with a very emotional reading of "Monk's Mood," an almost Dixie shuffle on the "Friday the Thirteenth" vamp, and a burning "Epistrophy." [SF]

I've begun to discover the deeper joys of Monk's music recently by playing his melodies, for example, "Jackieing" and "Crepescule with Nellie," on my cornet day after day. Something about the little pauses in the midst of phrases, the repositioning of harmonic elements to create overtones that echo after one phrase and into the next, is gradually letting me understand how both the processual and textural participatory discrepancies (see chapter 3) can be thought of as framing each and every sound. Time flows exist to show deliberation and intent. One of my favorite Monk LPs, heard for the first time on a visit to Steve, is the 1971 two-volume Black Lion sessions (rereleased on Mosaic) recorded in London with Art Blakey and Al McKibbon in firm support; it includes a great take of "Evidence." [CK]

p. 15 . . . *our encounters with Robert P. Armstrong* . . . Robert Plant Armstrong's trilogy on aesthetics and humanistic anthropology comprises *The Affecting Presence: An Essay in Humanistic Anthropology* (Urbana: University of Illinois Press, 1971), *Wellspring: On the Myth and Source of Culture* (Berkeley: University of California Press, 1975), and *The Powers of Presence: Consciousness, Myth, and the Affecting Presence* (Philadelphia: University of Pennsylvania Press, 1981). [SF]

p. 17 . . . *push through to mystical participation* . . . Books that discuss the possibilities of reclaiming participatory consciousness include Owen Barfield's
Saving the Appearances: Studies in Idolatry (Middletown: Wesleyan University Press, 1965) and Morris Berman's *The Reenchantment of the World*
(New York: Bantam Books, 1984). Much of Gregory Bateson's work moves
in the same direction; see *Steps to an Ecology of Mind* (New York: Ballantine
Books, 1972), *Mind and Nature: A Necessary Unity* (New York: Dutton,
1979), and *A Sacred Unity: Further Steps to an Ecology of Mind* (New York:
Cornelia & Michael Bessie Books, 1991). Issues of *The Trumpeter, Journal
of Ecosophy,* often have very helpful articles, for example, vol. 9, no. 2
(1992):43–88, with sixteen articles on the deep ecology movement and
the philosophy of Arne Naess. [CK]

p. 17 . . . *cream of Yoruba-ness* . . . For "cream of Yoruba-ness," see the Robert
Farris Thompson books cited on p. 34, at comment with reference to page
10, and the second half of Armstrong's *Affecting Presence,* cited on p. 40,
bottom. The stories of Amos Tutuola—such as *The Palm Wine Drinkard*
(New York: Grove, 1953), *My Life in the Bush of Ghosts* (London: Faber and
Faber, 1954), and *Feather Woman of the Jungle* (London: Faber and Faber,
1962)—and their use by Ulli Beier and Suzanne Wenger to inspire a whole
school of artists (notably Twins Seven Seven) in Oshogbo and Ibadan during the early 1960s represent a great "art world" synthesis that deserves a
loving description (see Harold R. Collins, *Amos Tutuola* [New York: Twayne
Publishers, 1969]). Chris Waterman's *Jùjú: A Social History and Ethnography
of an African Popular Music* (Chicago: University of Chicago Press, 1990)
contextualizes the main urban musical style very skillfully and contains a
fine bibliography. Henry Drewal and Margaret Drewal's *Gelede: Art and
Female Power Among the Yoruba* (Bloomington: Indiana University Press,
1983) and, more recently, Karin Barber's *I Could Speak Until Tomorrow:
Oriki, Women and the Past in a Yoruba Town* (Edinburgh: Edinburgh University Press, 1991) and Andrew Apter's *Black Critics and Kings: The Hermeneutics of Power in Yoruba Society* (Chicago: University of Chicago Press, 1992)
have explored other rich traditions within the Yoruba expressive universe.
For a classic interpretation of Yoruba religion in the New World see Roger
Bastide, *The African Religions of Brazil: Toward a Sociology of the Interpenetration of Civilizations* (Baltimore: Johns Hopkins University Press, 1978). [CK]

p. 18 . . . *a generally Marxist paradigm* . . . While applied Marxism in big states
seems to be slipping swiftly and deservedly into the historical archives,
Marxism as a theory of how the world works still has a lot to recommend
it: the focus on material conditions, class forces, historical sequences, oppressions and alienations, and a dialectical sensibility. Two short articles,
"Applied Ethnomusicology and a Rebirth of Music from the Spirit of
Tragedy" (*Ethnomusicology* 26, no. 3 [1982]:407–11) and "Culture, Music
and Collaborative Learning" (in *Dialectical Anthropology: Essays in Honor
of Stanley Diamond,* ed. Christine Gailey [Gainesville: University Press of

Florida, 1992]), the introduction and concluding chapter of *Tiv Song: The Sociology of Art in a Classless Society* (Chicago: University of Chicago Press, 1979), and chapters 5 and 7 here represent my best efforts to bring some Marxist assumptions into ethnomusicology. I have been less concerned with the correct political line and more concerned with correct praxis, working collaboratively (this book, the two on polka, and *My Music* are all collaborative efforts), while trying to keep the focus on working-class people who are neither often heard from nor generally credited with creating their own cultures. Whatever theoretical gains I've been able to make in ethnomusicology since graduate school have come from a slow absorption of basic Marxist and feminist tenets in working with my American Studies and Women's Studies colleagues at SUNY/Buffalo over the years, especially Liz Kennedy and Angie Keil, from team-teaching with John Shepherd and auditing his excellent lectures at Trent University (summers of 1982 and 1983), and from reading Ken Gourlay's "The Role of the Ethnomusicologist in Research," *Ethnomusicology* 22, no. 1 (1978):1–36, Chris Small's *Music: Society: Education* (London: John Calder, 1977) and *Music of the Common Tongue: Survival and Celebration in Afro-American Music* (London: John Calder, 1987), and many of John Blacking's books and articles. Basic Marxist axioms and a long British socialist tradition suffuse these writings, usually in a gentle and clarifying way that offers a corrective to the lack of sociological imagination in much American scholarship (see C. Wright Mills, *The Sociological Imagination* [New York: Oxford University Press, 1959]).

   Marxism and Art: Essays Classic and Contemporary, ed. Maynard Solomon (New York: Vintage Books, 1974), is an introduction to a host of original thinkers from a variety of European Marxist traditions. Graduate students still find it useful to trace the post-Marxist commentary on popular culture from Theodor Adorno and Max Horkheimer ("The Culture Industry: Enlightenment as Mass Deception," in *Dialectic of Enlightenment,* 120–67 [New York: Seabury Press, 1972]) through Raymond Williams (*Society and Culture 1780–1950* [New York: Harper and Row, 1958], *The Country and the City* [New York: Oxford University Press, 1973], *Problems in Materialism and Culture* [London: Verso, 1980], *Resources of Hope: Culture, Democracy and Socialism* [London: Verso, 1989], *The Sociology of Culture* [New York: Schocken Books, 1981], and *Raymond Williams on Television: Selected Writings* [London: Routledge, 1989]) to Stuart Hall (*Culture, Media, Language: Working Papers in Cultural Studies, 1972–1979,* ed. Stuart Hall et al. [London: Hutchinson, 1980]). [CK]

   Charlie's emphasis on dialectics and history in our early-1980s discussions, and his interest in the British critical tradition opened up a new window for me into John Blacking's scholarship, in both its ethnographic concern with the extraordinary humanity beneath the brutal realities of South Africa and its general concern with musical sociability and liberation. Blacking (1928–1990) developed a broad range of humanistic, scientific, and historical concerns linking the biological and cognitive aspects of musical experience with the shaping forces and structural dimensions of power. Among his many books and articles, I've often returned to *Venda Children's Songs: A Study in Ethnomusicological Analysis* (Johannesburg: Witwatersrand University Press, 1967); *How Musical is Man?* (Seattle: University of Washington Press, 1973); *"A Common-Sense View of all Music": Reflections on Percy Grainger's Writings on Ethnomusicology and Music Education* (Cambridge: Cambridge University Press, 1987); *The Anthropology of the Body* (London: Academic Press, 1977); "The Value of Music in Human Experience," *Yearbook of the International Folk Music Council* 1 (1971): 33–71; "Some Problems of Theory and Method in the Study of Musical Change," *Yearbook of the International Folk Music Council* 9 (1979): 1–26; "Political and Musical Freedom in the Music of Some Black South African Churches," in *The Structure of Folk Models,* ed. L. Holy and M. Struchlik, 35–62 (London: Academic Press, 1980); "Making Artistic Popular Music: The Goal of True Folk," *Popular Music* 1 (1981): 9–14; "The Problem of Ethnic Perceptions in the Semiotics of Music," in *The Sign in Music and Literature,* ed. Wendy Steiner, 184–94 (Austin: University of Texas Press, 1981); "The Biology of Music-Making," in *Ethnomusicology: An Introduction,* ed. H. Myers, 301–14 (New York: W. W. Norton, 1992). For overviews of Blacking's impact on music studies and full bibliographies of his extensive writings, see the obituaries by Jim Kippen in *Ethnomusicology* 34, no. 2 (1990): 263–70; John Baily in *Yearbook for Traditional Music* 22 (1990): xxii-xxi; and Jan Fairley in *Popular Music* 10, no. 2 (1990): 115–19, and the biographical interview with Blacking in *Ethnomusicology* 35, no. 1 (1991): 55–76. [SF]

p. 18 . . . *our symposium . . . at the ethnomusicology meetings . . .* We jointly organized a panel for the 1983 Society for Ethnomusicology annual meetings, in Tallahassee, Florida, on the comparative sociomusicology of classless societies. The goal was to develop a model for qualitative comparison of the interrelations between musical style and social organization. Presentations of papers by each of us and by Marina Roseman generated lively discussions. The symposium was published in *Ethnomusicology* 28, no. 3 (1984); two long papers (Steven Feld, "Sound Structure as Social Structure," 383–409, and Marina Roseman, "The Social Structuring of Sound: The Temiar of Peninsular Malaysia," 411–45) were followed by comments and critiques from Charles Keil, Ellen Basso, Judith and Alton Becker, Robert Knox Dentan, Kenneth A. Gourlay, William Powers, Carol Robertson, and Anthony Seeger (446–66). In subsequent years SEM panels have extended the framework of that session to class and stratified societies; some papers from those sessions, and others on our original topic, have since been published in the journal; e.g., Donald Brenneis, "Passion and Performance in Fiji Indian Vernacular Song," *Ethnomusicology* 29, no. 3 (1985): 397–408; Thomas Turino, "The Coherence of Social Style and Musical Creation among the Aymara in Southern Peru," *Ethnomusicology* 33, no. 1 (1989): 1–30; and John Kaemmer, "Social Power and Music Change among Shona," *Ethnomusicology* 33, no. 1 (1989):31–45. [SF]

p. 19 . . . *reading my Barfield and my Lévy-Bruhl* . . . A few of the older anthropological classics on participatory consciousness are Lucien Lévy-Bruhl, *Primitive Mentality* (New York: MacMillan, 1923), *The "Soul" of the Primitive* (New York: MacMillan, 1928), and *How Natives Think* (New York: Washington Square Press, 1966); Maurice Leenhardt, *Do Kamo: Person and Myth in the Melanesian World* (1947; Chicago: University of Chicago Press, 1979); and Bruno Snell, *The Discovery of Mind: The Greek Origins of European Thought* (Cambridge, Mass.: Harvard University Press, 1953).

Until I came across Owen Barfield's work, Kenneth Burke's many works on "dramatism" (e.g., *Language as Symbolic Action* [Berkeley: University of California Press, 1968]) and his visit to Buffalo, when he preached the gospel of "antiabolitionism" (that the agricultural, industrial, and informational revolutions have *not* abolished our collective "species being") were my main reference points for thinking about participation. Occasionally a new book pops up that makes the same point in a fresh way; for example, Rogan P. Taylor, *The Death and Resurrection Show: From Shaman to Superstar* (London: Anthony Blond, 1985).

William Blake and any good poetry puts me in a no-compromise mood about the value of participation. See Linda Levalley Cervantes, "Going West: Poetry, Poetics, and Anthropology," in *Dialectical Anthropology: Essays in Honor of Stanley Diamond*, vol. 2, *The Politics of Culture and Creativity: A Critique of Civilization*, ed. Christine Gailey, 249–80 (Gainesville: University Press of Florida, 1992). All of what we call "the arts," including "music," were once part of ritual. Rites filled with music-dance bound humans to nature and to each other and gave us our fullest sense of ourselves, our deepest identities. With each division and renaming of ritual into discrete arts, some degree of participatory consciousness was sacrificed. Participation is about consubstantiation; this is the lesson of *Tiv Song* and *Sound and Sentiment*. These ethnographies are about the primacy *and* destruction of prime or genuine cultures, about the forces that create and destroy social integration and pleasure in daily life. [CK]

p. 19 . . . *collaborative work with Buck and Bambi Schieffelin* . . . My first fieldwork in Bosavi in 1976–77 took place alongside the linguistic and ethnographic work of Bambi B. Schieffelin and Edward L. ("Buck") Schieffelin (they had worked previously in Bosavi in 1966–68). I was introduced to Kaluli people as Bambi's younger brother; this meant Buck and I were brothers-in-law and Zachary Schieffelin and I were mother's brother/sister's son, a special, named reciprocal relationship. Apart from learning to fulfill the Kaluli expectations for such relationships, we profited from each other's work in numerous direct and indirect ways. Although we had separate houses and most of the time pursued our work separately, we had meals together and were constantly in dialogue about everything from everyday village life and practical details of the Kaluli language to the specific nature of our linguistic, musical, and ethnographic projects. A wide range of information was routinely shared, and three voices usually meant that we stayed humbly mindful of the complexities that surrounded us. Although we have rarely presented our work together and even less frequently coauthored papers in the years following our initial fieldwork, we have consistently drawn on each other's expertise and special interests and routinely benefited from each other's insights, readings, and criticisms. The 1984 and 1990 linguistic projects I pursued with Bambi B. Schieffelin were specifically organized and funded as collaborations on Kaluli narratives and on a dictionary; we anticipate more coauthored work in those areas.

The main book-length statements from our collective Kaluli research are Bambi B. Schieffelin, *The Give and Take of Everyday Life: Language Socialization of Kaluli Children* (New York: Cambridge University Press, 1990); Edward L. Schieffelin, *The Sorrow of the Lonely and the Burning of the Dancers* (New York: St. Martins Press, 1976); Edward L. Schieffelin and Robert Crittenden, *Like People You See in a Dream: First Contact in Six Papuan Societies* (Stanford: Stanford University Press, 1991); and Steven Feld, *Sound and Sentiment: Birds, Weeping, Poetics and Song in Kaluli Expression,* 2nd ed. (Philadelphia: University of Pennsylvania Press, 1990). Each contains extensive references to other articles reporting on the Kaluli. [SF]

p. 19 . . . *"Hey, this music is about the earth . . ."* See Wendy Wickwire, "Theories of Ethnomusicology and the North American Indian: Retrospective and Critique," *Canadian University Music Review* 6 (1985):186–221. [CK]

p. 19 . . . *Marina Roseman hears it so clearly . . .* Marina Roseman's ethnographic and ethnomusicological research among the Temiar of Malaysia in the early 1980s takes up a number of themes relating nature and culture through music and thus provides, in addition to its intrinsic importance, a useful comparison to the Kaluli materials. Her work is reported in "The Social Structuring of Sound: The Temiar of Peninsular Malaysia," *Ethnomusicology* 28, no. 3 (1984):411–45; "Inversion and Conjuncture: Male and Female Performance among the Temiar of Peninsular Malaysia," in *Women and Music in Cross-Cultural Perspective,* ed. Ellen Koskoff, 131–49 (Westport: Greenwood Press, 1987); "The Pragmatics of Aesthetics: The Performance of Healing among Senoi Temiar," *Social Science and Medicine* 27, no. 8 (1988):811–18; "Head, Heart, Odor and Shadow: The Structure of the Self, the Emotional World, and Ritual Performance among Senoi Temiar," *Ethos* 18, no. 3 (1990):227–50; and *Healing Sounds from the Malaysian Rainforest: Temiar Music and Medicine* (Berkeley: University of California Press, 1991). [SF]

p. 20 . . . *symbolic analyses and . . . materialist . . . perspectives.* A variety of writings are useful for understanding the development of culture theory and, particularly, the shifting trends in the field during the 1970s and

1980s: Richard N. Adams, *Energy and Structure: A Theory of Social Power* (Austin: University of Texas Press, 1975); Keith Basso and Henry Selby, eds., *Meaning in Anthropology* (Albuquerque: University of New Mexico Press, 1976); James Boon, *Other Tribes, Other Scribes* (New York: Cambridge University Press, 1982); Pierre Bourdieu, *Outline of a Theory of Practice* (New York: Cambridge University Press, 1977); Ernst Cassirer, *The Philosophy of Symbolic Forms* (1923; New Haven: Yale University Press, 1955); James Clifford, *The Predicament of Culture* (Cambridge, Mass.: Harvard University Press, 1988); Benjamin Colby, James Fernandez, and David Kronenfeld, "Toward a Convergence of Cognitive and Symbolic Anthropology," *American Ethnologist*, 8, no. 3 (1981):422–50; Janet Dolgin, David Kemnitzer, and David M. Schneider, eds., *Symbolic Anthropology* (New York: Columbia University Press, 1977); Mary Douglas, *Natural Symbols: Explorations in Cosmology* (New York: Pantheon, 1971); Mary Douglas, ed., *Rules and Meanings: The Anthropology of Everyday Knowledge* (Hammondsworth: Penguin, 1973); Emile Durkheim, *The Elementary Forms of the Religious Life* (1905; New York: Collier, 1961); James Fernandez, *Persuasions and Performances* (Bloomington: Indiana University Press, 1986); James Fernandez, ed., *Beyond Metaphor: The Theory of Tropes in Anthropology* (Stanford: Stanford University Press, 1991); Clifford Geertz, *The Interpretation of Cultures* (New York: Basic Books, 1973) and *Local Knowledge: Further Essays in Interpretive Anthropology* (New York: Basic Books, 1983); Arnold van Gennep, *The Rites of Passage* (1909; London: Routledge and Kegan Paul, 1960); Anthony Giddens, *Central Problems in Social Theory* (Berkeley: University of California Press, 1979) and *The Constitution of Society* (Berkeley: University of California Press, 1984); Dell Hymes, ed., *Reinventing Anthropology* (New York: Random House/Viking, 1972); Roger Keesing, "Theories of Culture," *Annual Review of Anthropology* 3 (1974):74–98; Edmund Leach, *Culture and Communication: The Logic by which Symbols are Connected* (Cambridge: Cambridge University Press, 1976); Claude Lévi-Strauss, *The Savage Mind* (Chicago: University of Chicago Press, 1962) and "The Effectiveness of Symbols," in *Structural Anthropology* (New York: Basic Books, 1963); George Marcus and Michael Fischer, *Anthropology as Cultural Critique* (Chicago: University of Chicago Press, 1986); Marcel Mauss, *The Gift* (1925; London: Cohen and West, 1954); Sherry B. Ortner, "Theory in Anthropology since the Sixties," *Comparative Studies in Society and History* 26, no. 1 (1984): 126–66; Sherry Ortner and Harriet Whitehead, eds., *Sexual Meanings: The Cultural Construction of Gender and Sexuality* (New York: Cambridge University Press, 1981); Paul Rabinow and William Sullivan, eds., *Interpretive Social Science: A Reader,* 2d ed. (Berkeley: University of California Press, 1987); Roy Rappaport, *Ecology, Meaning and Religion* (Berkeley: North Atlantic Books, 1979); Marshall Sahlins, *Culture and Practical Reason* (Chicago: University of Chicago Press, 1976) and *Islands of History* (Chicago: University of Chicago Press, 1985); J. David Sapir and Christopher Crocker, eds., *The*

Social Use of Metaphor (Philadelphia: University of Pennsylvania Press, 1977); Richard Schweder and Robert Levine, eds., *Culture Theory: Essays on Mind, Self, and Emotion* (Cambridge: Cambridge University Press, 1984); Victor Turner, *The Forest of Symbols* (Ithaca: Cornell University Press, 1967), *The Ritual Process* (Ithaca: Cornell University Press, 1969), *Dramas, Fields, and Metaphors: Symbolic Action in Human Society* (Ithaca: Cornell University Press, 1974), and "Symbolic Studies," *Annual Review of Anthropology* 4 (1975):145–61; Victor Turner and Edward Bruner, eds., *The Anthropology of Experience* (Urbana: University of Illinois Press, 1986); and Roy Wagner, *The Invention of Culture* (Chicago: University of Chicago Press, 1981) and *Symbols That Stand for Themselves* (Chicago: University of Chicago Press, 1986). [SF]

p. 21 . . . *phenomenology of the senses and the social world.* Peter Berger and Thomas Luckman, *The Social Construction of Reality* (New York: Anchor Doubleday, 1967), is still a fine introduction to social phenomenology and the ideas of Alfred Schutz. For a deeper view see Schutz, *Collected Papers,* 2 vols. (The Hague: Nijhoff, 1970), *The Phenomenology of the Social World* (Evanston: Northwestern University Press, 1967), and *On Phenomenology and Social Relations: Selected Writings* (Chicago: University of Chicago Press, 1970). Schutz's often-quoted paper on "tuning up" and "tuning in" is "Making Music Together: A Study in Social Relationship," *Social Research* 18, no. 1 (1951):76–97, reprinted in *Symbolic Anthropology,* ed. Janet Dolgin, David Kemnitzer, and David M. Schneider, 106–9 (New York: Columbia University Press, 1977). Key texts for a phenomenological appreciation of cultural complexity include Maurice Merleau-Ponty, *The Phenomenology of Perception* (London: Routledge and Kegan Paul, 1962), *The Primacy of Perception and Other Essays* (Evanston: Northwestern University Press, 1964), *Sense and Non-Sense* (Evanston: Northwestern University Press, 1964), and *Phenomenology, Language and Sociology: Selected Essays* (London: Heineman, 1974). Also see Paul Ricoeur, *The Rule of Metaphor* (Toronto: University of Toronto Press, 1979) and *Hermeneutics and Human Sciences* (New York: Cambridge University Press, 1981); Martin Heidegger, *Poetry, Language, Thought* (New York: Harper and Row, 1971) and *Identity and Difference* (New York: Harper and Row, 1974); and Henri Bergson, *Dreams* (London: T. Fisher Unwin, 1914), *Introduction to Metaphysics: The Creative Mind* (Indianapolis: Bobbs-Merrill, 1980), and *Matter and Memory* (New York: Zone Books, 1988). [SF]

p. 21 . . . *the obsolescence of high culture* . . . On the obsolescence of high culture in music, Henry Pleasants, *Serious Music—And All That Jazz* (London: Victor Gollancz, 1969), and Christopher Small, *Music–Society–Education* (London: John Calder, 1977), present some of the main arguments. Roger Taylor, *Art, an Enemy of the People* (Hassocks, U.K.: Harvester Press, 1978), is another powerful warning about taking high culture too seriously. [CK]

p. 22 . . . *an emerging planetary culture* . . . In the opening paragraphs of my "Paideia con Salsa: Ancient Greek Education for Active Citizenship and the Role of Latin Dance-Music in Our Schools" (in *Becoming Human through Music,* ed. David McAllester [Reston, Va.: Music Educators National Conference, 1985]), I tried to spell out an agenda for "world peace and justice" through "planned cultural layering from a . . . world government point of view . . . biculturalism or triculturalism from an individual vantage point [and] a complex problem of cultural sequencing from an educational perspective":

> Many of us, especially those privileged white folks who profit most from planet rape, will have to develop at least two, probably three, layers of cultural awareness and loyalty. First, in relation to a local, satisfying, self-sufficient culture in depth where a passionate "us-ness" cannot lead to wars because it is small, localized—one of a great many such passions. Second, in relation to larger bio-regional watershed cultures that seem to be shaping up as Atlantic and Pacific "rims" now but that might reshape themselves into smaller regions later. Finally, some cosmic consciousness or a thin layer of planetary culture will probably be required of some or all of us so that regions or the peoples within regions do not drift back into aggressing, aggrandizing, state-building and empire expanding.

See also p. 339, comments following dialogue 3, "Commodified Grooves," at the reference to page 312. [CK]

p. 23 . . . *Amiri Baraka's "changing same."* Back when Leroi Jones was becoming Amiri Baraka and creating articles, reviews, plays, and books at a terrific pace, the "changing same" was a good description for both his own production and for black music generally (see his *Black Music* [New York: William Morrow, 1970], especially the last chapter, "The Changing Same [R & B and New Black Music]," and the last chapter of *Blues People* [New York: William Morrow, 1963]). If strong writing could keep black music whole and healthy in the face of commodification pressures, this writing would do it. [CK]

p. 25 *Isn't James a wonder?* For a basic James Brown biography and discography, see James Brown with Bruce Tucker, *James Brown: The Godfather of Soul* (New York: Macmillan, 1986). JB's classic 1960s recordings on King Records include singles of "Bewildered," "Lost Someone," "Night Train," "Please, Please, Please," "Papa's Got a Brand New Bag," "I'll Go Crazy," "Ain't That a Groove," "Money Won't Change You," "Cold Sweat," "I Can't Stand Myself," "Licking Stick," "Give It Up or Turn It Loose," "Mother Popcorn," "Sex Machine," "Talkin' Loud and Sayin' Nothin'," and "It's a Man's, Man's, Man's World." The King materials plus Brown's sides since the early 1970s have been reissued on numerous Polydor volumes; major anthologies include *Roots of Revolution, Soul Classics; Ain't That a*

Groove—The James Brown Story 1966–69; Doing It to Death—The James Brown Story 1970–73; Dead on the Heavy Funk—1974–76; Startime; and *Motherlode.* These anthologies include the tunes "Soul Power," "I Got You/ I Feel Good," "Night Train," "Hot Pants," "King Heroin," "Say It Loud I'm Black and I'm Proud," "Try Me," "I Don't Want Nobody to Give Me Nothing," "Out of Sight," "Don't Be a Dropout," "I Got Ants in My Pants," "People Get Up and Drive Your Funky Soul," "You Got to Have a Mother for Me." The *Live at the Apollo* sessions, perhaps JB's best known early recordings, have been reissued on Rhino. [CK and SF]

p. 26 . . . *dedicate the book to James and Aretha.* Aretha Franklin's early recordings, 1960–1967, are on several Columbia recordings. Her career took off in 1967 with the Atlantic album *I Never Loved a Man the Way I Love You* (with the songs "Do Right Woman," "Respect," "Drown in My Own Tears," "Dr. Feelgood," and "Change Is Gonna Come"), followed by *Aretha Arrives* (also 1967), *Lady Soul* (1968; with "Chain of Fools" and "Natural Woman"), and *Aretha Now* (1968; with "Think" and her cover of Ray Charles's "The Night Time Is the Right Time"). The climax of the Atlantic period is the 1971 *Live at the Fillmore* set (with King Curtis and Ray Charles) and the 1972 *Amazing Grace* double gospel album (with the James Cleveland Choir). Her Atlantic *Thirty Greatest Hits* recording collects her 1967–1974 chart busters. Her comeback recordings of the mid-1980s are on Arista; the most important are *Who's Zoomin Who?* (1985), *Aretha* (1986), and *One Lord, One Faith, One Baptism* (1987), a live volume recorded at the New Bethel church in Detroit with members of the Franklin family, the Staples Singers, the Mighty Clouds of Joy, and Jesse Jackson. A basic facts and figures fan biography and discography is *Aretha Franklin: The Queen of Soul,* by Mark Bego (New York: St. Martins Press, 1989). [SF]

p. 26 . . . *most of all Billie Holiday* . . . The autobiography of Billie Holiday (1915–1959), written with William Dufty, *Lady Sings the Blues* (1956; Hammondsworth: Penguin, 1984), was widely criticized as inaccurate and self-serving, but it is an extremely hard-hitting book and sure to promote reflection on racism, music, and the mythology of the tortured artist-victim in America. For a terse, poetic version of her life, see Alexis DeVeaux, *Don't Explain: A Song of Billie Holiday* (New York: Harper and Row, 1980), and Robert O'Meally, *Lady Day: The Many Faces of Billie Holiday* (New York: Arcade, 1991). For a sober scholarly review, see John Chilton, *Billie's Blues: The Billie Holiday Story 1933–1959* (New York: DaCapo, 1989). Most divide the essential Holiday recordings into two periods—the earlier work of the 1930s to early 1940s, illustrating the buoyant range of her spoken-sung melodies and microphrasing, and the hard-hitting, edgy, raspy, broken-voiced recordings of her last, alcohol- and drug-ravaged years, in the early and mid 1950s. Columbia has remastered and rereleased the early materials and Verve the latter, of which *Lady Sings the Blues,* with extraordinary versions of her most melancholy numbers—"Good Morning Heartache,"

"Strange Fruit," "My Man," "Don't Explain," "Love Me or Leave Me," and "Willow Weep For Me"—is a powerful reminder of how defiant and jubilant a broken and bitter voice can sound. Nat Hentoff's "The Real Lady Day," *New York Times Magazine,* 24 December 1972, responds to the mythologizing of Holiday in the 1972 Hollywood-Motown movie version of her autobiography, *Lady Sings the Blues,* which starred Diana Ross. [SF]

p. 26 *Like Ulahi in Bosavi.* Ulahi is one of the most prolific singer-composers I've met in Bosavi. In 1976, when I met her, she was working with Bambi Schieffelin on a study of her son Abi's speech development (see B. B. Schieffelin 1990:44–51). When Ulahi invited Bambi to come to her sago area in the bush to record Abi's speech, I went along to record her singing. Bambi and I were instantly taken with her musicality. I began regularly recording her songs and working with her to transcribe and translate them. She also served as one of my principal guides to the complexities of transcribing and translating women's sung-texted weeping. I've recorded and transcribed or translated about two hundred of Ulahi's songs, and at some point I hope to devote a long article or monograph to them. From recordings I made in 1976–77, 1982, and 1990, Ulahi can be heard singing her songs in the *heyalo, ko:luba, gisalo,* and *kelekeliyoba* genres on *Music of the Kaluli* (LP, Institute of Papua New Guinea Studies, IPNGS 001, 1981), "Voices in the Forest" (National Public Radio, 1983), *The Kaluli of Papua Niugini: Weeping and Song* (LP, Bärenreiter Musicaphon, BM 30 SL 2702, 1985), and *Voices of the Rainforest* (CD/cassette, Rykodisc, RCD 10173, 1991). [SF]

p. 27 . . . *like Louis Armstrong when he sings* . . . *Satchmo: My Life in New Orleans* (1954; New York: Da Capo, 1986) by Louis Armstrong (1900–1971) is complemented by earlier fan biographies like Max Jones and John Chilton's *Louis: The Louis Armstrong Story* (New York: Little Brown, 1971) and Hughes Panassié's *Louis Armstrong* (1969; New York: Da Capo, 1979). Later critical studies are essential reading: James Lincoln Collier, *Louis Armstrong: An American Success Story* (New York: Macmillan, 1985), and Gary Giddins, *Satchmo* (New York: Doubleday, 1988). Gunther Schuller's *Early Jazz* (New York: Oxford University Press, 1968) has a substantial analysis and appreciation of Armstrong's contributions to melodic structures, phrasing, and syncopation in improvisation. Armstrong's discography is enormous, but all the early essential works, including the Hot Fives and Hot Sevens recordings, have been remastered and rereleased by Columbia. Many of the later works have been rereleased by Decca and Verve; see the Collier and Giddins books for thorough discographical information. [SF]

PARTICIPATION IN GROOVES

1 MOTION AND FEELING THROUGH MUSIC

In *Emotion and Meaning in Music,* Leonard Meyer (1956) manages to fill much of the gap in our knowledge defined by the question, What is a musical experience? In attempting a very short sequel to his work, my purpose is to discuss an aspect of music that I feel has been neglected in his study. In doing so, I find it convenient to define my general position vis-à-vis the positions delineated so clearly by Meyer at the outset of his book and in his articles "Some Remarks on Value and Greatness in Music" and "The End of the Renaissance" (Meyer 1967:22–41, 68–84). To begin with, I am primarily concerned, as is Meyer, with teleological or goal-directed music, although I will try to demonstrate that the goals to which music may direct itself are not always as circumscribed as he would have us believe. Furthermore, we share an emphasis (in this discussion, at least) on understanding music itself, irrespective of any referential or extramusical content it may possess.

At this point, however, our positions diverge. Among those who are interested in "the understanding of and response to relationships inherent in the musical progress," Meyer distinguishes two points of view: "The formalist would contend that the meaning of music lies in the perception and understanding of the musical relationships set forth in the work of art and that meaning in music is primarily intellectual, while the expressionist would argue that these same relationships are in some sense capable of exciting feelings and emotions in the listener" (1956:3). *Emotion and Meaning in Music* demonstrates quite effectively that formalist and expressionist points of view tend to be complementary rather than conflicting, "for the same musical processes and similar psychological behavior give rise to both types of meaning." Meyer develops this thesis with materials from the Western compositional tradition, using the concept of syntax and such corollary concepts as norm-deviation and tendency-inhibition; the net effect is impressive. The thesis established, he attempts, with somewhat less success, I think, to transpose the theory into the musical systems of other cultures.

Meyer's relative failure to extend his generalizations to styles outside the Western stream stems at least partly from the fact that syntax and syntax alone determines the core of his theory; that is, he develops his thesis by first examining the form of music—a succession of tones—then relating this form via psychological principles to meaning and expression. This procedure assumes that for analytic purposes music can be fixed or frozen as an object, a score or a recording, and it implies not only a one-to-one relationship between syntactic form and expression but a weighting in favor of the former to the detriment of the latter. This tight equation of form and expression, which for Meyer represents "embodied meaning," yields results when applied to the generally through-composed, harmonically oriented styles of our own Western tradition, and in fact, with only a few reservations, we can say of this music, "Music must be evaluated syntactically" (Meyer 1967:36). But when this equation and the corresponding evaluative criteria are applied to non-Western styles or to Western compositions *in performance,* we often find that something is missing. It is that something, or at least an important part of it, that I will attempt to specify in some detail.

All music has syntax or embodied meaning. Consider, however, the system or style in action—music as a creative act rather than as an object—and remember that outside the West, musical traditions are almost exclusively performance traditions. In some music, and I am thinking specifically of African and African-derived genres, illumination of syntactic relationships or of form as such will not go far in accounting for expression. The one-to-one relationship postulated by Meyer will not hold; syntactic analysis is a necessary condition for understanding such music, but it is not in itself sufficient.

In addition to embodied meanings we must talk about characteristics of the ongoing musical process that can be subsumed under the general heading of "engendered feeling." For the sake of brevity and, I hope, clarity, several contrasts between these two aspects of musical experience will be enumerated at the outset (table 1). In making this list of polarities my primary reference points are Meyer's theory (as formulated for the Western compositional tradition) and the musical idiom that I am best acquainted with, jazz. I hasten to add that these contrasts are loose and fuzzy; they are meant to be thought-provoking rather than precise, hence the logical interconnectedness of the notions in either column is conjectural, to say the least.

Table 1. Table of contrasts

	Embodied Meaning	Engendered Feeling
1. Mode of construction	composed	improvised
2. Mode of presentation	repeated performance	single performance
3. Mode of understanding	syntactic	processual
4. Mode of response	mental	motor
5. Guiding principles	architectonic (retentive)	"vital drive" (cumulative)
6. Technical emphases	harmony/melody/em- bellishment (vertical)	groove/meter(s)/rhythm (horizontal)
7. Basic unit	"sound term" (phrase)	gesture (phrasing)
8. Communication analogues	linguistic	paralinguistic (kinesic, proxemic)
9. Gratifications	deferred	immediate
10. Relevant criteria	coherence	spontaneity

There are a number of valid objections to be met and ambiguities to be clarified with respect to this preliminary and rudimentary chart. Though I prefer to remain suggestive rather than explicit, I will try to de-lineate clearly what I mean by "engendered feeling." First, let me repeat that every piece of teleological music involves both syntax and an elusive quality designated here as "process." Any good composer, that is, tries to give some spontaneity to his forms, and conversely, any good impro-viser tries to give some form to his spontaneity (see contrasts 1 and 10). In either case, whether the notes are written or improvised, whenever music is performed the processual aspect becomes important.[1] Second, I am emphasizing less syntactic, underspecified aspects of music not sim-ply to reassert the formalist-expressionist split so carefully patched up by Meyer, but because my ultimate aim is to reveal that part of expression not inherent in form or syntax.

Third, the metaphysical specter of mind-body dualism seems to emerge from these polarities, specifically in contrast 4, mode of response. Al-though I am neither a philosopher nor a physiological psychologist, I would agree with Meyer that the mind-body duality is a somewhat con-trived, chicken-and-egg sort of issue. Yet I believe he resolves the dualism dilemma a little prematurely along Christian Science, mind-over-matter lines. I particularly take issue with the following paragraph:

> On the one hand, it seems clear that almost all motor behavior
> is basically a product of mental activity rather than a kind of

1. Performance and process are synonymous in the sense that the Embodied Meaning column relates to the score of a J. S. Bach cello suite while the Engendered Feeling column describes a Casals performance of that suite. In this light the presentation comparison (contrast 2) may seem confusing; I am arguing that in music composed for repetition,

direct response made to the stimulus as such. For aside from
the obvious fact that muscles cannot perceive, that there seems
to be no direct path from the receptors to the voluntary muscles
systems, motor responses are not as a rule made to separate,
discrete sounds but to patterns and groupings of sounds. The
more order and regularity the mind is able to impose upon the
stimuli presented to it by the senses, the more likely it is that
motor behavior will arise. Such grouping and patterning of
sounds is patently a result of mental activity. (Meyer 1956:81)

Common sense and day-to-day observation of children learning by
doing as much as by thinking cast considerable doubt on this assertion;
moreover, experiments have demonstrated quite convincingly that our
muscles are perceptive (Held and Freedman 1963; Penfield and Roberts
1959, Hebb 1949). And somehow muscles remember: once a bike rider,
always a bike rider; once a drummer or dancer, always a drummer or
dancer. Could it be that in many cultures children learn to listen while
they learn to dance? Watching an African father support his infant while
it pumps its legs up and down to the "highlife" coming over the radio,
one is tempted to think so. The nervous system is all of one piece and so
is the learning, remembering, expressive person.

This leads to a fourth possible objection: There appears to be a serious referential flirtation, if not an out-and-out romance, going on between music of the engendered feeling type and dance. The engendered
feeling entries above strongly imply a reference to music for dancing.
If this were a court of law, I would have to sustain this objection, but
would add three counterstatements and a summation: (*a*) In many cultures music and dance are so tightly intertwined that cleanly separating
the two seems as impossible and fruitless as separating myth from ritual,
or mind from body for that matter. (*b*) Styles of music intended for dancing have a way of evolving into music for listeners only. Take, for example, modern jazz; although Thelonious Monk (Farrell 1964) regularly
leapt from the piano to dance a chorus or two, and other jazzmen have
their characteristic stances and movements, the jazz audience now remains immobile save for some head-bobbing, toe-tapping, and finger-
popping. Yet the music's dance or motor element, though less visible, may
still be essential to an adequate analysis. (*c*) No less an avowed formalist
than Stravinsky stated, "The sight of the gestures and movements of the

---

"engendered feeling" has less chance, or, conversely, that the more the music is determined
by the improvisation of the performer, the more likely it is that "engendered feeling" will
prevail.

various parts of the body producing the music is fundamentally necessary if it is to be grasped in all its fullness" (Meyer 1956:80). Can we
then dismiss dance expression as extramusical?

Toward the end of his book Meyer paradoxically manages to make
this very point while missing the point altogether:

> Unfortunately little of the extensive research done in the field
> of primitive music is of value for this study. First, because
> the primitives themselves do not make musical creation a self-
> conscious endeavor, they have neither a theory of music nor
> even a crude "aesthetic" which might serve to connect their
> musical practices to their responses. It seems clear that on the
> most primitive level music is, on the one hand, so intimately
> connected with ritual and magic that its aesthetic content is
> severely restricted and, on the other hand, that it is so closely
> associated with bodily effort that its shape and organization
> are to a considerable degree products of the physical activities
> connected with ritual, labor or expressive behavior. (Meyer
> 1956:289)

May I suggest, first, that it may be our own notion of the aesthetic
that is crude and restricted, not that of the primitives. Must an aesthetic
be exclusively verbal? Can we not infer a great deal from choreographic
response or "symbolic action,"[2] from the "conversation" between dancers and musicians (stimuli and responses go in both directions, I suspect),
or that between player and instrument? If music "is so closely associated
with bodily effort," why not build a body-based aesthetic adequate to
the task? John Blacking, in his brief discussion of Hornbostel's "motor
theory" of African rhythm, has asked essentially the same questions, and
I strongly second his suggestion that greater attention be paid to this
problem (Blacking 1955; Hornbostel 1928).

Having answered objections with queries, let me turn to some termi-
nological ambiguities. Contrasts 1 and 2 are well amplified by the excep-
tionally articulate (musically and verbally) jazz pianist Bill Evans; the
liner notes he wrote for Miles Davis's album *Kind of Blue* (1959) are
worth citing at length, with references added to the contrasts in table 1:

> There is a Japanese visual art in which the artist is forced to
> be spontaneous [contrast 10]. He must paint on a thin parch-
> ment with a special brush and black water-paint in a such a

2. Kenneth Burke's works are well worth reading for anyone interested in elaborating a theory of music along the lines presented here. J. L. Moreno's *Psychodrama* (Beacon, N.Y.:
Beacon House, 1946) is also recommended, especially for its treatment of spontaneity.

way that an unnatural or interrupted stroke will destroy the line or break through the parchment. Erasures or changes are impossible. These artists must practice a particular discipline, that of allowing the idea to express itself in communication with their hands [contrasts 7 and 8] in such a direct way that deliberation cannot interfere [contrast 4].

The resulting pictures lack the complex composition and textures of ordinary painting [contrasts 5 and 6], but it is said that those who see well find something captured that escapes explanation [contrast 9].

This conviction that direct deed is the most meaningful reflection [contrasts 4, 7, and 9], I believe, has prompted the evolution of the extremely severe and unique disciplines of the jazz or improvising musician.

Group improvisation is a further challenge. Aside from the weighty technical problem of collective, coherent thinking, there is the very human, even social, need for sympathy from all members to bend for the common result. This most difficult problem, I think, is beautifully met and solved on this recording.

As the painter needs his framework of parchment, the improvising musical group needs its framework in time [contrast 6]. Miles Davis presents here frameworks which are exquisite in their simplicity and yet contain all that is necessary to stimulate performance with a sure reference point to the primary conception. (Evans 1959)

Cumulatively, this brief text might easily stand by itself as an expanded definition of process [contrast 3]. Further definitions of process can be culled from a recent interview with another outstanding jazz pianist, Paul Bley. Although he is talking about music in general, many jazz players would find his imagery particularly appropriate in describing a successful piece of music in their idiom:

Basically the body of music that exists is like a river meeting a dam—constantly accumulating. It'll find the weakest spot, and finally it will break through and continue—but it will still be a river. . . . You can approach a piece as an anti-piece for example. But whatever you use, there has to be *a groove to get into*. That's the hard part. Once you're into it, you don't have to keep deciding whether or not the next phrase is going to be good or not. A soloist can usually tell by the first phrase whether it's going to be a good solo. When you *get into something* to start with, don't worry about the rest of the set; it's going to be beautiful. If anything, just hold back, because it'll all come out eventually anyway. The important thing is getting on the *right track*—the *right pattern*—in the *right way* and exerting the control and practice necessary to get it. (Bley 1965:16–17; italics added)

The phrases I have emphasized in this statement, the extended river simile, and Evans's analogy to Japanese art do not add up to a very concrete definition of process, simply because, as used in this context, it is an abstract concept covering an infinite number of "vital drive" principles—which brings us to contrasts 4, 5, 6, and 7 and the empirical problems about which this theory revolves.

What is this groove, track, pattern, or way that Bley and other jazz performers feel is so important to get into? What is this thing called swing, vital drive, process? Aside from a close examination of the music itself, we have only a brief chapter from a book by French critic André Hodeir to help us. It is from Hodeir, in fact, that I have borrowed the term "vital drive." Although he designates the phenomenon and stresses its importance, he goes no further: "There is another element in swing that resists analysis and that I would hesitate to mention if my personal impressions had not been echoed by many jazz musicians. What is involved is a combination of undefined forces that creates a kind of 'rhythmic fluidity' without which the music's swing is markedly attenuated" (1956:207). All we have, then, from Hodeir is one more ambiguous term to add to our burgeoning catalogue. In all fairness, he does offer, before admitting defeat at the critical moment, a number of insights into process that will be incorporated here. His general failure evolves from a misordering of the elements in swing, which in turn is related to his initial denial of what I feel is a fundamentally sound assertion made by Joost Van Praag as far back as 1936: "Swing is a psychic tension that comes from the rhythm's being attracted by the metre" (quoted in Hodeir 1956:196). The word "psychic" here might involve us in more mental-motor controversy (contrast 4), so to avoid argument I propose "organismic," a general term but with strong motor connotations, as a temporary surrogate. The focus of Van Praag's definition is crucial—the tension generated by a complex relationship between meter and rhythm. But here again a qualification must be made by defining meter, à la Meyer, as "an awareness of the regular recurrence of accented and unaccented beats," which leaves room for a primary pulse, "an objective or *subjective* division of time into regularly recurring, equally accented beats"

(Hodeir 1956:102–3; italics added.) Quite clearly, this is the pulse to which the rhythms in Van Praag's definition of swing are attracted. It is a subjective pulse that Richard Waterman speaks of when he uses the concept "metronome sense" as the ordering principle in the polymetric rhythms of West African ensembles (Waterman 1952). In jazz groups polymeter or even a sense of polymeter may or may not exist, but the subjective pulse or metronomic sense remains the center from which all vital drives derive (Stearns 1956:11–12).

Vital drive may be generated in a number of different ways, and a more detailed look at the mechanics of this process as exemplified in jazz may prove serviceable in explicating contrasts 5, 6, and 7.

The best starting point is probably rhythm-section attack.[3] By attack I mean simply the type of contact the player makes with his instrument in the initial production of a note.[4] Every drummer has what is known in

---

3. Although not concerned with vital drive or swing per se, Hornbostel and Blacking justly place strong emphasis on attack. Hornbostel states:

> African rhythm is ultimately founded on drumming. Drumming can be replaced by handclapping or by the xylophone: what really matters is the act of beating; and only from this point can African rhythms be understood. Each single beating movement is again twofold: the muscles are strained and released, the hand is lifted and dropped. Only the second phase is stressed acoustically; but the first inaudible one has the motor accent, as it were, which consists in the straining of the muscles. This implies an essential contrast between our rhythmic conception and the Africans': we proceed from hearing, they from motion; we separate the two phases by a bar-line, and commence the metrical unity, the bar with the acoustically stressed time-unit; to them, the beginning of the movement, the arsis, is at the same time the beginning of the rhythmical figure. (Hornbostel 1928:26)

Elaborating upon this point, Blacking feels that "the contrast which Hornbostel suggests is therefore not so much one of procedure as of *attitudes* towards movements and the productions of sounds." Blacking documents this shift in emphasis by comparing the technique of a Chopi xylophone player with that of a concert pianist:

> One has a similar impression of downward "attacking" movements when one watches the performance of a virtuoso pianist. . . . Closer analysis of his movements will usually reveal that there is a constant lift, which makes the downward "thrust" more of a downward "drop." Some piano teachers insist that all the muscular effort must be made when preparing to play each tone, so that the note is actually struck during a moment of muscular relaxation. The fingers are allowed to fall on the keys rather than compelled to hit them; thus, contrary to what may seem natural, the louder one plays the more relaxed one is. (Blacking 1955:15)

The Adler system of drumming, once so popular with jazz percussionists, is derived from the same foundation of note preparation.

4. Characteristically, Hodeir relegates the crucial notion of attack to a footnote: "The rhythmic phenomenon is not simply a question of *time values;* the succession of *attacks* and *intensities* is also an important part of it" (Hodeir 1956:96).

the jazz argot as a distinctive tap, that is, a manner of applying stick to cymbal.[5] The basic tap may be notated approximately as in example 1 or somewhat more accurately as in example 2. But the fact is that taps cannot be adequately notated.[6]

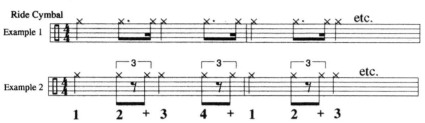

For syntactic purposes we might write down a reasonable facsimile of a tap with all its variations (and there are many) vis-à-vis the improvisations of a soloist, noting how the rhythmic structures of the two patterns complement each other and interact, but we would be talking about only a small part of what the drummer contributes to the music. The primary goal of his characteristic and internally consistent tap is to create as much vital drive as possible, to build a groove for the soloist to get into—and this is done by pulling against the pulse. Although each drummer has a personal way of doing this, for heuristic purposes we may distinguish players in terms of two common approaches or attacks; those who play "on top" of the pulse, and those who "lay back" behind it. The former school (Kenny Clarke, Roy Haynes, Billy Higgins, Jimmy Cobb, Frank Dunlop, Osie Johnson, among others) attacks the cymbal so close to the pulse as to be almost ahead of it or "above" it when dealing with those notes in the tap that fall on 1, 2, 3, and 4 of a 4/4 measure. It is primarily by "playing" with the syncopated beat between the pulses (see examples 1 and 2) that on-top drummers generate vital drive. Some drummers eschew the "middle" beat altogether on occasion, playing "straight four" on the cymbal and elaborating the pulse with sporadic accents on the snare or bass drum. In the hands of a master (for example, Louis Hayes, who uses rotary draw-away motions when applying this tap), straight-four technique may be dull as dishwater syntactically but electrifying as part of a process. Although it is difficult to generalize about the attacking motion, on-top drummers tend to keep the stick

5. I am speaking of jazz since the introduction of the "ride cymbal" in the 1930s.
6. Of course, no rhythm can be notated absolutely accurately—there is always a performance tradition that gives "life" to the notes (see Meyer 1956:80–82, 199–204)—but it has often been observed that the standard notation system is particularly ill-suited to the transcription of jazz (or African) rhythms.

close to the cymbal and the arm fairly stationary, with the stroke moving perpendicular to the cymbal, such that each beat lands on the cymbal in the vicinity of its predecessor.

Conversely, drummers of the "lay-back" school (Philly Joe Jones, Art Blakey, Pete LaRoca, Elvin Jones, Paul Motian, Tony Williams) seem to attack horizontally, so to speak, placing each beat on a different part of the cymbal as the arm moves back and forth slightly. In the pattern given in example 2, the lay-back drummer places a slightly delayed accent on the notes marked "+," letting beats 1 and 3 "lay back" still farther behind the pulse, so that only notes 2 and 4, the offbeats, seem to coincide with the metronome.[7] Following the motion described, the +1 and +3 parts of this tap are played on one side of the cymbal and the 2s and 4s on the other. I think lay-back drummers take more drastic (or less subtle, if you prefer) liberties with the pulse than their on-top compatriots.

This dichotomy by no means exhausts the typology of taps. Connie Kay, for example, employs what might be called a "flattened out" tap, in which the syncopation is almost but not quite eliminated; Frank Isola is perhaps the only other drummer that uses anything like Kay's attack. More recently some drummers (notably Sonny Murray, who uses thick knitting needles in place of sticks) have developed a tap that might be described as "reflex-textural." Murray seems to let his hand respond by itself to the music (provided by pianist Cecil Taylor), and while it is sometimes difficult to pick out any recognizable rhythmic pattern in his playing, the resultant echo-effect is certainly tension-producing.

Among bassists, a similar broad division can be made on the basis of attack or, in this case, pluck. This distinction is not formally recognized by jazz players in their argot, but I think it exists nonetheless. I would describe the opposition as "stringy," light, sustained, and basslike versus "chunky," heavy, percussive, and drumlike. The former school (Paul Chambers, Scott LaFaro, Ron Carter, Steve Swallow) plucks higher on the strings, away from the bridge, usually with the full side of the finger, and the tone "emerges." The latter group (Wilbur Ware, Henry Grimes, Percy Heath, Milt Hinton, Ahmed Abdul Malik, Gene Ramey, Eddie Jones, John Ore) plucks lower on the strings, nearer the bridge, usually more with the tip of the finger, and the tone "bursts."

Classifications of this sort are tenuous, for no jazz bassist or drummer attacks "time" in quite the same way as any other. Nevertheless, I would like to take the discussion a few steps further by examining briefly various

7. In actual practice beats 2 and 4 are usually reinforced by the "chap" of the sock-cymbal apparatus manipulated by the left foot.

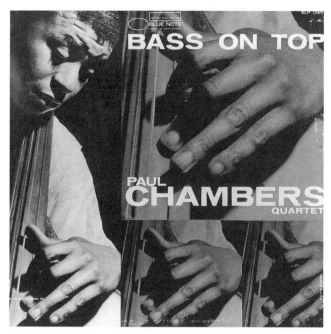

Paul Chambers, *Bass on Top,* cover. © 1957 Capitol Records, Inc.

Thelonious Monk, *Thelonious Monk in Italy,* cover, 1961. Riverside Records.

Table 2. Bassist/Drummer Combinations

	Bassists	
	Chunky	Stringy
Drummers: On-top	A. Malik / R. Haynes P. Heath / K. Clarke M. Hinton / O. Johnson J. Ore / F. Dunlop	P. Chambers / K. Clarke
Lay-back	W. Ware / P. J. Jones	P. Chambers / P. J. Jones S. LaFaro / P. Motian S. Swallow / P. LaRoca R. Carter / T. Williams

("Four-fold table schemes" are very much in vogue with social scientists but this one is simply illustrative and not statistically significant.)

bassist/drummer combinations (table 2), relating these rhythm teams to the "comping" or chording instrument (piano, guitar, etc.) found in most jazz groups and to the soloists.

In general, chunky bassists and on-top drummers combine effectively, while stringy bassists and lay-back drummers work well together. Although there are some notable exceptions, the groups led by Thelonious Monk and Miles Davis illustrate the general rule very nicely. Monk consistently preferred chunky bassists, almost invariably coupled with on-top drummers (Oscar Pettiford / Kenny Clarke, Ahmed Abdul Malik / Roy Haynes, John Ore / Billy Higgins, Butch Warren / Frank Dunlop, Sam Jones / Art Taylor),[8] the exceptions being some excellent earlier recordings in which lay-back drummers Art Blakey and Shadow Wilson are coupled with chunky bassists Percy Heath and Wilbur Ware respectively. Miles Davis's rhythm teams are organized on the complementary principle—he invariably employs stringy bassists and shows a marked preference for lay-back drummers (for many years Paul Chambers / Philly Joe Jones, more recently Ron Carter / Tony Williams)[9] although at one point Jimmy Cobb (a predominantly on-top drummer) and Chambers made up the rhythm team. Davis has occasionally brought a group into the recording studio that had a "Monk-type" rhythm section (Percy Heath / Kenny Clarke, Pierre Michelot / Kenny Clarke). These rhythm section preferences are guided, I think, by the manner of phrasing used by the leader-soloists. Not only is Monk's syncopation (phrases or "sound terms"; contrast 7 in table 1) remarkably irregular ("predictably unpredictable," as one writer puts it) even for a jazzman, but he places

8. A typical example: Thelonious Monk Quartet, *Monk's Dream* (Columbia CL 1965).
9. A typical example: Miles Davis Quintet, *Round about Midnight* (Columbia 949).

Ron Carter and Tony Williams, the rhythm team of the Miles Davis Quintet, of the mid and late 1960s. © Ray Avery Photo 1990.

his notes (phrasing) against the groove with vicious consistency; hence his preference for a firm, even heavy, rhythm team whose pulse is relatively explicit. Miles Davis is a melodist whose lyrical phrasing is inconsistent in the sense that during a given phrase some notes may fall behind the pulse, others ahead of it, still others directly on it. The distinction between syntactic phrase and processual phrasing is not easily made. He often tends to float around and above the groove rather than to attack it directly and thereby contribute to the cumulative vital drive. In other words, he needs a rhythm section that can swing well on its own, with or without him. Put another way, I hear Monk phrasing into or against the groove, while Miles is phrasing over or in-and-out of it.

I should point out here that in my opinion a *good* stringy/lay-back team can generate more vital drive by itself than the best chunky/on-top combination, although the latter teams are better in terms of consistency. For example, a soloist who wants to make a record in New York and has not been working regularly with any particular rhythm team, can be more confident of making a good showing by bringing together a chunky bassist, typically Milt Hinton or George Duvivier, and an on-top drummer, usually someone like Osie Johnson or Roy Haynes, even if the two men have not played together frequently prior to the recording. The three other possible combinations, if made impromptu, are somewhat risky. A chunky/lay-back team sometimes generates a sluggish vital drive (for example, some Wilbur Ware / Philly Joe Jones recordings), a stringy/on-top team usually doesn't lack for drive but may rush at fast tempos (Kenny Clarke / Paul Chambers),[10] and when a stringy bassist and lay-back drummer get together, anything can happen.

The foregoing examples are both impressionistic and oversimplified, for the best jazz performers are incredibly adaptable when faced with the task of generating a vital drive around a common pulse: in the words of Duke Ellington, "It don't mean a thing if it ain't got that swing." Charles Mingus, bassist extraordinaire, and Danny Richmond, drummer, have been known to create a number of different vital drives within a single piece; Mingus shifts his attack and Richmond adjusts accordingly, or vice versa.[11] One thinks also of Roy Haynes, normally a thoroughly on-top drummer, replacing Elvin Jones (who likes to lay back his tap as far as it will go) with the John Coltrane Quartet for a month or so; after a few nights' work his playing became practically indistinguishable from that of his predecessor, at least as far as the overall "engendered feeling" of the group was concerned. The Coltrane group by the way, features a unique yet illustrative process that would merit a monograph-length analysis if only we had a theory and method adequate to the challenge.[12] For when we add a third variable to the picture—a pianist whose placement of chords has a great deal to do with vital drive—and begin to talk about rhythm sections rather than simple teams, processual permutations become very complex indeed. Introduce more variables—soloists whose placement of notes may be just as important to process as the contributions of any rhythm section member—and one begins to see why jazz critics, with the exception of Hodeir, have studiously avoided the very essence of their subject matter.[13]

Returning to table 1, contrasts 5 and 6, the foregoing examples should facilitate the clarification of terms. In composed music the structure or architecture is obviously of great importance; broadly speaking, melody rests

10. *Bohemia after Dark* (Savoy MG12-17).
11. *Mingus Presents Mingus* (Candid 8005).
12. John Coltrane Quartet, *Coltrane* (Impulse Mono-A21)
13. Realizing, I suppose, that purely syntactic evaluations do not really do the music justice, this sort of criticism is generally avoided and, excepting the sometimes insightful semisociological work of Nat Hentoff, Martin Williams, and LeRoi Jones, jazz criticism is largely in limbo.

upon harmony and embellishment upon melody. For example, to the extent that an artfully embellished melody inhibits the tendency toward an expected harmonic resolution, we have embodied meaning. Furthermore, retention is important, for to properly understand a variation or deviation one must remember the theme or norm; it pays to know the score.

In improvised music, the analogy to a building does not fit. Paul Bley compared it to a river, Hodeir to a train: "Swing is possible . . . only when the beat, though it seems perfectly regular, gives the impression of moving inexorably ahead (like a train that keeps moving at the same speed but is still being *drawn ahead* by its locomotive)" (1956:198). To the extent that the rhythms conflict with or exhibit the groove without destroying it altogether, we have engendered feeling, and for a solo to grow the feeling must accumulate. Pursuing the contrast, it pays to keep careful track of the groove or pulse.

Finally, to comprehend syntax thoroughly it is necessary to focus on the vertical dimension, to examine the constituent notes of each chord, to be able to distinguish the various architectonic levels at any point in the progress, to assess the range of melodic variations possible over a given ground base. Something approaching complete comprehension of the processual aspect will only be possible when we are able to determine accurately the placement of notes along the horizontal dimension. Where is each musician placing his notes in terms of the groove? This is a difficult question to answer, but some progress might be made by asking a group of competent musicians to match their perceptions and intuitions with respect to a given rhythm section stimulus. Although the thought is somehow distasteful, it may be that instruments something like the melograph or the device used by A. M. Jones (1959:13) can be used to measure objectively the tensions between the attacks of drummer A and bassist B. How far back can the beat be laid, or is this phenomenon some sort of illusion? When is "on top" of the groove actually ahead of it? Quite obviously our explorations of this processual nexus have hardly begun.[14]

Another section of Meyer's text provides a good introduction to contrasts 7 and 8:

> A sound or group of sounds (whether simultaneous, successive, or both) that indicate, imply, or lead the listener to

---

14. In 1964 measuring devices were limited, but since that time Olavo Alén Rodriguez has used Winkler instrumentation in East Berlin to measure the phrasing of percussionists in the *tumba francesa* ensemble very precisely and J. A. Prögler has used a Mac Digitizer to measure the discrepancies between bass plucks and ride cymbal taps in jazz rhythm sections. Papers reporting these measurements will appear in the journal *Ethnomusicology*.

Learning to dance in Cuba. Photo courtesy of Olavo Alén Rodriguez.

Member of Icough women's dance ensemble, Tivland, Nigeria, 1966. Photo Charles Keil.

Men's Agatu dance ensemble, Tivland, Nigeria, 1966. Photo Charles Keil.

Spinning the polka across the generations; Buffalo, N.Y. Photo Charles Keil.

Baptism party at Methodios Taverna; Aghios Vasilios, Greek Macedonia. Photo Charles Keil.

expect a more or less probable consequent event are a musical gesture or "sound term" within a particular style system. The actual physical stimulus which is the necessary but not sufficient condition for the sound term will be called the "sound stimulus." The same sound stimulus may give rise to different sound terms in different style systems or within one and the same system. (1956:45ff.)

Meyer goes on to develop a language analogy—the meanings a word may have in different contexts, the meaningful relationships between sentences in a paragraph, and so on—but a stricter linguistic analogy can be made with equal or greater profit, for Meyer's "sound term" corresponds quite closely to the notion of a morpheme, his "sound stimulus" seems clearly on the phonemic level, notes may be considered as phones, and so forth. This analogy could be carried further.

On the processual side, a kinesic analogy can readily be made, and collaboration with researchers in that field may be of inestimable value. Birdwhistell, Hall, and others have demonstrated that a vast amount of communication is nonverbal, bodily, and largely unconscious (Birdwhistell 1952; E. T. Hall 1959, 1963). The problems they deal with in segmenting a continuum of body movement into significant units on the general linguistic model—kines, kinemes, and gestures—are very much like those faced in a processual analysis of music. When a man winks while gazing at a woman, is he attempting to remove a piece of dust from his eye, or is he making a pass? The answer depends upon what happens next. Similarly, when a jazz saxophonist comes up with a triple forte screech, is it reed trouble, or is it the climax of the solo? Only the gesture's place in the overall process can determine the answer. This illustration is gross and subject to distortion but suggestive, I think. The analogy between music and both kinesics *and* linguistics may be confusing at first, for while in face-to-face interaction a wink is a wink and a word is a word, in music the same note or set of notes may be both a "sound term" or phrase and a "sound gesture," phrasing. I am insisting on this relatively abstract distinction because in jazz, it seems to me, the net effect of an entire piece may focus on one or two significant gestures; indeed, a vital drive may be seen as a device for holding our attention and increasing our involvement so that a single phrase, "weighted just right," will have maximum impact—a good "break" in the earlier jazz styles, the few seconds of "squatting and tooting" that inevitably climax one of John Coltrane's half-hour solos, the solo in which the phrasing is consistently behind the groove and then for one dramatic instant squarely on top of it. The "gesture" suddenly bursting forth from the midst of "process" may be something of an illusion, for in some instances (those in which the jazz player is more a stylist than an innovator) it may be possible to show how an apparent bolt from the blue has actually been prepared for syntactically by the improviser. In general, however, an analyst who attempts to cope with the sound and fury of a contemporary (1964) jazz solo (by Cecil Taylor, John Coltrane, Ornette Coleman) in purely syntactic terms will be forced to quit in frustration; there is little in the way of a consistent terminology to be grasped, and the usual criteria of clarity, unity, and order are largely irrelevant. Careful, even microscopic, observation of the movements associated with music making, particularly the motions of those entrusted with the creation of vital drive, close attention to each participant's manner of phrasing and the characteristic "sound gestures" of the soloist—in short, a processual approach like that advocated here, applied with as much precision as our elementary knowledge allows—will lead eventually, I hope, to more intellectually and emotionally satisfying results.

If the primitive theory that I have outlined has any validity, it follows that we will need two distinct sets of criteria to evaluate music, depending upon whether the processual or syntactic aspect is dominant. In classical Indian music, to use a difficult example, syntactic criteria seem more applicable to the initial phases of a raga's development, whereas the accelerating rhythmic interplay between sitar and tabla during the concluding portion would require a predominantly processual evaluation.

In order to specify more concretely the relevant criteria for processual music, a discussion of gratifications seems unavoidable. In one sense, there are certain obvious parallels to be drawn from Meyer's discussion of value in music wherein he bestows the label "masterpiece" upon those works in which resistances, uncertainties, tensions, and the overcoming of obstacles manifest themselves most markedly; in good music, if I may paraphrase Meyer, resolutions must be anticipated and patiently awaited; gratifications must be deferred. His citation of Robert Penn Warren's definition of a good poem is apt: "A poem, to be good, must earn itself. It is a motion toward a point of rest, but if it is not a resisted motion, it is a motion of no consequence" (quoted in Meyer 1967:26). In syntactically organized music the points of rest are largely harmonic and the resistances and uncertainties are the product of melodic elaborations, usually reinforced with rhythmic deviations, to be sure. On the processual side, the pulse provides the resting points; the rhythms (in the sense not only of syncopation but of note placement) provide the resistances.

There are at least two levels of feeling to be distinguished, for to the extent that vital drive is constant throughout, as it usually is, the resting point is reached only at the conclusion of the music, while the soloist "landing on" the pulse at scattered intervals can release some tension at points within the piece as well. In improvised music uncertainty would also seem to be more constant; you never know from one performance to the next what shape a solo will take or when the significant gestures will emerge. Paralleling Meyer, then, the greater the processual tension and gestural uncertainty a jazz piece has, the higher its value.

In an important sense, however, music which emphasizes engendered feeling over embodied meaning as its primary goal also stresses immediate over delayed or deferred gratification. Somewhat paradoxically, I must admit, the pulse-meter-rhythm tensions of jazz are immensely gratifying, even relaxing in themselves, in a way that extended arpeggios in composed music are not.[15] To the extent that one feels like tapping one's foot, snapping one's fingers, or dancing, gratification is also constant, and a jazz fan who does not feel like doing this begins to question the merits of the group providing the stimulus. Similarly, a jazz buff who wants to convince you that a particular performer is great is likely to point to a single gesture or a portion of the music in which the musician is playing with the pulse in a particularly perverse manner and ask over the music, "Isn't that bit a gas?" To exaggerate slightly, a classics fan will wait respectfully until the piece is finished or, better still, put a score in your lap and ask, "Do you see how beautifully it all fits together?"

For music in which good process and spontaneity are the avowed goals, it seems unfair if not ludicrous to frame an evaluation exclusively in terms of coherent syntax and architectonic principles. Meyer's remarks with respect to this problem are particularly pejorative and reveal a restricted view of Freud that, as Meyer himself admits, borders on the puritanical. For example, "The differentia between art music and primitive music lies in speed of tendency gratification. The primitive seeks almost immediate gratification for his tendencies whether these be biological or musical." Or:

> One aspect of maturity both of the individual and of the culture within which a style arises consists then in the willingness to forego immediate, and perhaps lesser gratification, for

15. Hodeir (1956:206–7) quite correctly stresses the fact that "relaxation plays an essential role in the production of swing," although his argument that a great many blacks are naturally endowed with "complete neuromuscular relaxation" while whites invariably have to work very hard to attain it is extremely problematic, to say the least.

the sake of future ultimate gratification. Understood, generally, not with reference to any specific musical work, self-imposed tendency-inhibition and the willingness to bear uncertainty are indications of maturity. They are signs, that is, that the animal is becoming a man. And this, I take it, is not without relevance to considerations of value. (1967:33)

In Meyer's defense it must be added that by primitive he means music that is dull syntactically (repetitive, cliché-ridden, of small tonal repertoire) and not necessarily the music produced by nonliterate peoples.[16] Nevertheless, such statements are first of all rather silly from an anthropological perspective, for every culture demands varying sorts of conformity, toleration of uncertainties, and deferment of gratifications from its members; these demands are no greater for participants in our civilization than those made upon Kalahari Bushmen, though they may be somewhat different. Second, why should we assume that immediate gratifications are evil and brutish? Meyer insists that value correlates with the inhibition of natural tendencies and the overcoming of obstacles, and for syntactic music in which intellectual control is at a premium this may be so. But what of music where inhibition itself is the primary obstacle? In our culture (and perhaps in others where repression and oppression must be fought) it may be that music whose goal is engendered feeling, spontaneity, and the conquest of inhibition is of far greater value than music which aims to reflect our civilization and the repression-sublimation-Protestant-ethic syndrome upon which it is based simply because, like much great art, it offers an antidote, a strategy for dealing with our situation (again, see Blacking 1955; Hornbostel 1928), rather than reinforcing it. I suspect, as do other critics, that we admire many modern painters—Picasso, Klee, Kandinsky, Miró, Chagall, Pollock—more for their sophisticated childishness than for their maturity. Many modern jazz performers, notably Thelonious Monk, Sonny Rollins, and Charles Mingus, are equally serious about being infantile. At the very least, art of this sort deserves to be evaluated by canons other than those associated with a Meyerish concept of maturity (i.e., unity, control, clarity, variety), although admittedly such general concepts can be twisted to at least partially fit music of the processual sort. In a long, involved, and erudite sequel to Freud's *Civilization and Its Discontents* (1930) Norman O. Brown offers some interesting notions that may be

16. Even this qualified definition of "primitive" reveals the analyst's syntactic blinders; in music concerned with process, constant repetition, the use of clichés, and exceedingly small tonal repertoires can sometimes be employed to create great tension and vital drive.

suggestive in concluding this attempted sequel to Meyer's work. Although any crystallization of his thought into a few neat slogans does Brown a grave injustice, he argues generally for release from repression, resurrection of the body, and a return to the perverse, polymorphous playfulness (and immediate gratifications) of childhood. The latter qualities of childhood alliterated so playfully by Brown (and Freud before him) strike me as a peculiarly appropriate set of criteria for establishing value, if not greatness, in jazz. Just how one goes about measuring perversity or playfulness I am not at all certain. But where process and spontaneity are the ends in view, I think we must make the effort to analyze and evaluate in these terms, for, as Brown notes in speaking of art, "Its childishness is to the professional critic a stumbling block, but to the artist its glory" (Brown 1959:58).

Finally, I must ask myself the same nasty question that I have directed to Meyer: Will a theory based almost exclusively on one musical idiom, in this case jazz rather than classical music, have any validity when applied to the musics of other cultures? I am convinced, of course, that ultimately the answer will be an emphatic Yes. My conviction rests on two assumptions: first, that the vast majority of cultures around the world have musical styles that are performance-oriented, dance-derived, and at least partially improvised; and second, that a processual methodology will be developed in the coming years so that this rudimentary theory can be tested, elaborated, and refined accordingly.

2 COMMUNICATION, MUSIC, AND SPEECH ABOUT MUSIC

FIELD ELEVEN STEPS

Music has a fundamentally social life. It is made to be engaged—practically and intellectually, individually and communally—as symbolic entity. By "engaged" I mean socially interpreted as meaningfully structured, produced, performed, and displayed by historically situated actors. How this happens, what it means, how one can know about it—these issues focus on the nature of the music communication process, and to rethink them I turn back to the question posed often by Charles Seeger: What does music communicate? To answer that he also needed to ask, What does speech about music communicate? Through diagrams and dense prose, Seeger (1977:16–44) argued that to address the issue of what music communicates one must specify what it cannot communicate. Logical preoccupation with differences between the speech and music modes of communication led to his notion that speech is the communication of "world view as the intellection of reality" while music is communication of "world view as the feeling of reality."

In this essay I want to argue both for another approach to these questions and for another set of answers. Specifically, I am concerned less with the logical and philosophical distinction between the speech and music modes and more with the general question of communication, that is to say, with the process of meaningful interpretation explicitly conceived as social activity.

Seeger devoted great efforts to pointing out the potential distortions of music in verbal discourse about music. He felt that the "operational idiosyncrasies" (1977:7) of speech biased the study of music, and he endeavored to promote metalanguage and definitional postulates that were ontologically precise. He was concerned that speech about music overemphasized musical space while underemphasizing musical time, that speech about music ultimately valued event over process, product over tradition, and static over dynamic understanding. He continually reminded audiences of the shortcomings of linguocentrism in music scholarship. Rather than merely repeat his cautions, I want to address some of the consequences of studying how people routinely talk about music. But first I want to extend Seeger's query about what music communicates to talk about how this communication process takes place, how we participate in it, and how our participation invents, validates, circulates, and accumulates musical meanings.

A Communications Approach

Seeger concerned himself with rigorous definitional postulates, a precise and logical series of terms and denotata. As an overarching concept for music and speech he invoked the term *normenon* for any "class of manmade products that serves primarily a function of communication"; he further defined communication as "transmission of energy in a form" (1977:10, 19). We can refine this notion of communication by moving it from physicalistic exposition to more firmly social ground. Being fundamentally relational, communication is process, and our concern with it should be a concern with the operation of social determination in process. The focus is always on a relationship, not on a thing or entity; in the case of human expressive modalities, it is on the relationship between the origin and action of sensations, the character of interpretations and consequences. Communication in this sense is no longer ontologically reified as a transmission or force; it can only exist relationally, in between, at unions and intersections. To the extent that we take this notion as the grounding for an epistemic approach, we must claim that the origins and conditions of communication are multidimensional. Communication then is not located in the content communicated or the information transferred. At the same time it is not just the form of the content nor the stream of its conveyance. It is interactive, residing in dialectic relations between form and content, stream and information, code and message, culture and behavior, production and reception, construction and interpretation. Communication is neither the idea nor the action but the process of intersection whereby objects and events are, through the work of social actors, rendered meaningful or not.

The term communication rightly evokes process and activity, but I would also like to emphasize two other aspects, those of meaning and interpretation. We cannot speak of meaning without speaking of interpretation, whether public or conscious. Communication is not, in other words, a "thing" from which people "take" meanings; it is rather, an ongoing engagement in a process of interpreting symbolic forms which makes it possible to imagine meaningful activity as subjectively experienced by other social actors. Communication is a socially interactive and intersubjective process of reality construction through message production and interpretation. By "socially interactive" I mean that, whether events are face-to-face or mediated in some way, we apprehend the symbols and situations before and around us through various schemes of typification and, unless evidence to the contrary is in hand, we assume that these schemes are not whimsical or idiosyncratic but social (Berger and Luckmann 1967). Whether or not we think we know what things, events, or sounds are about, we assume, not infrequently, that they display the subjective intentions of others. We understand that these intentions may or may not be explicit and refined in the minds of the others; they may be equally vague and ambiguous to both actor and receiver, equally transparent and obvious to both, or at different levels of clarity with relation to each. To the extent that we apprehend scenes as meaningfully organized, we assume that others share our sense of reality, as well as our more specifically situated and finite sensibilities. At the same time we recognize that we might not all have the same idea, the same "take" on what is going on and what it means. We guess about what others are up to, what is on their minds. We guess about what they intend or whether they mean to intend, or mean to feign disinterest in intention (Worth and Gross 1974).

In responding to objects and events that are either familiar or exotic, both those to which we are frequently exposed and anonymous abstractions, we take some things for granted, as transparent, requiring no action or verification beyond their physical presence or existence. Other things invite engagement and choice; we make choices that extend typifications and, in so doing, engage an object or event to take it in knowingly. In all cases the importance of a communications perspective is in its focus on (*a*) the primacy of the social, interactive, intersubjective realm of these processes; (*b*) the fact that engagement in the processes shapes, defines, maintains, and brings forth tacit or explicit subjective realities for participants in the scene; (*c*) the way in which meaning fundamentally implicates interpretation; (*d*) the complex relation of production codes and producer's intentions to interpreted messages; and, because this nonisomorphic complexity cannot be reduced to purely logical or normative terms, (*e*) the need for socially situated investigation.

Communication or Semiosis?

Other recent models of musical and sociomusical analysis, following semiotic theories (Molino 1975; Nattiez 1975; Boilès 1982; Tagg 1982), have also invoked or evoked the concept of "communication." To help focus my concerns, let me briefly distinguish their approaches from mine, at the same time emphasizing that many of these ideas are indeed complementary to mine and perhaps reflect larger, shared goals.

The best known and perhaps most substantial proposals for rethinking the process of musical signification are raised (not entirely explicitly) by the tripartite model of musical semiology associated with Jean Molino (1975) and Jean-Jacques Nattiez (1975).[1] Recognizing the nonisomorphism of code and message, of artistic "intent" and produced "effect," of interpretations by producer and consumer or sender and receiver, Molino and Nattiez propose a model of musical signification which considers the vantage points of code production (*poiétique*) and message perception (*esthésique*) and posits a *niveau neutre,* an autonomous level of material

---

1. Jean-Jacques Nattiez's important book, *Fondements d'une sémiologie de la musique* (1975), the basis for so much discussion of the nature of a musical semiology, including that found here, has been largely reworked and greatly refined for the English version, *Music and Discourse: Toward a Semiology of Music* (Nattiez 1990). Nattiez has extensively read and reflected upon social theory and the anthropological analysis of music, and he takes great pains in the new version to clarify what he considers to be misunderstandings about his project and musical analysis generally by critics who have found his book to be an important springboard. He devotes a section of the new book to semiology and communication (1990:16–28), largely to discuss how they involve distinct issues and how Jakobson's and Eco's theoretical invocations of communication within semiology overlap his but are logically separate from the issues he and Molino wish to raise about the tripartition. He carefully responds to many of Lidov's criticisms in this section as well. The revised book displays an impressive erudition and sophistication, although Nattiez holds onto some ideas about the tripartition with a tenacity that is difficult to understand in light of the obvious enlargement of his sense of musical meaning. Indeed it is hard to read the new book without the sense that Nattiez both embraces his interlocutors' critiques of the autonomy of the musical object, and wants to convince us that he never meant musical objects to be quite so autonomous to begin with.

Nattiez's book is essential reading in the ongoing debate about the discourse of music, for he clearly has a broad and comprehensive vision of musical analysis, even if it is not entirely clear how he would integrate a truly cultural and hermeneutic dimension into his program. In rereading the present essay, originally written in 1983, a fundamental point still stands: virtually all of musical semiology privileges scores, sign logics, and a highly formalist notion of essentialized musical meanings. The communicational notions developed here are meant to raise critical questions as to whether this kind of semiological stance really helps one grasp the meaning-making processes that listeners use to engage with their musical experiences. The extent to which I see these notions as both oppositional and complementary to semiological projects remains much the same as when the piece was written, although I am happy to acknowledge that much recent semiological work has demonstrated a substantially greater desire to account for more of the problematics of human historical and social complexity.

structure where music is "text." Nattiez's book is largely an attempt to justify the autonomy and empirical validity of this "neutral level," holding the other two levels back for future exploration. Some commentators have found this cause for strong criticism. David Lidov, for example, argues that, in function and in practice, the *niveau neutre* can only constitute a retreat from musical meaning, as well as from communication: "If all descriptions of music have their origin in the facts of production and perception, how is a neutral description possible except as a vacuous hypothesis?" (1977:19).

Lidov's question is harsher than though related to my own, namely, Do semiotic approaches really analyze communicational processes or transacted social meanings? To answer, I think it necessary to distinguish communicational analysis from logical, philosophical, or other normative analyses that seek to establish typologies of signs and sign functions. For the semiotics of music, much activity seems to stress the taxonomy and form of sign types. Meaning is subjugated to logical relations, hence Nattiez's "intrinsic signification" and "symbolic signification" take over where Meyer's (1956) "absolutist/expressionist" and "referential/expressionist" left off. While these notions tease our concern for a real semantics and pragmatics, the issues of use and interpretation are never addressed socially and directly. I cannot escape the sense that the dominant concern still is with "cracking the code," with formalization, rather than with the code as a *fait social total.*

The analyses of Boilès (1982) and Tagg (1982) are more satisfying in some respects, but can also be differentiated from mine. Boilès follows the Peircian semiotic trichotomy and sets up a calculus of interpretive possibilities based on a relationship of interpreter, interpretant, sign-object, designatum, and thing-object. The benefit of such a calculus as a convenient way to map logical relations is clear. The problem is also clear: the image of listening experience projected by such a model is extremely simple. One can quickly and intuitively falsify it. Listening experience involves things that happen in time; such things change often and rapidly. To construct a model of this experience and a sense of its relation to how signs signify and how musical symbols mean, one must confront the dynamics of changeability and the interactions of form and content, of specific and general experience, and of background expectations and generalized interpretive routines. Once again it seems that form dominates content, taxonomy dominates real worlds of users and use, and logical types dominate ambiguities, heterogeneity, lived meanings, and the multi-functionalism and reception of signs.

Tagg (1982) eschews some of this formalism to situate his object socially within real worlds of audiences whose interpretive investments are
clear. But I still find his notion of communication bound to the idea that
a certain "something" exists within a music that can project itself outward onto its audience ("receivers"), which is affected by it. This effects-
reinforcement approach to musical affect tends to focus on structural
features of music and reified minimal units ("musemes") rather than on
engagement or the variety of ways sounds are consumed. Tagg presents
an ideological critique of the macroeffects of the musical messages he an-
alyzes (1982:62–63) but admits that he has not integrated this level
with his "textual analysis." This strikes me as the crux of the problem;
one cannot stay at a syntactic level of analysis and then project its results
to micro- or macrosemantics as if these were determined by a musical
text. Musical meaning cannot be reduced to the textual level of structural association, comparisons of musemes in one piece with phrases,
motifs, or patterns from others. While such associations may be part of
the microstructure of listening experience, they do not necessarily fix any
or much of a piece's meaning.

While these proposals are of great utility because of their clarity, formal explicitness, and concern with general theory, Clifford Geertz's critique of the semiotics of art seems to apply in degrees to their real or
potential problems:

> For an approach to aesthetics which can be called semiotics—
> that is, one concerned with how signs signify—what this means
> is that it cannot be a formal science like logic or mathematics
> but must be a social one like history or anthropology. Har-
> mony and prosody are hardly to be dispensed with, any more
> than composition and syntax; but exposing the structure of a
> work of art and accounting for its impact are not the same
> thing . . . . If we are to have a semiotics of art (or for that mat-
> ter, of any sign system not axiomatically self-contained), we
> are going to have to engage in a kind of natural history of
> signs and symbols, an ethnography of the vehicles of mean-
> ing. Such signs and symbols, such vehicles of meaning, play a
> role in the life of a society, or some part of society, and it is
> that which in fact gives them their life. Here too, meaning is
> use, or more carefully, arises from use. (1983:118)

In the perspective that follows I will try to illuminate a model compatible with some of the formal concerns illustrated in the work of these
semioticians. My focus however is not on logical or neutral analyses but

on what I see as the more specifically communicational processes of musical meaning and interpretation. In order to demonstrate the complementarity of these perspectives, I will approach the process of musical communication with an emphasis on the listening process rather than the score, composer, or code per se. By doing so I wish to subvert the usual assumption that a producer's intention is closer to some abstract rule determining significance in music than the ordinary feelings that arise from routine engagement on the part of the listener.

Dialectics of the Music Communication Process

Let us begin with the assumption that the presence of sounds in our social field will invite conventional patterns of attending, disattending, foregrounding, or backgrounding. The invitation proceeds dialectically through the structure of sound and its placement in historical and physical space and time. If I walk out of my office and cross the street I must attend to car horns in a particular way. I may or may not attend to them if their sounds come in through a closed or open window or emanate from a record or tape recording. I will attend to them in another way if there is no sound source to be heard but only a spectral chart or sonogram labeled "car horn" that I must use.

Similarly, I attend to the details of a performance in a certain way at a concert or club, in another way at home with a recording or score, if one exists for the sounds in question. These levels of experience can also be combined. Moreover, having attended to a sonic experience in any one of these ways, I am no longer able to attend to any of the other experiences in exactly the same manner as I did before. Experience is not only cumulative but interactively cumulative. We rarely confront sounds that are totally new, unusual, and without experiential anchors. Hence, each experience in listening necessarily connotes prior, contemporary, and future listenings. Engagement reproduces one's sense of meaningful pattern and experience.

Leonard Meyer's work (1956, 1973, 1989) takes on the issue of musical meaning and communication by arguing that our ongoing predictions of musical structures—in tension, drama, fluctuation, development, changes, constants, deflection, implication, suggestion, delay, and such—will be satisfied, frustrated, or surprised through the listening process in time. He argues that affective and emotional states in the listener are responses to these musical stimuli. Based on gestalt perceptual principles, Meyer finds inhibition or gratification of anticipated structures to be the basis of meaningful musical communication. Keil (chapter 1) argues that Meyer's emphasis on syntactically recoverable dimensions of music leaves out an entire dimension of performance dynamics, which, particularly in improvised, spontaneous, or nonwritten musics, are deeply linked to expressive and emotive feelings and responses on the part of the listener. Shepherd (1977b, 1982) and Lidov (1977, 1980) have discussed Meyer's treatment of a score as musical signifier and other problems in his framework with communicational implications. For instance, Meyer's theory does not distinguish the meaning of one musical item from another, does not address the meaning of "pieces" or "musics" but only of *music,* and does not probe structural domains besides drama and tension. Furthermore, the framework does not account for varied meanings of the same piece to different listeners, or of the same piece to a single listener over time. One must, in other words, differentiate the syntactic features which might be said to arouse a listener, from the range and variety of musical feelings the listener may have in experiencing the piece.

Rather than posit only psychological constants as the deep sources enabling music to express emotions, we must also acknowledge social experience, background, skill, desire, and necessity as central and complementary constructs that shape perceptual sensations into conceptual realities. To do so is to recognize the social character of the musical communication process: the listener is implicated as a socially and historically situated being, not just as the bearer of organs that receive and respond to stimuli. For this reason, a description and a theory of the musical encounter must be sensitive to the biographies of the objects, events, and actors in question. The encounter is not simply one between a musical text and the gestalt processing of patterns of tension, anticipation, fulfillment, and resolution. Rather, it involves engaging and making sense of music through interpretive procedures deeply linked to, but not synonymous with, the structure of concatenated sound events (Schutz [1951] 1977).

Each listening is not just the juxtaposition of a musical object and a listener. It is a juxtaposition—in fact an entangling—of a dialectical object and a situated interlocutor. "Dialectical object" reflects the fact that a sound object or event can only be engaged through recognition of a simultaneous musical and extramusical reality: the experience is mental and material, individual and social, formal and expressive. In short, any musical object embodies and provokes interpretive tensions. One cannot encounter the object without making associations; the character of the associations is musical and extramusical. One cannot encounter the object without turning percepts to concepts; the character of those concepts is musical and extramusical. The musical object is never isolated, any more than its listeners or producers are. Its position is doubly social; the object exists through a code, and through processes of coding and decoding. These processes are neither pure nor autonomous; neither is encountered at a strictly physiological level of experience, no matter how perceptual or physical the implication of the label one applies to them (Baudrillard 1981).

Enter the Listener: From Dialectics to Interpretive Moves

All musical sound structures are socially structured in two senses: they exist through social construction, and they acquire meaning through social interpretation. Both kinds of engagement are socially real regardless of the ultimate importance or value of the musical sound and regardless of how consciously it is formed, attended to, and understood. Interpretation of a sound object or event (that is, of a construction) is the process of intuiting a relationship between structures, settings, and kinds of potentially relevant or interpretable messages. When we first listen we begin to "lock in" and "shift" our attention, so that the sounds momentarily yet fluidly polarize toward structural or historical associations in our minds. The immediate recognition is that sounds are contextual and contextualizing, and continually so. We attend to changes, developments, repetitions—form in general—but we always attend to form in terms of familiarity or strangeness, features which are socially constituted through experiences of sounds as structures rooted in our listening histories.

When I hear piped-in music, I am first aware of it as generic piped-in background music, over and beyond whether it is a known or unknown tune or a known or unknown performer. But I recognize it neither from sound nor setting only. I must draw upon a range of typifications. If I am in the bank or an elevator I will be surprised if I hear piped-in Kaluli (Papua New Guinea) music, even if it is soft and perfectly obeys other structural features of Muzak. At the same time, I would be quite surprised if I hear what I structurally know to be appropriate background music played at a loud volume.

Interpretation always requires an active process, however unconscious, intuitive, or banal, of relating structure to ranges of potentially appropriate or relevant messages. In other words, the sound event draws my interpretive attention to the circumstances of meaning through the general features of being contextual and contextualizing. These features of the way we listen involve form-content and musical-extramusical dialectics. In the simplest sense what takes place in the experience of a piece of music is the working of some features of momentary experience into the context of prior and plausible experiences to interpret what is going on.

Take the example of listening to the American national anthem, the "Star Spangled Banner," performed in the minor mode. The recording I have in mind is the opening section of the Carla Bley Band's "Spangled Banner Minor" (Bley 1978). What happens in the process of listening? First, one makes some attentional shifts and adjustments within the dialectic of musical and extramusical features. As one listens, one works through the dialectics in a series of "interpretive moves," developing choices and juxtaposing background knowledge. Interpretive moves involve the discovery of patterns as our experience is organized by juxtapositions, interactions, or choices in time when we engage symbolic objects or performances. Interpretive moves—regardless of complexity, variety, intensity, involvement—emerge dialectically from the human social encounter with a sound object or event (fig. 1).

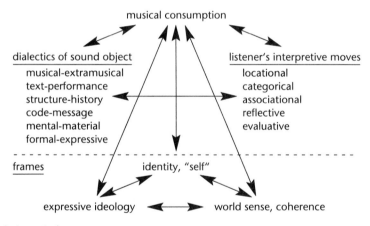

Figure 1. A musical encounter

Without establishing an order, sequence, or hierarchy of such moves, we can list some general categories. One kind of move is *locational,* placing the object that one is hearing within a subjective field of like and unlike items and events. In the case of "Spangled Banner Minor," such a move would vary significantly according to whether the listener was an American, a veteran, a prisoner, a dominated minority, a visitor, an immigrant. We would also expect an enormous range of responses within any one of these groups, no matter how much we assume members share common experiences.

One might also have certain more specific *categorical* interpretive moves, relating the piece to a class of things—anthems, and patriotic songs—or an even more specific set—parodies of "important" texts. Or one might think of nonstandard treatments of anthems that are not parodies, for example, Ray Charles's soul-gospel version of "America the Beautiful." Moreover, one might make various *associational* moves, relating or analogizing this item to particular visual, musical, or verbal imagery. For instance, one may conjure the image of a flying American flag; a Jasper Johns painting of the American flag; a photograph of Larry Flint in a wheelchair naked save for an American flag serving as a diaper; a burning American flag outside the U.S. embassy in Teheran; hippies and yippies of the 1960s dressed in American flags; the passing of a folded flag to the survivors of a deceased military officer at a funeral ceremony; a flag at half-mast. One may hear the particular recording while at the same time also imagining or even hearing the "correct" rendition of the same tune. Similarly, one might imagine or hear the words that go with the melody. Such moves, singly or in combination, may begin immediately or after a period of exposure or may fade in and out during an extended listening experience.

Additionally, one might make a variety of *reflective* moves, relating the item to social conditions, political attitudes (patriotism, nationalism), or personal experiences that include similar or dissimilar sounds, mediated or live. One could reflect on something as specific as a live performance of the same piece by the same band, on recordings of the national anthem by Jimi Hendrix, Grover Washington, or Aretha Franklin, or on versions performed at mass events. More generally one might reflect upon standardization and the range of aesthetic license different performers might take or have taken with this piece in different historical or performance contexts.

Perhaps one also makes some *evaluative* interpretive moves, instantly finding this funny, clever, distasteful, inappropriate, hip, immoral, or foolish. Students occasionally question the seriousness of my choice of "Spangled Banner Minor" or take offense at my making an academic exercise out of something they may consider abhorrent and unpatriotic. Others accept my forcing them to listen to it in class but feel real animosity toward the performers for making it. Others find it outrageously funny and wonder why it took so long for someone to come up with such an obvious parody.

As one listens and applies various interpretive moves—locational, categorical, associational, reflective, evaluative—certain issues arise. One must decide if this is an intentionally incorrect version of something usually experienced in a slightly different form. One might question the seriousness of the performers or their ability to play "correctly" or "in tune," and therefore doubt the deliberateness of the piece. Or one might decide that the articulation is skillful, carefully crafted, and intentionally different—a parody. Then there is the problem of the seriousness of the parody. Is it just a cute joke, mild fun or the like, or is some deeper political message or critique implied? We might consider why the joke has been made using a song that, while not sacred, has more rigidly fixed semantic parameters than most other tunes familiar to the majority of Americans and associated by others with America. It would be a different "kind" of joke if the same technique were applied to "Mary Had a Little Lamb" or "Amazing Grace."

It is therefore not surprising that parodies—whatever their initial text or reference—involve more fixed and preset musical semantic parameters than do other pieces; parodies involve conscious and intentional manipulations that require certain analytic prowess in the process of conceptualization and production. One must grasp the importance and tacit generality of the major mode to Western patriotic songs, anthems, and the like in order to alter just that while preserving almost every other typical code feature—brass instruments, stately pace, clear articulation—of a serious performance in the genre.

Through all this activity—however much takes place at the moment of listening and however much through subsequent reconstruction—the work, essentially social, is brought into the situation that I am calling musical engagement. In a sense then, interpretive moves act roughly like a series of social processing conventions, locating, categorizing, associating, reflecting on, and evaluating the work through various aspects of experience. Such conventions do not fix a singular meaning; instead they focus some boundaries of fluid shifts in our attentional patterns as we foreground and background experience and knowledge in relation to the ongoing perception of a sound object or event. Meaning then is momentarily changeable and emergent, in flux as our interpretive moves are unraveled and crystallized.

I do not mean to suggest that there is a specific order, hierarchy, or conscious articulation to these interpretive moves as they pertain either to specific pieces, genres, styles, cultural repertoires, or listeners. I also would not suggest that all varieties of interpretive moves are significant in equal proportion all the time. Further, there is no isomorphism between the density and involvement of interpretive moves and the importance, greatness, aesthetic value, or enduring quality of a piece as socially placed and understood. I am also aware that my example is particularly loaded. Many pieces or musics do not involve the range and variety of interpretive activity I have described for "Spangled Banner Minor." But what is always similar is the instantaneous, momentary dialectical impression, which is unraveled and developed, or fixed and held, through listening time. These caveats suggest that various social, cultural, and historic processes and constraints operate to provide these skeletal interpretive moves with nerves, muscle, veins, blood, and clothes—that is, with many layers of internal and external variability. An ethnography of musical communication which concentrates on musical meaning and interpretation should be concerned with explicating some of these lived epistemologies, these intertwinings of form and substance, these practices full of potential or realized coherence and contradiction.

To summarize: interpretive moves involve certain dimensions of communicative action. Recognition of certain features of code, genre, stylization, and performance instantly identify boundaries of the musical object that exist in a tension of ideational and material structure, musical and extramusical features. Codes articulate through acoustic patterns, and surely the recognition of acoustic pattern is central to communication; all sounds are structured, performed, and heard through organized patterns of anticipation. But notice how what is communicated is potentially much more than any of this, much more than a "parody of the national anthem" or "the national anthem rendered in a minor key." A range of social and personal backgrounds, some shared, some complementary, of stratified knowledge and experience, and of attitudes (about anthems, songs in general, parodies in particular, politics in all cases) enters into the social construction of meaningful listening through interpretive moves, establishing a sense of what the sound object or event is and what one feels, grasps, or knows about it. At the same time some very specific decisions (about seriousness, nonseriousness, intent, performer's attitude and meaning) can also be made by drawing on interpretive moves and other kinds of social knowledge. Some of these might relate to factors far outside the specific hearing, like knowledge of the performers and their body of work. Others might relate to factors closer to the specific hearing—the conditions surrounding a recorded presentation or other sound objects heard immediately before and after the one in question. In short, each hearing, like human social interaction generally has, as Erving Goffman (1983) insisted, a biography and a history, and these may be more or less important to the particular hearing in question at a specific time.

From Interpretive Moves to Boundaries and Frames

I have argued that the core of the music communication process involves two components. One is dialectic or tension that emerges as one recognizes and engages a sound object or event in time, the other the interpretive moves one employs to situate, entangle, and untangle this engagement and recognition process. These components are dynamically linked, and the linkage typically produces a boundary—what Gregory Bateson (1972) and Goffman (1974) called a "frame"—namely, a conceptual sensing of organizational premises and a foregrounding of the operational dynamics of a situation. This boundary or frame represents the notion that potentially very general and very specific messages emerge simultaneously in the consciousness of the interpreting listener. The boundary or frame is both a closed and open door to this process; it can lock in or compact a summary of all interacting interpretive constructs, or it can let them scatter and draw more attention to its own position among those elements. If interpretive moves provide the possibility both of digging deeply into referential and expressive dimensions of music hearing and of more limited, superficial engagement, the notion of a boundary or frame is meant to suggest the instantaneous possibility of abstracting the dynamism of the sound object's dialectics and the listener's interpretive moves to a general level, which can then be directed back toward specifics or fixed where it is. The question then is this: What sorts of constructs or tendencies are set up by this boundary-making and framing process? I think there might be three general types of these contextualizing frames.

One variety of frames has to do with *expressive ideology*. Through framing, music can communicate highly patterned aesthetic orderings. To the extent that a given frame suggests one mode of interpretation over other possible treatments of form and content, boundary making or framing involves value. A range of meanings as interpreted amongst others draws attention to one organizational premise—the extent to which the form or content is a preferred one. A second variety has to do with *identity*, the means by which music communicates sameness or difference of character as it exists among music makers, makers and listeners, individuals and groups. It draws interpretive attention to the character, the signature, of the "self." Musical practices typically either emphasize context by high redundancy of code, or emphasize code through a combination of contextual neutralization and low redundancy. Given the possibilities for very redundant codes in music, it is often the case that interpretive action moves elsewhere; redundancy and what it puts into focus can become a sort of identifying signature (see Jakobson 1960).

A third variety of contextualizing frame has to do with *coherence*, a term suggested in recent work by Judith and Alton Becker (1981). The coherence of a frame refers to the extent that it is indivisible from other ways of relating to the subjectively real world—a notion close, I think, to what Seeger had in mind by "world view as the feeling of reality." In this kind of frame, the musical mode may present the same orders of message that are presented, simultaneously or otherwise, in other modes. I am referring, then, to tropes and crossmodal abstractions, those figurative wellsprings that unify experience across natural, cultural, physical, and aesthetic fields of reference. Coherence systems involve organizing principles that are not unique to one social domain, symbolic system, or social practice, but are instead broadly epistemic and unifying, culturally axiomatic, implicated in social behaviors and praxis of all sorts.

Seeger often stressed that music is interesting because of the way generality allows for many levels or overlaps of conscious discovery in listening. Here is where our views are most compatible. The significant feature of musical communication is not that it is untranslatable and irreducible to the verbal mode but that its generality and multiplicity of possible messages and interpretations brings out a special kind of "feelingful" activity and engagement on the part of the listener, a form of pleasure that unites the material and mental dimensions of musical experience as fully embodied. It is in this sense that we might speak of music as a metaphoric process, a special way of experiencing, knowing, and feeling value, identity, and coherence. If our interpretations of musical sounds are general, floating frames and boundaries that exist simultaneously and instantaneously, it is because we momentarily apprehend value, identity, and coherence through the "thisness of a that or the thatness of a this" (Burke 1945), through the simultaneous recognition of relationship and difference. Because metaphors operate on meaning over form, they generalize in ways no taxonomy might, while specifying in ways descriptions rarely achieve. Instantaneous recognition of shared connotative and denotative features is the motion from interpretive moves to frames and boundaries.

Speech about Music

Recently, in a lecture series bearing Seeger's name, Klaus Wachsmann (1982) spoke to the problem of speech about music. He suggested that talk about music is a fact of life, worth turning into an object of study in its own right rather than a continual cause of musicological lament or embarrassment. He argued, along with Hugo Zemp (1979) and me (Feld 1981a, 1990), that the ways people talk about music can be a significant datum of musical concepts, theory, and experience and can be studied systematically. He addressed some ways in which any discourse about music is a window opening to metaphoric processes and synesthesia and therefore a potential way to explore—through the verbal mode—certain complexities of the musical mode stressed by Seeger's notion of music as the communication of "world view as the feeling of reality."

Yet when Charles Seeger talked of the qualities of speech about music, he considered only one dimension of verbal language, the referential or lexically explicit semantic character of speech, the dimension where words stand as proxies for denoted objects. It is true that musicologists and analysts use a very technical and referentially explicit lexicon to talk about music. But this theoretical, technical language is often closely related to metaphor, whether, as in many metalanguages, to a limited kind of polysemy or to a broader kind of linguistic creativity. Let me put that aside for now and argue that, at the very least, the "talking about music" that most people do, most of the time, whatever their technical knowledge, involves both lexical and discourse metaphor. This is at once a recognition of the nontranslatability of musical and verbal modes and the simultaneous multiplicity and generality of what is communicated. Metaphors involve the instantaneous recognition that things are simultaneously alike and unlike. And when most people talk about music, like and unlike is what they talk about.

Furthermore, when people talk to each other, to themselves, or to music analysts they often draw upon the stock of interpretive moves that I identified earlier. They *locate* and *categorize* musical experiences in relation to similar or dissimilar experiences. They *associate* musical experiences with experiences of other types. They *reflect* on how an experience relates to like or unlike imagery. And they *evaluate* the experience by relating it to their particular preferences. When people say, "It's different from . . . ," "It's a kind of . . . ," "It sort of reminds me of . . . ," and things of this sort, they are creating discourse frames with locational, categorical, and associational features. When they say, "Well, if I had to name it . . . ," "I mean on some level . . . ," "For me at least . . . ," "I really can't say but, do you know what I mean?" they are not necessarily tongue-tied, inarticulate, or unable to speak. They are caught in a moment of interpretive time, trying to force awareness to words. They are telling us how much they assume that we understand *exactly* what they are experiencing. In fact, we do understand exactly what they are experiencing. We take it as socially typical that people talk this way about music, stringing together expressives, and we assume that this confirms what we are all supposed to know: that at some level, one just cannot say with words what music says without them. Finally, when someone says of a piece, "It's not as good as . . . " or "What I really like is . . . ," they are making an evaluative move that draws on simultaneous recognition of other texts, experiences, or performances.

These common structures of verbalization (all of which can be found concretely in the Music in Daily Life project interviews; see Crafts, Cavicchi, and Keil 1993) tell us something about the nature of interpretation and the possibilities for speech about music. One engages and places an item or event in meaningful social space through ongoing interpretive moves. These moves do not fix or freeze a single meaning; meaning is emergent and changeable in relation to various combinations of moves made by specifically situated speakers. Interview data confirms both the importance of lexical and discourse metaphors for verbally expressing something about musical experience and its prevalence in representing such abstractions as value, identity, and world sense. Talk locates emergent processes of making meanings, and it is as social engagement and accomplishment that talk must be studied.

Here is where I most obviously diverge from Seeger. By equating the referential domain of the speech mode with primary verbal communication, he left aside much of how people routinely talk and certainly how they routinely talk about music. It was this emphasis on the referential that led him to assert that speech about music communicated "world view as intellection of reality." On the contrary, I think speech about music represents an attempt to construct a metaphoric discourse to signify awareness of the more fundamental metaphoric discourse that music communicates in its own right. What is to be gained by attention to speech about music is information about the construction of interpretive moves as a kind of metaphoric engagement. Locational, categorical, associative, reflective, and evaluative discourse attempts to identify the boundaries that sound objects and events present in their structure and social organization. Interpretive moves in talk, then, are attempts to recreate, specify, momentarily fix, or give order to emergent recognitions of the events that take place so rapidly and intuitively when we experience musical sounds.

For clarity, let me emphasize that verbal representations of these sorts are in no way necessary or essential to musical communication. Musical communication is a primary modeling system, to use John Blacking's (1981b) phrase, with unique and irreducible symbolic properties. These must be experienced and approached in their own right and, as Seeger said, empirically and conceptually freed from any notion that they simply translate or copy the speech mode. At the same time, speech about music clearly constitutes a source of parallel or exploratory information about metaphoric process, discourse, interpretive moves, and conceptual ideas or theories about sound.

Conclusion

What does music communicate? The question as articulated by Seeger places an emphasis on music as a contained universe that evokes meanings from an inner form to an outer social realm. To rethink this question I have replaced it with several others: What are the shapes of music's communication processes? How are these processes activated? How do they implicate interpretation? In answering these questions I have tried to explicate the role of listening as symbolic engagement in order to redress the imbalance common in analytic perspectives that equate musical communication with the extent to which a listener receives a composer's or performer's intentions, or receives what a music analyst can uncover in the score.

By communication I have meant a socially interactive and subjective process of reality construction through message making and interpretation. Communication is a dialectical process. The dialectic between musical structure and extramusical history is central to the study of human musicality in evolutionary, cross-cultural, and symbolic perspective. A communications epistemology addresses this dialectic not by choosing sides but by focusing on its consequences. Those consequences concern boundary making, framing, and contextualizing as universal perceptual features of the dialectical process. Furthermore, framing involves simultaneous recognition of generality and specificity, form and reference, through some combination of locational, categorical, associational, reflective, and evaluative interpretive moves. I sense that investigating the substance of these processes leads to the conclusion that music's major messages are general and multileveled and concern expressive ideology and value, identity and character, and coherence of world sense.

I have argued that what makes this possible is the process of boundary framing, the contextualizing turn that proceeds from the recognition of dialectically simultaneous musical and extramusical features experienced in engaging the sound object. I think that these constructs are, to varying degrees, accessible to intuitive and empirical investigation. At the same time, they may also be represented at the level of verbal interpretive moves that metaphorically locate, categorize, associate, reflect on, or evaluate music experience. A key to this is the differentiation of music, as instantaneously apprehensible metaphorical expression of one symbolic order, and speech about music, as metaphorical expression of another order that reflects secondary interpretive awareness, recognition, or engagement.

PARTICIPATORY DISCREPANCIES
AND THE POWER OF MUSIC

Bo Diddley Bo Diddley have you heard
My pretty baby said she was a bird.
                              —Bo Diddley

The power of music lies in its participatory discrepancies, and
these are basically of two kinds: processual and textural. Music,
to be personally involving and socially valuable, must be "out of
time" and "out of tune."

For *participatory discrepancy* one could substitute "inflection," "articulation," "creative tension," "relaxed dynamism," or
"semiconscious or unconscious slightly out of syncness." For
process one could say "groove," "beat," "vital drive," "swing,"
"pulse," or "push," and for *texture,* "timbre," "sound," "tone
qualities," "as arranged by," and so forth. The fact that these
musical essentials are barely "figured" in Owen Barfield's sense
(1965:24 ff., 188) and certainly not "collectively represented"
with any great clarity in language (Barfield 1965:41, 111, 122,
154–55) is evidence, I believe, of their original or active participatory power (Barfield 1965:28–45). Put another way,
wherever "lexical meanings" are various and ambiguous for a
particular phenomenon, one can assume a lot of collective and
individual unconsciousness and conversely a greater power for
"speaker's meanings" (Barfield 1984) to define situations.

The syntactic or structural aspect of all music (Meyer 1956)
but especially of through-composed Western and other civilized
musics, can create tensions, set up melodic-harmonic relationships that defer resolutions and gratifications, and thereby involve the listener in the music. But isn't this involvement more
analytic, sequential, and conscious than "participatory" in the
sense described by Lévy-Bruhl and Barfield? Syntax, even in
these civilized musical systems, does not invite the listener to
participate in the phenomena with the same powers that process
and texture have. It is really only in relatively recent periods of
Western music that a peculiarly rationalist approach to syntax

(Weber 1958) has managed to squeeze the mysteries of musical participation to the furthest corners of our awareness.

I am using the concept of "participation" as defined by Lévy-Bruhl and refined by Owen Barfield. The paradigmatic citation is from Lévy-Bruhl:

> The Bororo (neighboring tribe) boast that they are red araras (parakeets). This does not merely signify that after their death they become araras, nor that araras are metamorphosed Bororos, and must be treated as such. It is something entirely different. "The Bororos," says Von den Steinen, who would not believe it, but finally had to give in to their explicit affirmations, "give one rigidly to understand that they are araras *at the present time,* just as if a caterpillar declared itself to be a butterfly." (Lévy-Bruhl [1910] 1966:62)

And Barfield on participation:

> Participation begins by being an activity, and essentially a communal or social activity. It takes place in rites and initiation ceremonies resulting in [quoting Durkheim] "collective mental states of extreme emotional intensity, in which representation is as yet undifferentiated from the movements and actions which make the communion towards which it tends a reality to the group. Their participation is so effectively *lived* that it is not yet properly imagined."
>
> This stage is not only pre-logical, but also pre-mythical. It is anterior to collective representations themselves, as I have been using the term. Thus, the first development Durkheim traces is from symbiosis or active participation (where the individual feels he is the totem) to collective representations of the totemic type (where the individual feels that his ancestors were the totem, that he will be when he dies, etc.). From this symbolic apprehension he then arrives at the duality, with which we are more familiar, of ideas on the one hand and numinous religion on the other. (Barfield 1965:32)

All humans were full participants once upon a time, and I believe we still experience much music and perhaps some other portions of reality this way. I also believe we need more of this participatory consciousness if we are to get back into ecological synchrony with ourselves and with the natural world. At the very least, it is important to recognize this capacity in human beings to defy logic, to defy the so-called laws of contradiction, and to insist upon identity, to insist upon participation. We are all Bororos! We are all Araras! If you can participate once, in one song, dance, poem, or rite, you can do it more times and in more ways until you are "at one" with the entire universe or at least with very large chunks of it. The social moments where I get these "oneness" and "urge to merge" feelings most forcefully are when I'm dancing at polka parties (see Keil, Keil, and Blau 1992) or salsa parties, swept up in a black church service, or making music. When trying to conceptualize or explain these euphoric feelings of "polka happiness" or "blues mellowness," a theory and rhetoric of participation helps keep the good feelings alive. Positivism, and Marxism too (with its language of negation, contradiction, alienation, commodification, reification, mediation, etc.) tend to reify our problems still further, as they name and describe them, whereas the language of participation, poetry, invites participation and promises ever deeper and more satisfying knowledge of who we are.

Participation is the opposite of alienation from nature, from society, from the body, from labor, and is therefore worth holding onto wherever we can still find some of it, the two exceptions to this rule being those large-scale nation-state organizations with aggressive purposes, where participation becomes the very essence of fascism, and those participations fueled by fear and desperation, where cargo-cult beliefs can and often do have disastrous consequences. The rites of fascist participation are easily recognized (and, one hopes, avoided) because they are enacted on a large scale and heighten the inequalities: society over nature, society over other societies, men over women, men over other men. As ecocatastrophic and economic crises deepen, however, it may become harder and also more important to distinguish between participations that really revitalize, equalize, and decentralize as opposed to those that promise the equalities in the future if followers will only make sacrifices now.

Discrepant is as good a term as I've been able to find for the phenomena that make music a peculiarly powerful vehicle for participatory consciousness and action: "not consistent or matching; disagreeing [from the Latin] *discrepare*, to sound different, vary; *dis-* apart plus *crepare*, to rattle, sound" (American Heritage Dictionary 1969). It is the little discrepancies between hands and feet within a jazz drummer's beat, between bass and drums, between rhythm section and soloist, that create the groove and invite us to participate. I gave a preliminary description of these processual kinds of participatory discrepancies twenty years ago in "Motion and Feeling through Music." More recent explorations of the "push" or dynamism in Polish-American polka music reveal similar sorts of discrepancies drawing people to the music, onto the dance floor, into the festival. Here Ed Benbenik and Chester "Hoot" Filipiak describe Marion Lush's great band of the 1960s:

> As Ed put it, "Marion has always been hell on drummers; he knew what he wanted, the sound he wanted, and that's what he got. It was a relaxed, dynamic sound. Playing with other bands can be a lot of work, but with Marion it just flows along." Or in Hoot's phrasing of the same paradox, "The most important thing in a good polka band is relaxation, to push it hard in a relaxed mood. If the trumpets are playing tense, it can affect the whole band, and if anyone in the band is tense, the dancers can actually feel this on the floor. Lush's band was always relaxed."
>
> Hoot brought his drumsticks to the phone to beat out a comparison between "Jeep" Machinya's snare drum rhythms and Li'l Wally's. As he talked about the beat of each drummer— the differences between Hoot's beat and Jeep's and where Rudy Sienkowski's way with a snare drum might fit—it became clear that every polka drummer of any reputation, every band with any loyal following, has a unique "beat."
>
> Talking about polka rhythm sections overall, and Lush's "million dollar rhythm section" in particular, Hoot pointed out that the articulation of the bass line has also been a crucial variable in defining "beat" and style and sense of tempo. The amplified bass from a concertina dictates a "slower," looser pace and feeling than the bass from the accordion or the still "quicker" bass from a chordovox. The old combination of string bass and piano working together creates still another "time feel." (Keil, Keil, and Blau 1992:63–64)

Following Filipiak briefly (one could elaborate this conversation to thesis length), the idiosyncratic processual discrepancies—within a given polka drummer's snare-drum beat and between that beat and one of four or five other bass sources, each of which will be shaped by a personal touch—create "push" or "relaxed dynamism" that can be enhanced or hindered by the absence or presence of tension in the trumpet section. This seems so similar to the jazz processes described in "Motion and Feeling through Music" that the reader might wonder about my subjective biases or whether the Polish-American processes were the result of diffusion from Afro-America. Time and future research will tell, but I think "swing" or "push" is present to varying degrees in all musics and that old Polish grooves were simply enhanced by any Afro-American vibes picked up in the New World. Nick Timko's brilliant analysis (personal communication) of the ways in which the crisp and loose articulations (participatory discrepancies) of Eastern and Chicago styles respectively are falsely perceived by dancers as primarily differences of tempo ("Eastern is faster than Chicago," say a lot of people) opened my ears ten years ago to the range and complexity of polka processes; there is no reason to believe that things were any simpler in ages past; probably quite the contrary.

Certainly the textural or timbral participatory discrepancies tend to be wilder and crazier the further back and further out one listens. Or is it the further up? I'm thinking of all the pitch discrepancies in peoples' music all over the planet and out in the countryside, but especially in the mountain musics of Tibet, Appalachia, Epirus, the Tatras, the Alps. The driving dissonance of Goral singing and string playing from the Tatras have been gradually "toned down" in the New World. Degrees of out-of-tuneness, vis-à-vis Western bourgeois conventions, are noticeable in the basses of Polish-American polka bands, but textural discrepancies in the higher frequencies are subtle and not obviously celebrated as in Goral singing and fiddling. Could we trace textural losses and processual gains in the urbanization of various traditional musics around the world? The two-trumpet sound developed by Marion Lush and now utilized by most polka bands (even a quartet like the Bay State Four has two trumpets, accordion, and drums) is powerful, I believe, because the blended harmonics of two trumpets guarantee textural participatory discrepancies and a bright, happy sound that invites people to get up and dance. Paired alto saxophones in Papago-Pima polka bands and the pairs of wet-tuned reeds in a button-box accordion or concertina may have similar effects. The paired instruments of Tibetan monastery ensembles are perhaps the paradigmatic instance of pitches juxtaposed or rubbed against each other to maximize the intensity of matter, spirit, and energy coming together, to be sent, in this case, heavenward. As with process, every live or genuine music has varying kinds of textural discrepancies, and measuring these is uncharted territory. Within the jazz community there is a lot of informal discussion about the out-of-tune "edge" to the "tone" of players X, Y, and Z or the "sound" of groups A, B, and C. Similar talk exists in the polka world and probably in every musical community. Even in the perfection-addicted Western music world, what do the best piano tuners do when they want more brightness from each three-stringed note? How are the tubes of an organ made to resonate well? They are deliberately untuned a bit for better resonance.

But rather than multiply textural and processual examples, perhaps this is a good place to outline how a musicology of participatory discrepancies might proceed. Some broad queries follow:

1. *Listen and look for participatory discrepancies in the process and texture of a music and in its wider contexts.* I suggest that the analyst look as well as listen; the physical motions of music makers give important information, and the behavioral responses of people (for example, dancing) are a bridge to the audiovisual space-time tropes of a culture (Armstrong 1971; Keil 1979b). The best Chicago-style polka dancers are consistently way out of sync with the music, to my eyes at least; what is this discrepancy about? Similarly, in Cuba it seemed to me that the best dancers were consistently "between the beats" in their footwork, providing a hermeneutic or between-the-lines interpretation of drumming patterns that were certainly complicated enough and rich in discrepancies before the dancers added their moves to the mix.

2. *Discuss all possible participatory discrepancies with a variety of experts.* Some jazz and polka musicians can hear and describe the tensions

Bo Diddley and band, mid 1950s. Photo courtesy of MCA/Chess files.

Polka bellringers for Happy Richie and the Royalaires; Buffalo, N.Y. Photo Charles Keil.

Trumpet duo reach for polka brightness. Photo Dick Blau.

Polka harmonizing at an International Polka Association party. Photo Dick Blau.

and dynamism in any rhythm section. Others can say something about their personal touches and approaches. Many do not conceptualize the discrepancies at all and groove better without thinking about it. Some practitioners may also be organic intellectuals, like Nick Timko and Chester Filipiak, with clear theories about what is happening in their music. In any case, check out the best musicians and dancers ethnographically. What do they say they are doing? Where do they think the magic of participation is coming from? How do they "figure" and individually or collectively represent any possible discrepancies and the resulting grooves?

3. How do your perceptions (query 1) and expert perceptions (query 2) match up?

4. What laboratory measurements are possible to further confirm matchups between your perceptions and expert perceptions or to shed light on areas of disagreement? Can we wire up the contact points on fingers and drumsticks? Can we precisely graph the acoustical phenomena and measure actual discrepancies in time and pitch?[1] Within jazz and

1. See page 67, note 14. Progress has been made in measuring the processual participatory discrepancies, but how can we investigate textures empirically?

polka rhythm sections alone there are thousands of possible experiments that would combine expert perceptions and lab measurements to more exactly specify kinds and degrees of "swing" or "push." Confident that these participatory mysteries will never be more fully resolved than the mysteries of small particle physics or the further reaches of the universe, I'm ready to call in the engineers and start exploring.

5. *What do people "figure" and "collectively represent" to be going on in their music? How are the mysteries of participation kept mysterious?* You are by now aware that the best music must be full of discrepancies, both "out of time" and "out of tune." What was keeping you from this perception before? How did your soul get so fretted, bored, and well tempered? One can tease about the peculiar Western biases that have long kept us from a liberating musicology, but I suspect that every culture has its own blinders that protect participatory discrepancies and keep them as fully mysterious and as fully participatory as possible. Maybe that's why I didn't call in the engineers to finish the refutation of Meyer's syntax fixation in 1966. Commenting on my criticisms in "Motion and Feeling through Music," Professor Meyer argued that "swing" might be a matter of microsyntax. The tiny hesitations and anticipations could be notated and their contributions to the deferred gratifications of value and greatness in music assessed. Two decades later I would like to turn this notion around and suggest that musical syntax may just be macroprocess and macrotexture or, when written down, a petrified skeleton on which to hang the flesh and blood of actual music making.

One of the great works of twentieth-century music, "Bo Diddley," by the composer of the same name, is based upon "hamboning" rhythms that probably derive from the period when slaves without instruments used their bodies as drums. Placed in creative tension with the mechanical vibrato or tremolo of an electric guitar, these rhythms ushered in the era booming today out of boom boxes and disco systems everywhere, the era of mechanical participatory discrepancies. In "Bo Diddley" the mechanical guitar vibrato is not just a textural surface feature but the core of the process and shaper of structure as well.

Talking to Bo backstage at the Tralfamadore Cafe (Buffalo, 31 December 1985) I asked about the famous beat. The expert rejected both of my perceptions. On my hambone rhythm hypothesis Bo recited the traditional lyric, demonstrated the body drumming licks, and compared them to his own beat onomatopoeically, insisting in the face of their obvious (to me) similarity that "the only thing that makes the sound like it could be related to Bo Diddley's beat is the structure of the words: Hambone, hambone, have you heard, you see, Papa's gonna buy me a mocking bird, see. If you took off 'bird' it would change the rhythm set, you dig?" He demonstrated the hambone and Bo Diddley beats again for emphasis and said, "Two thousand miles difference!" I want to talk about milliseconds and Bo is talking miles. This dialogue continued:

> CK: And that mechanical guitar vibrato on that original song [I imitate the pulsed drag triplets]—that transforms it completely!
>
> BD: No. That has nothing to do with it. That's just something, a mechanical device that they made the armature of a tremolo [sic] and I used it. I don't know if that made the difference in the song, if it made the difference in rhythm pattern of the song or what. It could have made the difference, to have the notes being wobbly like that. I call it wobbly. 'Cause guys have copied the thing and they didn't have no tremolo and they made it with being straight . . . straight guitar licks. So I can't say what made it, but it's not hambone, it's not related. It's the word structure. . . . It's not the same thing.
>
> CK: But that wobble? When I was listening to the record before I came down here, I said, I want to find out, if I can, what's behind that.
>
> BD: [Sings the wobbly sound emphatically]
>
> CK: It's in sync with the rhythm. It's in triplets against that [singing Diddley beat].
>
> BD: It took me about three or four years to, ah . . .
>
> CK: . . . sync it up!
>
> BD: No, not to sync it up, it's to learn to sing with that. Because it's an offset beat. I call it offset. It ain't directly right on. You see there's a trick to that whole song, and I'll tell you what it is. See, I wanted to be a drummer at one time. And what I'm doing on the guitar is what I expected to do on drums.
>
> CK: So drumming is the basis of that guitar style?
>
> BD: Yeah, with me. Because you got to have a certain thing going on in your head in order to execute this.

I think Ellas McDaniel (Bo Diddley) is completely honest in his responses but also protecting his participatory discrepancies in this interview. We are probably both "right" about the Bo Diddley beat and simply sorting out semantic differences, trying to negotiate the names for an elusive reality, names that can only begin to describe its uniqueness and its universality. Here's another writer's effort to describe it:

> Bo's beat is there, fully realized; he sets it with his guitar, and maracas and drums played like congas are its underpinning. That beat has often been described as "shave and a hair cut, two bits," the joke rhythm you beep on your car horn at the drive-in. Nothing is further from the truth. Bo's beat is his own pulse made art. More than a signature, it is his ultimate statement, the stable matrix from which his music flows.
>
> Yet the beat, four-quarter time shoved off center like the beat kept by the claves in West Indian music, is complex and changing. Bo can syncopate it any way he wants to. His physical strength makes it profoundly sensual, and the maracas evoke Africa or Haiti. The beat is dense, but its ambiguity of shadings opens it up and keeps it moving. It is the Bo Diddley beat: "Everybody from New Orleans," Louis Armstrong once said, "got that thing." (Lydon and Mandel 1974:65)

Jelly Roll Morton called it "the Spanish tinge," a universal or at least circum-Atlantic groove, but as particular as Bo Diddley at any given moment on any given night. His recent performance in Buffalo found him shading his "beat" and "sound" from song to song with varying degrees of success in terms of getting the backup band into the groove and the dancers moving happily. Each statement is the ultimate or last. The matrix is not stable. The "Bo Diddley beat" takes a slightly or markedly different form each time out. In this music, at least, the process and texture are tightly meshed and dictate whatever syntax there will be.

Moreover, these transformations of the Diddley beat seem to be a perfect analogue in the area of "swinger's feeling" to what Barfield calls "speaker's meaning" in the field of historical semantics:

> It is a historical fact that those elusive norms we loosely call "meanings" are involved in a constant process of change. It would moreover not be very difficult to demonstrate that all mental progress (and, arising from that, all material progress) is brought about in association with those very changes. One can go further and say that the changes are made possible precisely by that discrepancy between an individual speaker's meaning and the current, or lexical, meaning. (Barfield 1984: 30–31)

I am uneasy about the notion of "progress" in Barfield's description; even "development" suggests that our "meanings" and "feelings" are somehow improving over time (when in fact they may only be continually improvised). Our crucial point of agreement, however, is that whatever historical change in language, music, dance, or culture is about, we can study it best, at its very point of creation, if we attend closely to the discrepancies that enhance participation and the contexts that generate these discrepancies.

I will stop here at the beginning of what could be a shelf of books about music in the era of mechanical reproduction (Benjamin 1969: 220–25). What has happened since Les Paul and Mary Ford put the echo effect into "How High the Moon" and Bo Diddley learned to sing with a separate little magnatone tremolo box of bubbling mercury is a lot! It is silly, in some ways, to be thinking about a liberatory musicology or a revolution in musicology when the technoelectrical applications of any theory I might invent have been going on at an accelerating pace for thirty years; when the synthesizers, drum machines, dubbers, scratchers, hip-hoppers, and mass producers have already technologized participatory discrepancies, have already discovered the degrees of space, echo, reverb, digital delay, double-tracking, semisyncedness, and the like that will make millions buy and move, move and buy; when the engineers have already arrived in force and taken control of the central dance sector in ongoing Afro-American music; when "this non-machine tradition" (Bennett 1964:53; Keil [1966] 1991:175) has been almost totally mechanized, down to the degrees of density in the synthetic "soul clap"; when the revolution in the music is long over, the barricades set up, danced upon, taken down, and repacked for shipment abroad. So, one goal for researchers is to catch up with this process of mechanizing the participatory discrepancies. We really have to get down to the recording studio or dance floor to groove a while and to ask people about what has been happening.

Another goal may be to connect participatory discrepancies, PDs as I have come to call them, to Particles Dancing—the imperfections of an unfolding universe; the physics of energy and matter; chaos and cosmos; the sense we humans have that, across cultural boundaries, music puts us in touch with the ultimate forces.

Between these two extremes—participation in the universe and the mediation-mechanization of grooves—PDs have everything to do with pleasure in the Public Domain: the presence of shared tradition and an ever deepening sense of the subtle ways in which wrights and rites, skills and events, craft and culture, are connected in public space and time. If the microtiming is not right among the *bata* players the *orishas* will not descend. If the textural brightness and processual relaxed dynamism of the paired trumpets are not there a lot of polka dancers may sit tight. There are plenty of researchable questions here for ethnomusicologists thinking about their chosen styles. We are also challenged to keep these powers of music alive in localities and to invent new PDs, participatory discrepancies in public domains, wherever the traditional blends of wrights and rites in playful delights have faded or disappeared. Unlike power-over relations and alienated living, the PDs, pleasure, participation, and play cannot be legislated or enforced from above. But they can be imagined and enacted anytime and anywhere that people feel the need.

4 AESTHETICS AS ICONICITY OF STYLE (UPTOWN TITLE); OR, (DOWNTOWN TITLE) "LIFT-UP-OVER SOUNDING": GETTING INTO THE KALULI GROOVE

STEVEN FELD

The present discussion [of sound patterns] is really a special illustration of the necessity of getting behind the sense data of any type of expression in order to grasp the intuitively felt and communicated forms which alone give significance to such expression.

—Edward Sapir

Insistence on the opposition between life and art is tied to the experience of an alienated world. And failure to recognize the universal scope and ontological dignity of play produces an abstraction that blinds us to the interdependence of both.

—Hans-Georg Gadamer

Groove, Sound, Beat, Style

In the vernacular a "groove" refers to an intuitive sense of style as process, a perception of a cycle in motion, a form or organizing pattern being revealed, a recurrent clustering of elements through time. Such consistent, coherent formal features become one with their content but are uniquely recognizable by the way they shape content to articulate specifically in that form. Groove and style are distilled essences, crystallizations of collaborative expectancies in time.

A variety of abstract, formal definitions of style, merging several distinguished traditions, are currently in circulation. In a widely influential statement in the general aesthetics literature, Leonard Meyer wrote, "Style is a replication of patterning, whether in human behavior or in the artifacts produced by

(A tape with all the examples cited in this chapter, as well as examples from other chapters in the book, can be obtained from S. Feld, Dept. of Anthropology, New York University, New York, NY 10003.)

human behavior, that results from a series of choices made within some set of constraints" (1987:21).[1] In a semiotic discussion of speech styles, Greg Urban defined style tersely as "a general form that is recognizable apart from specific instances in which it is used" (1985:312; see also 1991a:106). Backing up to anthropological ancestors, Franz Boas ([1927] 1955:144–80) took style to comprise those unconsciously formal elements selected and arranged to be, like the sound elements of language, characteristic of an expressive system. Ruth Bunzel amplified that notion: "Style is more than the arrangement or patterning of this material; it involves the whole approach to and conception of the esthetic problem in the chosen medium" (1938:569).

Later embellishments include Meyer Schapiro who, picking up the analogy with language, separated style into form elements, form relationships, and expressive qualities, then put them back together as "a qualitative whole which is capable of suggesting . . . diffuse connotations as well as intensifying . . . associated or intrinsic affects" (1953:304), and A. L. Kroeber (1963), who restated the central Boasian distinction of form and principles abstracted from content and substance in a broader historical perspective of symptomatic traits (see also Gerbrands 1969 for a restatement from a more material culture, museological viewpoint). Later, and in different contexts, Gregory Bateson (1972) and Roman Jakobson (1960) conceived style as a key element in communicative and metacommunicative framing by differentially foregrounding code from message. Like music and art historians and somewhat in distinction to literary theorists, anthropologists and linguists have defined style more in terms of shared conventions of form than of deviations (see Meyer 1987:34 n.26).

Taking us specifically to the musical groove, Leonard Meyer puts it all together when he says, "Style constitutes the universe of discourse within which musical meanings arise" (1967:7). Each culturally constructed "groove" is such a universe, regardless of whether a society is characterized by tendencies toward more singular monolithic style formations or toward multiple ones; has style tendencies in conflict and contest or acceptance and reproduction; situates style more generally in other cultural patterns of fission, fusion, flux, acceptance, and rejection.

---

1. Meyer stresses the importance of choice to dispute the notion that style is dependent on synonymy or reducible to variations in manner of representation. In this his argument recalls Nelson Goodman's concern (1975) with pointing to the necessary integration of form and content in an overall theory of style.

Instantly perceived, and often attended by pleasurable sensations ranging from arousal to relaxation, "getting into the groove" describes how a socialized listener anticipates pattern in a style, and feelingfully participates by momentarily tracking and appreciating subtleties vis-à-vis overt regularities. It also describes how a seasoned performer structures and maintains a perceptible coherence; Keil, in "Motion and Feeling through Music," relates the groove to the subjective processes of swing, vital drive, and metronome sense in jazz. Getting into the groove also describes a feelingful participation, a positive physical and emotional attachment, a move from being "hip to it" to "getting down" and being "into it." A groove is a comfortable place to be.[2] When Aretha Franklin (1967b) covered Sam Cooke's tune "Good Times," she changed the first line from "Come on baby and let the good times roll" to "Get in the groove and let the good times roll." And the way James Brown (1966) tells it,

> When your baby and you are tight
> And everything you say or do is mellow
> She keeps everything alright
> And you know that you're the only fellow
> Ain't that a groove!

Of course the musical "groove" here derives from a primary reference to the patterned indent spaces on a disc recording, observable lateral impressions in a record's surface. The music is mysteriously "in" these physical recesses, pressed into the vinyl, and listeners may imagine journeying there to merge right "into the groove." Styles are engraved and ingrained in cultures the way grooves are engraved and ingrained in record discs.

Related, more general labels for styles and their attentive processes include the idea of the "sound" or "beat" (in Francophone Africa, "cadence"), for example, the Philly sound, the Nashville sound, the Motown sound, the Austin sound, the reggae beat, and Afro-Beat. Names of places, record companies and studios, eras, genres, and fusions abound in these phrases. From Jamaica, accompanied by the pulsing bass-and-drum essence of reggae *riddim,* Rico (1982) sings:

2. John Miller Chernoff, ethnomusicologist and percussionist, provides some additional details on the groove: "To me, its reference is mainly to rhythm, i.e., that the bass and drum 'lay down a groove.' It also suggests coolness and calm, something effortless and smooth, as in 'groovin'.' In its physical aspect, it keeps you with it, 'in the groove.' In West Africa, incidentally, many people refer to reefer as 'groove' and smoking it as 'grooving'" (personal communication, 4 December 1987).

What you talkin' bout
You say you don't like the reggae beat
You must be cra-a-a-a-zy!

I use these sound-text examples to stimulate a sense of the intuitive
realness of the ideas of groove, sound, and beat as style statements, but
they are obviously loaded examples, both because the texts include the
terms "groove" and "beat," and because as we listen we hear these
words lean into the specifically referenced "groove":

While these examples are unusual, I would nevertheless contend that
all grooves and beats have ways of drawing a listener's attention; one's
intuitive feelingful sense of a groove or beat is a recognition of style in
motion. As Leonard Meyer says, "A musical style is a finite array of in-
terdependent melodic, rhythmic, harmonic, timbral, textural, and formal
relationships and processes. When these are internalized as learned
habits, listeners (including performers and composers) are able to perceive and understand a composition in the style as an intricate network
of *implicative relationships,* or to experience the work as a complex of
felt probabilities" (1967:116; italics added). Out of these relationships
arise the "expectations—the tendencies—upon which musical meaning
is built" (Meyer 1967:8; see also 1956:45–73, 1989:1–37).

Linguistic shorthands—terms like groove, sound, or beat—significantly code an unspecifiable but ordered sense of something (Meyer's
"implicative relationships" and "felt probabilities") that is sustained in a
distinctive, regular, and attractive way, working to draw a listener in.
Terms like these say that the perception of style is empirically real, but
that it is also necessarily general, vague, and physical, feelingfully ingrained in affective time and space. As Kenneth Burke says, "Once you
grasp the trend of the form, it invites participation" (1969:58, cited and
discussed in Bauman 1977:16). Meyer is in the same groove when he
says, "A style is *learned,* even by the composers who 'invent' it"
(1967:116; italics in original). So is Clifford Geertz when he writes, "Art
and the equipment to grasp it are made in the same shop" (1983:118).

"Lift-up-over Sounding": Getting into the Kaluli Groove

This paper elaborates a specific case example, and through it three ethnographically and theoretically intertwined propositions:

1. The Kaluli notion of *dulugu ganalan,* "lift-up-over sounding," is a style statement, a local Papua New Guinea groove, sound, or beat. The "lift-up-over sounding" sound is the Kaluli sound, a local gloss for social identity articulated through human sonic essences.

2. This sonic model, manifest most directly in Kaluli song form and process, also reverberates and echoes through other Kaluli expressive and interactional modes. The same trope that animates musical "lift-up-over sounding" is highly patterned in verbal, visual, and choreographic artistic expression, as well as in patterns of everyday conversation and social interaction. This patterning is explicitly linked by Kaluli to the acoustic ecology of the rainforest environment, indicating an aesthetic and ecological coevolution.

3. The process by which this groove comes to be felt as totally groovy in Kaluli participation is an expressive intensification of style, in which the beautiful and the natural become identical, intuitively inseparable in local imagination and practice. This is where aesthetics might best be understood as an iconicity of style, rather than a formal homology of sonic (musical, verbal, and natural), visual, and choreographic structures. The position I assume on the interface of sound structure and social structure, musical meaning and social meaning, has been stated succinctly by John Shepherd: "Music has meaning only insomuch as the inner-outer, mental-physical dichotomy of verbally referential meaning is transcended by the immanence 'in' music of what we may conceive of as an *abstracted* social structure, and by the articulation of social meaning in individual pieces of music. In this respect music stands in the same relationship to society as does consciousness: society is creatively 'in' each piece of music and articulated by it" (1977a:60).

The ethnographic materials here focus on the Kaluli people, who number about fifteen hundred and live on several hundred square miles of rich land at an altitude of about two thousand feet in the tropical rainforest of the Great Papuan Plateau in the Southern Highlands province of Papua New Guinea (for basic ethnographic description, see E. L. Schieffelin 1976). They hunt, fish, and tend land-intensive swidden gardens that yield sweet potatoes, taro, pandanus, pumpkins, bananas, and many other fruits and vegetables. Their staple food, sago, is processed from wild palms that grow in shallow swamps and creeks branching off of larger river arteries that flow downward from Mount Bosavi, the collapsed cone of an eight-thousand-foot volcano. Traditionally, Kaluli lived in about twenty distinct longhouse communities; most people resided in large communal houses, each comprising fifteen families, or sixty to eighty people. In recent years, under influence from evangelical missionaries and government officers, many have moved to smaller houses occupied by single families, or at most two or three families.

This is a classless society that has only begun to feel the impact of occupational specialization, stratification, and socially rewarded differentiation since the intensification of outside contact in the last twenty-five years. Overtly, the tone of everyday Kaluli life is strongly egalitarian in the social and political spheres. People hunt, gather, garden, and work to produce what they need, taking care of themselves and their families and friends through extensive cooperation—food sharing and labor assistance—informally organized through networks of obligation and reciprocity. While gender differences were overtly marked, there was, until recently, little stratification produced by accumulation of goods, rewards, or prestige. Traditionally, as E. L. Schieffelin writes, "Kaluli deference is based on such interactional things as intimidation or fear of shame, and is largely situational, and not structural in character" (personal communication, 5 April 1988). Although that is changing rapidly, there is still, our recent ethnographic experience shows, a general lack of deference to persons, roles, categories, or groups based on power, position, or material ownership. Obvious recent exceptions include pastors, Aid Post Orderlies, and government and mission workers; gender differentials are becoming more pronounced as well.

My use of the term "egalitarian" is not meant to be static and reified. Existing and emerging differentiation, subtle or overt, is a historically significant facet of Kaluli life, as is the emergent character of ranking as a "coordinating device, establishing reciprocal relations within the larger set" (Adams 1975:170). Nevertheless, Kaluli expressive and interactional styles still seem deeply bound to an expressly egalitarian local notion of the self and social life (for some of the ethnographic complexities of Kaluli egalitarianism and individual autonomy, see B. B. Schieffelin 1990; E. L. Schieffelin 1976:117–34; and Feld 1984:397–403).

In a Word . . .

The Kaluli term *dulugu ganalan,* "lift-up-over sounding," is a spatial-acoustic metaphor, a visual image set in sonic form and a sonic form set in visual imagery. The process and idea are familiar enough; for example, in English we speak of the harmonics of a fundamental tone as its "over-tones." Similar examples could be cited from musical vocabularies in many languages, as visual-spatial imagery is a common polysemic or metaphoric source of musical terminology. Certainly the verbal figure "lift-up-over sounding" alone provides much for the imagination. "In the case of metaphor," Owen Barfield writes, "it is the pure *content* of the image, not only the *reference*, which delights" ([1928] 1973:70; italics in original). The essence of this "pure content" is good to think, an imaginative, delightful figure and ground perception. Aristotle said that the contemplation of metaphor implies an insight into likeness, an insight Paul Ricoeur describes as a rapprochement of thinking, sensing, and feeling, "a model for changing our way of looking at things, of perceiving the world" (1978:150; see Goodman 1976, for a congruent view specifically focused on art).

How might apprehending Kaluli "lift-up-over sounding" change our way of sensing sound? To explore that thought-feeling process I will playfully recycle the dimensionality of "lift-up-over sounding" through some personal images, mixing both Freudian cognitive "condensation" and Empsonian poetic "pregnancy" to evoke something that cannot readily be glossed or paraphrased. As Roy Wagner says: "A metaphor is at once proposition and resolution; it stands for itself" (1986:11). For me, intuitively, "lift-up-over sounding" creates a feeling of continuous layers, sequential but not linear; nongapped multiple presences and densities; overlapping chunks without internal breaks; a spiraling, arching motion tumbling slightly forward, thinning, then thickening again.

To invoke a recording industry phrase, also appropriated by hip-hop rap and scratch DJs to describe their layered, multitrack sound work, through "lift-up-over sounding" Kaluli "fix it in the mix." The "mix" here is the way one creates or perceives horizontal juxtapositions by refiguring vertical ground, and the "fix" is the way the listener manages resultant simultaneous perceptions of part-to-part *and* part-to-whole relationships. "Lift-up-over sounding" is always interactive and relational. By calling attention to both the spatial ("lift-up-over") and temporal ("sound*ing*") axes of experience, the term and the process explicitly presuppose each sound to exist in fields of prior and contiguous sounds.

Idea to Action

Now to set those images slightly more on the ground and in the ear, "lift-up-over sounding" in fact is implicitly or explicitly discussed and realized by Kaluli in ways that implicate what an outsider can separate into four analytically separable dimensions of musical form and process.

1. relations within an instrumental sound among its own acoustical strata, and relations of this sound to other, surrounding sounds intentionally or unintentionally copresent;

2. relation of deliberately coordinated or simply copresent voice sounds, song, and talk;

3. relation of vocalizing to accompanying sounds of rattle instruments or work tools, whether the same or different actors are involved in the two activities;

4. relation of any of these to copresent environmental sounds (for example, thunder or sounds produced by rain, birds, animals, or insects).

Kaluli vocal and instrumental expression in ritual and everyday contexts, involves the varieties of "lift-up-over sounding" noted above. Typical examples, drawn from published recordings of all Kaluli genres and performance settings, follow:

> {1} *ilib,* hand drums, with sounding costume and *degegado* crayfish claw rattles (Feld 1987b:B3; also hear Feld 1985:B8, 1991:9). Several "lift-up-over sounding" layers are evident in ceremonial drumming: for each drum, the separation of fundamental tones and overtones; the staggered entrances and overlaps of the four drums; and the interlocking relationships of rattle and costume sounds with drum sounds, for each dancer and among the group members. These relationships are enhanced and multiplied by the shifting spatial configuration of the drummers, dancing up and down a longhouse corridor, sometimes as much as fifty feet apart, sometimes moving past each other, sometimes dancing in place side by side at one end or the other of the house.
>
> {2} *uluna,* bamboo mouth harp (Feld 1981b:A3; also hear Feld 1985:B7, 1991:5). The constant interplay of the mouth-resonated sounds with the physical pluck of the instrument and the interplay of the fundamental tone and its overtones constitute two interacting layers of "lift-up-over sounding."
>
> {3} *ko:luba* song[3] with cicadas (Feld 1985:B2). Ulahi's singing with the pulsing cicada background of the forest is "lift-up-over sounding"; the verbal-cicada onomatopoeia of the text and the mimetic vocal textures multiply the relationship.

3. In spelling Kaluli words, o: symbolizes phonetic "open o," the initial sound in "ought," and a: symbolizes phonetic "epsilon," the vowel sound in the word "bet." All other vowel and consonant symbols carry their phonetic values in the spelling and pronunciation of Kaluli words. See Feld (1990a:18–19) for details of Kaluli phonology and orthography.

{4} *heyalo* song at a waterfall (Feld 1981b:A4; also hear Feld 1991:6). Ulahi and Eyo:bo's voices are "lift-up-over sounding" with the background waterfall sounds. The reverberation that results from singing into the waterfall gorge amplifies the texture; additional layers are provided by the occasional sounds of children's voices and machetes.

{5} *heyalo* song accompanied by sago scraping and whistling (Feld 1985:B1; also hear Feld 1991:2). Misa:me and Fo:fo: sing *heyalo* in a "lift-up-over sounding"; two additional layers are provided by Misa:me's husband Deina, who begins scraping sago with a stone pounder in rhythmic counterpoint, then adds a whistled imitation of the bird whose name is cited in the song text.

{6} Women's *sa-ya:lab* ritual funerary wailing (Feld 1985:A3). Gania and Famu wail; their staggered entrances and overlaps as well as their breathy, creaky-grained vocalizations "lift-up-over" one another and the background din of children and adults crying and speaking in the longhouse.

{7} Women's ceremonial *kelekeliyoba* with *sologa* seed pod rattles (Feld 1981b:B5). The staggered voices of four women, Ulahi, Gania, Ea, and Eyo:bo, are "lift-up-over sounding" in relation to each other and cumulatively in relation to the hand-shaken seed pod rattles.

{8} *sabio* quartet accompanied by *sologa* seed pod rattles (Feld 1985:B6; also hear Feld 1981b:B7). The voices of four men, Wano, Gigio, Gaso, and Sowelo, are heard in pairs; the two voices in each duo "lift-up-over" one another, and each duo "lifts-up-over" the other duo with the droned "o" phrase endings. Rattles also "lift-up-over" the vocal sound. Gaso pointed out that the use of crescendo and decrescendo also enhances the temporal fullness of the "lift-up-over sounding" sound.

{9} *heyalo* quartet accompanied by *sologa* seed pod rattles (Feld 1985:B4). Four voices split; Kulu sings in a leading pattern, while Gigio, Seyaka, and Kogowe echo behind the same text and melody one octave lower; the octave split and the timbral contrast of falsetto-nasal/midrange-open amplify the "lift-up-over sounding." The singing is layered spatially by the uniformly thick texture of the background rattles, whose simultaneous metric pattern and continuous nongapped pulsation enhance the felt separation from the voices.

{10} Men's ceremonial *iwo:* accompanied by *degegado* crayfish claw and *sologa* seed pod rattles and ax handles (Feld

1981b:B1). A first voice, that of Ganigi, is echoed by a vocal chorus (Fagenabo, Deina, Kulu, Hawi) that also accompanies with rattles and ax handles, creating a multilayered "lift-up-over sounding" sound. Later another singer-dancer, Baseo, enters the house from a far entrance, shouting place names and pounding a club on the house floor, creating a variety of sounds and noises that further punctuate the primary ensemble.

{11} Ceremonial *ko:luba* duo, with *degegado* crayfish rattle in dance costume (Feld 1981b:B9; also hear Feld 1991:10). Amini and Mei sing while dancing face to face, creating a three-way "lift-up-over sounding" sound: vocally, with the echo between voices; instrumentally, with the sounds of the rattles included in the dance costume; and physically, with sounds of the costume streamers and stamping feet.

{12} *gisalo* sung by a spirit medium, with *sob* mussel shell rattle, chorus, and weeping interplay (Feld 1985:A1). A solo singer (here the spirit medium Aiba) accompanies his song with a mussel shell rattle; the interaction of voice and instrument is "lift-up-over sounding," as is their collective relation to the voices of a surrounding chorus, which, in usual Kaluli fashion, echoes the same text and melody a split second later. Another layer is added when the song moves a man to tears; he "lift-up-over" wails along with the medium and chorus, simultaneously a distinct, unique voice and part of the staggering musical density of the ensemble.

These twelve excerpts illustrate sonic forms resembling or intersecting patterns Western musicologists describe with terms like canon, hocket, antiphony, and heterophony. Alan Lomax has suggested more culturally and historically neutral descriptive terms—overlap, alternation, interlock—to distinguish types of form *and* process dynamics for the "social organization of the vocal group" (1976:86, 177–80; see also Feld 1984:391–92). Sometimes the term "echo-polyphony" seems most appropriate, given the overlapping repetition of identical or similar melodic and textual elements split seconds apart. For Kaluli, all of these things are *dulugu ganalan*, "lift-up-over sounding." At the same time, the term *dulugu ganalan* does not map perfectly to any one of these glosses, in part because the Kaluli idea does not really presuppose multiple voices or instruments. In cases of a solo voice, as in example {3}, or a solo instrument, example {2}, multiple densities, presences, or sources create a sense of strata, of a multilayered sound shape or mass in time; these are as much *dulugu ganalan* as the examples with multiple voices or instruments.

Participatory Discrepancies

Approaching the problem from the opposite perspective, there is one kind of sound—unison—that is obviously not heard in any of the examples. Unison is the antithesis of "lift-up-over sounding." All "lift-up-over sounding" sounds are dense, heavily blended, and layered; even when voices or sound types momentarily coincide the sense is that unison is either accidental or fleeting, and indeed it is entirely by chance. The essence of "lift-up-over sounding" is part relations that are *in synchrony while out of phase.* By "in synchrony" I mean that the overall feeling is of togetherness, of consistently cohesive part coordination in sonic motion and participatory experience. Yet the parts are also "out of phase," that is, at distinctly different and shifting points of the same cycle or phrase structure at any moment, with each of the parts continually changing in degree of displacement from a hypothetical unison.

Additionally, timbre, the building blocks of sound quality, and texture, the composite, realized experiential feel of the sound mass in motion, are not mere ornaments but dominate melodico-rhythmic syntax in "lift-up-over sounding"; performance and form merge to maximize interaction and the dialogic potentials of style. The multidimensionality of the sound examples is striking. Part of the stylistic core of "lift-up-over sounding" is found in nuances of *textural densification*—of attacks and final sounds; decays and fades; changes in intensity, depth, and presence; voice coloration and grain; interaction of patterned and random sounds; playful accelerations, lengthenings, and shortenings; and the fission and fusion of sound shapes and phrases into what electroacoustic composer Edgard Varèse called the "shingling" of sound layers across pitch space.[4] Also of prime importance to "lift-up-over sounding" is the quality

---

4. Invoking Varèse in this context is not a quick poetic fix. A very long discussion could be developed here about the articulation of these Kaluli style parameters and the musical ideas developed by the American avant-garde, especially in the 1930s and 1940s. Henry Cowell, Edgard Varèse, John Cage, Lou Harrison, Harry Partch and others are well-known for rupturing compositional and aesthetic norms by deprivileging harmony, codified canonic forms, and technical virtuosity, to oppositionally insist on the centrality of the temporal, the sonorous, the rhythmic, the timbral (including extramusical noises), and the improvised in new music composition and performance practices. The centrality of sound sensation over syntactic structure, so central to Kaluli ethnotheory, was thus clearly figured in much musical modernism of the interwar years. (As in other modernist art practices of the time, "primitivity" was promoted as something radical and fresh, although Asian musics were the specific influences in the cases of the composers named above.) This approach achieved even greater influence in the postwar work of electroacoustic, *musique concrète*, soundscape, and noise music performance artists. See the following note, on Grainger, for another example of this point.

acousticians call "rustle time," the mean time interval between clicks, noises, or nonpitched sounds, heard so prominently in the pulsating sound densities of Kaluli rattles and environmental sounds (Schouten 1968; a musical review can be found in Erickson 1975:6, 71–72).

Musicologists and ethnomusicologists familiar with both Western European and Pacific (particularly Polynesian) traditions have suggested to me that the term heterophony—indicating a multipart relationship resulting from simultaneous performance of slightly varied or elaborated versions of the same basic text, melody, or rhythm—is generally adequate for these *dulugu ganalan* examples. I have avoided using this term for three reasons: It cannot be applied to the solo examples, it misses the centrality of timbre and texture, and, perhaps most significantly, it misses the crucial processual dynamic in many of the multipart (vocal or instrumental) examples, namely, that the "lead" and "follow" parts are free to switch roles at any point and to continually and playfully change order.

While descriptors like "in synchrony while out of phase" and "textural densification" may initially seem awkward to musical analysts, there is no reason to assume that they are less generalizable than other terms inherited or more recently invented in musical discourse. In an attempt to clarify this issue, Charles Keil (chapter 3) offers the general term "participatory discrepancies" to focus on these dimensions of musical experience that are particularly unrecoverable, unanalyzable, or unattended in Western approaches to style analysis, approaches heavily weighted toward syntactic and hierarchic analysis of melody, harmony, and rhythm. In an earlier paper, Keil (chapter 1) took on the same problem, counterposing the notion of "engendered feeling" to Meyer's (1956) "embodied meaning." With that term Keil delineated some of the important formal and expressive properties of performative, processual, momentary, and improvised dynamics in the jazz idiom. These were contrasted to those implicative dimensions of architectonic drama, tension, and inflection which Meyer identified as bearing meaningful consequences in the listener's experience of musical structure. Updating that initial critique, Keil's concept of "participatory discrepancies" concerns two specific levels of creative tension in music making and listening: the processual and the textural. The former locates phenomena like beat, swing, or groove; the latter, phenomena like timbre and sound quality. For Keil it is the emergent "edge" created by varieties of out-of-timeness (process) and out-of-tuneness (texture) that generate music's vital force, as well as inviting and guaranteeing the active qualities of participation.[5] In the Kaluli instance, the framework for processual participatory discrepancies is the pattern I have called being "in synchrony while out of phase," while the framework for textural participatory discrepancies is what I have called textural densification. These processes are the dominant interacting style constants of *dulugu ganalan.*

Two further linguistic details are relevant to apprehending *dulugu ganalan* as a process of in-sync, out-of-phase textural densification in motion. First, the term *dulugu ganalan:* The imperative verb forms are *duluguma,* "lift-up-over," as when one places something above, as on a smoking rack in the longhouse, and *ganala:ma,* "sound," a generic unmarked for agent or variety. In the term *dulugu ganalan,* the second verb is always inflected with the continual-processual aspect suffix /-an/; hence the ongoing sense of sound*ing* emphasizes process, motion, temporality, continuity, and extension. The term is never given in a nominalized form (*dulugu go:no:*) even though it can be easily and grammatically formed in that way. Second, one cannot substitute Kaluli terms for "lead" or "follow" (*tamina hanan,* "going first"; *fa:sa: hanan,* "going in back") for any dimension of *dulugu ganalan.* My own use of these terms for synonym or paraphrase was always corrected, negated, or outright rejected by Kaluli, suggesting strongly that the issue of differentiated leader and follower roles is worked out and submerged in the participatory equality of making "lift-up-over sounding" sounds.[6]

5. Keil's remark calls to mind composer and folk music collector Percy Grainger's fascination with "kaleidoscopic density," "everchanging euphoniously discordant polyphonic harmony," and "inexact unison" (Grainger 1915:425, 429) as mirrors of naturalness in unwritten music: "Modern geniuses and primitive music unite in teaching us the charm of 'wrong notes that sound right'" (Grainger 1915:431). In the same article Grainger describes an experiment, a "Random Round" he wrote based on early recordings of South Pacific polyphony. Rehearsing the piece "several of those taking part quickly developed the power of merging themselves into the artistic whole" (Grainger 1915:432). Keil similarly discusses expression of an "urge to merge" in the language of participation, as does Owen Barfield, upon whom Keil draws. Barfield's use of discrepancy, at least in his earlier writings, seems more sweeping: "Poetic experience depends on a 'difference of potentials,' a kind of *discrepancy* between two moods or modes of consciousness" (Barfield 1973:54; emphasis in original).

6. In *Sound and Sentiment* (Feld 1990a:177) I somewhat inaccurately glossed *dulugu molab* as "singing lead" and *dulugu salab* as "speak first," "hold the floor," "lead discussion." My confusion stemmed from an inaccurate understanding of context. My understanding at that time, based on my 1976–77 fieldwork, was that "lift-up-over" could be glossed as a "part that stands out." I took "lift-up-over" to indicate some notion of "lead" because every time a prominent voice would emerge my assistants would tell me, "it is lifting-up-over *there.*" After fieldwork in 1982, which was oriented more toward environmental sounds than human ceremonial ones, I reviewed my earlier materials and realized that in every instance Kaluli used the *dulugu* notion more relationally and interactionally than I had suggested. Later publications (1984, 1990a:239–68, 1991) correct this and amplify the interactional qualities of *dulugu ganalan* and *dulugu molan* in Kaluli human and natural sounds.

Talking/Working Social Relations

Cooperative and collaborative autonomy: that is the Kaluli model of egalitarian interactional style. Imagine the notion of anarchistic synchrony as a nonoxymoron and you have an image of how Kaluli work. What I mean is that this particular interactional style simultaneously maximizes social participation and autonomy of self. Speaking of the vigorous and exuberant ways Kaluli generally address themselves to situations E. L. Schieffelin writes, "Kaluli assertiveness is grounded in an implicit sense of personal autonomy, or independence" and "Kaluli commands initiate action because they are exciting, noisy, and dramatic" (1976:121, 129). This mutualism is displayed in a participatory equality that often has a quality of suddenness, bursting into what is simultaneously work, play, and performance. Kaluli energy projections, often appearing as flamboyance in men, insistence in women, "are characterized by a high level of exuberance, crowding, and noise" (E. L. Schieffelin 1976:154; see also E. L. Schieffelin 1985a, for a further characterization of the Kaluli assertive ethos). Charles Keil says that "the presence of style indicates a strong community, an intense sociability that has been given shape through time, an assertion of control over collective feelings so powerful that any expressive innovator in the community will necessarily put his or her content into that shaping continuum and no other" (chapter 5, discussion of hypothesis 1). The next sound examples, of collective work coordinated through sound, explicitly affirm that idea:

> {13} Men cutting trees (Feld 1987b:A1; also hear Feld 1991:3). Whistles, yells, whoops, hollers, and snatches of song accompany background forest insects and avifauna as men work with axes to fell large trees at a garden site.
> {14} Women at sago camp (Feld 1987b:A1; also hear Feld 1991:2). Women and children interact verbally and vocally with "lift-up-over" voices and tools as they work scraping and pounding sago; insects and birds "lift-up-over" in the forest background.

For Kaluli, sound, like work, is essentially leaderless. "Lift-up-over" is an image of nonhierarchical yet synchronous, layered, fluid group action. The play dimension captures the expressly pleasurable aspect of work as participation in cooperative dramatic display. Working together "works out" and "works through" sounding together. It also works out and works through the tension between egalitarianism ("let's do it") and individualism ("I'll do it"). Indeed, "lift-up-over" is an image rather like "stepping out of" or "rising above" the crowd; it pinpoints that same egalitarian-individualist dialectic. The echo-sounding of working together reproduces the quality of "joining in" as a model of sociability, maximized participation, and personal distinction.

This is the case not only with musical and environmental sound but, as the previous examples indicate, with verbal sound as well. Kaluli conversational interactions "put talk together," *to kudan,* extending here the use of the same verb employed to mark laying sticks across one another to build a fire. Like fire sticks laid in contact, voices interlock, alternate, overlap, densifying to fill all space-time gaps. The Western normative concepts of individual speaker turns, floor rights, and turn-taking etiquette, rationalized in both speech act philosophy and conversational analysis, are absent from and analytically irrelevant to Kaluli conversation and narration. What might be heard as regular "interruption" is not that at all, but rather the tense yet collaborative and cocreative achievement of *dulugu salan,* "lift-up-over speaking." Kaluli language uses extensive metalinguistic labeling, and talk about talk is constant in the society, but neither Bambi B. Schieffelin (who has done Kaluli sociolinguistic work since 1975) nor I have ever heard terms for anything like "breaking in" or "interrupting," terms to characterize speakers who aggressively verbally interact in that way, or terms describing attempts to constrain such speaking.

Kaluli parents never admonish children for speaking at the same time; indeed, parents encourage and explicitly instruct children to collaborate by putting talk together with what other talk is at hand (B. B. Schieffelin 1990). This is another dimension of modeling participatory joining in as normative, obligatory sociability. Quietness, sullenness, the withdrawn voice, like the posture of aloneness or remove, are markers of alienation. Layered sound as the marker of "being there," socially connected, is indexed to the posture of the engaged actor. Developmentally, a socialization format for *dulugu ganalan* is manifest even in the interactions of children just learning language. Children develop patterned prelexical vocal contours that echo, interlock, or alternate with the talk around and to them. The use of such contours situates the child as an interactional partner and collaborator in the immediate social scene, whether or not a dimension of play or instruction is directed toward the child (B. B. Schieffelin 1983, 1990).

Talk must always make contact: "Kaluli enjoy interactions that have some creative tension in them, where the outcome is potentially

unpredictable and dependent on the individual's ability to be clever"
(B. B. Schieffelin 1986:180). Words rub up against each other, voices
link and cross; again the preference is for densification, the in-sync, out-
of-phase stylistic norm for cooperative, socialized behavior. Listening to
informal recordings of verbal interactions further illustrates this patterning, in the everyday contexts of family discussion and group argument,
as well as the more artistic performances of narrative storytelling and
spirit medium seances (the following examples are excerpted from unpublished field tapes recorded in 1984):

> {15} Family verbal interaction around food preparation
> and eating.
> {16} Adult argument about gossip.

In the first example simultaneous speech is constant, but nobody is fighting for "floor rights." In the second a large group of adults have gathered
to discuss a matter of gossip; multiple voices hold the floor simultaneously and parties address multiple others and agendas simultaneously,
without any voice continually dominating or organizing the stream of
discussion. Commenting on this matter, E. L. Schieffelin added:

> Looking over some of your *dulugu salan* stuff I am increas-
> ingly convinced of its centrality in the negotiation of tempo-
> rary advantage in everyday "egalitarian" social and political
> activity. The *wabalun kalu* ("one who is talked about," or
> "one lauded for deeds") attained his prominence not only
> through reputation for killing or generosity, but also through
> his ability to shout down his opponents in verbal intimida-
> tion, or outwit them or keep them verbally off balance in dis-
> pute. . . . Sogobaye once compared the *wabalun* to those
> ridges and hills visible from Tabili which rose somewhat
> above the others, like bigger or lesser waves upon the sea.
> Perfect image of what Western anthropology has called "first
> among equals." (personal communication, 9 May 1987)

In artistic verbal performance, the expectation for *dulugu ganalan* is
similar to its framing in musical arenas:

> {17} Heina tells a narrative (*malolo to*) to small group of
> adults and children (unpublished field tapes, 1984).

In this example Heina is constantly echoed, questioned, and overlapped
to the extent that there is virtually a continuous stream of talk, con-
firmation, challenge, and collaboration. Narrative storytelling is often

considered an example par excellence of monologic verbal performance, yet here the dialogic relation to the audience is highly evident. Socio-linguists Alessandro Duranti and Donald Brenneis have recently addressed these issues. "To give the audience coauthorship is more than an ideo-logical stand. It represents the awareness of a partnership that is neces-sary for an interaction to be sustained, but it is often denied by analysts and participants alike" (Duranti 1986:243). Brenneis's general comment reads well as a specific description of Kaluli *dulugu salan:* "While such occurrences might seem chaotic to outsiders, in practice speakers are usually attending carefully to each other and responding appropriately . . . speakers are, at the same time, subtle and attentive listeners . . . be-cause of this, it is often analytically difficult to sort out who is voice and who is audience" (1986:344). Similarly, during a Kaluli seance the audi-ence interacts with the spirit medium to cocreate and coinvent the pres-ence of spirits of the dead and of nearby lands:

{18} Spirit medium converses with the audience at a seance
at Sululeb (unpublished field tapes, 1976).

As E. L. Schieffelin writes, "The reality of the spirit world as it is embod-ied in the seance is not a result of the performance of the medium alone, but emerges in the *interaction* between all the people present and the spirits" (1985b:717; italics in original).

For talk, then, *dulugu ganalan* is not an absolute norm but a tendency with greater or lesser actualization in different types of verbal interac-tions and settings. Artistic verbal performances carry higher expectations and actualizations of *dulugu ganalan* and thereby place an important emphasis on audience participation, even where the situation is defined by a largely monologic form. In everyday verbal interactions—animated conversations, disputes, negotiations, exchanges of new information— the more focused character of the topics and events promotes a greater tendency for *dulugu ganalan* in interactions of assertion than of appeal, where the strategies of begging, enlisting, or making another feel sorrow on one's behalf do not involve as many participatory display dynamics.

Rainforest as Hi-fi Soundscape

One morning as Gigio walked alongside my house at dawn he noticed me sitting on the back porch tape recording out into the bush. Quickly he caught my eye, grinned, and called out:

dulugu ganalan a:na dadalega, wai! ni Bosabi nemo: ho:ida-ke!, a:la: asuluma:no:

Hearing it lift-up-over sounding out there, hey, my Bosavi is
really calling out to me! I'll be thinking like that.

What we were both hearing were sounds of mists, winds, waterways, insects, birds, people, pigs, dogs, all located in diffuse but auditorally copresent space:

{19} Forest at dawn (Feld 1987b: A1; also hear Feld 1991: 1).

Gigio's comment could have been made at any point during the day; examples from other moments in the daily rainforest sound cycle attest to
that:

{20} Forest at dusk (Feld 1987b: A1; also hear Feld 1991: 7).
{21} Forest *nulu usa,* "deep of night" (Feld 1987b; A1;
also hear Feld 1991: 11).

At the village edge, dusk brings sounds of birds, insects, people, animals,
and drizzling drops after a typical late afternoon rain. In the late night
or early morning hours, crickets, mists, and frogs are more sensually
present.

What did Gigio mean? Most obviously, that the rainforest is a tuning
fork, providing well-known signals that index, mark, and coordinate
space, time, and seasons. "The perception of creatures by their voices
and movements in the forest gives a peculiar sense of presence and dynamism to things that are unseen, to surrounding but invisible life. . . .
It is important to realize the remarkable impression of immediacy of
sounds and creatures heard amid the pervading stillness and immobility
of the forest" (E. L. Schieffelin 1976: 96). One never knows how many
sources are contributing to the dense, in-sync but out-of-phase textures;
whatever the number the quality of forest sound is simultaneously thick
and homogenous, multidimensional yet unified, redundant overall but
with no precise, moment-to-moment repetition.

Canadian composer and soundscape researcher R. Murray Schafer
calls soundscapes "hi-fi" when they contain favorable signal to noise ratios, that is, when the full dynamic range of sounds present can be heard
clearly and distinctly without crowding, pollution, or masking by intrusive noise sources (1977c: 43). Schafer terms "keynote sounds" those
continuous, basic, frequent, customary sounds that provide a sense of environmental center (1977c: 9, 48). These notions apply well to the Bosavi
rainforest soundscape, where sounds provide ongoing indexical information about forest height, depth, and distance. Kaluli interpret these
ever-present sound patterns as clocks of quotidian reality, engaging the

soundscape in a continual motion of tuning in and out, changing perceptual focus, attending like an auditory zoom lens that scans from micro to
wide-angle to telephoto as figure and ground shift and sound textures
change with the daily and seasonal cycles.

There also may be a synesthetic factor interrelating, in a sensually in-
voluntary and culturally conventional manner, features of sound, texture, space, and motion. In the tropical rainforest height and depth of
sound are easily confused. Lack of visual depth cues, coupled with different vegetation densities and ever-present sounds like water hiss, often
makes one sense depth as height dissipating as it moves outward. "Lift-
up-over sounding" seems to code that ambiguous sensation of upward as
outward. My own major adaptation to this environment was learning to
feel and distinguish the height and depth of a sound in the absence of visual correlates. Although I was aware of psychological evidence that humans are better at horizontal than vertical sound localization and often
subjectively sense high tones to be higher in space than they in fact are
(Roffler and Butler 1968), I was acoustically disoriented in the forest for
months. Kaluli laughed hysterically the first times they saw me look up
to hear a sound that was deep, whether high or low to the ground. And
they quickly learned to reach over to move my hand when I mistakenly
was pointing the microphone too far up to record a bird of the deep
forest.

The forest is also a mystical home of *ane mama*, "gone reflections,"
spirits of Kaluli dead. The presence of sounds thus implicates spirit presences with bird voices sonically "showing through." In this sense attending to the forest may engage strong feelings of nostalgia and longing,
even though Kaluli attribute no specific mystical power or force to the
forest per se. There is simultaneously a less cosmic, deeply pleasurable
way the forest engages Kaluli, as an image of place, of land as a mediator
of identity (for a parallel case concerning place and the poesis of expression, see Basso 1990:99–173). For Kaluli the forest is both good to
listen to and good to sing with; surrounding sounds provide both enjoyment and inspiration. This notion is nicely attested by E. L. Schieffelin:
"There is no mistaking the feeling of affection and warmth when two or
three men burst into song on arriving back at their own territory after an
absence of a few days at another longhouse. Singing is appropriate not
only because it projects the feeling of the singer but also because it is
something to be *heard*—of a piece with the sounds of the forest itself. Sound images are much more evocative than visual ones for the
Kaluli" (1976:149; italics in original).

Becoming part of the forest by singing along with it ultimately intensifies Kaluli sentiments about the comforts of home. This was evident in
the earlier examples of spontaneous musical and environmental interaction, which combine stimulation and appreciation. In example {3} a
woman sang with cicadas; the text of the song consisted of extensive cicada texture onomatopoeia. In example {4} two women sang at a waterfall chosen as an accompaniment. The text of the song in example {5}
was about a whistler bird, and the whistling introduced to punctuate
the beats of a stone sago scraper imitated the call of the particular bird.
As Schafer says, "Man echoes the soundscape in speech and music"
(1977c:40).

Acoustic Ecology: Insides, Underneaths, Reflections, Flow, and Hardness

The visible and invisible inhabitants of the Bosavi rainforest are always "lift-up-over sounding," and Kaluli practices of listening and
singing involve a participatory tuning in, appreciating, and interpreting
of what they call the *sa,* "inside," *hego:,* "underneath," and *mama,* "reflection," of these ever-present pulsations. These terms extend the notion
of "lift-up-over sounding," filling in some of its process and activity implications in terms of engagement. If *dulugu ganalan* is the overall Kaluli
metaphor for natural sonic form, *halaido: doma:ki,* "making hard," and
the resultant *halaido:,* "hardness," evoke its competent formation, its
achievement as emotional persuasion (like the phrase "Come Together"
in the song of that title by the Beatles [1969]). "Hardness" is force, the
attainment of that evocative, charged, energized state, where, to extend
the notion into English metaphoric spaces, one is "knocked out" or
"blown away." The continued holding power of this hardened state is its
a:ba:lan, "flowing." "Lift-up-over sounding" flows when it enters and
stays with you, residing in memory and consciousness in ways it once did
not. Engagement—getting into the groove—is the sensing of the *hego:,*
"underneath," and *sa,* "inside," of sound patterns that "lift-up-over"
and the interpretation of their *mama,* "reflection" or "shadow," by feeling their associational force and possibilities (for elaboration, see Feld
1984, 1990a). Notice here that "reflection" is not a strictly or even primarily visual notion, like that of a mirror image. The sense is more like
that of a reverberation, a projected image or shadowed essence that is
sensately internalized as a vibration, an idea, and a feeling.

Participation—again, getting into the groove—invokes a local cluster
of Kaluli interpretive moves: hear the "lift-up-over sounding," feel it

"harden," let it "flow," "turn it over," to find the "reflected" "insides" and "underneaths." Here metaphors not only have their own consistent linguistic playmates but those playmates help us understand the specific processual, participatory, interpretive, experiential, intellectual dimension evoked by the whole. While "lift-up-over" seems literally vertical, the Kaluli sense is one of a simultaneously vertical and horizontal groove in time, propelling, arching up and tumbling forward. The totalized spatial-acoustic coherence of "lift-up-over sounding" is scaffolded by its "insides," "underneaths," "reflections," "flow," and "hardness." The poetic of aesthetics becomes the aesthetic of poetics. The way in which these metaphors take us back to a sense of unified relatedness and experience recalls the dynamic sociological and musicological versions of getting into the groove provided by Alfred Schutz and Victor Zuckerkandl: "Sharing of the other's flux of experiences in inner time, thus living through a vivid present in common constitutes . . . the mutual tuning-in relationship, the experience of the 'we'" (Schutz [1951] 1977:115; also see Fernandez 1986a). Drawing similarly upon Bergson's *durée*, Zuckerkandl writes, "The hearing of a musical tone is always likewise a direct perceiving of time. The moment the tone sounds, it draws us into time, opens time to us as perceiving beings" (1956:253).

Seeing/Hearing "Lift-up-over Sounding" in Body Decoration and Body Motion

For Zuckerkandl, "The interpenetration of tones in auditory space corresponds to the juxtaposition of colors in visual space" (1956:299). If we substitute "media, textures, colors, gestures, and motions" where Zuckerkandl indicates only "colors," we have an accurate image of Kaluli transpositions. The color images in this book, of Kaluli ceremonial costume and dance, demonstrate textural densification in the visual and choreographic modes. Face paint styles from major Kaluli ceremonies, *gisalo, ko:luba,* and *ilib kuwo:* (costume styles of the latter are identical), indicate a singular principle. Deep earth red (*bin,* from the pods of *Bixa orellana* or from ground clay) and shiny tree resin soot (*ason*) are painted on the dancer's face in a figure and ground, with a white clay (*sowan*) outline between them to create relief, the juxtaposition creating a sense of layered density. As the paints dry the contrast of the shininess of the black and dullness of the orange-red intensify; this is also enhanced by the use of resin torch light, which picks up and reflects the highlights of the resinous black. Note the importance of the forehead and the nose area; hiding the eyes hides the singer-dancer's identity. The mask effect conceals and at the same time beams the gaze of the singer-dancer. This facial figure-ground is realized in both a shiny-dull texture contrast and a black-red color contrast (the oppositional nature of black and red in Kaluli color symbolism is treated in Feld 1990a:66–71). These contrasts visually mirror sonic "lifting-up-over," and the effect was identified as such by Kaluli commentators who viewed these pictures.

The overall *ilib kuwo:* and *ko:luba* costume mixes many types of materials: layered possum fur; a frame headpiece with white cockatoo feathers; painting of face, arms, belly, and legs in red, black, and white; a shell necklace surrounded and centered by woven cross bands reaching under the arm; flapping feathers strung from bamboo in arm, belt, and knee pieces; a belly belt with a *degegado* crayfish claw rattle attached in back, emerging through *fasela* palm streamers densified with bright cordyline leaf top pieces. Costumes project layered density. Sound comes from shells and streamers in motion as the dancer bobs up and down, "lifted-up-over" by the drum and rattle in *ilib kuwo:* or by voices and rattles in *ko:luba*. The bouncing sounds of stamping feet on the longhouse floor (120–130 beats per minute in an up-and-down motion) and the indexical swaying of the longhouse mix out-of-phase with the pulses of the shell rattles and the shimmer and flapping of costume streamers. The streamers and shells make high frequency sounds which evoke those of a forest waterfall. The voice and drums of the dancers are the voices of the birds (particularly that of *wo:kwele*, the giant cuckoodove, and other doves and pigeons with high descending falsetto voices) "lifting-up-over" the waterfall sound (Feld 1990a:81–82, 171–74, 180–81). The textural densification of costume, dance, and sound thus merges into an overall visual, bodily, sonic, in-sync, out-of-phase sensation.

The *gisalo* dancer's costume includes similar materials. The primacy of the streamers is matched by the use of the *sob*, the mussel shell rattle whose high frequency sounds pulse indexically to the dancer's up-and-down motion (Feld 1990a:170–74). As in *ko:luba*, the voice of the dancer carries over the high-frequency waterfall sounds of streamers and rattles as the bird dance movement arches up and down either in place or up and down the corridor. The black cassowary head feathers and the red Raggiana bird-of-paradise arm band feathers flap and flow with the dance motion, densifying the blur of the flowing yellow palm streamers, the body paints, and the woven string and shell ornaments. All materials are in layered visual, sonic, and kinetic figure-ground relationships.

These images indicate that while in-sync, out-of-phase relations and textural densification begin in sound, the principles serve as a Kaluli style trope in ceremonial visual and choreographic modes as well (for additional descriptions and photographs of Kaluli ceremonies, costumes, songs, and dance, see E. L. Schieffelin 1976; Feld 1990a).

Uptown: Aesthetics as Iconicity of Style

Aesthetics involves a twist on the perception of style: when the groove is completely groovy, or, as Gregory Bateson (1972) would have it, when the levels of the parts and the levels of the whole merge to index, or draw attention to each other—what Bateson called "modulations" of levels of redundancy. Nelson Goodman ([1968] 1976) has attempted to summarize this grooviness as the interplay of four factors: (*a*) semantic and syntactic density (subtleties of difference convey subtleties of distinction); (*b*) repleteness (multiplicity of significant relationships); (*c*) exemplification (symbols sample the properties they possess); and (*d*) multiple and complex reference (symbols alone more important than their referents, close to Jakobson's idea [1960] of poetic mode).

In a variety of recent ethnographic studies, notions of style as cross-modal homology have been used to finesse aesthetics along these modulating, dense, replete, exemplified, autoreferential lines. Gary Witherspoon (1977) thus writes of a Navajo world where the "dynamic symmetry" of verbal, visual, and musical aesthetics and the "dynamic synthesis" of intellect are inseparably connected. Likewise, for Western popular culture, Dick Hebdige (1979) and Paul Willis (1978) describe the bricolage of symbolic linkages between counterculture punk and bike-boy lifestyles and the clothing, decoration, and musical forms that serve to encode the same focal values. Adrienne Kaeppler, describing homology as "consistency relationships between various cultural and social manifestations and the underlying structures that they express" (1978:261), shows that Tongan visual, verbal, choreographic, and musical forms pattern abstractly as an interaction of *fasi* (melody, lead part, essential features), *laulalo* (drone, space definers), and *teuteu* (decoration, elaboration of specifics). Similarly, Charles Keil's analysis (1979b:200–58) finds "circles and angles" to be material and aesthetic organizing tropes that cut across media and modes in Tiv culture, manifesting themselves in roofs, compounds, land organization, pots, calabash decorations, body scarification, dance gestures, sculpture, drumming, narrative, and song. Cross-sensory, synesthetic (as well as anti–genre-specific) analyses have also been presented by Barbara Tedlock, who traces the Zuni opposition of *tso'ya* (multicolored, chromatic, clear, bright, sharp, dynamic, varied) and *attanni* (powerful, taboo, dark, muffled, shaggy, old, static, fearful) through color, decoration, song, ritual and cosmology (1984, 1986).

Twisting aesthetic levels and wholes, connectedness, and homology one more turn, Judith and Alton Becker, in their analyses of coincidence and cyclicity in Javanese calendars, shadow puppet theater, and music (J. Becker 1979; A. Becker 1979; Becker and Becker 1981), describe something much like the groove I discussed previously with their notion of iconicity: "We might call iconicity the nonarbitrariness of any metaphor. Metaphors gain power—and even cease being taken as metaphors—as they gain iconicity or 'naturalness'" (1981:203). Quite so: in the Kaluli case, the "natural" as the locus of nature and human nature becomes the "beautiful"—exactly and unquestionably as it should be. When what we call metaphors (like "lift-up-over sounding") are felt to be naturally real, obvious, complete, and thorough, then they become iconic, that is, they become symbols that stand for themselves (Wagner 1986), and are experienced as feelingfully synonymous from one domain or level of image and experience to another. In more sociological terms, from Howard Becker, "people do not experience their aesthetic beliefs as merely arbitrary and conventional; they feel that they are natural, proper and moral" (1974a:773). These kinds of ethnoaesthetic studies, of what Robert Plant Armstrong (1971) called "similetic equivalents," recall the late nineteenth-century German psychophysics that influenced the emergence of twentieth-century anthropology, linguistics, and ethnomusicology: "Since the sensuous is perceptible only when it has form, the unity of the senses is given from the very beginning. And together with this the unity of the arts" (Hornbostel 1927:89, cited in Merriam 1964:99).

Peirce's semiotics of similarity talked of three kinds of icons: image, diagram, and metaphor (Peirce [1893–1902] 1955). Using his terms, Kaluli "lift-up-over sounding" moves from being a metaphor of style (Peirce's similar form and meaning across signs) to being an image of identity (Peirce's singular sign directly recalling its denotatum). More socially, "lift-up-over sounding" moves from being a metaphor of the Kaluli groove to being what Meyer Schapiro called "a manifestation of the culture as a whole, the visible sign of its unity [that] reflects or projects the 'inner form' of collective thinking and feeling" (1953:287). Kaluli "lift-up-over sounding" is an icon of what Sapir, Whorf, and others spoke of as the *intuitive* nature of a felt worldview, what Paul Freidrich (1986) has described as the emotionally satisfying dimensions of poetic indeterminacy. This is the level of icon Gregory Bateson invoked in writing about psychic and social integration when he approvingly cited Buffon's "Le style est l'homme même" (Bateson 1972:130). But notice the extension by Voloshinov (Bakhtin?) in 1926: "'Style is the man'; but we can say: style is, at least, two men, or more precisely, man and his social grouping, incarnated by its accredited representative, the listener, who participates actively in the internal and external speech of the first" (translated and cited in Todorov 1984:62).

Freud's quip to the effect that analogies explain nothing but at least make you feel at home is also resonant here. Indeed, by becoming icons, metaphors help one feel very much at home, and the critical word is "feel," since the link between play, pleasure, cognition, and emotion is where one validates the groove by not only getting *into* it but getting *off* *on* it. "To *feel* in the emotional sense of the word," Ricoeur says, "is to make *ours* what has been put at a distance by thought in its objectifying phase" (1978:154; italics in original). That "making ours" is the overwhelming and seemingly spontaneous (whether predictable or not) pleasure that comes from a felt naturalness of the whole, as one finds oneself in and through the music and the music in and through oneself. The more iconic the metaphor, the more unconscious its coherence, the more affective its resonance, the more intuitive its invocation, and the more intense its radiance. "Art is the burning glass of the sun of meaning" (Wagner 1986:27).

Synthesis: Stereotype and Style

A piece of each style jigsaw is the play of stereotypes (see Keil, chapter 5). In *This Man and Music,* a semiautobiographical consideration of music generally and of his own secondary career as a composer, novelist Anthony Burgess writes: "Music is considered an international language, yet it tends to gross insularity. What makes English music English? An American conductor to whom I put the question said, cruelly, 'Too much organ voluntary in Lincoln Cathedral, too much coronation in Westminster Abbey, too much lark ascending, too much clodhopping on the fucking village green'" (1982:23). These stereotypes of English national style (here, perceived excesses of Holst, Elgar, and Vaughn Williams are the obvious targets) remind me of a comment about what makes Kaluli music Kaluli, recorded in the course of a discussion in August 1982 with Keith Briggs, an evangelical missionary resident at Bosavi from 1971 to 1991:

> KB: Well, I'll tell you one thing we've noticed over the years; these people just cannot sing together. Even when we count

before singing a hymn, they are all off in their own direction after just a few words.

SF: Is that because they don't know the hymns very well?

KB: Oh no; they love the hymns and sing them all the time
around the station. . . . They learn the words all right and
the young ones are quick to harmonize too. . . . They just
can't sing together, even brothers or sister can't. . . . I
reckon they'll keep the tune jolly well, [but] never in the
same place at the right time!

Briggs's comments are neither as cruel nor as clever as those of the
American conductor, but they illustrate a grasp of something essential
about Kaluli style. The force of the stereotypy, however, leads Briggs to
read the strength and tenacity of local stylistic coherence as a sign of musical inability and inferiority. Notice Briggs's choice of phrases: "cannot
sing together," "off in their own direction," "never in the same place
at the right time." Kaluli of course sing very much together and with a
common goal; however unison is about as unnatural in their music as
microtonal free improvisation would have been in nineteenth-century
Germany. Precisely what is *most* socially interactive about "lift-up-over
sounding" is read by Briggs as being "off" on an individual uncoopera-
tive tangent. But the essence of *dulugu ganalan* is to be together by being
in different places at the (same) right time so that each person's own direction feeds and builds a cooperative cumulative interaction.

Deep down, I suspect that what disturbed Briggs was that the Kaluli
could not be conducted, that he perceived a threat to his authority and
control over local Christians. I'm reminded of Elias Canetti's words in
Crowds and Power: "There is no more obvious expression of power
than the performance of a conductor" (1963:394; Canetti's analysis of
"the orchestral conductor" is quoted and discussed in detail in Keil
1979b:183–86). Missionaries are indeed much like orchestra conduc-
tors: small movements of their hands order some and captivate others;
willingness to obey is the message, and self-assurance is central to the
performance. It is, furthermore, essential that others believe that these
people live for something higher than themselves. Like a god or god-
surrogate, a conductor-missionary is omniscient, holding everyone's attention, knowing and hearing each follower singly.

As Kaluli face an increasingly confused and dominated future there is
no doubt that their style—of singing, working, and being—will increasingly come into conflict with other, intrusive social patterns, whether those
brought by Christian missionaries, the Papua New Guinea government,

other Papua New Guineans, or Kaluli who have themselves experienced and assimilated patterns of interaction from the outside Papua
New Guinea world. It is hard to predict whether *dulugu ganalan* will
be a key resource (conscious or unconscious) for Kaluli resistance to
encroaching inequalities, social differentiation, and heterogeneity or
whether the overall sonic form of *dulugu ganalan* can stay relatively
stable if its essentially egalitarian social context disintegrates, leaving an
expressive form whose sonic coherence is no longer iconic within its
social formation. What is clear from Briggs's remark however is that the
rhetoric of contrast is already in motion. Two versions of "doing things
together" are now set head to head, one favoring layered, egalitarian
process, the other favoring linear, hierarchically differentiated process,
each obstinately "natural" ("normal" and "right") to the specific groups
concerned. The potential impact of the latter is undoubtedly far more destructive in every way. One sees here the subtle dynamics of power inequality, particularly that of false consensus formation, which have been
analyzed, with reference to class domination, under the rubric of hegemony. While the term does not apply here in the classic Gramscian or
Marxist sense (Williams 1977:108–14), it is worth reviewing the emerging ideological tone of the confrontation. The mission promulgation of
the naturalness of linear, discrete, sequential, one-at-a-time, unison or
single-leader/group-follower roles and social interaction is an intrusive
style ideology that proclaims itself normal, superior, and authoritative.
By so doing it attempts to legitimize and naturalize a view of Kaluli as
noisy, unruly, disorganized, "off in their own direction," stubborn, and
unable to "do things properly."

Kaluli modes of expression are thus relegated to "custom," a term
found both in Australian colonial usage (with the same condescending,
romantic overtones as certain usages of "folklore") and in the Papua
New Guinea lingua franca, Tok Pisin, as *kastom* (on the complicated
politics of this term and its placement in Melanesian anthropology, see
Keesing and Tonkinson 1982; Jolly and Thomas 1992). "Custom" is
what Kaluli are requested, "allowed," and, occasionally, paid to perform—a half hour of ceremonial drumming, for instance, at the mission
station airstrip on Papua New Guinea Independence Day. By requesting
and tacitly sanctioning this version of expression, the mission people signal to visiting dignitaries (other mission officials, government agents, anthropologists) that the Kaluli (still) "have culture." But more subtly, they
communicate that *kastom* can be commodified, bracketed, controlled,
turned on and off, and exhibited at their command. This is the process of

hegemonic folkloricization: dominating outside parties legitimate condensed, simplified, or commodified displays, invoking, promoting, and cherishing them as official and authentic custom, while at the same time misunderstanding, ignoring, or suppressing the real creative forces and expressive meanings that animate them in the community.

Kaluli have not explicitly challenged this imposition by either increasing the everyday markedness of their own way of "doing things properly" or by increasing the specific markedness of these command performances and other interactions with the mission. Nevertheless, their expressive style is clearly no longer the only natural model; increased confusion, struggle, alienation, and resistance may be around the corner, particularly as mission and government sources begin to give money prizes for performances and insist that Kaluli activities fit into other organizational frameworks in order to be valid.

Futures: Stability as Vitality, "Progress" as Entropy

One thing that might bear significantly on the future of such a Bosavi style struggle is the great affinity of *dulugu ganalan* to the developing musical forms of pan-Papua New Guinea popular music, whether sung in Tok Pisin, Hiri Motu, or local languages. Blended voices in interlocked and overlapped polyphonies, in-sync and out-of-phase with strongly metric guitar or ukulele strums, characterize much of the contemporary urban string band music of Papua New Guinea and the Pacific area generally. This music has made its way out to Bosavi increasingly since the mid-1970s, through both radio (transmitted by Radio Southern Highlands, the provincial branch of the Papua New Guinea National Broadcasting Company) and cassettes brought home by Kaluli who have worked or gone to school outside Bosavi. Popular Papua New Guinea groups like Paramana Strangers, New Krymus, Helgas, and Barike are now known to many young Kaluli men, who bring cassette recorders back from work contracts and tend to control their use in the villages. They say they are attracted to the sound and texture of the voices and instruments they hear, and often use listening to cassettes to promote nostalgic discourse about their experiences outside of Bosavi. Yet whatever the listening context, comprehension of lyrics, most of which are in other local languages and not Tok Pisin, is entirely secondary and often not a consideration at all.

Along with radio-cassette players (whose numbers in the Bosavi area increased from three in 1976 to twenty-three in 1984 to around sixty-five in 1992), there are now a few ukuleles in many of the Bosavi longhouses, and Kaluli play them as percussive instruments, precisely as they play their hand drums and bamboo jaws harps. The player moves the fingers of the left hand as if to fret chords, but the result is sound clusters (consonant or dissonant, intentional or unintentional) rather than conventional Western chords. Players know the motion of changing finger positions; they do not know any fingerings for actual chords, nor do they know to tune the instrument's four strings. The right-hand strum is a loud and isometric stroke, without much variation in volume or dynamics. Kaluli use the instrument like the seedpod rattle, as a textural and metric device, not to accompany a song's melody. The desired effect is continuity of dense unbroken sound without gaps, pauses, or openings. Voices, which "lift-up-over" one another, also cumulatively "lift-up-over" this ukulele sound, which "lifts-up-over" itself, the decay of each strum overlapping the attack of the next. The sum is a vocal-instrumental textural densification, exactly as in all other examples of *dulugu ganalan.*

Listening to Tok Pisin and Kaluli renditions of Papua New Guinea pop music indicates how the "lift-up-over sounding" sound is easily realized by Kaluli in versions of popular string band music:

{22/23} "Wanpela Meri," with ukulele and *sologa* seedpod rattle; "Ga imilise," Kaluli text version of "Wanpela Meri" (unpublished field tapes, 1977).

Both examples were sung by the same group moments apart. In both Tok Pisin and Kaluli versions, the vocal and instrumental stylistic elements are identical, with overlapped voices, group echoed text and melody from a lead voice, and densified isometric accompaniment. Rudimentary vocal harmony is mission inspired, as is the realization of a vocal blending closer to unison. These can be compared with the original:

{24} "Wanpela Meri," recorded in Port Moresby by Krymus, a popular string band, in 1975.[7]

Notice here too that there is less temporal differentiation among the voices; the layered feeling deriving more from the vocal-instrumental interplay.

7. The 1975 Krymus Band trio version was released as an EMI 45-rpm disc. The song is credited to Sharon Ahuta, identified in the liner notes as the group "leader." The later version, more widely known today, was released in 1978 on the NBC cassette *Krymus Rua.* By this time the band had expanded to ten members and was known as New Krymus. The cassette credits the song to Viora Atabe, listed on the 1975 disc notes as Krymus's "chief vocalist and composer." In 1976–77 I knew of no Kaluli who owned cassette copies of "Wanpela Meri." Young men in Bosavi learned the song from others who had picked it up from radio broadcasts while out on labor contracts.

Kaluli place no fetish premium on musical "innovation," "progress," or "development" and make no assumption that change is synonymous with vitality or that stasis denotes degeneration, notions that James Ackerman (1962) and Leonard Meyer (1967) have carefully explicated and critiqued as components of the teleological ideology of "style change" in Western arts. Merging *dulugu ganalan* and contemporary Papua New Guinea string band style to feel them as one makes a strong statement about how Kaluli recognize stability as vitality. Kaluli-ized pan-Pacific popular music in fact involves simplifications (or at least nonelaborations) of the timbral, textural, and interpretive-performative subtleties basic to "lift-up-over sounding" as heard in the original Kaluli genres. But the basic stylistic resource is there for new nuances to develop as Kaluli become more experienced and involved in using, listening to, and sharing Papua New Guinea popular forms. This is precisely as Meyer observed in general terms: "Because intrastylistic change does not involve a modification of the premises of a style, but rather a realization of the possibilities inherent in such premises, intrastylistic changes are not necessarily linear and cumulative. Consequently, some works coming late in the chronology of a style may be actually less complex (more redundant) than those which preceded them" (1967:120).

"Voice Bosavi"

A final story speaks clearly to how well the *dulugu ganalan* sound works into popular Papua New Guinea expression at a more affective level. In 1976 Ho:nowo: Degili was learning carpentry at the Mendi Boys Vocational Training School, where he had been placed by Keith Briggs (the Bosavi missionary) in recognition of his linguistic and technical aptitudes. When Ho:nowo: returned to Bosavi for Christmas recess (which is when I met him for the first time) he brought work boots, sunglasses, and a ukulele with him, signs of his integration into the modern "town" world of Papua New Guinea. One night Ho:nowo: came to my house to sing Kaluli and Tok Pisin songs with Gigio, Seyaka, and some other young men. They accompanied themselves on the ukulele (which they took turns playing, each producing an identical sound, as described above) and a contemporary version of a Kaluli *sologa* rattle, made not from a gourd pod and seeds but from pebbles in an empty tin fish can.

When they sang there was a clear Kaluli "lift-up-over sounding" sound, with in-sync, out-of-phase voices overlapping, with alternating shifts to octave and falsetto parts, and the densified isometric pulsing of the rattle and ukulele never leaving a crack of unfilled rustle time in sonic space. At the end of one song, Ho:nowo: spontaneously switched into a radio announcer voice register and role, as if the group had been performing live on Radio Southern Highlands. In Tok Pisin he identified the previous selection, and, as the others giggled, he introduced each singer by longhouse community and name, prefaced by *Mista* ("Mister"). He concluded his announcement with a nostalgic sigh and, switching to English, "ah yes, voice Bosavi."

Ho:nowo:'s choice of the English word "voice" follows the use of the term by announcers on Papua New Guinea's provincial radio programs, as an identifier of local styles (Tok Pisin *bilong ples,* "of that place," i.e., locality, region, area; as in *tok ples,* "native language," local or village-level language; Mihalic 1971:157–58, 191). In this context the word "voice" carries the same idea captured by the terms "groove," "sound," and "beat." "Voice Bosavi" would indeed be a contemporary Papua New Guinea way to gloss the "Kaluli sound," the *dulugu ganalan* groove. "Voice Bosavi" is the distinct local flavor of Kaluli expression finding its *ples,* "place," its local identity in the larger worlds of the Southern Highlands Province and Papua New Guinea.

Moving Downtown: Style Lessons in Listening-up-over

Turning from the transformations of Kaluli music-making and identity marking to ways my own identity and practices are situated, a further extension of *dulugu ganalan* that requires explication concerns how Kaluli listened to me listen, and how they listened with me to music from my own orbit. A few anecdotes about casual interactions provide insight into the tacit naturalness for Kaluli of the *dulugu ganalan* style, as well as into overt Kaluli invocations of style as a bridge between aesthetic worlds.

I arrived for each visit in Bosavi with a cassette arsenal of "my music" (whatever I happened to like listening to at that particular time), imagining that these tapes would be a good antidote to Kaluli information overload, burnout, and culture shock and a means to "hook up" to something familiar. This hookup, of course, was both figurative—to "my" urban North American world of musical idioms—and literal—to headphones. What better way to remove my ears (hence mind and body *ensemble*) from the incredible ongoing density of Kaluli sound, interaction, and obligation! Headphones were my best "being there" way to not be there. Kaluli friends were willing to give me some space when it came to a need to hear my own tunes; they had no trouble recognizing that I would be nostalgic for my music and were at ease when I reminded them of that need. Besides, when Kaluli worked with me or the Schieffelins, we sat around a table wearing headphones, absorbed in the quiet of transcription and review, tuning out others and visibly signaling our need for separation and concentration. Headphones were thus generally understood by Kaluli as an unaggressive, typified, obvious signal of the desire to seal oneself off from most outside interruptions and interactions with others.

So when I wanted to listen to my music, I usually listened alone, with headphones, and in doing so pretty much withdrew from the surrounding scene. This, of course, was as thoroughly un-Kaluli behavior as might be imagined. Had I been operating their way, I would probably have brought a large boom box and kept it on, at medium to low volume, all the time (even if only to produce static), simply densifying the overall listening environment with "lift-up-over sounding" sounds to be differentially attended, foregrounded, or backgrounded according to what was going on or desired at a given moment. Virtually all Kaluli listening and most listening sources are public, however specialized or privatized the focus of what one or more listeners tune into. The social and sonic seal of headphones, and lengthy hours in sitting or lying positions wired to them, was a clear part of the reportedly *mada ko:le,* "very different," world of us *dogo:f wanalo:,* "yellow skins."

Kaluli want to be listening with others, and they want to be talking and multiply focused while they are listening. This follows from their being accustomed to "lift-up-over sounding" sound—environmental, verbal, and musical—as a multiply dense constant. While Kaluli were able to recognize that I might want to be alone with my music, they could not really imagine why I could not do that in my own head, without headphone prostheses. For Kaluli, the personalized experiences of listening and the ability to focus intensely when listening do not principally involve shutting one thing out in order to hear another. People must be available to one another while listening separately or together. For example, I found out the hard way that Kaluli transcription assistants worked less well and were less focused with greater sensory decontextualization. Thick-cupped earphones that shut out all other sounds were useless. Kaluli were far more productive, relaxed, and stimulated wearing loose, light headphones, slightly off center on the ear, and listening at lower volumes. Sound-for-focus juxtaposed with sounds from sources outside the headphones helped Kaluli listen most attentively. An edge or tension was present when they had to work to listen, engage to tune in. Additionally, with these headphones Kaluli could talk and listen at the same time, which was far more natural.

In any case, while private listening remained an occasional activity of mine, my stock of non-Kaluli music tapes did not remain private for long. Kaluli curiosity to listen along (or more appropriately, perhaps, listen-up-over) led me to disconnect my headphones and let the tapes play in the background while I was casually interacting with friends. Yet I dismissed many of my first experiences listening with Kaluli to other Papua New Guinea musics and Western musics. I think I found these moments superficial and somewhat obviously transparent. In retrospect I should have tape-recorded and closely studied those interactions and the spontaneous remarks that Kaluli offered. They probably contained superb indications of what I later began to closely monitor and attend to, namely how Kaluli commentary on non-Kaluli music indicated the centrality of *dulugu ganalan* as something to listen for and remark upon, in both descriptive and evaluative discourse.

The single most forceful experience in this regard occurred one day when I casually played a tape of selections by the Miles Davis Quintet of the late 1960s. In addition to Davis on trumpet, the band included Wayne Shorter on tenor saxophone, Herbie Hancock on piano, Ron Carter on bass, and Tony Williams on drums. Many of the compositions the band recorded were by Shorter, including one entitled "Nefertiti," from an album of the same name (Davis 1967). This recording stopped Kaluli ears in their tracks. The song is a sixteen-bar melody with a strong feeling of subdivision between the first eight bars and the second eight. On the recording these sixteen bars are played sequentially thirteen times by the ensemble. The form is thus unusual for small group jazz improvisation in that the players do not explicitly play a melody (usually called the "head") and improvise solo choruses on the chord structure accompanied by the rhythm section ("blowing" or "playing changes"), closing with an ensemble reprise of the head.

The "Nefertiti" recording consists instead of the head played over and over by the ensemble. Yet it involves tremendous subtleties and differences in each of the thirteen choruses and in the contrast of the first and last eight bars of each chorus, which often exploits a tension-relaxation principle. Many of the subtleties involve textural differences in the relationship of the horns (trumpet and tenor saxophone); others involve continual changes in the densification of rhythm section parts (piano, bass, and drums), "comping" (accentual patterns of piano chords), "walking" (bass runs contrasting melody and timekeeping functions with soloistic material), and "fills" (drum accents and embellishments off the basic 4/4 cymbal "tap" and time groove). Throughout the piece, changes in volume and balance between the horns, between the horns and the rhythm section, and within the rhythm section add to the sense of nuanced repetition with development.

The first chorus is played just by the tenor sax and rhythm section. They continue into the second chorus, but the trumpet joins the sax in unison for the last eight bars. The next three choruses develop a swinging 4/4 groove, with the horns in unison and the rhythm section alternating light and dense sections of accompaniment; the rhythm section additionally gets louder throughout and adds more fills, accenting its role in every chorus during the last two bars of the sixteen-bar phrase, where there are no horn melody notes. The sixth chorus finds the volume way down, the piano virtually mute during the first eight bars, then back in for the second eight. The seventh is louder and the rhythm section is more active, leading to a strong focus on the drums in the last eight bars. The eighth starts louder, then becomes softer to focus on the bass in the last eight bars. The ninth chorus feels like the apex of rhythm section solos within the cycle, accented first by rolling piano block chords in six-against-four and three-against-two patterns with the bass and drums, then in the last eight bars by strong drum soloing playing off of similar cross-rhythmic motifs. In the tenth chorus the horns play the melody in staggered, overlapping echo at the beginning, coming back closer to a unison statement at the end, then varying the echo technique and more typical unison statement throughout the eleventh chorus. The twelfth is played just by the rhythm section: rich block chords from the piano, walking bass lines, and highly polyrhythmic drum fills overlay the basic groove. The final chorus finds the horns back in unison, with some slight echo effects, and the recording ends with a rhythm section fade.

Kaluli listeners attended to a number of dimensions of this performance of "Nefertiti" and applied the notions of "lift-up-over sounding" and "hardening" to comment on their sense of the form and performance dynamics. *Dulugu ganalan* was employed to comment on (*a*) the relationship of the melody as stated by the horns to the simultaneous accompaniment by the rhythm section; (*b*) the figure-ground contrasts and tensions between more ensemblelike and more soloistic moments, especially the shifts in the piano and drum playing; (*c*) the motion from unison melody statement to staggered echo statement by the horns; and (*d*) the continual changeability of the sound and emphasis on overall and section-internal volume contrasts. Additionally, the notion of "hardening" was applied to the overall structure, the climax coming in the transition from the loud, agitated rhythm section work at the end of the ninth chorus to the overlapped echo horn statement in the first eight bars of the tenth chorus.

Undoubtedly, the thinning and thickening of textures, and the subtleties of the group being simultaneously together yet with each player partially off in solo space is central to an appreciation of the band's performance here. From the vantage point of the experienced jazz listener the aesthetics of the piece rest on a playful subversion of the classical jazz distinction between ensemble and solo artistry. In an overt sense "Nefertiti" has no solos—certainly none of the classic improvised jazz type—but there are solos throughout, and the players move in and out of solos together. In effect, the role of the sixteen-bar melody progresses, as does the head in a typical jazz performance, from contextual to textual to subtextual to pretextual to textual functions.

I doubt this is what Kaluli heard, and I would not suggest that they experienced "Nefertiti" at all the way sophisticated or novice Western jazz listeners might. But they also did not just hear it as something from afar. While the melodic, harmonic, and rhythmic idioms of the piece and the genre are entirely alien to them, the elements that they heard and labeled as "lift-up-over sounding" are specific relational process elements replete with textural densification, and in-sync, out-of-phase patterning. In effect, "Nefertiti" made sense to Kaluli because it *sounds* like their kind of groove.

Further Downtown, in the Treetops: Kaluli Groove-ogenesis

The formation of the Kaluli "lift-up-over sounding" sound proceeds from a dual dialectic, between sounds and environment on the one hand, sound and social relations on the other (fig. 2). The first side involves a process of adaptation. The fluidity of environmental awareness as musical inspiration, environmental perception as musical appreciation, lies in the motion between nature and "naturalness," the sensate and the sensual. The music of nature becomes the nature of music. The second side involves a process of rationalization. The fluidity of musical consciousness as social identity, idea performed to ideation formed, is the motion between the "natural" and human nature, the sensual and the sensible. Now the nature of music is "doing what comes naturally." The simultaneous feeling of being "in it" and "of it" is the emergence of "lift-up-over sounding" as synonym-image for Kaluli cooperative work, sound making, and soundscape, each echoing the same pattern, turning the same groove, and echoing outward, toward interaction and talk in *dulugu*

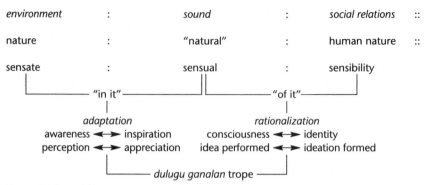

Figure 2. The Kaluli groove

salan, "lift-up-over speaking," as well as toward textural densification and in-sync, out-of-phase costume-dance-sound relationships.

Meanwhile, Back Uptown . . .

In an extraordinary trilogy on anthropological aesthetics, Robert Plant Armstrong (1971, 1975, 1981) laid some foundations for a humanistic anthropology that might put aside "art" and "the beautiful" and look at culture "as a pattern-in-experience" and at works of "affecting presence" as "a direct presentation of the feelingful dimension of experience" (1975:18, 19). Armstrong's quest is to understand affecting qualities and works in terms of presentation, not representation; immediation, not mediation; and metaphor, not symbol.

Armstrong treats metaphor as "the being of the work of art; through metaphor it exists [as] the actual, incarnated being of . . . non-verbal affective life" (1971:xxi). He argues that affecting presences, as works or events witnessed, are "constituted, in a primordial and intransigent fashion, of basic cultural psychic conditions—not symbols of those conditions but specific enactments—presentations—of those very conditions . . . the affecting presence is not a 'semblance' but an actuality . . . in cultural terms it presents rather than represents" (1975:24). The media of such affecting presences are the minima of this presentational state, and metaphor is the mode of affecting existence, "a process by means of which the artist creates in various spatial and temporal media states of affective being" (1975:62).

Packed into Armstrong's concern with revealing the conditions of a work's powers of invocation is a strong critique of approaches which transparently equate art and beauty with excellence of execution and aesthetics with the conditions of virtuosity (1981). He sees such an approach to aesthetics, like those that interpret works principally as signs of their times, as exteriorizing and ethnocentric. In place of such formulations he wishes to examine works of affecting presence as direct forces and sensibilities, through which one might grasp "the very consciousness of a people, the particular conditions under which their human existence is possible" (1975:82). This is why he is so concerned with affect as a kind of knowing linked to power, or the efficacy of such conditions of feeling. For Armstrong "the affective realm is the universe of man's interiority, and its mode of address is direct" (1971:43). Hence works of affecting presence are not only physically identical to what they immediately present but metaphorically identical to the emotions transferred through their witnessing.

Armstrong's phenomenology is dense and elegant and often takes one far from real worlds of people, physical works, cognized affect, and enacted metaphor. But at the same time he has done more theoretically than anyone else to situate metaphor and emotion at the center of ethnoaesthetics and to elaborate a critique of anthropological crypto-aesthetics. He does this in part by reinvigorating the notion of tropes and showing how tropes transmute core cultural patterns through formal metaphoric properties, modalities, and media as a "projection *of* consciousness *in* consciousness" (1975:45). "Style may . . . be seen to be a composite of media and their structures, *in terms of* the *discipline* to which those media and structures are characteristically subjected in enactment" (1971: 51; italics in original). Through similetic equivalences in different media and modes, the sensate and feelingful dimensions of affecting presences gain iconic force. "Style is affecting when it can be asserted that it is integral to the presentational being of the work" (1971:51).

Here too Armstrong seems to be one of the few anthropological aestheticians to transcend a false dichotomization of cognition and emotion, knowing and feeling. For him, the viewer's affect is never caused by the artist's sensibilities packed into work; rather, the viewer's feelings are drenched in comprehension of enacted sensibilities that live in the work. Armstrong thus joins other philosophers and aestheticians (Solomon [1976] 1983:192–93; Bouwsma [1954] 1970; Goodman [1968] 1976: 245–52) who challenge "expression" theories of art and concomitant hydraulic theories of the emotions: "In aesthetic experience the *emotions function cognitively.* The work of art is apprehended through the feelings as well as through the senses . . . Cognitive use involves discriminating and relating them in order to gauge and grasp the work and integrate it with the rest of our experience of the world" (Goodman 1976:248; italics in original). While critics have found work like Armstrong's or Good-man's outside the tradition of ethnographic and political grounding, it is worth noting how this placement of emotion in fact forges a link to the neo-Marxist "structures of feeling" notion of style and aesthetics found in the work of Raymond Williams: "We are talking about characteristic elements of impulse, restraint, and tone; specifically affective elements of consciousness and relationships; not feeling against thought, but thought as felt and feeling as thought: practical consciousness of a present kind, in a living and interrelating community" (Williams 1977:132).

Coda: Style and Groove Re-Fused? Re: Fused? Refused?

How do the implications of aesthetics as iconicity of style bear on why getting into the groove feels so good? That question ended the orig-inal formulation of this paper. When I tried to answer it at Rice University, drawing on Armstrong as above, Michael Fischer pointed out the implicit connection to another question: What does *dulugu ganalan* do to help us put distanced uptown aesthetic theory in critical relief? As I meditated on that, Charles Keil sent one answer to both questions, "lifting-up-over" earlier drafts:

> Getting into the groove feels so good because it frees us of a lot of abstractions, logics, "culture," "knowledge," aesthet-ics, iconicities, etc., and all the forces that both separate and fix music from dance, myth from ritual, recipe from food, etc., etc., etc. Guess I'm suggesting that you push it further downtown and toward applied sociomusicology in conclu-sion rather than saying that we need to think through the fixed concepts in order to grasp the groove. It's the reverse; we need to groove more in order to break open some con-cepts, drop others, keep all mere ideas at a safe distance. (per-sonal communication, 7 November 1986)

Another way to say it is that as a down-home stylistic sensibility the *dulugu ganalan* groove feels so right because it accomplishes the Kaluli social idea or goal of maximized participation. Each voice in a stream of collaboration is at once a self-referenced "hardness," an attested skill, competence—a presence that is rewarding and revealing. Simultaneously, each voice is socially ratified as cooperative agent, linked and immersed in a myriad of human relations that continually activate the pleasures of identity. What feels good is the familiarity of local ethos—a Kaluli emo-tional tone that supports as it challenges, agitates as it invites, stimulates as it soothes. *Dulugu ganalan* is about play, about control and letting go, about being loose and being organized, about being poly- and -phonic, together but always open to reconstituting relationships, about being synchronously in and out of time together. Simply put, it feels good to know how to feel good.

Getting back to uptown aesthetic theory and Michael Fischer's question, *dulugu ganalan* is, at the least, a forest of trees falling, crashing down, and shaking the grounds of any general aesthetics that privileges vision, visual objects, and visualism, product over process, melody and rhythm over timbre and texture, syntax over semantics, structure over emotion, form over participation, linearity over simultaneity, force over flow, transcendental over temporal, top-heavy over egalitarian, vertical harmony over the moving groove. Keil (chapter 3) and Gadamer (1986) have concisely provided the gist of an extended answer: *dulugu ganalan* takes us in numerous nonalienating play, performance, process, and participation directions, exploring forms and expressions while creating them, intensifying Schutz's "tuning-in," Armstrong's "projection *of* consciousness *in* consciousness," Ricoeur's "projection of new possibilities of redescribing the world" (1978:152).

When I closed on that note at Columbia, Dieter Christensen suggested another use for *dulugu ganalan* that takes the critique back to "music," that consummate uptown invention that possesses all our "musicologies." To his ears, the *dulugu ganalan* groove again challenges assumptions of and tendencies toward reified usages of "style" in Western music history. Style is often taken as an unproblematic notion implying specialness, continuity, persistence, established boundaries, mild dynamism, and self-generated reproduction. Along such traditional musicological lines, style is, in its crudest classificatory usage, whatever is unique and individuated about a piece, what any set of pieces are situated "in," or what they flow "out of" or "into." Style is the clustering of traits which make each work a token ("piece") of and in a type ("opus"). In this sense, style may denote those sound patterns of a period, epoch, location, or composer that are most redundant, recurrent, transparent, or formally consistent, a core reflection of a place or time that evolves, is mastered, then discarded or superseded. Style too can be the mark of what makes one piece greatly creative, another minimally so; in this view, style may be viewed as analytically transparent, something deduced purely and uniquely from "the notes," a transcription or a score. For example, claiming in its first sentence to be "old and derivative" and thereby standard and consensual in approach to style, LaRue's score-centric *Guidelines for Style Analysis* "presents a framework for understanding music based directly on the notes themselves" (1970:vii). On the creative individuated identity, Dickenson's definition in the opening lines of *A Handbook of Style in Music* is typical: "Style is the reflection of the individual essence of a work of art which gives it its *identity*. This identity is the result of a distinctive *conjunction* of components, coupled with distinctive *emphases* among the components. Style is thus the crystallization of the traits of a work, characteristically adjusted in one comprehensive individuality—the creative personality of the work" (1965:3, italics in original).

While some musicologists and theorists have critiqued such typological or trait-cluster approaches to style (for example, Hatten 1982, who in an argument drawing on Chomsky and Culler urged musicologists to approach style as competence and stressed how stylistic competence is not transparently reflected in a score), it is clearly Leonard Meyer's work on style and style change (1967:104–33, 1987, 1989) that constitutes the broadest and most rigorous reassessment of assumptions about musical style, specifically the confusion of stylistic classification with stylistic analysis. Meyer argues that "knowledge of style is usually 'tacit': it is a matter of habits properly acquired (internalized) and appropriately brought into play. . . . It is the goal of music theorists and style analysts to explain what the composer, performer, and listener know in this tacit way." Moreover, "what the theorist and analyst want to know about, then, are the constraints of the style in terms of which the replicated patternings observed can be related to one another and to the experience of works of art" (1987:31).

Ultimately, and unfortunately, Meyer lets this position devolve into an overly internal and physicalistic notion of behavior and rules, leading to the notion that one can only study the nature of choices and constraints from the behavior of players as manifest in "the invariable laws of human cognition" (1987:33). In doing so, he subjugates the inevitable social complexity of style and misses the unique and fundamental role of cultural analysis to interpret the richness and thoroughness of style as collective representation, as human resource, as evolutionary adaptation. More obviously, he misses the *stylistic centrality* of extramusical and sociomusical markings for an explication of what is specifically articulated in the sonic-musical. The problem, of course, is that a thorough analysis of style precisely pinpoints the artificiality of a triangulation that distances the sonic-musical, extramusical, and sociomusical, finally liberating the subject back into its fundamental unity. Some fifty years ago,

M. M. Bakhtin precisely located the parallel problematic of stylistic analysis for literature:

> The separation of style and language from the question of genre has been largely responsible for a situation in which only individual and period-bound overtones of a style are the privileged subjects of study, while its basic social tone is ignored. The great historical destinies of genres are overshadowed by the petty vicissitudes of stylistic modifications, which in their turn are linked with individual artists and artistic movements. For this reason, stylistics has been deprived of an authentic philosophical and sociological approach to its problems; it has become bogged down in stylistic trivia; it is not able to sense behind the individual and period-bound shifts the great and anonymous destinies of artistic discourse itself. More often than not, stylistics defines itself as a stylistics of "private craftsmanship" and ignores the social life of discourse outside the artist's study, discourse in the open spaces of public squares, streets, cities and villages, of social groups, generations and epochs. Stylistics is concerned not with living discourse but with a histological specimen made from it, with abstract linguistic discourse in the service of an artist's individual creative powers. But these individual and tendentious overtones of style, cut off from the fundamentally social modes in which discourse lives, inevitably come across as flat and abstract in such a formulation and cannot therefore be studied in organic unity with a work's semantic components. (Bakhtin [1934–35] 1981:259)

Transposed to the musical, Bakhtin's admonition forcefully situates an appreciation of *dulugu ganalan* as an ethnomusicological critique of the historical reification of constant forms and fixed elements, as well as a critique that more specifically implicates musicocultural analysis to locate the power of style in the social imagination as "a concrete embodiment or projection of emotional dispositions and habits of thought common to the whole culture" (Schapiro 1953:305). Phrasing this from the Kaluli perspective, style (as *dulugu ganalan*) is more than the statistical core reflection of the place or time, or patterned choices made within constraints. It is the very human resources that are enacted to constitute the reality of social life in sound. Style is itself the accomplishment, the crystallization of personal and social participation; it is the way performance and engagement endows humanly meaningful shape upon sonic

form. Style is an emergence, the means by which newly creative knowledge is developed from playful, rote, or ordinary participatory experience. Style is the way an internalization and naturalization of felt
thoughts and thought feelings guides experience; more than just main-
taining the *dulugu ganalan* musical order, it creatively produces and sus-
tains it by allowing Kaluli the pleasures of feeling actualized potential,
resources, skills, and desires, through careful listening no less than actual
performance.

With *dulugu ganalan*, the emergent Kaluli camaraderie, sound, and
sensation are cognitively and emotionally integrated in the deepest sense,
not just as metaphoric equivalents, but as a felt iconic wholeness. In that
sense, style is a gloss for the essence of identity; which is why Kaluli *dulugu ganalan* mediates individual creativity and collective experience,
and why grooves or styles are universes of discourse (Meyer), pervasive,
rigorous unities (Schapiro), assertions of control (Keil), and algorithms
of the heart (Bateson) essential to affecting presences (Armstong).

GROOVING ON PARTICIPATION

SF: In "Motion and Feeling through Music" you contrast engendered feeling as a performative and improvisational mode to embodied meaning as the compositional mode, but you acknowledge that music which is composed is also performed. So tell me more about engendered feelings in the Western European art tradition.

CK: Even the most through-composed, penned-down, no-improvisation, no-cadenzas, nothing-in-the-way-of-spontaneity piece still has to be put into motion and given feeling. I love the example of the Casals cello suites because everybody thinks of that as a transformation of old Bach, in which J. S. Bach disappears in the fury of Casals getting his feeling into those notes and transforming them. And that is what all the mystique of the conservatory is. Henry Kingsbury's book on that world gets us closer to seeing how, when you get right down to the nitty-gritty, somebody has to inject feeling into those notes, and how, out of an almost mystical awareness of whether a person has feeling or talent or the right touch at the keyboard and all that stuff which is impossible to evaluate objectively, the conservatory is separating out people who will become concert pianists from those who will be accompanists. All that sorting out is done around motion and feeling questions, performative issues. Do they have enough touch? Can they put enough legato and mist into the Chopin, enough fog into the Debussy? Is there enough moonlight in the Moonlight Sonata? All of that has got to be done by touch. So all musics must be evaluated processually, groovily. All that engendered feeling means is to "groove": engendering groove, creating groove. How are the touches on cymbals and string bass achieving lift-off, achieving some kind of groove that other musicians can interact with? I talked about jazz in that article, but the same goes for any other style, including a ponderous symphony orchestra. Somebody has got to get that machinery cranked up in a tempo with some kind of tension.

SF:At the time you wrote this piece ethnomusicology as a field was quite different. Alan Merriam's *The Anthropology of Music,* in 1964, was a radical challenge in many ways but it wasn't addressing musicologists like this piece does. Merriam was proposing . . .

CK: . . . better contexting—that's what was going to anthropologize the musical . . .

SF: . . . but here you don't engage in a discussion with Merriam and his program for a more culturally contexted musicology. Instead, you posit that analysis and evaluation have something to do with each other, a notion which is a much more radical challenge to ethnomusicology and one that taps into the critical agenda of musicology. I find that interesting because you are saying that one can ethnomusicologically evaluate jazz in ways like art music audiences and critics evaluate compositions. However, you're proposing that it can't be done from a text, that it must be based in performative, improvised, emergent, processual structure. And you're claiming that jazz players and audiences do it all the time. Looking back, that is one of the fascinating things about the article to me, how different it was compared to most of the ethnomusicological literature at that time. Why weren't other ethnomusicologists taking on Meyer and, in a larger sense, taking on the best of Western theory on its own turf and terms?

CK: Because most of them were inside the Western way of thinking. They were evaluating music syntactically. Merriam, when he's getting to the nitty-gritty of how to analyze music, is still back there with Kolinski, transcribing and then counting intervals, trying to tell you the ratio and significance of where the first note is in relation to the end note, and so forth. And these were very simple structural comparisons, such as counting the number of minor seconds. That was the methodology.

SF: But by then, performance ethnomusicology was already off the ground. Mantle Hood was already doing his thing, had his students playing music. There was more going on than Kolinski's or Herzog's type of interval analysis . . .

CK: . . . but what Merriam said about the people who were playing music was right: they would get into playing it, without telling you *how* they got into it. The how of it and what they had to do, what

"Lift-up-over" face painting for *gisalo* ceremony; Bosavi, Papua New Guinea, 1984.
Photo Steven Feld.

"Lift-up-over" costume and painting for *ko:luba* ceremony; Bosavi, Papua New Guinea,
1982. Photo Steven Feld.

Ceremonial drumming; Bosavi, Papua New Guinea, 1982. Photo Shari Robertson.

Ko:luba performers with dance streamers flowing like waterfalls; Bosavi, Papua New Guinea, 1982. Photo Shari Robertson.

Gisalo singer, waiting his turn to dance; Bosavi, Papua New Guinea, 1984. Photo Shari Robertson.

Gisalo singer-dancer performing; Bosavi, Papua New Guinea, 1984. Photo Shari Robertson.

Bird of paradise in display like costumed dancers; Baiyer River Sanctuary, Papua New Guinea. Photo Duncan MacSwain.

Gulusa waterfall, flowing like dance streamers; Bosavi, Papua New Guinea, 1984. Photo Steven Feld.

they had to unlearn in order to be a proficient gamelan player or whatever, was not getting articulated very clearly.

But to answer your question about why I didn't bring in historicist, positivist, relativist, or any other anthropological schools of thought in relation to Meyer, I really wanted to go right to the heart of the issue and say that we were ignoring the most basic part of music. The only thing I didn't get in the article that I wish I had is the textural thing, the sound of massing strings, the sound qualities, textures, and timbres. To me the textures are as important as the processes.

SF: You get at that a little bit when you use words like "chunky" and "stringy" to describe the bass players. Those sorts of ethno-textural concepts prefigure the participatory discrepancy paper, but they're still more on the processual side . . .

CK: My final point was to go after the deferred gratification—I think of it as "defurred," have the touch and feel taken out of it—the Protestant-ethic stiffness of the Meyer schemata, by counterposing a more Freudian liberation psychology. Playful, polymorphous, perverse. Be a child, be playful, let the grooves fall where they're going to fall. That was my final appeal: not for an anthropological corrective to musicology, but for a psychoanalytic one.

SF: Juxtaposing jazz rhythm sections with the canon's masterpieces was a hip move in terms of both ethnomusicology and race and culture politics in the mid-sixties. There's a debunking in that which resonates with the contemporary critique now leveled at musicology by ethnomusicologists and some musicologists like Susan McClary and Gary Tomlinson. And you addressed the high culture crowd in their own *Journal of Aesthetics and Art Criticism,* too, just as Judith Becker does in her "Is Western Art Music Superior?" piece in *Musical Quarterly.* Her line is that musicology's contribution to colonialism is the idea that no other musics have the degree of sophistication of Western art music.

CK: The way I try to put that, in the participatory discrepancy paper, is to ask if we will think, fifty years from now, of Kenny Clarke's tap or John Coltrane's tone as a process and a texture comparable to the structure of Beethoven's Ninth Symphony. This processual thing that Kenny Clarke had, and the sound that Coltrane had, are as magical to me as anything that has ever been structured or "syntacted" in music. But I don't think that particular aesthetic has really won through. I assumed when I wrote this article that it would blow the cover of Western musicology, show that the emperor has no clothes, take care of this whole music department obsession with syntax, order, sequencing, and deferred gratification. I thought it was a good theoretical statement against all that. But I didn't go and try to do the measurements to prove that these gaps exist, to prove that the chunky-stringy thing is happening.

SF: Is that what Lenny wanted you to do?

CK: His response was that if these things are there, we can notate them in micro-microsyntax, in dotted-dotted-dotted-eighth notes. He argued that we can capture Kenny Clarke's tap with a notation system, but I don't think that's true. Some jazz musicians I've talked to perceive the gaps, perceive that people are fooling with the time, and can tell you, for example, that the bass player is ahead of the drummer with the pianist like a pendulum in between. Yet other perfectly accomplished jazz musicians hear it all as absolute time: The rhythm section gets better the tighter we are, and the more together we are, the better we get . . .

SF: Aren't they using the term "together" as an encompassing metaphor to cover all their discrepancies, their differences in articulation?

CK: . . . my point is that the engendered feeling skills and the articulation skills are variably perceived by the craftsmen inside the tradition . . .

SF: . . . variably articulated verbally, as well . . .

CK: Right. These things are out of awareness, or variably in awareness. It's a kind of liminal area. And since that article we've not just talked to jazz musicians but have measured the participatory discrepancies and can say how many milliseconds this cymbal tap is ahead of the bass pluck. Olavo Alén from Cuba did some measurements in East Berlin where he shows how the different bell patterns breathe or flex . . .

SF: . . . wait a minute, Charlie. Why do you need the measurements? Aren't you doing an about-face and taking Meyer's position? You make such a strong claim that this is about feeling, that a feeling is a subjective inner state which is physically and culturally constructed, that listening sophistication and awareness and involvement as part of a musical community all develop over time as part of involvement in the music, that there is this wonderfully complex, subjectively constructed dimension of what engendered feeling is.

Isn't measurement just a way of microdotting those eighth notes? Why is it so important to measure all this stuff? Just to *prove* it?

CK: I think so. It has to be proved to the music schools of the world and to all the people who are training little kids. This is about simply showing that, yes, things have to be in tension, that your touch on the piano has to be your own touch . . .

SF: . . . so you're arguing simultaneously that these things are so objectively real that they are measurable, and that they are so subjectively real that any musician socialized in these patterns of playing will intuitively recognize them . . .

CK: But don't you see what the point is, of proving it in different cultures, as Olavo's measurements do? I think that having independent verification that *all* musics have to be out of time to groove is important. We don't have to do it many times, and we don't have to do it for all musical styles, although it would be interesting to see. Are all those notes behind the abstract pulse, or ahead of the abstract pulse? In which cultures? And so on. There's a lot to do there to demonstrate what the feel is, what the engendered feeling is. Is it some mystical thing? Yes, but it's also quite precise. This is certainly the beauty of Olavo's measurements. He shows that you have a lot of latitude on this one bell beat, maybe way ahead, or maybe as close as twenty milliseconds before, but never on it or behind. This other bell beat, however, has to be almost exactly on the pulse, with only a twenty- or thirty-millisecond margin of error. Certain notes have to be very accurate, others can be played almost anywhere as long as they come before the abstract pulse. I think those are important things to know because they tell every single child, potentially, it's *yours.* It's not by some abstract rule out here. You've got to tune up to this performance tradition, and your time sense is crucial. It's going to be out of time, it's going to be out of tune. You don't have to have perfect pitch. Do you see how that liberates people? The notion that you're tone-deaf disappears as a dismissal. The same motive animates this paper and the participatory discrepancy paper. I want to liberate the music-making from the strictures that say you must know how to read it, you must follow the score, you must be in absolute synchrony.

SF: But anybody who is well trained in Western European art music knows those strictures are baloney anyway. No musicians are really *just* following the score. And there's plenty of improvisation at earlier moments in Western art music . . .

CK: . . . the further back you go, the more there is, but it really got squeezed out . . .

SF: But what about the person who accepts your analysis as right-on for jazz, but insists that you don't need to denigrate the complexity of all Western art music just to prove it? We know that Western art music is harmonically more interesting and complicated than it is rhythmically. If you can count three or count four, you can play it. So is the key thing you've done here to insist that theorists can pay attention to jazz because . . .

CK: . . . jazz is more like the rest of the world's musics than is Western art music. In theory, all of Western music could be liberated from the Weberian rationalization and demystification, which allows for no more improvising, no more cadenzas, no more leeway, everything in the hands of the conductor. Actually going back through the centuries, retracing Western art music's history, you do find more improvisation, more leaving the phrasing of fiddle parts to the fiddle sections, more of the concert master conducting instead of a conductor. I think Chris Small's work showing how much leeway, how many ad libitum passages and cadenzas there once were—the bravura piano style right up until the 1920s and 1930s that came to be dismissed as flowery and romantic—it all shows the steady diminution of engendered feeling in Western music historically, the effort to move it increasingly into the hands of the conductor and into the heads of theorists, Platonists. Then you punch out the mistake, like Glenn Gould making his recordings perfect by putting just the touch he wants on the piano note and punching that in. And once he's recorded those things just the way he wants them, he doesn't ever have to play them again. Isn't that the position he took after a while, that the definitive version has been done?

SF: But so did Thelonious Monk. When you listen to the Orrin Keepnews's Riverside digital reconstruction of the *Thelonious Himself* sessions, you hear a half hour of Monk in the studio, at the piano, working out an arrangement of "'Round Midnight." He plays four bars, eight bars, a phrase, gets into something and doesn't quite like it. So they stop rolling tape, call a new take, Monk takes it from the top of the phrase and goes on. So you hear the whole process, and then you hear the original release, which you come to realize was not improvised in one run, but was spliced together from many phrases and sections from all the takes.

CK: But the ethical, aesthetic, moral, political, and all the larger value dimensions of Western through-composed music are towards the perfect performance ideal. Think of Rahsaan Roland Kirk who, when he hears the question about what happens if the guy playing the nose flute gets a booger in it, yells down the bar, "It's all part of the music!" That part of the aesthetic is not there: a booger in the nose flute is not part of the Western aesthetic. You're trying to get perfection, abstract, clear, note-for-note perfection . . .

SF: . . . come on. Lots of musicians in various places are into some kind of idea of perfection . . .

CK: . . . the best swoop, the best "lift-up-over," but not in that same sense of a crystallized, totally civilized thing, never to be done again because it's been done so perfectly—*the* realization of Beethoven's ideal composition . . .

SF: Don't you think that Cecil Taylor or Anthony Braxton are interested in that for their musics? What about gamelan or koto players?

CK: Cecil, probably no. Anthony Braxton, probably yes. Koto players, yes, because it's a preoccupation of their civilization to get the perfect performance. Might be Balinese religious gamelan, no, and Javanese court gamelan, yes! I'll bet that the Japanese have an aesthetic standard for "That was the perfect rendering of three deer in the bamboo" on the *shakuhachi.* But it's a function of class society and hierarchy: perfectionism and "Only the talented can do this" . . .

SF: . . . but when every music in the world meets the recording studio and record producers, and when people gain some consciousness of the degrees of new and heightened control they have through recording technology, something else sets in. And the mediation becomes part of the aesthetics in new and potentially very liberating ways. I don't think you can do a West versus the rest number on any of these issues . . .

CK: I do! I think the Western perfection preoccupation is embodied in the recording studios. And you are right, whenever a Western recording studio meets Sunny Adé, not such good things happen. Things that had been negotiated in a living tradition and in a public space are all of a sudden being negotiated in a recording studio with layers and tracks and dubs and splices and samples . . .

SF: I don't go for that at all. It just seems like an overdone version of folky protectionism or you being suspicious that the technology is screwing up the music . . .

CK: You put the two together, a Western perfectionism and the recording studio's capacity to *give* that to you, and it's a deadly one-two punch for a whole lot of "spill drink" musical traditions, where spilling the drink was part of the sound.

SF: I think you're making this too much into a game of absolutes. Why can't you imagine that the recording studios embody simultaneously the power to thin out *and* to augment a lot of musical potentials?

CK: But you see, I would argue that wherever that recording thing happens, perfectionist, classicizing, Apollonian dream realizations are creeping in. We listened to Abdullah Ibrahim's *African River* recording this morning, and it was like a classicized, ethereal adaptation . . .

SF: Why shouldn't he be allowed to do that?

CK: No, no, that's all good. It's just that when I think of the honking saxophones of the taxi jive fifties, that old Mace LP I wore out, with those short, punchy tunes by the Big Heads, the Fast Drivers, the Snake Bites—so powerful, so raw, so clear, no studio polish *at all*—I feel loss . . .

SF: . . . but Abdullah Ibrahim's music is such a vital, nuanced, edgy blend of South African tunes, gospel and vernacular harmonies, Ellington's horn section sound . . .

CK: . . . but it's a classicized thing. It's been perfected, dreamified, it's a different studio world.

SF: Duke Ellington wanted a dreamified world, too. And even the raucousness of Charles Mingus's bands could create that dreamified world, like the ballads on *Mingus Mingus Mingus Mingus*—"Celia" or "I X Love" or "Goodbye Porkpie Hat" . . .

CK: I agree. And that same Ellington could rock the live house with "The Hawk Talks" or "Jam with Sam" on the Seattle concert LP. All I'm arguing is that we recognize what happens in recording studios as a classicizing, perfecting, dream-world thing, and that takes it away from the dancers, which takes it away from public space, the streets, clubs . . .

SF: Maybe—but to return to "Motion and Feeling," it's the only piece in the book that wasn't written in the 1980s. Here's Chuck, way out there, twenty years before critical cultural studies, saying that analysis and criticism *do* have something to do with each other and that, contrary to the ethnomusicologists and cultural relativists who don't want to evaluate anything, there is a way to talk about what's a *good* groove completely apart from Meyer's deferred gratification.

It's an article that could have been as seminal twenty or twenty-five
years later . . .

CK: To me, it is important that the statement is there in the mid-sixties,
on the eve of big changes in the U.S. . . .

SF: . . . and big changes in the music education world; this is the moment where both jazz and ethnomusicology were struggling for
some validation . . .

CK: . . . so this wasn't coming totally out of left field. John Coltrane's
music was peaking at that time. He was in Chicago, and I was
there every night for six nights listening to his music. That was the
impetus to argue with Meyer, and to say, "This matters," to set it
straight. It's not about syntax. It's about grooving. So in that sense,
it's not some premonition of an eighties understanding of things. It
actually was contemporary with Coltrane's music and the revolution of sensibilities that it implied.

SF: Tell me about the response to it.

CK: The article went into a void. It was not cited that much, although
it did get reprinted in Tom Kochman's anthology *Rappin' and Stylin'
Out* as a manifestation or example of the sensibility of black culture.
But it didn't stimulate a lot of response in the academic music departments of the world or in ethnomusicology. Where it usually
resurfaces is as an obligatory footnote in popular music rebuttals,
starting with John Shepherd's pieces in the 1970s. People writing
an article about popular music and how it is not understood and
has its own aesthetics and so on might cite this article and Andrew
Chester's "Rock Aesthetic" articles, where he talks about the "inten-
sive" and the "extensive." He was trying to get a handle on the
same thing, that there's a whole other way of apprehending non-
Western or non-high-culture music. But it's not like these popular
music writers really took the article seriously either, to go out and
investigate where the groove is actually coming from. There is
something about the popular music, mass-mediated music, and
cultural studies people that remains theoretical and outside of the
actual music. They don't want to get into the music and figure out
how it actually works. Which is again why I think that *some* amount
of measuring and comparing of how participatory discrepancies
work in different kinds of styles, of how engendered feeling gets
engendered, is very important.

SF: But the difference, of course, is in the personal and ethnographic
grounding part, and that is also absent from a lot of cultural studies.

That's one reason that it's surprising to me that in this article you never mentioned that you are both a bass player and a drummer, that you have an experiential basis in lessons, in playing, and in listening to analyze the bassist-drummer grooves and interactions the way you do. Put a record on and here's Chuck, playing the air cymbal and getting the feel of the drummer's tap, or fingering the air bass and getting the pull or push of the pulse. You've played along with records. You've picked up the bass or sat at the drums and grooved with these guys as they were grooving. Why is that personal and experiential knowledge base overtly absent from this piece?

CK: I assumed that to say that I know this from inside my head *and* hands, from having plucked basses and tapped cymbals, wouldn't carry much validity in the world of either the social sciences or the humanities.

SF: But the article talks about the physical reality of engendered feelings and about the dance and the motion, about how it's all in the body. But it is in *your* body, too, which is not talked about here. Obviously that was a different time; people were not writing as personally or reflexively in the mid-1960s.

CK: Right, and the real source of this understanding is in all the very pleasurable and problematic relationships that I've had over the years, as a drummer with bass players, and as a bass player with drummers. What was my relationship to Steve Swallow in the summer of 1959, and how were we not hearing the beat the same way? Or my relationship to a piano player not comping in a way that would help my tap? You try to solve problems in a rhythm section to make it groove at all tempos, and you've got to become aware of all these issues. But you're right. I didn't put that in the article.

———

CK: What prompted you to write "Communication, Music, and Speech about Music," Steve?

SF: Largely my affiliation with the Annenberg School of Communications at the University of Pennsylvania in the early 1980s. I was constantly feeling a kind of tension around uses of the communication concept there. It was an important concept to me, but I wanted to relate it to the process of experiencing music. I was increasingly

worried that the concept of communication was taken to be synonymous with production, and with valorizing the meanings and
intentions of those who produced works, in whatever media. So in
the case of music, communication was being addressed from the
point of view of the makers of the music, focusing on composers
and performers and their intentions, and not addressed to the listeners, except in terms of mass-audience research. I was feeling
that in order to talk about communication, I had to talk about dialectics of production and reception, message form and content,
code and context, rephrasing the process from the point of view of
the listener. What does a listener do? Any listener? And from that
starting point, I tried to think about a general logic of the listening
experience. At the time, I was teaching a course on musical communication at Annenberg, and that was what gave me the context
to take all the communication models, literature, and paradigms
and think them through for the musical process.

CK: That's a wonderful thing to have happened, that you were in that
communications school, because forcing yourself to think in that
communications mode probably put you outside of a whole lot of
baggage that a music department or anthropology department
would want you to carry on this trip. When I first read this paper, I
was somewhat resistant to the long series of words that seemed to
try to cover the whole territory, like "engaged" as "interpreted as
meaningfully structured, produced, performed, and displayed."
That would happen seven or eight times in the opening pages,
where all the possibilities are being covered. At the time, I thought
you were trying to cover too much. What does each one of these
verbs mean? But in retrospect, I think it really is as complicated as
every one of those listings suggests. When these things—dialectics
of the sound object and the listener's interpretive moves in locational, categorical, associational, reflective, and evaluative modes—
can all be happening at the same time or in odd sequences, how
do you sit down with somebody, listen through a piece of music together, and make inferences that would fill out this map in any particular case? It seems like a real challenge.

SF: Like lots of people in the 1980s, I was growing less comfortable
with the abstract, symbolic model of shared culture that was
around in anthropology, even though I had worked in a very small-
scale society where it was possible to use pieces of that model with
some success. But I wanted a model that expressed more of the

complicated dialectics of what is shared and what is completely individuated in experience, more of the distributive and complex
quality of meanings, and more of how those meanings were connected to actual listening activities and practices. So I went from
reading Goffman and Schutz and phenomenology to introspecting
about my own experiences of listening to music—how I listened,
how it was different each time I listened—and how I might get a
handle on this cumulative, interactive, biographical, and historical
process of what listening socialization in musical traditions might
be about . . .

CK: . . . but you're also saying that you *want* some sort of shared culture model. You're looking for schemes of typification, evidence
that they are not whimsical and idiosyncratic. I'm thinking that
they could be *very* whimsical and idiosyncratic . . .

SF: Yeah, that's the other side of it. Consider R. D. Laing writing *The
Politics of Experience* or Berger and Luckman writing *The Social Construction of Reality* entirely in terms of *music.* Then where would this
shared versus individuated thing be? It seemed that there was
nothing in the musical literature which problematized that. When
I did look at the musical literature I realized that communication
was being modeled in a very referential way, related to the theory
of meaning, which was all syntax. The notion of interpretive moves
that I use was just a way of trying to problematize what a musical
experience is. I think I'm responding, like you do in "Motion and
Feeling," to Lenny Meyer's question: What is the musical experience? Both of us are saying that it is not primarily a referential,
syntactically driven emotional experience. It calls forth all the dimensions of interpretation and intersubjectivity, which make this
shared versus individuated thing as problematic as possible.

CK: Let me make it still more problematic for you. One of the things
that came out of puzzling over Tiv songs and the emotions associated with them was that I couldn't find any emotional correlates in
the way Tiv were talking about music. They always talked about
it in terms of craft, perfection, clarity, glowing. All the adjectives I
could collect: "He sings a song clearly, brightly, in detail." And I
would ask, what about singing a song "sadly" or "passionately"?
The response was always, "No, one would hardly ever say that." In
testing out all these frames, I found that Tiv just weren't interested
in the emotional, metaphorical stuff. They were only interested in

the techniques behind really good songs. When I'd ask whether a song sung at a funeral was a sad song, the response was no, the song could be sung the next day at a dance and then it would be a happy song. Or, an elder who locks himself in his hut and sings the songs that made him happy in his youth, might now be really sad. So it was perfectly clear to the Tiv that there were no emotional reference points that could be tied with any degree of reliability to the syntax or to the song itself. Everything was dependent upon the individual.

Then I come to a wonderful interview in the Music in Daily Life project that we did, where we had a couple hundred people talking about music in their lives. One woman, an oboist being interviewed by her boyfriend, gets really pissed off at him in the course of the interview. She says, "You're trying to tell me that I should hear music a certain way, and I'm telling you that when I listen to a Bach cantata, some mornings it makes me silly, laughing, giggly, giddy, and I just think it's the brightest, sunniest thing I've ever heard. The next morning, I can put the same Bach cantata on, and I am in tears, totally devastated. It's the saddest thing I've ever heard. And this is the same piece of music, and that's how it is for me, and you can't say how it should be." And her boyfriend argues that this is counterintuitive, and they have this wonderful argument. So she is a Tiv, right? She is saying that the music is absolutely neutral. How does the oboist and the Tiv take, that the music is neutral and all the rest is in the ear of the "behearer," fit with your "interpretive moves"?

SF: I don't think there's a necessity for a level of verbal articulation to go with each level of perceptual reality. It's much more complex than that. The reason why the interpretive moves framework is kept as general and as vague as possible is because I think the most important thing about the metaphoric tendency is that our minds work in associational, categorical, and locational kinds of ways. So I'm trying to ask, How can we get a handle on some of those general, intersubjective tendencies? I'm as concerned as you are with theorizing why we don't hear exactly the same thing. Social phenomenology reduces this simply: You have your experience, and I have mine. I have my experience about your experience, and you have your experience about mine. But I don't have your experience, and you don't have mine. But of course there is more . . .

CK: . . . layers of overlap, of conjoining possibilities at any given moment . . .

SF: . . . yeah, that we talk or tap our feet or nod our heads in the same way, or get together on the dance floor in a certain kind of way, or are in the music together without ever saying anything to each other, or that we can coordinate this conversation with a whole bunch of head nods and back-channel cues which keep telling us that we're talking together and in the same interlocking groove. Of course, all that is socialized and very cultural. What I'm saying here is that there is a kind of stylistics of listening that intersects and in a way completely neutralizes the false dichotomy of the musical versus the extramusical . . .

CK: . . . and gets away from this stupid referentialism that tries to tie it down . . .

SF: A general model of a musical experience lets us ask if something like this intuitively happens to you. The distinction that needs to be drawn is between how people use music and how people perceive music. I'm not making any claims about the hard-wiring of the brain or how people perceive music auditorally. I'm interested here in the social process; that begins with perception, but it centers in engagement, in meanings being made through listening experiences as they are woven into the fabric of daily life . . .

CK: But I'm confused, because they all seem the same to me: to perceive it, to engage it, to hook into it?

SF: Lenny Meyer and the psychologists want to hook this ultimately to the physiological apparatus of musical perception. They want to tie these kinds of syntactic questions to a cognitive theory of what it means to hear and to perceive music. But I'm not just talking about ears hard-wired to brains here. I'm not talking about any kind of physiological autonomy from the subjective processes of cultural construction. I'm saying that the discursive possibilities—how people talk about music—are as culturally constructed as the social dimensions of its perception. And that is why one kind of musical pattern might potentially be linked to a variety of emotional states, not just one.

CK: Sure, and not just to an opposition, such as I'm happy / I'm sad.

SF: "Interpretive moves" is just an attempt to throw as many cultural monkey wrenches as possible at any kind of more autonomous cognitive modeling of the musical perceptual process. It is not to say that those models are entirely useless, just that we shouldn't assume that culture and experience will be modeled any better in cognitive theory than they have been in music theory.

CK: But you're not denying the physical basis of sound . . .

SF: The physical dimensions of the sound are undeniable. I just want to keep problematizing all of the ways in which researchers separate off the psychological, physiological, musicological, text-centric, syntax-centric forms of analysis from what we are calling culture and experience. Cultural analysis, which is about experience, about what people hear and how people hear it, is worked through the socialized, biographical, the historical process of lives and of people living and relating.

CK: And we sure as hell don't know enough about that.

SF: Ironically, I'm a devoted reader of all the music psychology journals. I like reading research on musical memory, auditory illusions, perceptual universals, all those laboratory experiments. All of that is fascinating to me, but in a model of musical communication I don't want to privilege those perceptual things as autonomous from the complexity of culture, experience, and interpretive moves.

CK: In the *My Music* interviews, I've heard it over and over again about people using music to match a particular mood or to help them get out of it. It's a standard Aristotelian catharsis. But nobody has the same music, and nobody has the same moods. It's hard work to get shared communication about how this music is doing its thing, to specify further *how* is it working, what's at work there.

SF: I hope that the interpretive moves framework gives people a particular language for thinking about the necessarily vague, general, and nebulous dimensions of the experience of music. Like the "groove." What I find fascinating is that you can find the locational, associational, and categorical—the range of interpretive moves—in talk which is utterly vague, nebulous, inarticulate, not explicit at all. We have to separate out the analytic ability to track interpretive moves from the notion of articulateness of speech. Vast amounts of discourse are not very articulate, yet they contain incredible clues to the emergent complexities of interpretive moves.

CK: And we have got to be tolerant and curious about how it is that people can or cannot articulate their meaningful musical moments. I keep thinking about the talk last night with Greg Urban about having music in his mind all the time, or other people who always have a sound track on. Talk about interpretive moves! Something is on there, something is in their brains, and we didn't realize until a

couple of years ago that this phenomenon even existed. We don't
know if it works cross-culturally. Are there Kaluli people hearing
music all the time?

I wanted to ask you earlier, too, about emotional correlation. For
the Kaluli, it must be that some of the *gisalo* songs that prompt the
burning of the dancers are tied to an emotional state, right?

SF: Sure.

CK: Then there's some kind of fixity there between the musical process
and an emotional flow? Whenever you hear that kind of song,
you're tuned in to a whole range of references and missing people.

SF: Studying something like the *gisalo* ceremony for what it indicates
about the relationship between sadness and anger reveals many
subtleties that will not be revealed directly in the variety of anger or
sadness terms in the Bosavi language. Those feelings are embodied,
formed, and performed through form, performed into feelings that
are enacted. So for me, there is an aesthetics of emotion, and a
presentation or performance of emotion, which is a powerful cultural dimension. It transcends the extent to which one can talk
about emotion vis-à-vis consciousness, rationality, and the extent
to which emotions are culturalized at that level. It isn't the fixity of
musical process that's the key here; it's the staging of song performance as an arena for the aesthetics of emotional display, confir-
mation, and circulation.

CK: It's an old cliché that music in some way codes the language of
emotions. After reevaluation counseling and studying that theory a
bit, I have a little better sense about how grief can move to anger,
then maybe to laughter. We know that there are sequences of emotions that people in a culture go through, which are part of purging themselves of past hurts or past losses or of emerging from
death and separation anxieties. I think we are just lifting the lid on
all that. When we sit here and talk about this, I realize that there
are thousands of studies still to be done about these musical, emotional mixes and sequences in every culture in the world. Why is
soul music bittersweet, or blues bittersweet? People always talk
about that. It is bitter *and* sweet. I think that is true. The truth is
that it is about emotional mixes in people's minds. It's not just that
the oboist hears the Bach cantata as sad on one day and happy the
next. There is probably a happy-sad balancing act going on at any
given moment. The happiness part predominates at one moment,
but all of a sudden the teeter-totter shifts and the nostalgia for

home or family that comes up around that music takes over, like nostalgia for home and family takes over at certain moments in a Kaluli song. Jung said that you build a unique self out of ego-stuff, that your stay on the planet is really all about that emergent self. But music is an even better summarizer of all of that stuff . . .

SF: That was the point I wanted to make too. Because music does this in directly feelingful ways. It's the physicality of being in the groove together that brings out a lot of this emotional copresence and co-construction. James Brown's point is great, that we are hearing it before we are seeing it, and that physically the sense of seeing is something apart, out there, whereas you feel the resonance of your voice inside of your head and chest. The sense of touch, the sense of feel, the sense of sound are so deeply and thoroughly integrated in our physical mechanism. James is onto it, the Kaluli are onto it, and we're just trying to get communicational and cultural theory onto it.

SF: When did you write the "participatory discrepancies" piece?

CK: I wrote it right around the Bo Diddley moment, so to speak, and I just whacked it out in a few days. I got the urge to go down to talk to Bo when he was in Buffalo, playing New Year's Eve at the Tralfamadore Cafe. I talked to him backstage, and I thought the interview was so hilarious. I was busy being the scholar, trying to analyze this thing, and take the four-letter words out of there—it's a little bowdlerized. I was so amused by the fact that I thought we understood each other, yet he was protecting his PDs pretty carefully, saying, "You really don't have a handle on my groove, buddy. That's my groove."

SF: How did you choose these two words, participatory discrepancies?

CK: In Latin, *discrepare* is to rattle, a sounding apart, a separation. It kind of captures this notion of sounding split seconds apart and the way that these discrepancies bring people into the sound in a totemic or presymbolic mode.

SF: That they invite participation.

CK: Right, *discrepare* describes pretty well those rattles and shakers and all the things that shamans are using in all those cultures. It's about rattling and shaking, and hissing high-hats that open and close . . .

SF: . . . about a driving force in some sense. And "participatory," that comes from Barfield?

CK: It especially comes from Lévy-Bruhl, who is using *participation,* the French word, which I think is the one Barfield is going on, too. I could just as well be using "deep identification," in terms of Arne Naess's "deep ecology," where he talks about our need to return to a deep identification with the natural world. It has been formulated a lot of different ways by a lot of different thinkers. Part of the problem of saying one is a participation theorist is that the field is rather diffuse. Nobody has ever consolidated it into one theory. Lévy-Bruhl probably wrote the most about it, but he was ridiculed a fair amount of the time, or was seen as a lackey of imperialism because he was theorizing that there were different ways of thinking, interacting, and participating. Participation was seen as a primitive, negative, illogical mode for most of the twentieth century. Only now, with the ecological crisis, are we beginning to see that it is absolutely necessary to get some of that specific totemic participation and collective acknowledgement of diversity back if we want to live in balance with the natural world.

SF: You start off very simply by saying that the power of music is in its participatory discrepancies and that these are basically of two kinds, processual and textural. Twenty years before this, in the "Motion and Feeling" paper, you laid out the beginnings of critical approach to the processual aspect. Why did it take twenty years to catch up with the textural aspect? What made you feel that out-of-tuneness is as important as out-of-timeness?

CK: I think it was meditating on Tibetan monastic music and trying to figure out why it is not groovy. It does not have a hell of a lot of process that is going to make you snap your fingers or get up and shake your bootie. Syntactically, there are no compelling structures there that invite you to defer gratification or not. I began to wonder what was at stake with this music. These monks have been practicing up there for eight hundred years, every day, and this is what they have come up with. It is very timbral and textural, with an emphasis on harmonics and overtones. And I realized that their pairing of the conch shells, pairing of the shin-bone trumpets, pairing of the shawms, pairing of the bass trumpets, that all those pairings of instruments share one goal: to maximize overtones, harmonics, and "beats," the throbbing of pitches rubbing against each other. I think that is one goal of music, to maximize timbres, textures,

overtones, and harmonics. It puts you into the spiritual or supranat-
ural, above the Himalayas, in a spatial head. If you wanted to account for what was powerful about Tibetan music, you would have
to have a theory of texture and timbre that was just as powerful as
any theory about process or syntax.

SF: Did this strike you as an instrumental issue only? Were you also
thinking about the texture and timbre issues in relation to the
voice?

CK: Well, another source of this thinking was from Goral music in
southern Poland, where they sing in a deliberately out-of-tune way.
It also came from listening to the Epirus subtone clarinet. Once I
got it into my head that timbres and textures were involved in the
magical part of Tibetan music, I could hear the magic in a lot of
musics. I noticed that the polka bands in Buffalo all had two trumpets and I wondered, why did two trumpets evolve as the preferred
sound? In the Bay State Four, there are four guys: a drummer, an
accordionist, and two trumpeters. You must have two trumpets to
get polka happiness. To get that polka brightness in the sound
those two trumpets have to be rubbing together. So in my mind, I
do see it as a mainly instrumental phenomenon. But I hear what
you're saying about the voice, like with Louis Armstrong or Billie
Holiday. Is it in the growl, or in the whine, or in the grain . . .

SF: . . . in the fluidity, the liquidity, and the vibration recipes of the
voice . . .

CK: It is very powerful, and it comes out of the voices first. Of course
the monks in Tibet are alternately chanting and playing instruments, but they use the voice with the same purpose of maximizing the overtones and the harmonics. So it was becoming clear to
me that texture deserved as great a place as process in the theory
of how music involves people and draws you into deep identification, total participation, past the logical contradictions of separation from the Other. I don't want to say that music "stands for,"
because I want to get past the symbolic. I think your iconicity idea
does that, says that this identification is more than symbolic. You
now *are* the Other, or the Other is *in* you. You are *in* the music. The
music is *in* you. Clearly the textures are just as powerful for drawing
you into music, and it into you, as are the processes. Probably some
combination of the two is the most effective. That is why the point
about Bo Diddley at the end of the article is very important, that he
uses that tremolo effect as both process and texture. In the end, all

these analytic aspects of syntax, process, texture, lyric, and context
are simply abstractions, the pulling apart of something that is really
a unified whole. In its performance, in its ongoing energy, it is a
unified thing. Timbre becomes process, texture becomes groove,
and syntax is shaped by both of them or used to hang both of
those things out there.

SF: You have a rap in here about participation which involves a certain
idealization of participation as the nonalienating, positive, antifas-
cist, antidominating aspect of music . . .

CK: . . . except that it is fascist. This is a point that I have trouble with
whenever I'm lecturing in the classroom, whenever I'm arguing
with people over the dinner table about why participation theory is
so important to me. Participation is fascism. It becomes the bundle,
all the rods united for greater strength, with the sum of the parts
being greater than that of the individuals. When it's done nation-
state style, it is a horror. That is what the Holocaust was about, and
every genocidal nationalism is about this false participation, if you
will, in which the nation-state turns solidarity into a state apparatus.
So yes, you are playing with fire when talking about participation.
My notion is that we have got to make the world safe for small-
scale, decentralized, diversified participations, so that the big participation of uniforms, tanks, and kicking ass on alien peoples never
happens. People have to be satisfied in their localities and to feel intense local involvement, participation, and deep identification, or
else those energies will be channeled into statist nightmares. Everybody requires participatory consciousness. That is how we evolved,
and we are tuned up to participate. The people who are not getting that, who are not involved in music and dance and trance lo-
cally, are susceptible to false identifications and participations, to all
the nonsolutions to their problems that the State offers.

SF: To pick up on an earlier issue, tell me about Olavo Alen's measurements and how you think they confirm the point you are driving at
in this piece.

CK: Olavo Alén's measurements are discussed in his 1986 book *La
Música de las Sociedades de Tumba Francesa en Cuba*. The importance of Olavo's measurements is they provide a certain confirma-
tion completely independent from my theorizing. He measured the
relationship between two or three drums in an ensemble and a bell
pattern in different Cuban traditions. He took his tapes to Berlin

and worked on them for a year and a half of micromeasurement, using some strange machine that I still can't fathom the nature of. He was able to get very precise measurements as to what degrees of latitude there were for each note in a repeating bell or drum pattern, where they are in relationship to each other, and where they are in relationship to some absolute sense of measured time.

SF: These are natural recordings, done in context?

CK: I think so. So he can determine that there is a great deal of latitude on the second bell beat, while there is not much at all on the middle bell beat. That there is a kind of breathing in this phrase, some slack in the first third, some slack in the last third, but the middle has to be tight. Or that, in another style, the slackness is in the middle, and the ends have to be tightly in sync. A lot of subtle things that you can kind of feel can be more firmly established by measurement. And again, for me the most important thing is that this all takes away the power of perfectionism, of addiction to perfection, the notion of music as absolute Platonic forms just partially realized by mere performers. If we confirm that everything has to be a bit out of time, a little out of pitch to groove, then approximations will do just fine till you find your own groove with others. It reverses the whole aesthetic. It makes clear that everybody is musical, that every single child born on the planet has a physiological need to be tuned up in this loose-tuning, loose-timing way. The very lifeblood of music, in all cultures, has to do with discrepancies. And that is why I want to use the "negative" term. I want to keep that open, somewhat chaotic, somewhat diversified, differentiated, nonperfect, evolving—an emergent universe.

What's at stake in the premise that PDs are where the juice, the groove, the funk, and the delights of music, and of life, are, is a real basic worldview that says that the universe is open, imperfect, and subject to redefinition by every emergent self. Every individual on the planet has a different time feel, just like everyone has a different signature and everyone dances differently. I will never forget bringing friends, two couples, to a polka dance. I figured they would have to get used to the dancing, that it would take a while before they could get into the groove. The minute they stood up and started dancing, I could see that they had their styles. One guy had a nice hesitant stutter step going, while the other one had a big, loose stride. And their wives had to keep up with this initiation.

But after they had been out on the floor for a couple of minutes, I could see a style emerging, and that each couple had a unique way of dancing. I think that every single person on the planet has this emergent, expressive self, and that notions of perfection, of in-tune and in-time, are part of a conspiracy to shut them up, to pacify them and leave them in a corner appreciating the "true" talents. That's all bullshit. I'm sick of it. So for me it is really important to insist that the discrepancies are discrepant, and that everybody can be allowed to find their own time feel and their own sense of pitch, timbre, and voice.

———

CK: Steve, why do we have to have uptown, high theory? Why do I have to share you with Bob Armstrong? I want you all to myself, only downtown, in the participatory groove.

SF: You know, the uptown-downtown part got cut out of the title when the piece was published in the *Yearbook for Traditional Music* because the editor, Dieter Christensen, thought it was too mystifying for an international publication. Fine for the New York City slickers, not so hip in Eastern Europe.

CK: But that is the whole point of the article. Or is it? Why do you think having both versions of the groove is so important? Are you trying to reconcile idealism and materialism again?

SF: It's an attempt to reconcile scholarly and vernacular, theorized and the on-the-ground local grooves. It tries to juxtapose some heads on the high theory side—Armstrong, Meyer, Roman Jakobson— with "lift-up-over sounding" on the Kaluli side, with the vernacular, PDs, the worlds of James Brown, Aretha Franklin, the dance floor, and the rainforest, the feelingful sonic, the directly articulated, the embodied, the primal, downtown.

CK: You say "aesthetics as iconicity of style." Style, iconicity, and aesthetics become overlapping abstractions by the end of the article, so that each has a bit of separation from the other, yet they are also the same at some level?

SF: Not quite. The idea is that aesthetics is more than the fineness of execution, virtuosity, beauty, or any type of evaluative judgment in the sense of holding your thumb up to a painting. By iconicity of style, I simply mean the multiple representations of one idea: how the visual, the verbal, the musical, the choreographic, the ritual, the ceremonial, the everyday, and the mythological are all interwoven and layered in Bosavi. They create a whole, a naturalized whole, that is a centerpiece of Kaluli identity. So when you unpack the dense meanings of "lift-up-over sounding," you see how that one idea is the trope for Kaluli style.

CK: Why do you need the word "iconicity" when you can just use "trope" and "base" and have the Armstrong terminology?

SF: I want to align the style concept with the important insight from semiotics that you can have several varieties of these very direct, very feelingful resemblance relationships between things which we might otherwise refer to as symbols. There is a particular kind of symbolic realm where there are feelingful, interpenetrated relationships, felt resemblances, imaginative connections between the thing-out-there, and the feeling-in-here. What I want to capture in the term "iconicity" is this bringing together of perception and feeling, the abstraction and the unabstraction of it.

CK: So this does the job of Bateson's "ecology of mind" or Berman's "enchantment of the world" or any of these participation understandings of reality where the sound and the sentiment, the music and the people, are consubstantial at some profound level which is not symbolic, not "standing for." So the title could also say "aesthetics as iconicity *as* style"?

SF: Yes, except that here I use style as the master notion for the expressive, like the way an anthropologist uses "culture" or the way a linguist uses the word "grammar." Style is to expression what grammar is to language and what culture is to social behavior.

CK: One of the nice points that I like here is that bringing the emotions and the cognitive back together is important—the emotional resonances and the cognitive grasp, carnal knowledge, body knowledge. This is a way of knowing, an emotional, musical way of knowing. Can you elaborate on that a bit more?

SF: "Lift-up-over sounding" is the most basic Kaluli idea about music, but it is also an important general idea about nature, about talking, about interacting, about what a costume is, about what a dance is. It is as broad and profound for Kaluli as the idea of "harmony" is for the West and covers a lot of the same metaphoric space. What I like about this is that such a profoundly resonant and insightful concept is also, at the surface, vague and unexegetical. That is why it is like the notions of "groove" or "beat"—say no more; what it is is what it is. "Get in the groove and let the good times roll."

"Lift-up-over sounding" invites participation the way the groove does. And this is what leads to the idea of an emotion, a feeling state, as a way of knowing, evaluating, understanding.

CK: But how is it a way of knowing? How is it like a cognitive mapping of reality?

SF: Because participation models style, reinforces the feel of the groove, strengthens the naturalness of it, keeps it from the realm of abstraction, keeps it in practice. "Lift-up-over sounding" is only a metaphor, only an abstraction in its glossed, English manifestation. Out there in Bosavi, it's an attitude, a resource, a style, a predisposition, a stance, a posture, a tendency. This is the importance for me of the cognitive and the emotional, the way the feelingful dimensions are reinforced and experientially grounded, what you call "engendered feeling" or what Bob Armstrong called "form incarnating feeling" . . .

CK: . . . the schooling of the emotions, so to speak, the channeling, the controlling, the expression . . .

SF: . . . as well as the presentationality of them, the aesthetics and expressive display of emotion . . .

CK: . . . but "lift-up-over sounding" is not superserious either. With your Gadamer quote up front and your downtown take on the subject you are insisting that it's playing, basically, that people are playing with the participatory discrepancies and playing with each other . . .

SF: Well, play works out tensions, and is an important socializing force. The impulse to "lift-up-over" sound, to be interactive, is a highly social impulse, just as the impulse to play is a highly social impulse—to overlap a little more, a little less, go from fission to fusion, to dip and bend a note a little more this minute, pull it back to center in the next . . .

CK: I was puzzled by the figure near the end of the essay, with these ratios of environment to sound to social relations, nature to "natural," to human nature, sensate to sensual to sensibility. I kind of had the feel of what all that is about, though the word "natural" in quotes gives me a bit of a problem. But when I get to "in it" and "of it," I'm less sure. What does all that map again?

SF: That diagram is just a structural summary that begins with three analytically separable things: the environment, sound, and social relations. These are the domains that are cognitively and emotionally integrated and united by this "lift-up-over sounding" trope.

The environment is the experience of nature. Sound is the sensing of nature, of the natural, of what is there. Social relations are the conventionalization of human nature. So just as sound, environment, and social relations are related, nature, the natural, and human nature are also brought together and integrated. Similarly, the environment is experienced sensately; sound is a sensual experience; and social relations are about the sensibility of experience. So what is sensate, what is sensual, and what is sensible are also brought together in this formulation.

Sound is the centerpiece of a dual dialectic, with the environment on the one hand, and social relations on the other. This dual dialectic articulates the relations between people and place, articulates the naturalization of place and experience, and emphasizes the central position of the senses in those processes.

CK: They are sharing sounds, so to speak.

SF: Right. So the dialectic between the sound and the social is the rationalizing of what it means to be *of* this place. Rationalization, in Weber's sense, involves a tension between consciousness and identity, between a performed idea and the formation of ideation or ideology. That is the dialectic of sound and the social world. On the other hand, there is a parallel dialectic between the sound and the environment. The environment is the world of nature and of the sensate, but sound is always in a particular relationship to it, because sound is the perceptual means through which one experiences that natural sensuality, through which one is *in* it. What it means to be *in* it is to experience the fluidity between what is nature and what is natural, between what is sensate and what is sensual. That is a process of adaptation, parallel to the process of rationalization. So people are adapting to their environment as they are rationalizing it. They are dealing with being *in* it, parallel to dealing with being *of* it. Identity formation is the rationalization, the notion that you are of this place. Adaptation embodies a fluidity of awareness and inspiration: the perception of a world becomes the appreciation of it . . .

CK: . . . right—perception, appreciation, awareness . . .

SF: The sense of being *in* a place and the sense of being *of* a place is a meeting point for a materialist ecological perspective and a symbolic aesthetic one.

CK: Using the Weberian concept of rationalization, you are arguing— which I think is bold and beautiful—that participation is rational, not, as Lévy-Bruhl says, prelogical or not quite conscious. You are arguing that the rational way to be of the world is to keep all these ratios in balance and in one place. From that you could argue, like Bateson and Berman do, that everything else is schizoid, making divisions where there don't have to be divisions, making logical contradictions where there don't have to be any. So you are arguing for the rationality of participatory consciousness and for deep identification through sound.

SF: I am arguing that adaptation and rationalization are parallel and intersecting, and that every dimension of the dialectic of sound and the environment is parallel to the dialectic between sound and social relations. Sound is more than a mediator. It is oscillating between the environment and social relations. Sound is the locus of the tension between what it means to be in a place and of it. That is what I see as the intersection, or the rub, the tension, between the Weberian notion of rationalization and the biological or evolutionary notion of adaptation.

CK: So if this is how it works for Kaluliland, then what the *hell*—and I use the word deliberately—do you do with *our* social relations, sound and environment connections? Do you think you can put this map on the West and then show the distortions?

SF: No, why should I?

CK: Because I want this for us . . .

SF: . . . and I want it for them! . . .

CK: . . . I want to get us back in sync with the natural world, hearing the birds and the waterflows of our place. We have so many screens between us and that kind of a balancing. What is the corrective? What do you learn from the Kaluli that we can apply here?

SF: Well, I'm interested in the potential of these ideas for critiques of civilization but . . .

CK: . . . but once critiqued, what do we do to get some kind of measure? But what about us?

SF: Well, the hell with you!

CK: Here we are back at hell!

SF: Let me put it this way: What's wrong with honestly acknowledging that this is a passionate exploration of what it might mean to be a very different kind of human being than the one I am? That is what I get off on. I don't want to *be* Kaluli, just to explore . . .

CK: . . . but you *do* want to be as much a part of Kaluli culture as you can . . .

SF: I want to have an experience of that place and those people which challenges the ordering of my senses, the nature of my thinking, the logic of my musicality, the experience of just how profound cultural difference can be . . .

CK: . . . so there is no Kantian categorical imperative, or a moral or political implication or generalization from your Kaluli work that you want to venture outside of your own understanding?

SF: Of course there is an imperative . . .

CK: There has to be, because the Kaluli have been changing dramatically over the years. All of a sudden, Chevron is there; a big money economy has plunged in, and people have stopped doing the ceremonies. Even if it was not a question for what you tell us back here, it is a question for the Kaluli. How are they going to keep their capacity to shock you if they get culture-shocked by the incoming Western onslaught? Both directions—what is happening to the Kaluli and what is happening to us—make it seem like you will have to extend your Kaluli understandings of things into our world, the world that they are being plunged into willy-nilly. I still believe in a future classless revolution or something. We have to break out of the civilization trip into something like a rediversification of cultures in their bioregions. That is on my mind all the time . . .

SF: . . . mine too. Let me clarify it this way: I would *love* to challenge people to be inspired by this, but I don't want to tell them *how* it should inspire them.

CK: Very often you start the day by listening to the birds in Kaluliland conversing on *Voices of the Rainforest,* right?

SF: That gives me a lot of focus; if I concentrate and listen carefully, I can hear something new and different with each listening. I find that humbling and inspiring. So sure, it acts as some sort of corrective to the intellectual arrogance of business-as-always university life.

CK: But that brings me back to my basic question: Why do you feel that you have to live uptown, in a world of high theory? I have kind of rejected that, thumbed my nose at it and said that I am going to be a philistine and a troglodyte, and sit here under a rock and snipe at it. Why do you have to be involved with that at all?

SF: What's so terrible about talking about Meyer, Sapir, Jakobson, and Armstrong *and* James, Aretha, Miles, and Kaluli "lift-up-over sounding" in the same article or, for that matter, the same sentence? Can't you feel the liberating, resistant vibe I get from doing that?

CK: You want to keep it one world?

SF: No! I want to force the issues about uptown and downtown, about "high" and "low," theory and ethnography, about academic and vernacular discourses—like what we're doing here in dialogue. Theory provides one set of interpretive exercises, which come out of a particular cultural and historical situation. Ethnography is a way of depicting a culture, the Kaluli world, as I experience it emerging from practices, ideas, history, biography, and all of that rooted stuff. So what is happening out there on the ground, in the trees, in the rainforest not only can that be part of a dialogue with our theoretical uptown world; it also has something to say to it. It puts a spin on the concept of style, on the notion of aesthetics, on iconicity, on the groove. It talks back and puts a spin on all of those things, a spin which is uniquely and distinctively Kaluli but at the same time speaks to us about the reality of all those theorizations of style. And that spin does have a lot to do with the music that moves me everyday at home, and what I like to dance to . . .

CK: So there is no advocacy that I can tease out of you, no advocating that we do this or that we do that, or that more anthropologists do this, or musicologists do that. You simply do what you need to do to bring the Kaluli and the . . .

SF: This *isn't* advocacy? Give me a break, Chuck!

CK: It could be taken that way, as a version of Kaluli-Western realities and a reconciliation of the cultures . . .

SF: . . . it is an interpretation of the Kaluli world which is permeated by who I am. Dig: I live in a world of listening to Miles Davis at home. I took the world of listening to Miles Davis out there to the rainforest, and when we hit the tenth chorus of "Nefertiti" some Kaluli said, "It's lift-up-over sounding, right *there*," and our worlds collided in a whole new and special and wonderful way. I came back and reread Meyer and Zuckerkandl and Bergson and then said, "Oh, it's lift-up-over sounding, right *there*." Isn't that advocacy— to dissolve uptown and downtown, to read high theory ethno-graphically, through another language, another set of tropes, to hear through another set of ears?

CK: You got to check it all against somebody's—against some cul-ture's—reality. But those uptown guys don't theorize about grooves as such. Do you find any of them, aside from your buddy across the table, theorizing about grooves? Sometimes I think you and I are a little mutual admiration society of two, grooving on each other, voices "lifting-up-over" each other, while the rest of the world could give less than a damn. We don't have a tribe, just a duet going here. Do you really think that grooving is part of the Gadamer play concept?

SF: I think you have more of a sense of mission about all of this . . .

CK: . . . and you don't have that sense?

SF: . . . while it is a long, continuous ethnographic shock for me . . .

CK: . . . but once shocked, you have a mission. You have a mission! Don't be coy with having no mission here! When you say, "Come on down to Austin and let's lift-up-over," you want to transform scholarship, you want to transform the whole way that high theory is authenticated and comes down from the mountain on the tablets. You want to cut through a lot of that to make it more Kaluli-like, the way knowledge gets perceived and generated. Let's get the emotions back into it, and let's get the whole picture here!

SF: OK! Yes, I find it inspiring that in the Kaluli world multiple voices have to do with engagement. I like everybody telling their story at the same time. What other people might find to be the cacophony of this society is what I find to be the profound sociability of it, the thing that gives me a certain sense of how there can be a wonderfully intense pleasure verging on disorder. And scholarship for me is also about the humility of dealing with this level of disorder . . .

CK: . . . discrepancy, disorder, difference. You value those things too . . .

SF: . . . exactly . . .

CK: When you came back last time from Kaluliland, you were in tears to me on the phone. You were choking, because things that you had assumed were the Kaluli style, were the way, nonunisons and so on, were going fast. The ukuleles were now beginning to strum in unison, and what had been cooperative basketball—let's all help each other put the ball in the basket—had begun to get a competitive edge. Or you could see everybody looking to Chevron for a salary in the future, and asking can we get everybody into a mission school fast enough to learn enough English to get jobs. You are going to have something corresponding to nostalgia or hurt or pain if you go back to Kaluliland next time and they strum the ukuleles like Freddy Green instead of like Kaluli.

SF: Yes, there's pain, a new and different kind of chaos for me, a confusion about why people are making the choices that they are making now. How many of those choices are being imposed and how much of it are they doing themselves? How much of what I am about to experience in Bosavi will I not be ready for? After all, I have depicted the Kaluli as having a musically coherent kind of universe. And the question that you can throw at me is, if it's so damn coherent, why aren't they resisting, why aren't they out there blowing up the oil fields and doing their "lift-up-over sounding"? Why isn't "lift-up-over sounding" helping them stay strong? Why do they want to give up gardening, give up the forest, and buy tinned fish at the store? Why does everybody want cash? What does that have to do with this particular model of social relations and sociability that I've laid out? To what extent are people making choices now that are in any way adaptive? Or are we just seeing something which is an extremely profound pattern in Papua New Guinea, where people are extremely dramatic and expressive and make a lot of quick changes, like dropping ceremonies and then reviving them?

CK: The beauty of this fellowship is that you are going to be able to be in and out of there to ask those questions at this absolutely crucial moment of the Kaluli dialectic with the West.

Further Comments

p. 151 . . . *the mystique of the conservatory* . . .Henry Kingsbury, *Music, Talent, and Performance: A Conservatory Cultural System* (Philadelphia: Temple University Press, 1988). [CK]

p. 152 . . . *still back there with Kolinski* . . . Mieczyslaw Kolinski (1901–1981) worked with Erich M. von Hornbostel from 1926 to 1933, completing his Ph.D. in 1930. Fleeing Nazism he moved from Prague; lived in Belgium from 1938 to 1951; settled in New York in 1951, where he worked as a composer, pianist, music therapist, and educator; and later moved to Canada, teaching at the University of Toronto from 1966 to 1976. Kolinski is best known for his voluminous transcriptions and his rigorous methods for the description and analysis of scale, contour, tempo, and meter. Some of Kolinski's best-known methodological and analytic studies are found in "The Evaluation of Tempo," *Ethnomusicology* 3 (1959):45–57; "Consonance and Dissonance," *Ethnomusicology* 6 (1962):66–74; "The Structure of Melodic Movement: A New Method of Analysis," in *Studies in Ethnomusicology,* ed. M. Kolinski, 95–120 (New York: Oak Publications, 1965); "Recent Trends in Ethnomusicology," *Ethnomusicology* 11 (1967):1–24; "Barbara Allen: Tonal vs. Melodic Structure," *Ethnomusicology* 12, no. 2 (1968):208–18, 13, no. 1 (1969):1–73; and "A Cross-Cultural Approach to Metro-Rhythmic Patterns," *Ethnomusicology* 17, no. 3 (1973):494–506.

Further perspective on Kolinski's analytic work can be gleaned from the festschrift dedicated to him, *Cross-Cultural Perspectives on Music,* ed. Robert Falk and Timothy Rice (Toronto: University of Toronto Press, 1982). Also see the obituary by Beverly Cavanaugh in *Ethnomusicology* 25, no. 2 (1981):285–86. Alan P. Merriam's method of musical transcription and analysis was derived from Kolinski and mediated through his teacher Melville Herskovits, for whom Kolinski transcribed many African and African-American musical materials. Merriam's approach is most apparent in the analysis section of his *Ethnomusicology of the Flathead Indians* (Chicago: Aldine, 1967); see Kolinski's review in *Ethnomusicology* 14, no. 1 (1970): 77–99. Although they disagreed on many aspects of ethnomusicology, Merriam defended Kolinski's emphasis on comparison; see Merriam, "On Objections to Comparison in Ethnomusicology," in *Cross-Cultural Perspectives on Music,* ed. Robert Falk and Timothy Rice, 174–89 (Toronto: University of Toronto Press, 1982).

Marcia Herndon's paper "Analysis: The Herding of Sacred Cows?" *Ethnomusicology* 18, no. 2 (1974):219–62, was a major critical reassessment of Kolinski's approach. Kolinski replied in "Herndon's Verdict on Analysis: *Tabula Rasa.*" Ethnomusicology 20, no. 1 (1976):1–22; Herndon answered with "Reply to Kolinski: *Taurus Omicida,*" *Ethnomusicology* 20, no. 2 (1976): 217–31; Kolinski responded again in "Final Reply to Herndon," *Ethnomusicology* 21, no. 1 (1977):75–83.

Related to Kolinski's approach is that of George Herzog (1901–1984). Herzog was an assistant to Erich M. von Hornbostel at the Berlin Phonogram-Archiv and emigrated to the United States in 1925. He studied with Franz Boas at Columbia and was at the University of Chicago from 1929 to 1931 and Yale from 1932 to 1935. He received his Ph.D. from Columbia in 1937, with a dissertation on Pima and Pueblo musical styles, and taught at Columbia until 1948 when he went to Indiana University, there establishing an anthropology department. From Berlin Phonogram-Archiv materials he had taken first to Columbia, he later founded Indiana's Archives for Traditional Music. He continued to work on southwestern American Indian music, as well as African and European musics, retiring from Indiana in 1962. Herzog's approach to music analysis developed differently from that of Kolinski because of his fieldwork, his training as a linguist and anthropologist, and his interest in the relationships between melody and text, or language and music more generally. His influential analytic papers include "The Yuman Musical Style," *Journal of American Folklore* 41, no. 160 (1928):183–231; "Speech Melody and Primitive Music," *Musical Quarterly* 20 (1934):452–66; "A Comparison of Pueblo and Pima Musical Styles," *Journal of American Folklore* 49, no. 194 (1936):284–417; "Drum Signalling in a West African Tribe," *Word* 1 (1945):217–38, reprinted in *Language in Culture and Society,* ed. Dell Hymes, 312–29 (New York: Harper and Row, 1964); "Song," in *Standard Dictionary of Folklore, Mythology and Legend,* ed. Maria Leach, 2:1032–50, (New York: Funk and Wagnalls, 1950). See also Bruno Nettl, "George Herzog: An Eightieth Birthday Appreciation," *Ethnomusicology* 25, no. 3 (1981):499–500, and David McAllester, "George Herzog: In Memoriam," *Ethnomusicology* 29, no. 1 (1985):86–87.

On the application of Herzog's analytic framework and transcription methods, see the work of his students, especially Bruno Nettl, *Music in Primitive Culture* (Cambridge: Harvard University Press, 1956) and *Theory and Method in Ethnomusicology* (New York: Free Press, 1964); also the analysis in David P. McAllester, *Peyote Music* (Viking Fund Publications in Anthropology, no. 13, 1949) and *Enemy Way Music: A Study of Social and Esthetic Values as Seen in Navaho Music* (Cambridge, Mass.: Peabody Museum, 1954; Papers of the Peabody Museum of American Archeology and Ethnology, Harvard University, vol. 41, no. 3, Reports of the Rimrock Project Values Series, Number 3). [SF]

p. 152 *Mantle Hood was already doing his thing . . .* Mantle Hood (b. 1918) completed his Ph.D. on Javanese modal practices in 1954. He taught at UCLA from 1954 to 1975 and initiated and directed its Institute of Ethnomusicology beginning in 1961; during this period he worked closely with Charles Seeger. Since 1976 he has taught at the University of Maryland. His

emphasis on the role of performance practice in ethnomusicological training and on ethnomusicological institutes as international conservatory
environments made a major impact on the field in the 1960s and 1970s.
Hood's perspectives on performance and on field and laboratory methods
are expressed in a number of influential publications: "Training and
Research Methods in Ethnomusicology," *Ethnomusicology Newsletter* 11
(1957):2–8; "The Challenge of 'Bi-Musicality,'" *Ethnomusicology* 4, no. 1
(1960):55–59; "Musical Significance," *Ethnomusicology* 7, no. 3 (1963):
187–92; "Music the Unknown," in *Musicology,* ed. F. Harrison, C. Palisca,
and M. Hood, 215–326 (Englewood Cliffs: Prentice-Hall, 1963); "Ethnomusicology," in *Harvard Dictionary of Music,* ed. Willi Apel, 298–300, 2d
ed. (Cambridge: Harvard University Press, 1969); "Universal Attributes of
Music," *World of Music,* 19, no. 1/2 (1977):63–69; and especially, *The
Ethnomusicologist* (New York: Macmillan, 1971; Kent, Ohio: Kent State
University Press, 1981). [SF]

p. 153 . . . *a more Freudian liberation psychology.* The liberation psychology I
have in mind is described by Norman O. Brown in *Life against Death: The
Psychoanalytic Meaning of History* (New York: Vintage, 1959), *Love's Body*
(New York: Vintage, 1968), and *Closing Time* (New York: Vintage, 1974).
Dorothy Dinnerstein's *The Mermaid and the Minotaur: Sexual Arrangements
and Human Malaise* (New York: Harper Colophon, 1976) is in many ways a
sequel to the Brown books and a great way to start thinking about the origins and increasing virulence of sexism, the nurturance of children across
cultures and historical periods, and the possible importance of early musical learning in relation to patriarchy. See also further comments following
dialogue 3, "Commodified Grooves," at the reference to page 311.

I have been wondering for some years now about the conspicuous lack
of research and writing about music and sex across species and cultures.
Few ethnomusicologists are exploring the implications of the male hump-
back whale's apparent monopoly on song and the fact that male birds do
most of the singing, probably for fear of being labeled biodeterminist or
worse, but no one knows what the long whale song will turn out to be
about or why some bird species have songs "in excess" of known or as yet
conceivable biological functions. There have also been no detailed comparisons of the "flute house complex" in Papua New Guinea and the Amazon, and little refinement or revision of Alan Lomax's hypotheses about
vocal qualities, socialization and sexual repression. Why has there been no
Music in Nightly Life project to parallel our Music in Daily Life work at
SUNY/Buffalo? [CK]

Music and sex across cultures? Let's start with the voice. Reading the
chapter on "Hearing" in F. Gonzalez-Crussi's *The Five Senses* (New York:
Vintage, 1989), 35–61, I was struck by his references to the eroticism of
the voice and his account of the dramatic rise in telephone pay-for-sex/
fantasy call-in lines. I could find no real information about how this kind of

erotic vocal performance worked, so I called some 900 numbers advertised in the Austin newspapers and, after a lot of bumbling (ever try explaining that your particular turn-on isn't pretending to be a professor interviewing a sex worker?), finally convinced a few people to just talk with me about their work. In the first half-dozen interviews one thing was very clear: the women who do this work know a lot about voice texture and quality. They imitated different kinds of voices for different turn-ons and told me that many of their clients included talk about smoking cigarettes or drinking liquor in their fantasies. The husky, sexy deeper voice, associated with smoking, pouting lips, and exaggerated sucking lip gestures, was one iden- tifiable complex. Another was the smooth, liquid, sing-song higher voice, connected to drink and licking or rimming the tongue around the lips. These sorts of connections between voice types, mouth, lip, and tongue gestures, and inhaling or drinking are just a beginning in what might be an elaborate set of body competencies and performance styles relevant to this line of work and to some extent shared by other sorts of vocal performers who manipulate acoustic features to communicate intimacy, desire, sensu- ous involvement, and pleasure. [SF]

p. 153 . . . *the contemporary critique now leveled at musicology* . . . A survey of the current critical musicology literature includes Carolyn Abbate, *Unsung Voices: Opera and Musical Narrative in the Nineteenth Century* (Princeton: Princeton University Press, 1991); Jacques Attali, *Noise: The Political Econ- omy of Music* (Minneapolis: University of Minnesota Press, 1985); Christo- pher Ballantine, *Music and Its Social Meanings* (New York: Gordon and Breach, 1984); Judith Becker, "Is Western Art Music Superior?" *Musical Quarterly* 72, no. 3 (1968): 341–59; Georgina Born, "The Ethnography of a Computer Music Research Institute: Modernism, Postmodernism, and New Technology in Contemporary Music Culture" (unpublished Ph.D. disserta- tion; Department of Anthropology, University of London, 1989); Alice Cash, "Feminist Theory and Music: Toward a Common Language" (con- ference report), *Journal of Musicology* 9, no. 4 (1991): 521–32; Michael Chanan, "The Trajectory of Western Music; or, As Mahler Said, The Music is Not in the Notes," *Media, Culture, and Society* 3 (1981): 219–41; Marcia Citron, "Gender, Professionalism, and the Musical Canon," *Journal of Musi- cology* 8, no. 1 (1990): 102–17; Catherine Clément, *Opera: or, The Undoing of Women* (Minneapolis: University of Minnesota Press, 1988); Richard Lep- pert, *Music and Image: Domesticity, Ideology and Socio-Cultural Formation in Eighteenth-century England* (Cambridge: Cambridge University Press, 1988) and "Music, Representation, and Social Order in Early-Modern Europe," *Cultural Critique* 12 (1989): 25–55; Richard Leppert and Susan McClary, eds., *Music and Society: The Politics of Composition and Performance* (New York: Cambridge University Press, 1987); Susan McClary, *Feminine Endings: Music, Gender, and Sexuality* (Minneapolis: University of Minnesota Press, 1991); Susan McClary and Robert Walser, "Start Making Sense: Musicology

Wrestles with Rock," in *On Record,* ed. Simon Frith and Andrew Goodwin, 277–92 (New York: Pantheon, 1990); Christopher Norris, ed., *Music and the Politics of Culture* (New York: St. Martins Press, 1989); Charles Seeger, *Studies in Musicology 1935–1975* (Berkeley: University of California Press, 1977); John Shepherd, *Music as Social Text* (London: Polity Press, 1991); John Shepherd, Phil Virden, Graham Vulliamy, and Trevor Wishart, *Whose Music? A Sociology of Musical Languages* (New Brunswick: Transaction, 1977); Christopher Small, *Music–Society–Education* (London: John Calder, 1977); Ruth Solie, "What Do Feminists Want? A Reply to Peter van den Toorn," *Journal of Musicology* 9, no. 4 (1991):399–411; Rose Subotnick, *Developing Variations: Style and Ideology in Western Music* (Minneapolis: University of Minnesota Press, 1991); Richard Taruskin, "The Pastness of the Present and the Presence of the Past," in *Authenticity and Early Music,* ed. N. Kenyon, 137–210 (London: Oxford University Press, 1988); Gary Tomlinson, "The Web of Culture: A Context for Musicology," *Nineteenth Century Music* 7 (1982):350–62, "The Historian, the Performer, and Aesthetic Meaning in Music," in *Authenticity and Early Music,* ed. N. Kenyon, 115–36 (London: Oxford University Press, 1988), and *Music in Renaissance Magic* (Chicago: University of Chicago Press, 1993); Leo Treitler, *Music and the Historical Imagination* (Cambridge: Harvard University Press, 1989), and "The Power of Positivist Thinking," *Journal of the American Musicological Society* 42 (1989):375–402; Peter van den Toorn, "Politics, Feminism, and Contemporary Music Theory," *Journal of Musicology* 9, no. 3 (1991): 275–99. [SF]

p. 154 . . . *the better we get* . . . I have been doing interviews over the past two or three years, mostly over the phone, with jazz rhythm-section players (Jimmy McGriff, Jimmy Gomes, Steve Swallow, Red Mitchell, Milt Hinton, Donald Bailey, Vernell Fournier, Herb Ellis, Ray Bryant, Jackie Bayard, Joe Blum, Maurice Sinclair, and Sabu Adeyola, among others), and each person has a different version of where the groove comes from. [CK]

p. 154 . . . *These things are out of awareness* . . . See Edward T. Hall's books for more on out-of-awareness culture: *The Silent Language* (Garden City, N.Y.: Doubleday, 1959); *The Hidden Dimension* (Garden City, N.Y.: Doubleday, 1966); *Beyond Culture* (New York: Doubleday, 1976); *The Dance of Life* (New York: Doubleday, 1983); and his recent autobiography, *An Anthropology of Everyday Life* (New York: Doubleday, 1992). [CK and SF]

p. 156 . . . *Weberian rationalization and demystification* . . . Max Weber, *The Rational and Social Foundations of Music* (Carbondale: Southern Illinois University Press, 1958), is largely about the history of tuning the piano to eliminate the participatory discrepancies. Ferenc Feher views Weber's argument as a polemic against Nietzsche's *The Birth of Tragedy* and reviews the efforts of Adorno and Bloch to salvage Western music; see Feher, "Weber and the Rationalization of Music," in *Dialectical Anthropology: Essays in*

Honor of Stanley Diamond, ed. Christine Gailey, 309–26 (Gainesville: University Press of Florida, 1992). See also Hugo Zemp's 1986 film *Yootz and Yodel,* documenting the decline of the wild Swiss "yootz" into tame choral yodeling; Roderic Knight's analysis of "Vibrato Octaves: Tunings and Modes of the Mande Balo and Kora," *Progress Reports in Ethnomusicology* 3, no. 4 (1991):1–49; and Chris Small's discussion of William Billings and the open choral traditions of North America in "A Different Drummer," chap. 6 in *Music-Society-Education* (London: John Calder, 1977). Wherever bourgeois values go, the effort to squeeze the life out of sounds and turn them into rational, controlled notes is sure to follow. [CK]

p. 158 . . . *spilling the drink was part of the sound.* "Milwaukee," chap. 5 in Charles Keil, Angeliki Keil, and Dick Blau, *Polka Happiness* (Philadelphia: Temple University Press, 1992), contains an analysis of why Slovenian style polkas in the smooth, streamlined Frankie Yankovic manner became hegemonic in that city. To make a long story short, there is an Apollonian or "proletarian perfectionist" tendency in many people's-music traditions that is highly intolerant of "false starts," "swooping glissandos," "broken strings," and "spilled drinks." Both the recording studios of mass culture and the bourgeois idealism of high culture can reinforce that proletarian perfectionist tendency in a variety of contexts. [CK]

p. 159 . . . *a whole other way of apprehending non-Western . . . music.* John Shepherd, Phil Virden, Graham Vulliamy, and Trevor Wishart, *Whose Music? A Sociology of Musical Languages* (New Brunswick: Transaction, 1977); Andrew Chester, "For a Rock Aesthetic," *New Left Review,* no. 59 (January–February 1970):83–87, and "Second Thoughts on a Rock Aesthetic: The Band," *New Left Review,* no. 62 (July–August 1970):75–82, reprinted in *On Record,* ed. Simon Frith and Andrew Goodwin (New York: Pantheon, 1990). In the latter article, Chester argues that, in contrast to extensional Western classical music, "rock however follows, like many non-European musics, the path of *intensional* development. In this mode of construction the basic musical units (played/sung notes) are not combined through space and time as simple elements into complex structures. The simple entity is that constituted by the parameters of melody, harmony and beat, while the complex is built up by modulation of the basic notes, and by inflection of the basic beat. (The language of this modulation and inflection derives partly from conventions internal to the music, partly from the conventions of spoken language and gesture, partly from physiological factors.)" Chester does not develop the ideas of "modulation of basic notes" (what we call texture and timbre) and "inflection of basic beat" (our process and groove) much beyond this single, suggestive, parenthetical sentence before going on to analyze rock genres and class forces, but this does seem to mark the emergence of a "motion and feeling through" model in British criticism. [CK]

p. 161 . . . *the point of view of the makers of the music* . . . A good overview of
the theories of communication that shaped the field in the 1960s, 1970s,
and 1980s can be found in John Fiske, *Introduction to Communication Stud-*
ies, 2d ed. (New York: Routledge, 1990). Good readers include Michael
Gurevitch et. al., eds., *Culture, Society and the Media* (London: Methuen,
1982), and Richard Collins, ed., *Media, Culture and Society: A Critical Reader*
(Beverly Hills: Sage Publications, 1986). Also see John Fiske, *Television Cul-*
ture (London: Routledge, 1989), and Constance Penley and Andrew Ross,
eds., *Technoculture* (Minneapolis: University of Minnesota Press, 1991). For
a more comprehensive overview see Erik Barnouw, ed., *Encyclopedia of*
Communications, 4 vols. (New York: Oxford University Press, 1989); the
journals *Media, Culture and Society,* and *Journal of Communications* usually
carry interesting debates and case studies. [SF]

p. 162 . . . *I went from reading Goffman* . . . Erving Goffman (1922–1982)
developed an approach to interactional dramaturgy that profoundly
affected the course of microsociology, ethology, and the anthropology of
interaction. His most influential statements are *The Presentation of Self in*
Everyday Life (Garden City: Doubleday, 1959), *Stigma: Notes on the Man-*
agement of Spoiled Identity (Englewood Cliffs: Prentice Hall, 1963), *Interac-*
tion Ritual: Essays on Face-to-Face Behavior (New York: Doubleday, 1967),
Strategic Interaction (Oxford: Blackwell, 1970), *Relations in Public* (New
York: Harper and Row, 1971), *Frame Analysis: An Essay on the Organization*
of Experience (New York: Harvard University Press, 1974). *Gender Advertise-*
ments (New York: Macmillan, 1979), and *Forms of Talk* (Philadelphia: University of Pennsylvania Press, 1981). [SF]

p. 164 *Lenny Meyer and the psychologists* . . . On the relationship of Leonard
Meyer's framework for style analysis to its cognitive implications, see
Bertram Rosner and Leonard B. Meyer, "The Perceptual Roles of Melodic
Process, Contour and Form," *Music Perception* 4 (1986):1–39, and
Leonard B. Meyer and Bertram Rosner, "Melodic Processes and the Percep-
tion of Music," in *The Psychology of Music,* ed. Diana Deutsch, 316–41
(New York: Academic Press, 1982).

    The general literature on music cognition, psychology, and perception is
vast, but some of the basic reading can be found in two journals, *Music*
Perception, and *Psychology of Music,* and in the following books: MacDon-
ald Critchley and R. A. Henson, eds., *Music and the Brain* (London: William
Heinemann Medical Books Ltd., 1977); John Booth Davies, *The Psychology*
of Music (London: Hutchison, 1978); Diana Deutsch, ed., *Psychology of*
Music (New York: Academic Press, 1982); Manfred Clynes, ed., *Music, Mind*
and Brain (New York: Plenum, 1982); P. Howell, I. Cross, and R. West, eds.,
Musical Structure and Cognition (New York: Academic Press, 1985); Fred
Lerdahl and Ray Jackendoff, *A Generative Grammar of Tonal Music* (Cam-
bridge, Mass.: MIT Press, 1983); Mary Louise Serafine, *Music as Cognition*

(New York: Columbia University Press, 1988); Wayne Slawson, *Sound Color* (Berkeley: University of California Press, 1985); John Sloboda, *The Musical Mind: The Cognitive Science of Music* (New York: Oxford University Press, 1985); John Sloboda, ed., *Generative Processes in Music: The Psychology of Performance, Improvisation and Composition* (New York: Oxford University Press, 1988); Carol Krumhansl, *The Cognitive Foundations of Musical Pitch* (New York: Oxford University Press, 1990); and Albert Bregman, *Auditory Scene Analysis* (Cambridge, Mass.: MIT Press, 1990).

For a perspective which includes an explicit ethnomusicological slant, see W. Jay Dowling and Dane Harwood, *Music Cognition* (New York: Academic Press, 1986). Also see Dane Harwood, "Universals in Music: A Perspective from Cognitive Psychology," *Ethnomusicology* 20, no. 3 (1976): 521–33; James Kippen, "An Ethnomusicological Approach to the Analysis of Musical Cognition," *Music Perception* 5, no. 2 (1987):173–96; Edward Kessler, Christa Hansen, and Roger Shepard, "Tonal Schemata in the Perception of Music in Bali and the West," *Music Perception* 2, no. 2 (1984): 131–65. [SF]

p. 165 . . . *music in his mind all the time* . . . During the Music in Daily Life project we came upon a few people who claimed to have music going on in their heads constantly: a young concert violinist ("May" in Susan Crafts, Daniel Cavicchi, Charles Keil, eds., *My Music* [Middletown, Conn.: Wesleyan University Press, 1993]); Andy Byron, drummer and student in one of the research seminars; and three or four others out of almost two hundred people interviewed. A larger number of other people, myself included, have a melody or "riff" of some kind going on almost all the time. I also whistle tunes a lot without being aware that I am whistling (people say hello to me from around corners as they hear me coming). I suspect that surveys and future research will show that "music in the head" or "on the brain," a constant or almost constant "sound track," accompanies a lot of lives without intruding. If we were trying to interpret this sound track in any way it would probably drive us nuts. [CK]

p. 166 . . . *studying something like the* gisalo *ceremony* . . . The Kaluli *gisalo* (alternate spelling *gisaro*) ceremony is described in Edward L. Schieffelin, *The Sorrow of the Lonely and the Burning of the Dancers* (New York: St. Martin's Press, 1976). Yasuko Ichioka's Japanese public television film, *Gisaro: The Sorrow and the Burning* (Tokyo: NAV, 1986), is based on this book. A complementary musical analysis can be found in "Song that Moves Men to Tears," chapter 5 in my *Sound and Sentiment: Birds, Weeping, Poetics and Song in Kaluli Expression*, 2d ed. (Philadelphia: University of Pennsylvania Press, 1990).

Additional information about Kaluli emotion, especially the social construction of Kaluli anger, can be found in Bambi B. Schieffelin, *The Give and Take of Everyday Life: Language Socialization of Kaluli Children* (New York: Cambridge University Press, 1990); Edward L. Schieffelin, "Anger, Grief and

Shame: Towards a Kaluli Ethnopsychology," in *Person, Self and Experience: Exploring Pacific Ethnopsychologies*, ed. G. White and J. Kirkpatrick, 168–82 (Berkeley: University of California Press, 1985). [SF]

p. 166 . . . *how grief can move to anger, then maybe to laughter* . . . Reevaluation counseling is a peer counseling self-help movement that has developed an impressive body of theory about discharging feelings in order to free thinking and behavior from the rigidity caused by past hurts. For more information contact Rational Island Publishers, P. O. Box 2081, Main Office Station, Seattle, Washington 98111. [CK]

p. 167 *Jung said that you build a unique self* . . . See the discussion of Carl Jung in Morris Berman, *The Reenchantment of the World* (New York: Bantam, 1984). See also Jung's own writings: *The Essential Jung*, ed. Anthony Storr (Princeton: Princeton University Press, 1983); *The Spirit in Man, Art and Literature* (New York: Bollingen Foundation, 1966); *Man and His Symbols* (Garden City: Doubleday, 1964). In William McGuire and R. F. C. Hull, eds., *C. G. Jung Speaking: Interviews and Encounters* (Princeton: Princeton University Press, 1986), Jung reveals his exhaustion and irritation with music because it is "dealing with such deep archetypal material, and those who play don't realize this" and his hatred of "background music" as one of many mediated distractions reducing the ability of children and adults to concentrate (McGuire and Hull 1986:274, 249). [CK]

p. 168 . . . *Arne Naess's "deep ecology"* . . . Is it just a coincidence that David Rothenberg, an improvising philosopher-musician with an ear for grooves, is the person to translate Arne Naess into English? See Naess, *Ecology, Community and Lifestyle: Outline of an Ecosophy* (Cambridge: Cambridge University Press, 1989). See also Rothenberg's book of interviews with Naess, *Is it Painful to Think? Conversations with Arne Naess* (Minneapolis: University of Minnesota Press, 1993). [CK]

p. 169 . . . *two trumpets to get polka happiness.* For more on polkas see Charles Keil, Angeliki Keil, and Dick Blau, *Polka Happiness* (Philadelphia: Temple University Press, 1992); Victor Green, *A Passion for Polka* (Berkeley: University of California Press, 1992); Charles Frank Emmons, "Economic and Political Leadership in Chicago's Polonia: Sources of Ethnic Persistence and Mobility" (unpublished Ph.D. dissertation, University of Illinois at Chicago Circle, 1971); Robert Dolgan, *The Polka King: The Life of Frankie Yankovic* (Cleveland: Dillon/Liederbach, 1977); James Leary, *Polka Music, Ethnic Music: A Report on Wisconsin's Polka Traditions* (Wisconsin Folk Museum, Bulletin 1, 1991); James P. Leary and Richard March, "Dutchman Bands: Genre, Ethnicity, and Pluralism in the Upper Midwest," in *Creative Ethnicity*, ed. Stephen Stern and John Allan Cicala, 21–43 (Logan: Utah State University Press, 1991); Robert Walser, "The Polish-American Polka Mass: Music of Postmodern Ethnicity" (paper presented at the Sonneck Society sixteenth annual conference, Toronto, 1990); Janice Ellen Kleeman, "The Origins and

Stylistic Development of Polish-American Polka Music" (unpublished Ph.D. dissertation, Department of Music, University of California at Berkeley, 1982); Mary Spaulding, "The Irene Olszewski Orchestra: A Connecticut Band" (unpublished M.M. thesis, Department of Music, Wesleyan University, 1986). [CK]

Rob Walser suggested juxtaposing the points in these dialogues about the energy of polka parts "rubbing together" with Susan McClary's discussion of erotic friction in seventeenth-century Italian music in *Feminine Endings* (Minneapolis: University of Minnesota Press, 1991). Discussing the historical character of gender encoding in musical structures, she writes that like Shakespeare's erotic dialogues—analyzed by Stephen Greenblatt as aesthetic analogues to the medicinal theory that male and female partners had to be mutually aroused to ejaculation in order to conceive and reproduce—the textures of composers from Monteverdi to Corelli involve "trios in which two equal voices rub up against each other, pressing into dissonances that achingly resolve only yet into other knots, reaching satiety only at conclusions. This interactive texture (and its attendant metaphors) is largely displaced in music after the seventeenth century by individualistic, narrative monologues" (McClary 1991:37). McClary refers to the seventeenth century in the West; yet the global prevalence of nonindividualistic, narrative dialogues, duels, and textural interactions and discrepancies is precisely what Keil finds compelling in so many popular and regional styles through the ages and is clearly the centerpiece of Kaluli "lift-up-over sounding" as well (chapter 4). [SF]

p. 172 . . . *on the high theory side . . . Roman Jakobson*—Roman Jakobson (1896–1982) came to the United States in 1941 and taught at Columbia University from 1944 to 1949, at Harvard from 1949 to 1966, and at MIT from 1957 to 1982. His impact on the development of linguistics and semiotics continues to be extraordinary and his enormous corpus of writings has been gathered and republished in a multivolume series, *Selected Writings*, appearing in stages between 1962 and 1987. In the context of the development of poetics see especially vol. 5, *On Verse, Its Masters and Explorers* (The Hague: Mouton, 1979), and vol. 3, *Poetry of Grammar and Grammar of Poetry* (The Hague: Mouton, 1981). These volumes include his classic papers on the autoreferentiality of poetics and on the pervasiveness of grammatical parallelism. The parallelism concept, in which Jakobson details how canons of repetition with slight variation exist at all linguistic levels, is about as close as any linguist has come to the notion of the "groove": patterned expectancies in time established by regularities of sonic, syntactic, or semantic elements set the ground for emergent figures. This patterned modification of existing elements in alternation with their expected repetition defines the particular groove Jakobson called "poetics."

Comprehensive reviews of Jakobson's contributions to anthropological and linguistic concerns in poetics can be found in James Fox, "Roman

Jakobson and the Comparative Study of Parallelism," in *Roman Jakobson: Echoes of His Scholarship*, ed. D. Armstrong and C. H. van Schooneveld, 59–90 (Lisse: Peter de Ridder, 1977), and Steven Caton, "Contributions of Roman Jakobson," *Annual Review of Anthropology* 16 (1987):223–60. On significant extensions in linguistic anthropology see Michael Silverstein, "Shifters, Linguistic Categories, and Cultural Description," in *Meaning in Anthropology*, ed. Keith Basso and Henry Selby, 11–55 (Albuquerque: University of New Mexico Press, 1976), and "On the Pragmatic Poetry of Prose: Parallelism, Repetition, and Cohesive Structure in the Time Course of Dyadic Conversation," in *Meaning, Form and Use in Context: Linguistic Applications*, ed. Deborah Schiffrin, 181–99 (Washington, D.C.: Georgetown University Press, 1984). Also see Dell Hymes, *Foundations in Sociolinguistics: An Ethnographic Approach* (Philadelphia: University of Pennsylvania Press, 1974). [SF]

p. 173 . . . *important insight from semiotics* . . . Semiotics, the study of sign phenomena, encompasses two intellectual strands, one deriving from the linguist Ferdinand de Saussure, whose *Course in General Linguistics* (1916: New York: Philosophical Library, 1959) proposed a dyadic signification process relating signifier (sign vehicle) and signified (meaning), and the other from the philosopher Charles Sanders Peirce, whose *Collected Papers* (Cambridge: Harvard University Press, 1931–58) proposed a triadic relationship between representamen (sign vehicle) and the object to which it points, as perceived by an interpretant.

On the Saussurean stream, its literary and critical as well as anthropological deployment, see Roland Barthes, *Elements of Semiology* (London: Cape, 1968); Jonathan Culler, *Saussure* (London: Fontana, 1976); Pierre Guiraud, *Semiology* (London: Routledge, Kegan Paul, 1975); T. Hawkes, *Structuralism and Semiotics* (London: Methuen, 1977); Edmund Leach, *Lévi-Strauss* (London: Fontana, 1974); and J. Woollacott, *Messages and Meanings* (Milton Keynes: Open University Press, 1977).

On the Peircian stream, with particular emphases on the variety and diversity of iconic (physical resemblance) and indexical (spatial-temporal contiguity) signs in language and other cultural forms, see Thomas Sebeok, ed., *A Perfusion of Signs* (Bloomington: Indiana University Press, 1977) and *Sight, Sound and Sense* (Bloomington: Indiana University Press, 1978); Elizabeth Mertz and Richard Parmentier, eds., *Semiotic Mediation: Sociocultural and Psychological Perspectives* (New York: Academic Press, 1985); and Greg Urban, *A Discourse-Centered Approach to Culture* (Austin: University of Texas Press, 1991) and "Semiotics and Anthropological Linguistics," *International Encyclopedia of Linguistics*, 3:406–7 (New York: Oxford University Press, 1991).

For broader overviews, see Umberto Eco, *A Theory of Semiotics* (Bloomington: Indiana University Press, 1979); Thomas A. Sebeok, ed., *Encyclopedic Dictionary of Semiotics*, 3 vols. (Berlin: Mouton de Gruyter, 1986);

Thomas A. Sebeok, *The Tell-Tale Sign: A Survey of Semiotics* (Lisse: Peter de Ridder, 1975) and *Semiotics in the United States* (Bloomington: Indiana University Press, 1991); Winfried Noth, *Handbook of Semiotics* (Bloomington: Indiana University Press, 1990); Victorio Tejera, *Semiotics from Peirce to Barthes: A Conceptual Introduction* (New York: E. J. Brill, 1988); Robert Hodge and Gunther Kress, *Social Semiotics* (Cambridge: Polity Press, 1988).

On semiotics of art and aesthetics see Paul Garvin, ed., *A Prague School Reader on Esthetics* (Washington, D.C.: Georgetown University Press, 1964); Ladislav Matejka and Irwin Titunik, *Semiotics of Art* (Cambridge, Mass.: MIT Press, 1976); Wendy Steiner, ed., *The Sign in Music and Literature* (Austin: University of Texas Press, 1981).

Some significant musicological and ethnomusicological excursions into semiology and semiotics include Jean-Jacques Nattiez, "The Contribution of Musical Semiotics to the Semiotic Discussion in General," in *A Perfusion of Signs*, ed. T. A. Sebeok, 121–42 (Bloomington: Indiana University Press, 1977), and *Music and Discourse: Toward a Semiology of Music* (Princeton: Princeton University Press, 1990); David Lidov, "Nattiez's Semiotics of Music," *Canadian Journal of Research in Semiotics* 5, no. 2 (1977): 13–54; Charles Boilès, "Processes of Musical Semiosis," *Yearbook for Traditional Music* 14 (1982): 24–44; John Blacking, "The Problem of Ethnic Perceptions in the Semiotics of Music," in *The Sign in Music and Literature*, ed. Wendy Steiner, 203–15 (Austin: University of Texas Press, 1981). [SF]

p. 178 . . . *uptown and downtown, . . . theory and ethnography* . . . On high and low, elite and vernacular, see Lawrence Levine, *Highbrow-Lowbrow: The Emergence of Cultural Hierarchy in America* (Cambridge: Harvard University Press, 1988); George Lipsitz, *Time Passages: Collective Memory and American Popular Culture*, chaps. 1 and 2 (Minneapolis: University of Minnesota Press, 1990); Andrew Ross, *No Respect: Intellectuals and Popular Culture* (New York: Routledge, 1989); and Jon Weiner, *Professors, Politics and Pop* (New York: Verso, 1991). [SF]

p. 179 . . . *strum . . . like Freddy Green instead of like Kaluli.* The Kaluli will probably be doing the "Hawaiian strum" or the "Pacific rim strum" long before they tune into the Basie band. Near the beginning of a wonderful interview with bassist Red Mitchell (14 June 1992) he told me this story about Count Basie's rhythm guitarist, Freddy Green, which seems to belong in a book called *Music Grooves*:

"The Basie band was in Stockholm and I was invited to this party and there was Freddy Green sitting alone at a table for two, so I got up the nerve to sit down with him. I started off like this, I said something like, 'You should really be in the Guinness Book of Records as the human being who has played the most swinging quarter notes of anybody ever.' At that time he'd been playing for over fifty years, only quarter notes, and I never heard him play one that didn't swing. And to let him know where I was I started off with this little poem that goes like this:

It isn't really rigid metronomic time that counts
It's sound and soul, communication, love, support, and bounce.

"He said, 'Yeah, I couldn't have said it better than that.'
"And I said, 'Can you verbalize how you do what you do?'
" 'Well, you gotta get the first beat right.'
"I said, 'You mean one of each bar?'
"And he said, 'No, the very first beat of the whole tune. If you get that right you got a good crack at the second. If you don't, forget it.'
"So I said, 'Well, OK, how do you get the first beat right?'
"He was very specific. The way to set a groove is for somebody, whoever it is, the leader or the melodist . . . if it's a singer, it really ought to be the singer that sets the groove, or the bass player. No matter who the melodist is, the bass player has to live, has to sort of sleep with the groove, make love to it."
"Freddy was talking about Count Basie setting grooves and how he did that. He and Basie understood each other really well. Basie was able to communicate a tempo with just the lift of an eyebrow. For us normal mortals, leaving Basie in heaven where he is, it usually involves the melodist or somebody in the band hearing the melody internally. If it's a singer then the tempo should come from how the words feel in the mouth. If it's an instrumentalist . . . there's usually one part of a tune that dictates the tempo, it could be the end of the bridge, very often it's just the title line. If you sing the title line to yourself you'll hear how you want to hear it, and that will depend on how you feel at the moment, which in turn will depend on what you just finished playing, might even depend on what you plan to play after that." [CK]

p. 180 . . . *why aren't they resisting . . . ?* On cultural disruption, mining, and resistance from an anthropological perspective, see R. Godoy, "Mining: Anthropological Perspectives," *Annual Review of Anthropology* 14 (1985): 199–217. On conflicts between mining companies and indigenous peoples in Papua New Guinea and Irian Jaya, see Sean Dorney, *Papua New Guinea: People, Politics and History Since 1975* (Sydney: Random House Australia, 1990); Peter Ryan, *Black Bonanza: A Landslide of Gold* (Melbourne: Hyland House, 1991); John Connell and Richard Howitt, eds., *Mining and Indigenous Peoples in Australasia* (Sydney: University of Sydney Press, 1992); George Monbiot, *Poisoned Arrows* (London: Sphere, 1989); David Hyndeman, "Mining, Modernization, and Movements of Social Protest in Papua New Guinea," *Social Analysis* 21, no. 3 (1987): 33–41, and "Melanesian Resistance to Ecocide and Ethnocide: Transnational Mining Projects and the Fourth World on the Island of New Guinea," in *Tribal Peoples and Development Issues: A Global Overview*, ed. John H. Bodley, 281–98 (Mountain View, Calif.: Mayfield, 1988); Richard Jackson, *Ok Tedi: The Pot of Gold* (Port Moresby: World Publishing, 1982); C. O'Faircheallaigh, *Mining and Development* (London: Croon Helm, 1984); Hank Nelson,

Black, White and Gold: Goldmining in Papua New Guinea 1878–1930 (Canberra: Australian National University Press, 1976); R. J. May and Matthew Spriggs, eds., *The Bougainville Crisis* (Bathurst: Crawford House Press, 1990); M. Howard, *The Impact of the International Mining Industry on Native Peoples* (Sydney: University of Sydney, Transnational Corporations Research Project, 1988); and Colin Filer, "The Bougainville Rebellion, the Mining Industry, and the Process of Social Disintegration in Papua New Guinea," *Canberra Anthropologist* 13 (1990):1–40.

The effects of mining on aboriginal human and land rights in Australia is taken up in several papers in the Connell and Howitt volume above and in D. Cousins and J. Niuewenhuysen, *Aboriginals and the Mining Industry* (Sydney: Allen and Unwin, 1984); T. Libby, *Hawke's Law: The Politics of Mining and Aboriginal Land Rights in Australia* (Perth: University of Western Australia Press, 1989); and R. A. Dixon and M. C. Dillon, eds., *Aborigines and Diamond Mining* (Perth: University of Western Australia Press, 1990). The literature on similar issues in South America, and particularly in the Amazon, includes Catherine Caufield, *In the Rainforest* (Chicago: University of Chicago Press, 1984); Susanna Hecht and Alexander Cockburn, *The Fate of the Forest: Developers, Defenders and Destroyers of the Amazon* (London: Verso, 1989); Adrian Cowell, *The Decade of Destruction: The Crusade to Save the Amazon Rainforest* (New York: Holt, 1990); David Cleary, *Anatomy of the Amazon Gold Rush* (Oxford: Basingstoke, 1990); June Nash, *We Eat the Mines and the Mines Eat Us* (New York: Columbia University Press, 1979); and Michael Taussig, *The Devil and Commodity Fetishism in South America* (Chapel Hill: University of North Carolina Press, 1980).

A regular flow of information about mining projects, indigenous peoples, and rainforest destruction may be obtained through the publications of Cultural Survival (215 First Street, Cambridge, Massachusetts 02142) and the Rainforest Action Network (450 Sansome, Suite 700, San Francisco, California 94111). [SF]

I have distributed dozens of copies of Bernard Nietschmann's "Militarization and Indigenous Peoples: The Third World War," *Cultural Survival Quarterly* 11, no. 3 (1987):1–16. This article includes basic information about the world situation that every person should have but that most do not. [CK]

p. 180 *The beauty of this fellowship . . .* The reference is to a five-year fellowship from the John D. and Catherine T. MacArthur Foundation awarded to Steve on the morning we recorded this dialogue. [CK]

MEDIATION OF GROOVES

PEOPLE'S MUSIC COMPARATIVELY:
STYLE AND STEREOTYPE,
CLASS AND HEGEMONY

In the field of ethnomusicology, whatever revolutionary potential there was in the "folk music" movement and among its scholarly promoters, notably the Seeger and Lomax families, seems to have been swamped by the usual liberal perspectives, professional standards, and technical emphases as represented in the founding of the Society for Ethnomusicology in the early 1950s. There is a most enlightening history to be written of the Seeger and Lomax families and their efforts to define and create an American "folk music" that could serve revolutionary purposes. I can't attempt a chapter of that book here.

I can say that the "folk" idea has been bothering me ever since I first gave the concept serious thought (Keil [1966] 1991), and further discussions (Keil 1978, 1979a; Dorson 1978) have clarified the issues but only deepened my frustration. I can agree with Richard Dorson, William Sturtevant, and others that everyone participates to some degree in folk subcultures centered on sports, modes of transportation, hobbies, musical tastes, and so forth; people from all classes and ethnic backgrounds pass along jokes and anecdotes and narrate personal experiences peculiar to their time, place, or vocation. Augmenting the peasants and primitives, who are the people most often turned into folk by folklorists, we are all part-time folk in that we share values and consciousness with various groupings whose processes of culture creation are not usually studied by scholars. Singing the unsung, mapping the hidden strategies of daily life, may be a worthy enough goal for folklorists, but without a dialectical sense of class relations and power differentials, "folk," "folklore," and "folk music" feel like concepts in search of content, a discipline searching indiscriminately for data.

For these reasons and in order to define a space between "folk" (with its strong connotations of "rural," "illiterate") and "popular" (with its denotation today of "mass-mediated") I like to talk about "people's" music. The following analysis, comparing blues and polka as people's musics evolving in the twentieth century, has been presented in various forms to various forums over the years and no major objections to its formulations have been raised. I hope it gives some sense of what a dialectical ethnomusicology might be like.

Around 1928 both blues and polka appear on record for the first time in clean, modern, authentic form. Around 1952 "dirty" blues and "honky style" polkas emerge from Chicago to challenge the established norms. Why this parallel pattern? How do economic trends and modes of production, the dominant culture's stereotypes, working-class recreational needs and, most important, the necessities of style combine to shape African-American and Polish-American music? Some simple Marxist assumptions ground these questions and my answers, but an older Apollonian-Dionysian dialectic is at work as well.

In the course of reviewing Robert Palmer's book *Deep Blues* I came upon a page of information that suggested the need for a radical revision of blues history and a more complex understanding of any style of people's music in the twentieth century. Palmer describes the earliest blues on record as follows:

> Phonograph records had existed since 1897, when the National Gramophone Company introduced them as an alternative to the recorded cylinders invented by Thomas Edison in 1877. A few black artists who hoped to appeal to a white audience were recorded during the late 1890s and early 1900s—vocal ensembles singing formal arrangements of spirituals, or "Negro novelty" performers like George W. Johnson, whose biggest hit was "The Whistling Coon." But apparently the idea of making recordings by and for blacks hadn't occurred to anyone in a position to do anything about it when the so-called blues craze hit around 1914–15, so Handy's "blues" and the blues of other popular tunesmiths, black and white, were recorded by whites, many of them specialists in Negro dialect material.
>
> Such recordings are rarely heard today, but some of them probably reflected contemporary black folk styles with at least a modicum of accuracy. One of the few examples available on LP (on the album *Let's Get Loose: Folk and Popular Blues Styles from the Beginning to the Early 1940's*, issued by New World Records) is "Nigger Blues," copyrighted by a white minstrel entertainer from Dallas in 1913, and recorded

in 1916 by a Washington lawyer and businessman, George O'Connor. The dialect is grotesquely transparent, and O'Connor further betrays his racial identity by singing perfectly articulated major thirds, without a hint of "blue" pitch treatments. But the verses were already traditional among blacks. One would later figure in a memorable recording by the Delta bluesman Robert Johnson.

> You can call the blues, you can call the blues any old thing
> you please
> You can call the blues any old thing you please
> But the blues ain't nothing but the doggone heart disease.

(Palmer 1981:105–6)

I haven't done much research on the earliest blues recordings but what I have heard makes me want to speculate extensively on the implications of the fact that for at least five years all the mass-mediated versions of the blues were white. I strongly suspect that eventually we can call the blues a white "heart disease" to which blacks had no immunity, and which only a truly black music could cure. (This diagnosis may be in complementary opposition to Ishmael Reed's notion of jazz as infectious "jes' grew," a jittery bug that enlivens its host organisms and is still seeking its text.) Following Palmer's account, it was some years after the "blues craze," circa 1920, that black women, billed as contraltos, were finally allowed to record vaudeville versions of the blues in "novelty" lyric form. Another few years passed before Blind Lemon Jefferson recorded in 1925, and it was not until 1927–1928, fifteen years after O'Connor's "Nigger Blues" was copyrighted, that a blues record was a really big hit with black people. Perhaps it took that long to adapt the stereotype, work it through, master it, and turn it into a black identity. Interestingly enough it was the clean, relaxed, sophisticated—in a word, modern—blues style of Leroy Carr and Scrapper Blackwell's "How Long, How Long Blues" that established the music as belonging to a large black audience. It was the Carr-Blackwell model that T-Bone Walker developed in the thirties and forties, B. B. King perfected in the fifties, and Bobby Bland consummated in the sixties.

The rest of Palmer's book and a fair number of other blues books and articles over the years have documented the "country" blues, the "downhome" blues, the "deep" or "real" blues, referring to the rougher, dirtier style of Mississippi, Memphis, and Chicago as if it were the "true" version, while the style most appealing to African-Americans from 1928 to the present (to the extent that blacks continued to be interested in blues

at all) is heard as something like a gloss, cover, or substitution for the
real thing. I don't dispute the possibility that a rural Mississippi blues
style may have existed before the first white recordings or the fact that
a peculiarly powerful version of the blues has been a continuing tradition in the delta from the 1920s to the present. But considering that the
blues idiom since the late 1960s has "ended up" with an almost entirely
white audience and more white performers than black ones, it might be
worth exploring the related hypotheses that music called "blues" was
originally or primarily (*a*) an urban phenomenon, (*b*) a white idea about
blacks, and (*c*) most influential in both black and white cultures as a
recorded or mass-mediated form. Eventually we may come to see 1928
to 1968 as a golden age of African-American blues bracketed by white
blues epochs.[1]

Certainly, listening to the upsurge of electric delta blues in Chicago,
circa 1951–1952, one could hear these three hypotheses being retested
and proved out. It is urban music. The worst white ideas about blacks
are accepted a second time and worked through with a vengeance in the
personae of Muddy Waters, a natural force like the Mississippi, a rolling
stone with mojo powers; Howlin' Wolf, a raging beast, the tail dragger
humping around on all fours; Sonny Boy Williamson, pushing sixty
when he first recorded for Chess but still a "boy" whose smiling face
could sell King Biscuit Flour. Never very popular with black audiences in
Chicago (I remember having a Sonny Boy performance all to myself in a
West Side joint in the early 1960s; Muddy and the Wolf played to audiences of fifteen or twenty people, up to seventy or eighty on a weekend
night, at Pepper's Lounge or Silvio's in the same period), the Chess
recordings by these men launched the key British rock groups—Rolling
Stones, Cream, Led Zeppelin—that continue to define the core of that
idiom. Most influential in recorded form, the sound of Chess studios and
Willie Dixon's garage is still echoing in rock bands today.

Why the emergence of the first black blues on record circa 1928 and
the reassertion of a dirtier blues identity circa 1952? In other words, why
accept the stereotype twice, and why at those specific times? Before we

---

1. Bruce Harrah-Conforth's research into the etymology of "blues" as a name for sad
emotions traces it back through centuries of English usage to sixteenth-century Scotland.
His work on sheet music has uncovered white "blues" tunes complete with flatted thirds
and sevenths in the 1880s. The first sheet music compositions by African-Americans with
blues in the lyrics or title "have almost no accidentals at all in them" and appear decades
later (personal communication, 28 May 1984). These and related arguments are part of a
1984 M.A. thesis in folklore at Indiana University, "Laughin' Just to Keep from Cryin':
Afro-American Folksong and the Field Recordings of Lawrence Gellert."

subject these events to closer analysis, consider the fact that the same pattern is audible in Polish-American polka music.

I believe that 1928 is the year when Ed Krolikowski of Bridgeport, Connecticut, made his first recordings of polka music in a distinctively American style, influenced by Dixieland jazz and years as a conductor-violinist with vaudeville and burlesque pit orchestras. At about the same time, similar bands were formed in Hartford, Connecticut, Springfield, Massachusetts, and Chicago, putting out new Polish-American music (accents on the hyphen and American) over radio and on records. Prior to this time a variety of Polish music, vocal and instrumental tunes for every conceivable variety of dance, was recorded in Poland and in the United States, but one listens in vain for any coherent style or a sound that is not "old country." Once Polish-American polkas began selling well in the late 1920s (one of Krolikowski's first records, "Baruska Polka," was so popular he recorded a swing-era version in the early 1930s; it later became "She's Too Fat For Me"), a style became audible, grew in popularity, and was brought to perfection in the late 1940s. Arrangements became more and more complex and tempos got faster and faster in the big bands of Walt Solek, Frank Wojnarowski, Ray Henry, Gene Wisniewski, and Bernie Witkowski. This "Eastern style" came to a climax just as the rock and television era dawned and upset all previous patterns of music and dance recreation.

As in the evolution of blues, however, a dirtier, deeper, disreputable style emerged from within the community that challenged established taste and preferences. In 1951–1952 Li'l Wally Jagiello made the first of a string of hit records on his own Jay Jay label in a style based on oral traditions, the village songs that people around him sang at weddings and picnics and in the taverns along Division Street, or "Polish Broadway." This music had its expert practitioners in Chicago before Wally came along, notably concertina player Eddie Zima, but Wally popularized it north and east of Chicago, touring incessantly, and within a decade this "Chicago" or "honky" style had pushed aside almost all the Eastern bands. The usual reason given for this is that the slower tempos made dancing easier, and that's true enough, but the acceptance of "honky style"—no written music, loose phrasing, old-fashioned concertina, from-the-heart vocals, anything-goes atmosphere—also represented an acceptance, working through, and transcendence, by working-class Polish-Americans, of the "honky" or "polak" stereotype.[2]

2. For a more conventional musicological view of polka evolution in terms of competing "folk" and "urban" models see Janice Ellen Kleeman, "The Origins and Stylistic

With this brief sketch of the evolution of African-American blues and Polish-American polkas in mind I would like to discuss the following hypotheses about people's music processes in twentieth-century America:

1. Style is a reflection of class forces.

2. Style has its basis in community recreation through ritual.

3. In class society the media of the dominant class must be utilized for the style to be legitimated.

4. For a working-class style to grow and prosper, the dominant culture's stereotypes must be accepted and transcended.

5. The first efforts of ethnic working-class communities to work through the dominant stereotypes using the dominant media borrow from both "high culture" and "popular culture," while second efforts toward the same goals tend to repudiate these borrowings.

6. Style always has hegemonic thrust as it works out the implications of form in terms of inclusion and exclusion principles.

7. A vital style always has Dionysian and Apollonian aspects competing for primacy.

8. Both the thrust toward hegemony and the play of Dionysian and Apollonian processes are confused and confusing due to the pervasive influence of mass mediation on music in this century.

As I hope will become clearer, these eight hypotheses are just analytically abstractable aspects of one complex process: the struggles of "peoples," ethnic segments of the working class, to keep control of their social identities in music.

1. *Style is a reflection of class forces.* I am using the concept "style" to mean something like the essential pattern within Sapir's "genuine culture" (Sapir 1924), a deeply satisfying distillation of the way a very well integrated human group likes to do things. Given the penetration of capitalism throughout the world, well-integrated, style-sustaining groups find it harder and harder to survive, and style may be thought of as a best available substitute for "genuine culture" or "primitive wholism" (Diamond 1974). The presence of style indicates a strong community, an intense sociability that has been given shape through time, an assertion of control over collective feelings so powerful that any expressive innovator in the community will necessarily put his or her content into that shaping continuum and no other.

Style may or may not be said to exist in classless societies where one broad way of music making tends to prevail and everyone is an innovator within it; the culture is the style and all members are stylists. In such a community of feeling there are no competing group interests to satisfy, unless of course styles linked to gender and division of labor can be distinguished. It is surprising how ignorant we are about questions like this—are separate men's and women's styles discernible in all, some, or many classless societies? However we choose to think about style in the classless world, style's presence anywhere seems to evoke that unity of feeling, and this is probably where much of the hegemonic thrust or energy in every style originally comes from. Once out of classless society, the human experiment can be heard or seen as a search for the primitive, a quest for community-unifying style which can end in state fetishism, Wagnerian opera, large scale fascism, or in the revolution that will make the world safe once again for decentralized, human-scale, genuine cultures.

One reason we may feel uncomfortable using the concept "style" in the context of classless societies is that we are accustomed to recognizing style through constant, consistent, perceptible changes over time. We don't know about style in classless societies because we can't measure stylistic changes in a people's music before the impact of imperialism. Broadly speaking, however, archaeological records suggest that the presence of style as we know it, changing through time, is an urban or civilization marker, and I assume that musical styles, plural, within a culture emerge at the same time. Musically, we have to study style retrospectively and "retroaudially." You can't know the template or paradigm until you've seen some or most of the implications worked out. To use an organic analogy, you can't really know a lot about the growth or maturity of a style until it begins to decay.

Certainly in all class or feudal societies there are at least two competing efforts to assert control over collective feelings, the well-known great and little traditions, as well as certain negotiated compromises, like Chinese opera, where peasant and aristocratic styles meet and mix. From the Renaissance until World War I in the West, style is like an idée fixe or lodestar for the dominant class, and we are well into this century before the decay of various bourgeois arts raises basic questions about what style is or represents. In music, the presence or absence of style and its meaning have only begun to be discussed in any penetrating way during the past decade or so. One conclusion I have drawn from this discussion and from my own research is that style in twentieth-century America is almost entirely an ethnic working-class phenomenon (Keil and Keil 1977); after World War I the owning classes can't seem to buy or subsidize an evolving musical style any more.

2. *Style has its basis in recreation through ritual.* "Recreation" can be read here in the usual sense, but our polka research over the years has required the development of a new area of theory to complement Marxism (on creation/production) and feminism (on procreation/reproduction). This theory of recreation/preproduction is also one of "participation" in Lévy-Bruhl's ([1910] 1966) sense as opposed to one of "negation" in critical theory, and I will be arguing that the lack of revolutionary theory and practice in this primary mode of our species being (existence before class and gender, play before work or sex, curiosity before value or desire) has been responsible for keeping joy from topping the list of revolutionary priorities. Indeed, without this primary theoretical development "happy consciousness" has gotten a bad name. "Ritual" requires no fancier definition either, just an assurance that secular rituals are as important as sacred ones. This allows us to put blues and polka performance events on a par with church services as processes that insure the opportunity for participation and catharsis to each member of the community.

In terms of the origins of blues and polka this second hypothesis is more like an article of faith. That recreation through ritual has sustained these styles, once started, is documentable in detail and need not occupy us long in this discussion. The one puzzle for me in comparing blues and polka along this dimension is the role of dance in shaping the rites of style. For polka, dance is primary, and it is in order to keep the dancing couples whirling ever more happily that drummers add bass kicks from rock, clarinetists listen for places to put a thrilling trill, bass players try to put more pulse into their amplified throb. It is in constant response to the expressed and implicit needs of the dancers passing before their eyes that tunes are chosen, tempos fixed, and the broad stream of musical style subtly elaborated from weekend night to weekend night in each polka locality over the years. What are the comparable forces shaping blues? Why are traditional African interactions between musicians and dancers conspicuously absent from many blues performances? Did a dance style or configuration of styles fit with Carr and Blackwell's club work in the 1930s or T-Bone Walker's in the 1940s? Perhaps blues is better thought of as two separable rites, the "boogie shuffle" (from John Lee Hooker's juke-joint dance rhythms through the rhythm 'n' blues of Wynonie Harris and Louis Jordan to all of rock) on the one hand, and on the other, the slow "dramatic testimonial" in which a singer's calls and instrumental responses are shaped through time by the committed "shouting" audience that yells to him immediately when he has touched a nerve. In both kinds of blues and in polka, immediate and constant feedback loops, in a habitual, tightly patterned form that I would dignify with the term "ritual," are what a vital style requires to keep growing, what a community requires to keep knowing itself well, and what each individual needs to be recreated as a member of that community.

3. *In class society the media of the dominant class must be utilized for the style to be legitimated.* With the arrival of radio and records in the 1920s, musical styles could be split schizophonically (Schafer 1977c:90) from their specific ritual-recreational, community-building sources, and analysts seeking cause and effect are placed in a long hall of funhouse mirrors and echo chambers filled with uncertainties. The new media required messages, markets, profits, and advertisers. And diverse ethnic segments of America's working class seem to have needed fresh identities in the face of this culturally homogenizing force. The way the old Polish-American band leaders of Bridgeport, Connecticut, and Springfield, Massachusetts, describe it, people demanded that they form larger, more public bands. It was the leading figure in Bridgeport's Polonia who suggested to Ed Krolikowski in 1929 that he line up some sponsors—a furniture store, a meat market, a travel agency, a monument maker—and do a radio broadcast with a band put together to play polkas, waltzes, and obereks. Workers at the local Columbia pressing plant suggested to their bosses that Ed should make records. Listening to Ed Krolikowski and his wife talk about those years, it almost feels as if the people, radio stations, and record companies called forth the Polish-American polka with one voice. The challenge to Krolikowski and the other bandleaders was to do something Polish *and* American, something Polish immigrants would recognize as theirs that would also be suitable for radio and records, something bigger and more organized than a three- or four-piece wedding band, something that could appeal to other Americans as well. I think it was in meeting this challenge that Polish-American polka bands and polka style were born. Wedding bands performed for a responsive community before and after the emergence of "radio-recording orchestras," but "the polka" as a distinctively American style of music could not be created and legitimated outside of the new mainstream channels of communication.

I don't have as much information on the 1928–1930 emergence of a blues style popular with African-Americans. "Country blues" scholarship is still piling up but I don't know what Carr and Blackwell were doing in Indianapolis before their big hit recordings. Were they popular in the clubs or did recordings make them popular? When and how did black radio make its start in Indianapolis, Memphis, and Chicago? With an "hour" here and there on the regular stations? Were the Carr-Blackwell records played? Did they do live broadcasts? The legitimating function of records and radio for "the blues" is less clear, but we do know that the two best-known Delta bluesmen, Robert Johnson and Muddy Waters, learned their first blues on guitar by copying the Carr-Blackwell record (Palmer 1981:104, 111–12). Texas old-timer Mance Lipscomb acknowledged that the first music *called* blues that he ever heard was around 1917, presumably on record (Keil [1966] 1991:58–59). And I have a feeling that all the best-known blues artists from 1930 forward learned as much or more from records as from oral transmission; witness B. B. King's huge record collection, over thirty years in the making.

4. *For a working-class style to grow and prosper, the dominant culture's stereotypes must be accepted and transcended.*

5. *The first efforts of ethnic working-class communities to work through the dominant stereotypes using the dominant media borrow from both "high culture" and "popular culture," while second efforts toward the same goals tend to repudiate these borrowings.* Hypotheses 4 and 5 can be discussed most parsimoniously as a pair. We have already described the pattern of stereotype acceptance for blues, but the polka data are less clear for two reasons. First, the dominant culture's stereotypes had had less time to form and had not been given such audible, visible public shape; a century of minstrelsy had not defined the "happy polak," though vaudeville and burlesque doubtless furnished some examples. Second, a place for "polaks" and polkas had to be found in the context of the jazz age in which various versions of African-American styles were all the rage. It was not long after his first radio appearances and records that Ed Krolikowski was being called "the Polish Paul Whiteman." I think this means not only that Krolikowski legitimated Polish music as Whiteman legitimated black styles, but also that Krolikowski gave polkas a jazz flavor. The mediated polka style had to respond to both the dominant culture's definition of "polak" and its definition of "nigger" at the same time. Pictures of Ed's band show them in tuxedos and reading music. The records let you hear a sliding trombone and jazz drum set.

This sort of double definition or triangulation vis-à-vis the dominant culture is even clearer in the early 1950s when Chicago-style polkas proudly take on the label "dyno" or "honky," defying the old Eastern-style norms and saying, in effect, We used to be immigrant peasants who had to prove our respectability with legitimate American jazz-influenced music; now we know we are despised immigrant workers, and we must dig a little deeper for a "soul music" of our own and do it our way.

Li'l Wally, the primary force behind "honky style" was aware of what was going on across town in the Chess brothers' studio in the early fifties and has spoken to us of his admiration for their business sense. Wally would probably not admit to having created and promoted a polka equivalent of the dirtier down-and-out Chess blues product, but to my ears the "Wolf beat" and Wally's loose bounce have a crucial common denominator: rejection of established forms, measures, and controls and the assertion of juke-joint and gin-mill joy against all high culture and pop culture conventions. They share a sense that the groove is primary, that written musical arrangements are irrelevant, and that the vocal and instrumental textures of the taverns can be unleashed in recording studios without shame.

It may well be that this is just an anthropologist's culturological comparison that glosses over other crucial shifts in mode of production circa 1950, for example, (a) the displacement of AM radio by television as the dominant communication channel, (b) the emergence of FM radio and alternative programming, (c) the abandonment of ethnic or restricted markets by the major record companies, (d) the emergence of many smaller independent labels to serve those same constituencies, and (e) access to tape technology as a way of making recordings without big radio and record companies. We face the same sort of puzzle as we did regarding 1928–1929: Does the simultaneous opening up of the radio and record industries invite the "down-home" blues and "village" polkas out of the little taverns into a redefined, more subtly mediated public space, or do these rough-and-ready styles rudely push themselves forward from the bottom up? Would these new (if apparently old-fashioned) blues and polka messages have been heard eventually without small record companies and FM radio? Is this really a "deeper acceptance of stereotype" once the electric media are diversifying, subject to a bit more community control, and members of the dominant culture are no longer listening? Or is it an emergence into appropriately "little media" of folk or people's processes that were always there? Is it a conscious or even an unconscious rejection of "high" and "mass" models? Or is it just an exploitation of residual cultural resources by petty capitalists, postwar recycling of African-American and Polish-American musical leftovers? Are the styles still legitimated if they are not mediated by major labels, AM radio, and TV?

Clarification of these related questions is further complicated by the facts that (a) the African-American community was becoming more concentrated and ghettoized in the 1950s and 1960s, while the Polish-American community started to diffuse to the suburbs, and (b) dirty blues did not displace the classic tradition within black communities even as it attracted wider white audiences, while "honky" polkas displaced the Eastern style within Polish America but never reached a mainstream audience. In other words, "honky style" polkas became more and more of an in-group solidarity symbol, while "deep blues" increasingly symbolized black ghetto life more to outsiders than to insiders. The mass media finally sucked up the blues sound but ignored the polka, co-opted and incorporated the threatening black third world while dismissing or laughing at the white ethnic working class.

So the acceptance and transcendence of stereotypes by African-Americans and Polish-Americans, viewed from recent stylistic end points, has not been the same sort of process. Dominated blacks and dominant whites have been in a continuing dialectic or negotiation of identities for centuries, whereas dominated Poles may be listening to dominant whites and resisting blacks but are ultimately talking to themselves and to a few other white ethnic workers in certain cities (Keil 1982b; Keil, Keil, and Blau 1992:129–51).

6. *Style always has hegemonic thrust, both as it works out the implications of form and in terms of inclusion and exclusion principles.* I'd like to use "hegemony" as the name for a sociocultural process of merging, enlarging, and consolidating people into a bigger and supposedly better "us." In the usual Marxist sense of the word, the tendency of the dominant class to bond people together through its ideology tends to be the only focus, and indeed bourgeois ideology is as powerful and hegemonic today as ever. But it is not just the ideological aspect of culture that has hegemonic properties; musical, religious, and other aspects may function that way as well. Bourgeois music has not held together as well as bourgeois ideology; ironically it is probably only the Communist Party in China, the remnants of the old left, and a few music conservatories in Japan and Korea that still truly believe in bourgeois music. In the twentieth century, however, the spread of jazz as "pop" music and rhythm and

blues as "rock" has given African-based forms of music hegemony over European forms.

Thought of from this general perspective, the very purpose of style is to establish a hegemony of feelings, and the naming of musics as "blues" or "polka" is itself a declaration of consolidation. A broad variety of early twentieth-century African-American musical activities are pushed aside as songsters and dance musicians become "bluesmen," compressing more and more experience and energy into one twelve-bar form. Similarly, mazurkas, krakowiaks, redovas, polonaise, and fifty other Polish dances were pushed aside by "the polka" in the 1930s.

An exclusion principal or focus on a sharply limited form or set of forms marks the beginning of a style, but it grows by inclusion, assimilating to its purposes the instruments, techniques, and ideas of other significant styles within earshot. One of the mysterious joys of ethnomusicology is to hear a style develop in this way over the years, feeding on what it needs without losing its stylistic identity. The power of a style to incorporate influences increases its claim to hegemony up to that point or phase where the exclusion principle applies again, and musicians decide, for whatever reasons, to pare away the excesses and get back to essentials. Whether or not one can call this phase a new style or not varies with circumstances and can probably only be known some years after the fact. Hegemony, like truth, is what more people come to believe, so we can't really know what is or was at stake in a style until it has run its organic course.

Or until, you might think, one style runs into another. "Blues" and "polka" do not really challenge bourgeois music; they take the harmonic frameworks utterly for granted (Shepherd 1982) and simply flow around or past institutionalized music as they keep to their own proletarian purposes. Nor do blues and polka really challenge each other; one style does not flourish within the working class at the expense of the other, although "country" and "soul" mass-mediated styles have been competing for influence in the Top 40 mainstream since the early 1950s. There has been some competition for adherents between different ethnic versions of the polka in various cities (Keil 1982b; also in Keil, Keil, and Blau 1992). An important move by some Polish-American bandsmen, notably Eddie Blazonczyk, has been to incorporate "country and western" music so thoroughly into "polka" that country fans might be won over to the polka style. But to date these are probably musical hegemonic sideshows. Peoples' musics remain tied to ethnic working-class communities or are relentlessly commodified. As long as economic and political hegemony remains in ruling-class hands we probably cannot expect any more basic shifts in stylistic allegiance. Music seems already far ahead of other aspects of class consciousness, and it is not at all certain that these styles can continue to grow and change without parallel shifts in the political economy.

7. *A vital style always has Dionysian and Apollonian aspects competing for primacy.* As important as the dialectical class struggle for ideological, religious, or musical hegemony may be, and as important as the struggle between different ethnic segments for hegemony within the American working class may be, I think it would be a mistake to interpret changes in blues and polka styles circa 1928 and 1952 only or primarily in these terms.

Let me spell out two possible class analyses of the blues and polka pattern. In the first interpretation one could portray the early blues and polka forms as a co-optation of nascent proletarian styles to respectable standards via the new corporate-controlled media. In this view, the resurgence of disreputable blues and polka styles in the 1950s becomes a tough reassertion of working-class identity. A second interpretation, however, might be that the first emergence in the 1920s is proletarian, folk forms transformed by urban craftsmen to meet new working-class needs, and that capitalist media profit from this process simply as a matter of course. In this interpretation, the later styles might be viewed as a lumpen proletarian reaction, entertainers on the fringe of their communities peddling novelty, eccentricity, and rougher stereotypes in a last ditch effort to make a few bucks before television closes down minstrelsy and vaudeville altogether. Neither of these explanations satisfy me. B. B. King may say that he's middle class and just wants to make the blues respected. Li'l Wally thinks of himself as a businessman or salesman and might be insulted by the proletarian label, much less the lumpen interpretation. But whatever they think they are doing needn't upset our outsider's class-analytic estimates of what forces their styles represent in world historical perspective.

I would like to keep all these stylists squarely within the working class, and to do this I will argue that what might appear to be folk-urban fluctuations or bourgeois co-optations and lumpen reactions are really manifestations of two forces first identified by the ancient Greeks as they approached class society but best described in dialectical terms by Friedrich Nietzsche a few millennia later as Apollonian and Dionysian. Unfortunately the terms came into anthropology without Nietzsche's insistence that these forces are dialectically intertwined in the creation of vital styles. Ruth Benedict may not have been entirely unjustified in using one concept or the other to describe a specific non-Western society or culture-and-personality configuration, but it is as contending forces that they explain the power of Greek tragedy at its peak and the seemingly contradictory tendencies of blues and polka evolution.

In Nietzsche's "The Birth of Tragedy Out of the Spirit of Music" he describes an "Apollonian art of sculpture, and the non-imagistic, Dionysian art of music . . . separate art worlds of dreams and intoxication," the Apollonian perfection and *principium individuationis* contrasted with Dionysian loss of self, immersion in fellow man and nature. The Apollonian is a frozen moment of dreamlike perfection, the illusion or ideal of perpetual life in separation from nature, while "Under the charm of the Dionysian not only is the union between man and man reaffirmed, but nature which has become alienated, hostile, or subjugated, celebrates once more her reconciliation with her lost son, Man" ([1872] 1967:33, 37). The bittersweet merging with the all, with mother and earth, with the reality of life and death at once, may be what all people's music strives for; it is certainly the feeling of blues and polka though they approach it from different (stereotypically "sad" and "happy") starting points. Perhaps polka is more expressive of the primal dithyramb, collective song and dance intoxication in a pretragic form, while blues is more focused upon tragic individuation and the dream, but both styles have required a balancing of both forces to grow.

Listening to the Apollonian perfection of Walt Solek's classic recordings in the Eastern style, you might never know that he was the clown prince of polkas, ready to climb into huge-titted drag, play the butcher of stolen kiska, or pull his pork from baggy pants in the form of a puppet piglet if that would get the crowd waving hankies and flipping out. Similarly, T-Bone Walker's classic dream-state recordings of the blues do not give a single clue to the amazing stage show in which he did flying splits while playing the electric guitar behind his head. These two culminators of blues and polka styles in the 1940s may or may not have been ambivalent about the clown role but they were very clear in their dedication to crafted recordings. The jester leader of the Dionysian or Bacchic revel was always beneath the surface of the earlier blues and polka on records, but in the 1950s the forces were reversed or rebalanced as crazy Li'l Wally tried to capture veteran's hall echoes and some of the in-person easy ecstasies in his recordings, and Chess records, with their rotten amplifiers and garagelike acoustics, set the stage, as it were, for Sonny Boy

T-Bone Walker and Lottie the Body. Photo courtesy of the
Helen Oakley Dance Collection.

Williamson to tour England in a black-and-tan piebald suit and homburg
hat. I think also of Howlin' Wolf posed in a beret with meerschaum pipe,
the philosopher caught in a moment of deep contemplation, reassuring
us that even the Wolf could attain an Apollonian detachment from the
world once his Dionysian frenzies were behind him. I don't know what
to make of all the audiovisual contradictions and reversals but peoples'
musics are full of them.

Walt Solek in drag at a U.S. Polka Association festival. Photo Charles Keil.

8. *Both the thrust toward hegemony and the play of Dionysian and Apollonian processes are confused and confusing due to the pervasive influence of mass mediation on music in this century.* If the late-1920s emergence of authentic blues and polka took an Apollonian form, and if the 1950s resurgence of "delta" blues and "village" polka does represent a resurfacing of Dionysian forces held in check before that time, we still must wonder why these major changes surfaced in 1928 and 1952, in periods of marked political conservatism. It seems to me that in

Howlin' Wolf in repose. Photo courtesy of MCA/Chess files.

addition to the broad effect of postwar economic booms on cultural florescence, the aforementioned shifts in specific modes of production, radio
and records, were decisive factors. For as long as big record companies
and AM radio legitimated these styles, their Apollonian aspects remained
primary. As soon as radio and record companies diversified, the atmosphere of local taverns could be mediated. Before we can sit back and
relax with these simple generalizations, putting *B.B. King Live at the
Regal* or the Dynatones' *Live Wire* on the turntable and taking a cold
beer from the fridge, we must pause to consider in closing the fact that all
recordings are inherently Apollonian just as all live performances tend
toward the Dionysian. Why have there been so few "live" recordings of
blues and almost none of polkas? Because early on, I believe, all participants in the rites of blues and polkas heard the recordings not as mere
echoes but as perfected echoes of their live experience. Record companies

Li'l Wally Jagiello singing and playing from the heart; Lakawana, N.Y. Photos Dick Blau.

Leroy Carr, blues singer and boogie-woogie pianist. Photo courtesy of Toby Byron, Avalon Archives.

never have cared that much about what was put on record as long as it sold, so I suspect that the perfectionism in blues and polka recordings is an expression of people's preferences, musicians and their audiences wanting the cleanest and most sophisticated versions of their music in public space. Once norms are established, recorded blues and recorded polkas take on a perfectable Apollonian dream life of their own. In polkas, for example, bands routinely record with upright string bass and a regular piano twenty years after these instruments disappeared from live performances because "that's the way polka records should sound." Many polka bands rehearse only when they have a recording session to prepare; the shared tradition of evergreen standards can sustain any band in live performances without rehearsing and through any changes in personnel.

Much more could and should be written about the subtle but important distinctions and interactions between the live and recorded styles—for instance, (*a*) the characteristics of repeatable, predictable recorded songs that may shape expectations and influence responses "live," as well as (*b*) the ways in which perfected recordings may challenge or free a band to be rowdier and full of surprises "in person" and (*c*) the ways in which lessons learned playing live about what works on people do or do not find their way into recordings—but Nietzsche's original point is still valid. It is the two principles acting upon each other that insure continued stylistic vitality and exert whatever hegemonic power a style may have. As enacted on the polka dance floor and in the rites of blues catharsis, the intoxicating Dionysian urge-to-merge and the dream of Apollonian individuation are not in conflict and all the old individual-versus-society clichés are laid to rest in a "libertarian sociability" (if not socialism) that can always include more people. Radio and records give more people easier access to the music—big hegemonic possibilities there—and over time these media replace written music (and all the control implicit in writing) by offering that permanent version and perfected echo of live performance. The experience of recorded music is much more magical and Apollonian than looking at a score or written arrangement can ever be, and normative recordings intensify live performance as something extraordinary, abnormal, and magical as well.

In sum, working-class styles of music arrived on the scene with the new media in the decade of "high culture" fragmentation following World War I and went on to resynthesize their internal Apollonian-Dionysian dialectics in divergent ways (polka exerting hegemonic claims within the working class and blues making claims outside it as well) in the decade of media diversification after World War II. I'm not certain how to weigh variables or restate this pattern in terms of causal explanation, but it seems as if the changes in broader economy and modern modes of communication invite a reverification of class and ethnic identities in terms of style formation processes and human rites that have ancient roots.

6   RESPECTING ARETHA: A LETTER EXCHANGE

14 March 1988

Dear Charlie,

I'm going to try setting out why I haven't done anything about your request for an article on Aretha Franklin for *Echology 2*. Basically, I've been an Aretha Franklin fan for twenty-three years. Her work has moved me, grooved me, provoked me, helped me smile and cry, made me want to dance or fall out, and made me anguish about black music, white America, and who I am. I think my heaviest studio-days music fantasy was to work on an Aretha date. I went through a whole political phase flipped on the way Aretha took soul songs about romantic rights/rites and turned them into anthems of civil rights. Ten years later I learned to hear her do civil rights songs and give them conjugal rights readings. On the gospel front, the experience of spending some Sundays at New Bethel in Detroit in the early 1970s, and listening to Aretha's record with the James Cleveland choir remain the closest I've gotten to imagining why anyone might care about being religious.

So what's my hang-up? If I'm such a committed fan why am I resisting writing about Aretha? One place to start is with the other stuff I do: I think I'm a victim of taking ethnography too seriously. I mean, after all these years of listening to the whole Aretha Franklin output, reading every interview and article about her, scrutinizing the songs, the texts, the cover versions, the soul repertory, talking to lots of people—after all this, I have never been able to talk with this woman. It makes me feel like a voyeur to contemplate writing seriously about her when I've never spoken to her. That must come from the fact that the other musics I write about are ones where I have carefully talked with the makers and listeners and been part of the scene in that close, grounded, ethnographic way.

Well, big deal; Aretha has a reputation for reticence and reclusion with regard to writers. Obviously this doesn't plague other people with things to say. Peter Guralnick has never spoken with her either, and he has a wonderful chapter about her in *Sweet Soul Music* (1986). And lots of good critical work is done from a distance. So am I an incurable purist cutting off my ear to spite my brain? Why should personal contact be necessary to ratify an article anyway? Have I created a reified ethic out of ethnography just because I feel that I've lucked into getting so close to the Kaluli in New Guinea, even though they are so distant in space and time?

Maybe this is also a bit of a cover for being uptight about attacks from feminists. Who wants to be labeled a white, middle-class academic voyeur/pimp for writing about black women, and specifically about mediated experiences of black women's voices and bodies, sexuality, emotion, evocation? Well, all that on the table, here are a few things that I've been thinking and wondering about Aretha Franklin over the years, some in the form of questions.

1. How does Aretha's emergence on the soul scene involve extension, ambiguation, and transformation of soul music's well-established male textual themes and male, secularized gospel performance styles? It seems to me that in her work unflinching lyrics are ambiguated, male centers reversed, sexual meanings given political and civil rights readings and vice versa. Yet at the same time many of the songs she sings maintain and reinforce the imagery of male-dominated love and sexuality that are standard in the soul repertoire. How do we understand the politics of this repertoire and her performance choices? (I'm playing off your "Style and Stereotype" paper here [chapter 5] because I see these questions about Aretha Franklin in terms of two larger themes in your formulations for blues and polka, that (*a*) dominant stylistic tendencies can and must be utilized in order to ambiguate and deny old meanings and to suggest and legitimate new ones and (*b*) dominant stereotypes can and must be accepted, restated, and centrally available in order to be potentially eclipsed.)

2. Why do some feminists read contradictions—and negatively, almost moralistically, so—into Aretha's work, while other feminists see her work as saturated with resistance (sometimes equally moralistically)? How do we, whether male or female scholars, analyze subtleties and ambiguities and contradictions without privileging a white, middle-class, academic moralistic/judgmental stance?

3. In the secularization process that creates soul we have texts that replace both the Lord and the Devil with the Woman. Ray Charles and James Brown are the classic examples here (both influenced no doubt by

Louis Jordan). These texts have something to do with black male preaching and the lifestyles of black male preachers. Aretha Franklin grew up in a world dominated by eloquent black men, especially her father, Rev. C. L. Franklin. By all accounts he was both a profound spiritual leader and a dapper ladies' man. There was also a series of press rumors and other nasty stuff in the early 1970s concerning C. L. and Aretha's turbulent relationship over several of her early years on the preaching road circuit. How do we understand the impact of black male preaching styles, texts, and lifeways, and their secularization in soul music, on the layers of Aretha's textual meanings and performance work?

4. "Respect" was the first song on *I Never Loved a Man the Way I Loved You* (1967b), the disc that broke things wide open for Aretha Franklin in 1967. When Otis Redding sang the song the opening lines were "What you want, baby you got it / What you need, baby you got it," but in Aretha's cover the lines are "What you want, baby I got it / What you need, baby I got it." But respect is ambiguous when it is the woman giving the man all her kisses and all her money. Even more so when the way she asks for it is by leaning hard into the phrase "Whip it to me when you come home." The juxtaposition of "R-e-s-p-e-c-t / Find out what it means to me" with the chorus singing "Sock it to me" intensifies the effect. Does "Sock it to me" mean fuck me or fuck off? Then there is the chorus's use of "Ree Ree Ree," both the first syllable of "respect" and Aretha's usual first name (Ree, or Miss Ree); it comes with the phrase "just a little bit." The juxtaposition of Aretha's strong calls ("Whip it to me when you come home," "Respect") and the diminutive chorus responses ("Ree Ree," "Just a little bit") mixes up the postures of demanding and begging, boss and infant. "Respect" comes at the height of civil rights tensions and in the middle of a brutal personal relationship between Aretha Franklin and Ted White. How do we understand all the male-female and black-white levels and contradictions of "Respect"?

5. The same record that opens with the cover of "Respect" closes with a cover of Sam Cooke's "Change Is Gonna Come." During the success of the record in 1967 and its follow-up Aretha traveled with the Reverend Dr. Martin Luther King, Jr. (an old friend of her father's), and played "Precious Lord" by his side at rallies. When Detroit declared Aretha Franklin Day in 1968, King presented her with the Southern Christian Leadership Conference award. She cut "Think" ("Think / What you're tryin' to do to me"; the bridge consists of the word "freedom" sung eight

times) right before King was assassinated. Are Aretha's civil rights messages and meanings from the late 1960s more straightforward and accessible than other messages? Why has there been a critical tendency to see more assertive messages here and more submissive ones elsewhere in her work?

6. Peter Guralnick has a great description of Aretha Franklin's appearance with C. L. Franklin on the David Frost show in 1971. Frost: "What sort of gospel do you sing?" AF: "My father's gospel." Frost: "Which father?" AF: "Both fathers." When she got loose playing "Precious Lord" she shouted "I wish other people knew him like I do." The next year C. L. appeared briefly on Aretha's live *Amazing Grace* gospel disc (1972). He tells the assembled: "The truth is, Aretha never left the church." This stuff came right at a time when Aretha was being very reclusive, highly hassled, going through a lot of personal transitions and the moment of the press rumors about her relationship with her father. How do we read the gospel activity and the family solidarity vis-à-vis the assaults?

This is starting to get long and I have questions like this about virtually every record. I'll just zoom it up to the present with one more:

7. *Who's Zoomin' Who?* (1985) was a major comeback album. The duo with Annie Lennox of the Eurhythmics on "Sisters Are Doing It for Themselves" is as tough and assertive as Aretha Franklin ever has been. It is full of the intertextual stuff I've loved. Like when her voice breaks through the cyclic refrain at the end and says "Thank you I'll get it myself." James Brown's 1969 soul–civil rights anthem comes right to mind: "I don't want nobody/To give me nothing/Open up the door/I'll get it myself." On "Sisters" we hear the sound effect of a door thudding shut behind Aretha and she adds a "Thank you." Once again good stuff for thinking about intertextual links between black-white and male-female themes.

Yet the same disc had a bigger hit with "Freeway of Love," about riding a freeway of love in a pink Cadillac (the video features a Caddy with the license plate RESPECT). "Jump in/Ain't no sin/Take a ride in my mach-i-ine" is followed later by the spoken "I think we're going for an extended throwdown/So drop the top baby, and let's cruise on into it's better than ever street." All semi-innocuous stuff if you put aside the potential double entendre (the street vernacular use of "pink Cadillac" to refer to a black woman's mouth and genital lips). Is it just that Aretha's stuff has always been both about sisters doing it for themselves and sisters getting done to? How do we understand the complexities linking politics and sexuality?

Questions out front, here is part two of the problem. Even if I could talk to Aretha Franklin and her circle, how dare I ask her about some of this stuff!? What would she or I gain? Would it not be insulting? Anyway, she's writing her own book; shouldn't I wait for that? Maybe it will be as juicy as Tina Turner's. But maybe it will be as jive as James Brown's. Then what? How can we read these books anyway? Looking through quotable quotes from Aretha interviews I'm full of a sense of ambiguity. Like in these two juicy ones from the interviews in Gerri Hershey's great "A Woman's Only Human" chapter of *Nowhere to Run* (1985): "The song doesn't matter . . . it's just the emotion, the way it affects other people." And, "Music, especially the kind I make, is a very emotional thing. As an artist you're happy when people get involved, you know. But what they hear and what I feel when I sing can be very very different. Sometimes I wish I could make them understand that."

I guess I'm trying to tell you that I haven't written what I know and feel about Aretha Franklin because of a double bind. One side is that without access I feel like a voyeur. The other side is that getting to her would soothe one problem and provoke some deeper ones.

So why am I writing to you? In part because you are a landed male, white, middle-class academic like me and have taken the time to anguish over black music and white racism more than anyone else I know. I guess the other reason I decided to write to you is that *Echology* 2 will probably be seen by a lot of women interested in feminist music projects. Maybe one of them has a solution or line on understanding Aretha Franklin that will emerge in part out of ruminating on my questions. But having written that sentence I also know that I've been grossed by some of the moralistic, uptight white, middle-class stuff feminists have written about *Who's Zoomin' Who?* So why should I believe that a feminist critic-scholar will have any more to say than me?

Writing to you also is a way of asking why you haven't written about Aretha. In fact you're the only person I know who has interviewed her— even in the way back when! And you were creeped out by Ted White too.

I'm still confused Chuck, but full of hope, and certainly still full of r-e-s-p-e-c-t for Aretha Franklin and her music.

Love,
Steve

Aretha Franklin. Photo courtesy of Arista Records.

20 March 1988

Steve,

I *really* appreciate the candor, the courage to jump into the song and sexuality issues that I've been afraid to write about too! I immediately tend to translate and sublimate the energies I get from Aretha and her sisters. I'll write you a letter.

Maybe we should get together a group and try to think-talk our way through issues that are too weird and threatening to handle in scholarly or meditative isolation.

30 March 1988

Dear Steve,

I'm trying to get this *Echology* to the printer and can't answer your letter with the breadth and depth it deserves.

I haven't written about Aretha or John Coltrane's quartet because words seemed a lot more inadequate than usual whenever I tried to describe those particular experiences in the 1960s. Twenty years have somehow passed since 1968, the year after leaving Nigeria and the bloated eviscerated Ibo bodies by the sides of the roads, the year we moved to Buffalo because the university would pay me something without withholding war taxes. Our daughter Aphro was 3, our son Carl was born, the Nigeria-Biafra war turned genocidal, the Vietnam war was raging, I tried to write a paper for the anthropology meetings on Moynihan's blame-the-broken-black-family theory and got choked up on my rage.

Our children were so beautiful and those Biafran children were being starved to death day after day.

Very few African-Americans and even fewer in the old or new left were able to struggle through the contradictions of a big African nation-state pogromming and starving a minority into submission with bipartisan support from the U.S. and USSR. Biafra was the beginning of Africa's slide into pogroms, civil wars, famines. My hopes for African humanism, African socialism, African music-dance-sociability inspiring the world were shattered and scattered (and I'm still trying to pick up the pieces).

No Malcolm X. No Coltrane. No clear thinking and no catharsis of the kind that nourished me in the early 1960s. Except Aretha's voice. (And Elis Regina's voice too; I can remember dancing around to her "oopa negrinyo" song with Aphro in one arm and Carl in the other.) I would sit and cry by the speakers listening to Aretha sing "And It Won't Be Long" from her first album: "Mr. Engineer, don't you keep me waitin' . . . hurry . . . hurry . . . HURRY . . . HURRY!" On the lyric surface, it's a corny song of sexual frustration—"he's a lonesome rooster, and I'm a lonesome hen"—but for me it was the restoration of sanity, impatience with an imperfect world shouted out and contradicted: "Baby here I am!/By the railroad tracks/Waitin' for my baby/He's a coming back." I had "Precious Lord" on two sides of a 45 to help me through. And "Respect." The summer of 1969 David Ritz and I tried to put together an anthology of black lyrics to be called "Spirit in the Dark" but the power we felt in the lyrics wouldn't translate to our satisfaction as visual poetic forms on the page and we couldn't peddle it with conviction.

What has changed in twenty years?

Something like five thousand Kurds were gassed to death, men, women, and children, a few days ago, just barely noticed in the news. Muhammadu Marwa and about ten thousand of his followers, men, women, and children, were slaughtered during a thirty-six-hour period in Kano, Nigeria, a few years ago and it went virtually unnoticed. The killers subsidized by the American right are roaming Mozambique and wiping out whole villages. Rainforests and rainforest peoples under attack everywhere. The massacres, administrative and nonadministrative, continue.

Tax time is coming up and until I can fill my life with the religious mission of converting people to the 12/8 Path I guess I will have to pay again.

Last weekend Aphro sang "It Won't Be Long" over the breakfast table with Joe and Sandy Blum and I doo-wopping and BaMbuting in support. Felt great. She did a Balkan encore that could be heard from Queens to northern Epirus.

Two days ago the *Wall Street Journal* had a long editorial on how very right Moynihan was to blame black men for the failures of the black family and how very wrong it was for the Kerner Commission to blame American society and government for failing to provide justice and equal opportunity to all Americans.

Is Jesse Jackson the only candidate who can talk common sense and hope because he grew up out of touch with his father? Should we thank James Baldwin's father and Marvin Gaye's father for beating up on the boys so they could give us "great art"? Does Aretha sing for the many thousands of her sisters who are survivors?

Thanks to a lot of reevaluation counseling I can cry with many more singers today, including white men like George Jones and John Conlee, but black gospel still does it best, "it" meaning having the capacity to put us in touch with our deepest feelings about our common humanity and the urgency of creating a world of peace and justice. There is no question that many of the voices that inspire today are the voices of the survivors, the people who have seen, heard, and worked through personal pain (*Hertzschmerz*) and the world's pain (*Weltschmerz*) without being destroyed by it. How much of the thrill you and I experience as listeners can be traced to Ike beating up Tina or Ted beating up Aretha we can't know, but we can say that whatever the histories of suffering behind the special voices we would gladly trade the "thrill" or "edge" in their expression for their wellbeing as people now and their happiness then. Reject the castrati principle in all its contemporary forms! We can say we are passionately committed to creating a world of full, equal, and diminishing employment (from the thirty-hour to the twenty-hour week) with great musical day-care centers at every workplace so that parents, cousins, aunts, and uncles can both provide for and spend lots of time grooving with their children.

And twenty years later "soul music" is still not presentable or translatable as "text" or "discourse." I thought "r-e-s-p-e-c-t" was just a spelling lesson for Head Start kids. It is possible to share meanings in these patterned sounds we call music, share meanings in the words too, and you can ask anyone, many people of all walks, what Ree's lyrics mean to them or what James Brown's "mother popcorn" and "lickin' stick" are all about. But the glory of music is that it *is* Heraclitus's river of time that can't be stepped into twice. The river is the river yet each of us swims in it differently. Unique signatures, fingerprints, dance moves from each of us and, as you have so clearly pointed out (chapter 2), a plethora of "interpretive moves" possible from each of us each and every time in response. So why do you or I need to talk to Aretha? Ree is right; "The song doesn't matter . . . it's just the emotion, the way it affects other people," e.g., us do-right men.

Love,

Chas

7 ON CIVILIZATION, CULTURAL STUDIES, AND COPYRIGHT

While art lives, it belongs to culture; in the degree that it takes on the frigidity of death it becomes of interest only to the study of civilization.

Civilization as a whole, moves on; culture comes and goes.

It is easier generally speaking for genuine culture to subsist on a lower level of civilization.

—Edward Sapir, "Culture: Genuine and Spurious"

Civilization originates in conquest abroad and repression at home.
—Stanley Diamond, *In Search of the Primitive*

But I am saying that we should look not for the components of a product but for the conditions of a practice.
—Raymond Williams, "Base and Superstructure
in Marxist Cultural Theory"

A lot of what passes for Cultural Studies is actually turning culture into civilization. This is inevitable actually, since all writing commits the sin of reification, but then there are reifications of reifications of reifications that obfuscate and lead nowhere or, worse yet, to still more of the same. My favorite multiple reification—six levels and counting—is the trend in advanced music education research to measure statistically the success or failure of psychopedagogical methods of teaching kids to appreciate the recordings of written-down Western music played in class. "Say, advanced music educator, could I just beat this drum a coupla times?"

Well, critical theory, Frankfurt schoolishness, deconstruction, semiotics, poststructuralism, postmodernism, and who knows what else are just as stuck to the tar baby of Western Civilization as those advanced music educators as far as I can tell. If this is what Cultural Studies is going to be about, then I want to work up some aphorisms to supplement those wonderful Sapir sentences that date back to before the impact of electronic media:

227

Civilization is the crap that culture leaves behind.
Civilization, as a whole, piles up; culture gets smothered.
Being more civilized means having more museums and libraries;
    culture is giving yourself to prime and present time.
Conversation is cultural; writing is civilized.
Culture is yeasty, fermenting, a single germ or seed generating a
    growth process; civilization is the wine bottled, labeled, and corked.
Improvising is cultural; following the letter of the law or the law of the
    letter is civilized.
Civilization is all grasp; culture is reach.

What I really want is a bumper-sticker-length message:

SNIVELIZATION REIFIES!
SIEVELIZATION LACKS JUICE!

Civilization has always been the enemy of culture. We cannot reach and grasp at the same time. Capitalist civilization with its capacities for mechanical reproduction and commodification of everything may eliminate culture once and for all. It delivers more goods than we can consume, plastics that won't biodegrade, fixed musics and big arts that refuse to die and decay. Beethoven impersonators and Elvis impersonators may never go away!

Studying culture, calling things "cultural" and writing about them, turns living practices into civilized products and is "part of the problem" much of the time. Civilizational Studies might be part of the solution.

———

Once you have come to the conclusion that music is in its very essence communal, spiritual, the opposite of private property, and at its best a totally shared experience, like love, a number of strong and clear positions on "the music industry" can be stated: There shouldn't be a music industry. Music shouldn't be written or mechanically reproduced and mass-mediated. Music should exist live, for the moment, in present time, and its makers should be rewarded with happiness and barterlike reciprocities.

Virtually all the music written or recorded has been turned into things for sale. Writing or recording music and copyrighting the results as property to be sold for profits is a process that human beings in general, but certainly all ethnomusicologists, should oppose in principle and try to combat in practice.

As ethnomusicologists we could take some of the following actions for people's music processes and natural world echological principles:

1. Oppose all copyright laws applying to music and lobby for their repeal.

2. Oppose any laws that attempt to limit the damage that media technologies do to each other. Home cassette taping replacing LP or CD buying is a good process. Letting MTV videos run their decadent, mechanical course may eventually convince people that commodified music is bad for mental health.

3. Support and lobby for the easing of restrictions on radio stations' licenses so that more stations with low-powered local transmissions can support cultural diversity and political alternatives on both AM and FM.

4. Oppose all subsidies to arts and artists. People's music and musicians have rarely if ever benefited from state agencies and private foundations, while bourgeois art forms are given artificial respiration with big doses of workers' tax dollars annually. Why should operas and symphony orchestras receive money from all citizens when polka, salsa, and funk do not?

Note that these efforts can be phrased as libertarian deregulation and laissez-faire to Republicans and as equality of opportunity and broader participation to Democrats with equal validity. State support of the Musical-Industrial Complex is the weak link that we as ethnomusicologists and citizens can do something about.

_____

Rites : Rights :: Wrights : Writes
REITs (Real Estate Investment Trusts)

This formula tries to express the idea that the collapse of ritual and ceremony into constitution, custom into law (rites:rights), is paralleled by the collapse of craft into art/aesthetics, the doing and making replaced by theories and statements about doing and making, production becoming ever more programmed, creativity replaced by criticism (wrights:writes). In both collapses we tend to lose the body in action, the whole person creating, to a visual fixation; people looking into TV and computer screens for a law or a text are not grooving on reality but having a substitution inscribed on the brain via the eyeball. REITs, below the "bottom line," divides everything above the line, underlies the common denominator of commodification, turning rites, rights, wrights, and writes into property. Capitalism has done this to us and is doing it to the rest of the planet. How to undo or reverse it?

I know that ratios and fractions probably don't work this way in real mathematical life, but I'd like to think that a rebalancing above the line will give rites and wrights much greater weight again and eventually turn the equation over so that REITs are better divided up by rites, rights, wrights, and writes. We will control capital, not it us. In the aural/oral world I want to revive, the five-way pun disappears in fun, wryte? A poem is simultaneously a human right-write-wright-rite and collective property, an investment, a trust, the moment it is spoken in public. Yet it is only in the visual world of reading, writing, and arithmetic that we can see the puns and problems spelled out and can magnify them with further constructions and deconstructions.

Recalling the warning against participation-as-fascism at the beginning of chapter 3 and our discussion of this issue in the second dialogue, it should be clear that I want to increase the rites-to-rights ratio with more dancing and not by declaring martial law; I want to improve the wrights-to-writes ratio by distributing musical instruments and appropriate technology, not by burning books. Worldwide we need human rights protections, the rule of law, and literacy campaigns more than ever before, if only so that we can all think clearly about minimizing global civilization and maximizing local cultures where participatory consciousness can flourish. But in those parts of the world where capitalism and its protective bureaucracies are firmly entrenched we do have to roll back law and find alternatives to courts and prisons, we do have to roll back text and find alternatives to schools and universities that have also become "holding facilities." I used to make music in the streets of Buffalo, but a liberal lawyer passed a law *for* us buskers (he said) and now I have to pay a license fee and observe twelve regulations or spend time/money/energy repealing the law if I want to play in the city (see page 339, comment with reference to page 314). Many times the legal world does replace the natural world and they can't coexist; then we may want to burn a lawbook and dance in its light.

Rites and wrights are about feeling and form, participatory discrepancies, holism, and "drawing on the right side of the brain." Rights and writes are about sequencing, segmenting, logic, analysis, adversarial processes, and "left hemisphere functions"—a very important half of our minds but only half. Of course the corpus callosum connects these two sides of the brain constantly and it may be that reintegration of the brain horizontally across the hemispheres and vertically, getting in touch with our mammalian and reptilian centers, is what will accomplish this re-balancing. Interesting in this respect that the prime peoples dance the birds, mammals, and reptiles in season while we do not. It is time to re-work our "ratio-nality" (McLuhan's concept of a balanced sensorium in *Guttenberg Galaxy*); undoing the "colon-ization" of rites by rights and wrights by writes, we will put property in its place, subservient to a hor-ribly interrupted but now renewed coevolution and diversification of cul-tures and species.

From R. Crumb's Diatribe on Modern Music

We're including R. Crumb's "Diatribe on Modern Music" in this section because many of these individual panels summarize so neatly what is wrong with industrial civilization, amplification, electrification, music as property. The musicians who sweat behind the King's courtly similes, the woman turning the corner on the Menudo clad lad with the boom box, the typical lout, the mortified little Dutch girl, the sleazeball promoter, the tough-minded pig on the couch, have all become characters who speak to me whenever I find myself in R's shoes puzzling over civilization, copyright, and the immeasurable loss of musical pleasures in our times.

WHERE HAS IT GONE, ALL THE BEAUTIFUL MUSIC OF OUR GRANDPARENTS?

IT DIED WITH THEM... THAT'S WHERE IT WENT...

THEN CAME PROGRESS. LIFE GOT MORE COMPLICATED. THERE CAME EMPERORS, KINGS, QUEENS, PRINCES, POPES, DUKES, DUCHESSES AND SO ON. THESE ARISTOCRATS PUT HEAVY DEMANDS ON MUSICIANS. THEY WANTED SOOTHING, REFINED MUSIC AS BACKGROUND FOR THEIR ROMANTIC INTRIGUES, OR WHILE SCHEMING UP NEW WARS OF CONQUEST, OR BOTH...

MADAME, HOW AM I TO EXPRESS THE VIVIDNESS OF MY FEELINGS FOR YOU, IF ONLY TO COMPARE THIS GLOW IN MY HEART TO THAT WHEN I FELT OR THE GLORIOUS DAY WHEN MY MINISTERS CAME TO ME WITH THE JOYFUL NEWS THAT OUR GREAT ARMADA HAD SUCCESSFULLY LANDED AT CALAIS!? ♪♫

SIR, YOUR WORDS ARE MOST ELOQUENT BUT YOUR SMILE I FIND A BIT STRAINED. ...KNOW DO TRY AGAIN...

AT THE SAME TIME THE HUMBLE PEASANTS, THE POOR PEOPLE OF THE WORLD, STILL HAD THEIR LOW-DOWN FUNKY MUSIC. WHEN THESE PEOPLE GOT OFF WORK, THEY LIKED TO PARTY HARD...THEY WOULD DANCE AND JUMP AROUND ALL NIGHT OR UNTIL THEIR NOSES BLED.

THINGS HAVEN'T CHANGED ALL THAT MUCH, YOU MIGHT SAY, BUT WAIT...THERE ARE SOME SUBTLE DIFFERENCES. MUSICIANS DIDN'T HAVE MICROPHONES OR AMPLIFIERS IN MEDIEVAL TIMES SO THEY DIDN'T NEED ROAD MANAGERS TO HAUL THEIR EQUIPMENT AROUND FOR THEM. ALSO, THEY DIDN'T HAVE TO WORRY ABOUT VIDEO RIGHTS OR MERCHANDISING CLOUT, THINGS LIKE THAT.

SOME MUSICIANS IN OLDEN TIMES WERE DISREPUTABLE CHARACTERS WHO WANDERED FROM TOWN TO TOWN JUST LIKE NOW, BUT MOST WERE ORDINARY PEOPLE WHO HAD STRONG TIES TO THEIR FAMILY, VILLAGE, REGION... THEY PLAYED IN THE LOCAL STYLE, LEARNED FROM THEIR RELATIVES AND NEIGHBORS. COMMON PEOPLE OF THE LOWEST CLASSES SPOKE ON THEIR FIDDLES WITH A FIERCENESS AND BEAUTY THAT COULD MOVE AND EXCITE THE HEART AS DEEPLY AS ANY OFFICIAL "MASTERPIECE" BY MOZART OR BEETHOVEN*

* DON'T TAKE MY WORD FOR IT...LISTEN TO SOME OLD RECORDS PUT OUT ON REISSUE ALBUMS...

AND WHILE THE OLD WAYS OF PLAYING MUSIC (NOW CALLED "FOLK" MUSIC) DIDN'T CHANGE VERY MUCH OVER THE CENTURIES, THE ABSENCE OF FORMALISTIC RESTRICTIONS LEFT THE MUSICIANS A LOT OF FREEDOM TO EXPRESS THEIR OWN UNIQUENESS. THIS IS HOW IT WAS RIGHT UP TO OUR GRANDPARENTS' GENERATION! ...AND THEN, AS MY DEAR OLD MOTHER ONCE TOLD ME ~

I REMEMBER BACK IN THE 'TWENTIES, MY MOTHER AND FATHER PLAYED MUSIC WITH THEIR FRIENDS ON WEEK-ENDS... OLD STRING-BAND MUSIC, Y'KNOW...... ON SUMMER EVENINGS THEY'D PLAY OUT ON THE FRONT PORCH...'

ALL UP AND DOWN OUR STREET ON TH' WEEK-ENDS YOU COULD HEAR THE PEOPLE PLAYING — BUT NONE OF US KIDS EVER PICKED UP AN INSTRUMENT... MY FATHER TRIED, BUT WE WEREN'T INTERESTED... WE LISTENED TO "OUR" MUSIC ON THE RADIO... ARTIE SHAW, BENNY GOODMAN... WE WERE JITTERBUGS... THE STUFF OUR PARENTS' PLAYED WAS STRICTLY CORNY TO US... WE WERE A BUNCH OF "HEP CATS"...

...WITH A HEY NONNY NONNY AND A HOT CHA CHA!*

* WATERED DOWN NEGRO JIVE TALK

EVERYTHING IS CHANGING SO FAST.. WHEN YOU'RE YOUNG YOU GOTTA BE HEP TO THE JIVE OR YOU'RE DOOMED.... TO BE "CORNY" IS TO BE A LOSER, OUT OF THE RUNNING, FINISHED, —BOOM!—KAPUT! THE KIDS WILL HAPPILY THROW THEIR PROUD HERITAGE ON THE GARBAGE HEAP IF IT MEANS BEING WITH IT, UP-TO-THE-MINUTE. THEY'LL SHIT-CAN IT EAGERLY, WITHOUT A MOMENT'S HESITATION, THEY "NEVER LOOK BACK."

HEY! GET SMART, YOU BUMPKIN!!

OH GOSH!

THIS PROCESS IS GOING ON ALL OVER THE WORLD TODAY, IN 1985... WHEREVER TECHNOLOGY INVADES A CULTURE, YOU FIND THE YOUTH EMBRACING IT, GOING FOR IT, DISDAINING THE OLD WAYS. THEY WANT THE GOODIES, THE SHINY TOYS, THE PROMISE OF ALL THAT GLITTER, THE COMFORT, THE CONVENIENCE, THE SOPHISTICATION—IT'S ONLY NATURAL!

ENVY OF EVERY KID IN THE VILLAGE

MENUDO

WELL, SO WHAT, YOU SAY? WHAT ARE THEY S'POSED TO DO, GO BACK AND SAY THEIR PRAYERS IN DIRT FLOOR HUTS?? WHAT'S WRONG WITH MODERN POP MUSIC? THEY'RE HAVING A GOOD TIME, WHAT TH' HELL'S THE DIFFERENCE? WHY ARE YOU IN SUCH A DITHER ABOUT IT ???

GRRR DIRTY DOG!!

I DUNNO... I GUESS I GOT THIS WAY FROM LISTENING TO OLD RECORDS TOO MUCH..THESE ECHOES OF THE PAST... A LOST WORLD, TRUE ENOUGH... THE LOSS OF THESE RICH AND ANCIENT MUSICAL TRADITIONS... WELL, IT BREAKS MY FUCKIN' HEART!!

WHAT HAPPENED? WHAT HAPPENED TO THIS MUSIC??

AAH, YER SO FUCKIN SENSITIVE!

ACTUALLY, ONE NIGHT RECENTLY I WAS SITTING IN THE BLUEBIRD NIGHTCLUB IN FORT WORTH, TEXAS, TAKING IN THE SCENE. I WAS KINDA GETTING WITH THE MUSIC—A MEXICAN BLUES BAND—TWO ELECTRIC GUITARS, ELECTRIC BASS, AND TWO SAXES—I WAS SORTA DIGGING IT.

WELL AWRIGHT!!

BUT AFTER AWHILE, I STARTED GETTING THAT OLD FEELING OF IRRITATION, AND THEN I ENDED UP VEXED, DISGUSTED... WHY DOES IT HAVE TO BE SO GODDAMN LOUD ?? IF THEY WERE PLAYING ACOUSTIC INSTRUMENTS, THE MUSIC WOULD SOUND SO MUCH BETTER! THIS ELECTRIC SHIT IS WAY OVERDONE—THAT'S A LOT OF WHAT IT COMES DOWN TO ...

END

8 NOTES ON "WORLD BEAT"

"It is simply incontestible that year by year, American popular music has come to sound more and more like African popular music." Charles Keil's bold pronouncement in *Urban Blues* ([1966] 1991:45) was certainly true, but it reflected just the A side of the emerging world beat record, because at the same time, on the B side, African popular musics had come to sound increasingly like American popular music. This complex traffic in sounds, money, and media is rooted in the nature of revitalization through appropriation.

Musical appropriation sings a double line with one voice. It is a melody of admiration, even homage and respect, a fundamental source of connectedness, creativity, and innovation. This we locate in a discourse of "roots," of reproducing and expanding "the tradition." Yet this voice is harmonized by a countermelody of power, even control and domination, a fundamental source of asymmetry in ownership and commodification of musical works. This we locate in a discourse of "rip-offs," of reproducing "the hegemonic." Appropriation means that the question "Whose music?" is submerged, supplanted, and subverted by the assertion "Our/my music."

The dual character of appropriation is typically located in stories like this: Mick Jagger and the Rolling Stones obviously contributed to the fame, income, and recognition of Muddy Waters when they recorded his song (cowritten with Bo Diddley) "Mannish Boy," utilizing many aspects of his original, recorded performance style from the 1950s. Jagger said that he idolized Muddy Waters and wanted to record great songs associated with him to draw attention to rock's debt to blues. For his part, Muddy Waters's later recordings of the tune, and his performances of it (largely for audiences of young white people), incorporated a few Jaggerisms of vocal inflection, as well as some rock instrumental influences. And Waters said he liked the versions recorded by the Stones and the seriousness with which British rockers played blues.

For some, the homage paid to Waters by the Stones' use of his material speaks to the true affection white rockers had for black urban blues styles. They also point out that Waters's record sales, concert tours, and record contracts were greatly helped by the "free" publicity spun off from the Stones' cover version and that white rock created a spotlight and larger market generally for black music. However, it is clear that the economic rewards and recognition of artistic status that accrued to the Rolling Stones greatly outweigh those that accrued to Muddy Waters for the original recording. Additionally, there is considerable cultural arrogance in the notion that it takes a recording by the Rolling Stones to bring recognition to the artistic contributions of a Muddy Waters. How then does one evaluate this type of trade, where original creative product by primary tradition bearers is appropriated in exchange for symbolic respect and possibly some lesser, trickle-down economic payback, advancement or crossover in the marketplace? Such a payback, when it occurs, itself reproduces the pattern of marketplace domination from above.

These questions are particularly poignant when we look at the international music scene, where worldwide media contact, consolidation of the music industry such that three enormous companies dominate world record sales, and extensive copyright controls in the hands of a few Western countries are having a riveting effect on the commodification of musical skills and styles, and the power of musical ownership. These issues add a complicated layer to the simpler recognition that American music is Africanizing while African music is Afro-Americanizing, a recognition that is "simpler" only because of the exact, identifiable, concrete nature of the waves of musical products, influences, styles, genres, and musicians that have circulated back and forth in the African and African-American sphere.

Take, as a brief example of both the overt traffic in style reinvigoration and the complexities of appropriation, Paul Simon's *Graceland* record. Released in the fall of 1986, *Graceland* has been an ongoing international success; it has won awards on every continent, sold millions of copies, and been celebrated variously as a melding of mainstream "world" pop and African "folk" musics, the major antiapartheid consciousness-raising and publicity event of 1987, and a major international market breakthrough for the South African musicians whose local pop styles (Soweto township jive, *mbaqanga, kwela, mbube, isicathamiya*) form the instrumental and general musical basis for much of the record's distinctive sound.

Paul Simon, *Graceland,* cover, 1986. Warner Brothers Records.

Maskanda street musicians doing the Zulu blues; Umlazi Township, Natal, South Africa, 1993. Photo Charles Keil.

"These are the days of lasers in the jungle," sings Paul Simon. "This is the long-distance call." These connecting, us-and-them images in *Graceland*'s opening song are the gestalt of a postmodern African/African-American/American musical melange that overdubs quirky 1960s Long Island/Brill Building Simon lyrics; pedal steel guitar riffs from a Nigerian *jùjú* band player conversant with Nashville recordings; vocals from Senegalese Youssou N'dour, on break from recording projects with British pop star Peter Gabriel; and everything from Synclavier samplers and drum machines to the Everly Brothers and Linda Rondstadt—all over the voices and instruments of South Africa's best-known township musicians—bands like Stimela, Boyoyo Boys, General M. D. Shirinda and the Gaza Sisters, and a cappella chorus Ladysmith Black Mambazo. What makes it fit all together? Simon tells us in the record liner notes and in interviews (the following quotes come from one in *Rolling Stone*, 23 October 1986) that when he heard South African township music, "It sounded like very early rock and roll to me, black, urban, mid-fifties rock and roll like the great Atlantic tracks from the period. . . . The way they play the accordion it sounds like a big reed instrument. It could almost be a sax." Of course, the reason it sounded that way had much to do with the steady stream of African-American rhythm and blues records that have circulated in South Africa and the way South African pop styles emerged in the context of a record industry with strong links to the American jazz, blues, gospel, and soul markets. These influences are unmistakable in the styles of the South African groups, and it is not surprising that the music sounded familiar and not at all exotic to Simon. South African pop music is full of African-American soul, rhythm and blues, gospel, and jazz influences, largely from 1950s and 1960s American recordings.

It is clear, however, that something more than the music's familiarity is involved in Simon's attachment to South African pop. There is energy, vitality, and some mysterious politically transcendental stuff about which he is at a loss for words. Simon's respect for these South African forms is obvious, and the fit between his fast-moving imagist poetics and the bouncing, up-tempo grooves of the South African bands is clear. The strongest blending of musical forms on the record—the a capella "Homeless," with words (in English and Zulu) and music cowritten with Joseph Shabalala (leader of Ladysmith Black Mambazo)—is also the most political ("Strong wind destroy our home/Many dead, tonight it could be you . . . We are homeless, homeless/Moonlight sleeping on a midnight lake"). Add to this that Simon worked with many South African groups, paid them top price plus standard royalty cuts, gave music credits to his cowriters, then toured the world with the participating groups plus black South African musicians Hugh Masakela and Miriam Makeba, produced a record for Ladysmith Black Mambazo on his label (Warner Brothers, a major move for the group from small independent label Shanachie, which had licensed material for North American release from Gallo, the South African state company that made all of LBM's recordings), and donated lots of money from these projects to African and African-American causes.

At the same time we must scrutinize Simon's role from the point of view of the overall ownership of the product (Simon's name above the title, "Produced by Paul Simon," "All Songs Copyright . . . Paul Simon") and how this ownership maintains a particular distance between his elite pop star status and the status of the musicians with whom he worked. All of the performance styles, grooves, beats, sounds, and genres are South African in identity, whatever other influences they synthesize and incorporate. The contribution of Simon's lyrics is clearly important and clearly acknowledged, but the distinct, formative influence of these appropriated musical forms on the quality and particularity of the record is downplayed, both conceptually, in the presentation, and physically, in the audio mix. The musicians fill the role of wage laborers. Of course, one could not find musicians in New York or London to do what they do because they are *not just* wage laborers but the bearers and developers of specific musical traditions and idioms. That no significant ownership of the product is shared with them beyond base royalties and their wages for recording studio time (triple union scale, the same price that the best players in New York receive) reflects the rule of elite artistry. What statement does this make about the role of Paul Simon the international pop star vis-à-vis the roles of the musicians without whom the record would have been impossible? It seems to draw the boundary line between participation and collaboration at *ownership*. Whose music? Paul Simon's music.

To look at the situation from another angle we might turn to the last two cuts on the record, recorded in the United States with exemplars of zydeco (black southwest Louisiana creole rhythm and blues) and East Los Angeles Chicano rock and roll—both connected to the South African cuts by the prominence of the accordion as a melody and rhythm instrument. "That Was Your Mother" was recorded in Louisiana with popular zydeco singer-accordionist Alton Rubin, Sr. (Rockin' Dopsie), and his

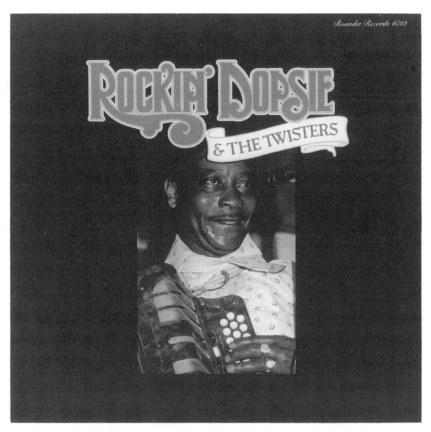

Rockin' Dopsie, *Rockin' Dopsie and the Twisters,* cover; 1977. Rounder Records.

band, the Twisters. The lyrics were written and sung by Simon, with instrumental accompaniment provided entirely by Dopsie and company. The music is clearly the kind of up-tempo straight zydeco groove with which Dopsie has been long associated. In fact, the music is virtually an exact copy of a tune called "Josephine" which Dopsie had recorded previously. Why then do the liner notes say, "Words and Music by Paul Simon," and why does Paul Simon hold the copyright? The musical dimensions of the song—the melodic line, chord progression, zydeco rhythmic groove, instrumentation, and performance quality—are all contributions of the zydeco tradition and specifically of Dopsie's band. These players are the tradition bearers, the ones who created the zydeco sound that Paul Simon overdubbed with his words.

Similarly, "All around the World; or, The Myth of Fingerprints" was recorded with the rock group Los Lobos. Again the lyrics were written and sung by Simon, with occasional vocals by Cesar Rosas and David Hidalgo of Los Lobos. The basic instrumental material is by Los Lobos, with some guitar and percussion parts added later by Simon and studio percussionists. Again the credit reads, "Words and Music by Paul Simon," and the copyright is held by Simon. In the April 1987 issue of *Musician* magazine, Los Lobos members Cesar Rosas and Louis Perez spoke about the process of the recording session with Simon: "So we got into the studio, there were no songs. After a while we started feeling like idiots: 'when is he going to show us the song?' . . . We expected him to have a song ready for us to interpret when we met him in Los Angeles, but he said, 'You guys just play,' and we said 'Play what?' We just worked up a bunch of stuff that he eventually got a song out of, and that was it. . . . We felt a little detached from the finished piece; we didn't have any real involvement in it."

In both cases the actual music—the structure and performance of the song materials—seems to owe much more to the bands than to Simon. He was using them much like he used the Boyoyo Boys music for "Gumboots" earlier on the record, as background material for his lyrics. Yet on that cut, and on "I Know What I Know" and "The Boy in the Bubble," the music writing credit is shared with the band members. While Simon's studio technique and tune credits are not unlike those of reggae "dub" artists who perform their lyrics to existing melody and rhythm tracks, it is curious that he acknowledges the unique musical contributions of the South African bands but does not do so with the American groups. Perhaps, being closer to these pop traditions, Simon felt that these songs were in fact more his own, or at least less anyone else's.[1] Or perhaps the fact that variants of the first nine songs had been previously *recorded* by local groups in South Africa marked those performers' original contributions more obviously, leading to the cocredit lines.

All these forms and processes of appropriation—some more direct, some more subtle, some more overtly arrogant and linked to control of the means of production, others more complex and contradictory in that they accommodate both parties and may strike each as fair trades— could be detailed song by song, style by style for *Graceland*. Recent

1. Simon may have found the zydeco musical form familiar to his project, but it is ironic if not bizarre that nobody pointed out to him how clearly the text of "That Was Your Mother" indicates ignorance of life in Louisiana. He sings of dancing with "Cajun girls" to zydeco music, but unless there have been big changes in Lafayette race politics recently, Cajun women are not the ones you're likely to meet at Creole bars that feature bands like Rockin' Dopsie and the Twisters.

recordings by other international pop stars, for example, Peter Gabriel's *So* or Talking Heads' *Naked*, could also be approached through this kind of archaeological stylistic stratigraphy, revealing layers and varieties of appropriation, circulation, and traffic in musical grooves, and concomitant embeddings and solidifications of musical ownership.

Ultimately of course, Paul Simon and other pop stars can't do much about the fact that the profit and artistic value structure surrounding their work precisely reproduces the typical three-cornered hat of the music business (as analyzed in Frith 1981): *Record companies* make the most money from single products with extremely high sales volume (seven million copies of one record make much more money than seven records that each sell one million copies). *Major contract artists* are only granted the possibility of producing their own work and taking economic and artistic risks commensurate with their sales. *Musicians* are laborers who sell their services for a direct fee and take the risk (with little expectation) that royalty percentages, spinoff jobs, tours, and recording contracts might follow from the exposure and success of records with enormous sales. This structure has particular consequences in the international marketplace, where the infusion of new blood into the record business—which exercises vertically and horizontally integrated control over the media and technologies for recording and reproduction and over publication rights to texts and music—simultaneously drains and distances those whose creative labors are central to making the music. Talent as labor can be imported, commodified in appropriated form, and exported with a new label, asserting the artistry, cleverness, and uniqueness of the star who brought it all together.

Getting back to Keil's old assertion, and how the A and B side of the old disc are now all one side—appropriately, increasingly on that non-sided and nongrooved new laser in the jungle, the CD—it seems that the Africanization of world pop music and the Americanization of African pop are complexly intertwined, particularly since the Second World War. At the same time that world music is homogenizing and human musical diversity shrinking, the new, the exciting, the revitalized, the "long-distance call," epitomized on the world musical map by Africa, is still the mark of otherness. Elite pop artists are in the strongest artistic and economic position in the world to appropriate what they like of human musical diversity, with full support from record companies and often with the outright gratitude of the musicians whose work now appears under a new name.

It is clear, however, that the flow of products and the nature of ownership is differentiated by market valuation factors. When James Brown broke down complex African polyrhythms and incorporated them into dense funk and soul dance tracks, critics didn't speak of a powerful African-American star moving in on African musical turf. And when, ten years later, Fela Anikulapo Kuti seized the essence of the James Brown scratch guitar technique and made it the centerpiece of his Afro-Beat, critics didn't speak of a powerful African star moving in on African-American turf. That's because the economic stakes in this traffic were small, and the circulation had the revitalizing dynamic of roots. But when Talking Heads moved in on both James Brown and Fela Anikulapo Kuti and used scratch, funk, Afro-Beat, and *jùjú* rhythms as the basic grooves for *Remain in Light,* something else happened. The economic stakes, however much attention was drawn to the originators as a result, were increased, the gap between the lion's share and the originator's share enlarged, and the critical discourse on race and rip-offs was immediate and heated.

I'm suggesting then that the revitalizing cycle of Africanization/Afro-Americanization in world beat comes to be increasingly entangled with issues of power and control because of the nature of record companies and their cultivation of an international pop music elite with the power to sell enormous numbers of recordings. These forces tend to draw upon and incorporate African and African-American materials, products, and ideas but stabilize them at the levels of labor, talent, or "influences," levels at which they can be continually manipulated for export and recirculation in made-over forms. The politicized aesthetic of a record like *Graceland* then looks more and more like an ink-blot test whose projection is a much too literal map of the black and white of world music.[2]

2. I wrote these notes in the months immediately following the release of *Graceland.* Since the piece was published, researchers with experience in South Africa have written equally anxious academic reviews of the issues treated here, analyzing the historical, biographical, and ideological situation of South African musicians. Their work should be consulted for details that extend and amplify the issues I raise about ownership and cultural equity. Materials I wish had been around in 1986–87 include Veit Erlmann's articles and book (1989, 1990, 1991), Charles Hamm's book (1988) and his exchange (1989) in *Popular Music* with Dave Laing (1990), Helen Kivnick's book (1990), and Louise Meintjes's superb analysis of *Graceland*'s meanings in and out of South Africa (1990).

9 MUSIC MEDIATED AND LIVE IN JAPAN

CHARLES KEIL

Edison invented the recorded cylinder in 1877. Mediated musics, sounds schizophonically split from their sources (Schafer 1977c:90), have been with us then for over a century. Phonograph records have been commercially available since 1897. Radio and records have been an extremely powerful means of disseminating music to people since the 1920s. Wire recordings, reel-tape recordings, and, more recently, cassette tapes have transformed listening habits and musical cultures throughout the world. Recordings may have been the single most important factor in getting the discipline of ethnomusicology started; freezing musical processes from the oral-aural traditions as objects of study was a precondition and remains an essential, if largely taken for granted, frame of reference.

Studies examining human interaction with mediated music processes are, however, surprisingly few and far between. How do people actually use this machinery and their record and tape collections? What social interactions occur around them? What exchanges of goods, services, and information? Americans, on the average, spend over a quarter of their waking hours interacting with television sets and I've never been able to find a good article about that process! Do people talk to each other very little or a lot while watching? Does this vary much with ethnicity and social class? Why is the sound usually off when the TV is on in local taverns? These kinds of questions, hundreds of them, about media and humanity in the concrete quotidian, are not asked very often and are studied even less. There is much media theory to read, and communication departments exist at a number of universities. There are plenty of product-related reports, and elaborate ratings systems can determine the number and kinds of listeners or viewers for any given station at any given moment. But the quality, the nature of people's listening and viewing, the social life in which media reception is embedded, does not receive much attention.

Why? I think that in capitalist America we just assume isolation, "individualism," passivity, mindless consumption—a lot of inert little black boxes out there into which mediated stimuli are pumped. It is assumed that the only responses that matter can be measured by sales of products and numbers of people tuning to different stations. And if social scientists and communications theorists are largely indifferent to what is actually happening in media-people interactions, why should ethnomusicologists care? Of course, in addition to the blinders capitalist culture gives us all, a whole series of partially examined ethnomusicological biases keeps us from making musical mediations a top priority in our research: (a) a traditional focus on non-Western music, (b) a concern with folkish authenticity, and (c) a privileging of live performance, both in descriptive work and in ethnomusicological performance group replications of traditional styles.

In my own case I know I have nurtured a deep ambivalence, at times masking outright hostility, toward all media for many years. I treat records badly; they aren't real music. I resent the accumulation of tapes I haven't listened to since the day I recorded them. I dislike rock concerts, and "sound systems" annoy me at any concert or performance. I've resisted the use of amplifiers in my own music making until the past decade or so. Once upon a time, I trashed the family TV unilaterally, dropping it two stories off the back porch. Until a few years ago my position on all electronic media was basically Luddite, a desire to smash it all on the grounds that it substituted machines for people, replaced live music with canned, further alienated us from our already repressed sensoria, and enabled capitalists to sell us back our musical and emotional satisfactions at a profit.

It was in the course of a visit to Japan in the summer of 1980 that I began thinking about these phenomena differently. In two weeks of wandering around Tokyo I experienced a variety of mediated-and-live musical scenes that revealed a very different cultural adaptation to electronically mediated music. Let me describe four of these scenes in hopes that this will stimulate some thought about what the significance of this adaptation might be.

My first day in Tokyo I went to a shrine where veterans of World War II were commemorating the dead. Strings of yellow lanterns, paintings hanging from ropes, rows of fine flower arrangements in cases, group photographs being taken by the great gate, a running display of traditional and popular music and dance traditions at a pavilion off to one side—in short, a panorama of Japanese music in a rich cultural setting—swamped my senses. The first note I put into my little book was "took pictures of two older men singing songs in front of the lanterns; a record player starts them off, but this is turned down as they sing into microphones, amplification somewhat distorted." Somehow the old veterans singing seemed to be a center of the festival in time and space, and I was disturbed that the record player was needed to supply context, tempo, a starting point for the singers. Even though the volume was turned way down as the old men gained strength, making it seem as if they were singing almost alone, I thought to myself that this song should be live or recorded but not both at the same time.

At the next festival I attended, *bon* dancing was done to 45-rpm records and live drumming. A little old lady put the records on the advanced stereo while a team of drummers up on the dancing platform took turns flailing away at a half a dozen big barrel drums. It would be hard to imagine this tradition without both the sound of live drums and the visual excitement of swinging arms in counterpoint to the dancing, but apparently at some point it was possible to substitute records for the rest of the live orchestra. I have not been able to determine whether the records played were specifically designed to be filled in by drummers. The *bon* records I bought in stores sound light on percussion but are not, to my ears, obviously "empty" or missing any parts. The vocals are prominent, and I can't remember now whether the singing at the festivals I attended was supplied mostly by the record or by the dancing public. It would be interesting to know the history, stage by stage, of the way recordings replaced some parts of the live tradition but not others. Did musicians protest this change when it occurred? Was there first an attempt at total substitution and then a gradual renegotiation of a balance? Do the recordings used for such festivals show shifts in vocal and instrumental balances in any patterned way through time? The scenes I witnessed seemed very traditional in the sense that there was no visible friction between live drummers and the older woman at the record player; the atmosphere suggested that this was the way it is always done.

The most surprising instance of mediated-and-live music came to my attention when I sought out a group of *chindonya* or street musicians. I'd heard that their typical role was to open pachinko (Japanese pinball) parlors or celebrate their reopening after temporary closings to avoid taxes, but the group I was finally able to locate was opening a small supermarket in the Tokyo suburbs. The group consisted of one man

Local karaoke bar scene; Tokyo, 1980. Photo Charles Keil.

Rural karaoke parlor scene; Ki-Hanto, Honshu, Japan. Photo © 1989 Christopher Smith; courtesy of Impact Visuals.

Chindonya street musicians opening a new supermarket in the Tokyo suburbs, 1980.
Photos Charles Keil.

dressed in old Japanese style playing a portable rack of two small drums and a gong, another tall man in clown costume beating a bass drum, and a woman portraying a huge-headed doll or puppet with tambourine in hand and a cassette player, hooked up to a battery-powered megaphone, under her skirts providing the instrumental and melodic half of the street music. The men drummed along, and we circled the hot, quiet suburban neighborhood with very little response, a few curious children peeking out from their yards or stepping forward to shake hands with the doll lady. At small apartment complexes the leader would stop and detach the megaphone from the recorder to announce the new supermarket and its offerings, usually without any response whatever. At the end of the tour I had the feeling that the days of *chindonya* were numbered, and an interview confirmed that working conditions were steadily worsening and the number of musicians involved declining. An attempt at a union folded five years earlier. Retired pensioners might continue the tradition, but there was not enough money in it to sustain younger people full-time. The leader of this group was apparently making more money giving dance lessons. The cassette-megaphone arrangement replaced two or three horn players and can be seen as an ingenious compromise that keeps smaller groups of musicians working in an idiom that might otherwise disappear.

The fourth and by far the largest category of mediated-and-live performances occurs in small bars all over Japan called *karaoke* or "empty orchestra." Behind the bar you find a complete cassette-tape stereo with mixer and echo effects and a library of specially recorded tapes that are missing the lead vocal parts, two to four songs per tape for quick access. On the bar itself there is a microphone and songbook-catalogues that provide lyrics and locate the song you want to sing. During the evening the microphone passes from hand to hand and every individual present can be a star in turn. People applaud after each vocal segment but they also go on with their own conversations; the music volume is not too high, so the atmosphere is relaxed, appreciative of the singer but not focused on each person's efforts. The goal of each singer seems to be a perfect replication of a specific star in a specific style, but research might uncover nuances and variations on standard star models that are valued variously in different karaoke contexts; bars are known to be oriented toward a particular style or mix of styles, ranging from *minyo* (folk) and *enka* (urban) to U.S. blues and country, with all the European, American, and Japanese pop styles in between. Some of these contexts might prize individual interpretation more than others. Each small bar tends to have a steady clientele and regular patrons often have their name on a personal bottle of whiskey behind the bar, to be called for as needed in entertaining friends.

More recently *Time* reports (28 February 1983) that karaoke tape sets have moved into Japanese homes in a big way: "In 1982 sales of home units zoomed to $265 million, more than was spent in the U.S. on, for example, gas ranges. . . . *Karaoke* sets are turned out by most of Japan's major electronics firms. One $4,000 top-of-the-line model includes synthesizers that can create a bossa nova or waltz beat, a computerized music memory system and two giant 5-ft. speakers. For $1,000 more, vocalists can add a small black box that grades their singing by scoring how well they stay on pitch and keep time with the beat of the electronic accompaniment."

What I find striking in these instances of mediated-and-live musical performances is, first, the humanizing or, better still, the personalization of mechanical processes. Japanese are not afraid to match themselves against the perfection and strictures of prerecorded accompaniment or to match their own voices against bright star models in public. *Time* titled its article "Closet Carusos," but the point of this phenomenon is just the opposite; these singers are not locking themselves away from the world but are contending against the world's best singers with the support of friends at the bar or their families at home. As Americans we are likely to be concerned by the conformist aspects of this process—the adaptation to the machine, the preset accompaniment, the star model followed closely—but in its own context this singing can be interpreted as an assertion of individualism, skill, and personal competence before others, in a demanding situation where any slip or hesitation will not be compensated for by the "empty orchestra." From my field notes: "People really do *hold* the microphone. They put it very close to the mouth and seem to treasure the moment. Faces work into impassioned expressions. You pour your feelings into it, glancing at the words in the book before you as necessary." There is something very Japanese about karaoke singing, an extension perhaps of all those old upper-class Zen self-disciplines leading to "expertness in which there is not the thickness of a hair between a man and his deed." "This act is effortless. It is 'one-pointed.' The deed completely reproduces the picture the actor had drawn of it in his mind" (Benedict [1947] 1967:241, 236). This principle of perfect mimesis, the execution of image in action, to the extent that it suffuses

Japanese culture in its transition from feudalism to what might be called feudal capitalism, could be a theme connecting musical mediated-and-live practices to the well-known ascendancy of Japanese factory production and technical achievements.

It would be tempting at this point to begin connecting evidence from *bunraku* puppet theater practices, from stylized movements in Kabuki and Noh theaters, from the delicate interplay between actors and musical accompanists, from the whole range of Japanese culture and behavior, in order to build some deeper explanation of why their mediated-and-live music making seems so natural, even traditional. Perhaps colleagues here and in Japan who are more conversant with these matters can give closer attention to mediated-and-live music in its various contexts as a recent phase of an old but still developing cultural pattern. But in concluding I would like to ask a few questions about "M & L" music as it exists closer to home.

Why haven't I paid any ethnomusicological attention to the fact that since I was a teenager I have spent more time playing bass or drums to records than I have playing with other people? My late uncle, Hop Rudd, used to carry a record player and set of drums south each winter to entertain himself and a few others with Dixieland classics mediated-and-live. I suspect these instances are not anomalous and that there are many people playing along with records, mostly in the closet for lack of appreciative contexts, missing the Japanese support systems but doing it nonetheless and not being studied by us. It's interesting that drum-along and sing-along are the two modes of "empty orchestra" in Japan, whereas it's my impression that the Music Minus One records here have been used primarily by jazz instrumentalists. How well have those records sold over the years? Are any trends apparent? Why have these private practices not become more public?

The most important parallels in the West may be the recently evolved "rap" style in African-American soul music and the "dub" versions of reggae. I don't know enough about the actual practice of either tradition to develop this point, but adding voice-over to prerecorded musical tracks or danceable disco records seems to be a challenge that more people like to hear being met. Perhaps it gives people a sense of reclaiming the music from the record companies and their machinery. Adding a "rap" or mixing recorded tracks differently in "dub" puts the individual back in control of the process, or at least gives the illusion of such control. Even though the microphone may not be passing from hand to hand as in Japan, the principle of a live performer matching and mastering the mechanized, unchanging "accompaniment" remains the same. Whether or not the rapidly increasing amount of mechanically reproduced music at rock concerts is part of the same phenomena is even more of a puzzle that I'm sure the rock press will devote endless copy to sorting out. Given the impact of mediated music this past century and the emergence of mediated-and-live styles the past decade, we should think about making further research in this area a top priority.

––––––––––

Thinking about these issues ten years later, in 1993, I am still struck by how little research or scholarship I've seen on mediated-and-live music. Karaoke has spread to the United States and to Europe; a friend, Mike Frisch, reports that the Italians have a microphone at every table and sing along as a group with the action on multiple television screens, a dramatic modification of the Japanese stress on nuanced individual mimesis. More and more people are singing along with the media. Is anyone asking them why, or how it feels to do so?

More performers are singing along as well. In the past few years, since Milli Vanilli, the duo that lip-synced their way to fame and fortune, many best-selling albums have been based on the aesthetic illusions of mediated-and-live phenomena. The recent best-selling rap albums are studio productions that echo the mediated-and-live performances of 1979–1982; we are supposed to imagine strutting MCs with microphones in hand and DJs running the technology behind them, but it is a mediation of mediated-and-live that we are hearing and when the group appears on TV the MC is most likely lip-syncing and the DJ doing air-technology, just making believe he is at the controls. So our sensibilities slip easily into mediated-and-mediated music and, via sampling of voices and instruments, into double schizophonia, sounds split from their sources picked up and split again from the original recordings; a scratch-guitar lick from a James Brown hit record blends with an "oooo" from an Aretha groove (transposed into a keyboard scale of "oooo"s in the studio) to become background for the image of a motor-mouth boy from the neighborhood threatening murder and mayhem.

Sitting here in Buffalo, New York—the "city of no illusions," local T-shirts claim—I know that mechanization, automation, the information revolution, closing factories, flight of capital, and declining schools and neighborhoods have devastated the city generally (average family income has dropped from $29,000 in 1979 to $18,000 today) and the African-

American community in particular, where average family incomes are much lower. Claims of control over energy, machinery, weaponry—the white man's tricknology—asserted symbolically in state-of-the-art rap performances, and over knowledge, asserted in lyrics, seem a lie, a balloon of hot air in the superstructure when the political and economic base for the African-American community has practically disappeared. There is no reality check built into mediated-and-mediated music to prick this balloon, no touch on the tonearm, no live-action test of MC-DJ coordination, no crowd response, only the appearances, the idolatry, and the dollar-denominated commodity.

Maybe mediated-and-live is just a skillfully negotiated and very Japanese compromise that can't last, an interim or transitional phase on the way to mediated-and-mediated, as the civilized fixation of culture triumphs over nature completely. Gene-splicing is certainly analogous to sound sampling; original species, artists, and recordings become less and less relevant as new creatures and artifacts are invented and proliferate, replacing reality with "virtual reality." Maybe we are witnessing the imagination run amok, the whole global civilization moving beyond mimesis of nature to physically replacing life as we have known it with versions of life-as-art designed by us and for us. Maybe all the mass mediation and academic overtheorizing about it is conditioning us to accept that this process of bioengineering and moral relativism in the free market is inevitable or even natural. It is not.

10 FROM SCHIZOPHONIA TO SCHISMOGENESIS: ON THE DISCOURSES AND COMMODIFICATION PRACTICES OF "WORLD MUSIC" AND "WORLD BEAT"

STEVEN FELD

> In every society the production of discourse is at once controlled, selected, organized, and redistributed by a certain number of procedures whose role is to ward off its powers and dangers, to gain mastery over its chance events, to evade its ponderous, formidable materiality.
>
> —Michel Foucault

> Struggles over musical propriety are themselves political struggles over whose music, whose images of pleasure or beauty, whose rules of order shall prevail.
>
> —Susan McClary

This chapter concerns "struggles over musical propriety" in the "production of discourse[s]" on "world music" and "world beat." In the first part of the essay I'm concerned to reveal a complex layering of representations and investments from voices who position themselves variously as academics, journalists, fans, musicians, indigenous peoples, critics, music industry insiders, and consumers. This overview of discursive practices, through critical reading and textual juxtaposition, reveals a play of shared and contested assumptions about what outcomes are at stake and about who is perceived to speak authoritatively and thus allowed to characterize, implicitly or polemically, such relative positions as "inside" versus "outside," "elite" versus "vernacular," "theoretical" versus "experiential," "progressive" versus "mainstream," "hegemonic" versus "counterhegemonic." The intertwining of these discourses indexes a social process of meaning negotiation; I employ the trope "schizophonia to schismogenesis" to describe some dynamics of the mutualistic process by which ever more commercial and noncommercial music is subsumed under the heading of "global culture" (Featherstone 1990).

The second part of the paper infuses the discussion with a specific example of world music commodification, as I review my role in producing a commercial CD representing a "remote," "ethnographic" music culture and environment. My concern here is to locate the problematics of the larger narrative trope not merely as abstractions about discursive elsewheres but concretely in the practices surrounding the production and distribution of recordings. In the current "global ecumene" (Hannerz 1989), where cultural interactions are characterized by increasingly complex exchanges of people, technology, money, media, and ideology (Appadurai 1990), transcultural record productions tell specific stories about accountability, authorship, and agency, about the workings of capital, control, and compromise, and about the strategies and possibilities for valuing indigeneity as something more than essentialized otherness or generic opposition and resistance. By telling one such story I insert my own reflexively contextualized range of meanings into the discursive formation analyzed in the first part of the paper. My personal account is thus meant to traverse and link two sets of participatory spaces—that of the reader, analyst-critic, and consumer, and that of the producer, author, and advocate.

"Schizophonia refers to the split between an original sound and its electroacoustical transmission or reproduction," writes Canadian composer Murray Schafer, introducing his terminology of soundscape research and acoustic ecology in *The Tuning of the World* (1977c:90). While the tone of the term indicates Schafer's suspiciously anxious view of the impact of technology on musical practices and sound environments, it also has the familiar devolutionary ring of mass culture criticism. Schafer laments a deterioration in world acoustic ecology from hi-fi to lo-fi soundscapes, a proliferation of noise corresponding to the increased separation of sounds from sources since the invention of phonographic recording. His scheme is straightforward: Sounds once were indexically linked to their particular times and places, sources, moments of enunciation, and human and instrumental mechanisms. Early technology for acoustic capture and reproduction fueled a preexisting fascination with acoustic dislocations and respatialization. Territorial expansion, imperialistic ambition, and audio technology as agent and indicator increasingly came together, culminating in the invention of the loud-speaker. Then came public-address systems, radio expansion, and after the second world war, the tape recorder, which made possible a new and unprecedented level of editing via splicing manipulation such that sounds could be endlessly altered or rearranged yet made to have the illusion of seamless, unbroken spatial and temporal contiguity. Summarizing his concept Schafer writes:

> I coined the term schizophonia in *The New Soundscape* [1969] intending it to be a nervous word. Related to schizo-phrenia, I wanted it to convey the same sense of aberration and drama. Indeed, the overkill of hi-fi gadgetry not only con-tributes generously to the lo-fi problem, but it creates a syn-thetic soundscape in which natural sounds are becoming increasingly unnatural while machine-made substitutes are providing the operative signals directing modern life. (Schafer 1977c:91)

If Schafer were writing his book now, he would no doubt see digital sampling, CD-ROM, and the ability to record, edit, reorganize, and own any sound from any source as the final stage of schizophonia—total portability, transportability, and transmutability of any and all sonic en-vironments. But for the moment forget this after-the-deluge rhetoric and the many social complexities Schafer ignores, such as the occasional hi-jacking of musical technology to empower traditionally powerless people and to strengthen their local musical bases. Rather, focus on the sense of nervousness in Schafer's lovely and precise *schiz-* word and what it means to evoke: mediated music, commodified grooves, sounds split from sources, consumer products with few if any contextual linkages to the processes, practices, and forms of participation that could give them meaning within local communities.

Schafer's schizophonia idea recalls Walter Benjamin's celebrated essay of forty years earlier, "The Work of Art in the Age of Mechanical Repro-duction." Although Benjamin's concern with the transformation from unique to plural existences centered upon visual-material art objects, his critical interest in "aura"—what is lost from an original once it is repro-duced—first raised the assumption that also anchors Schafer, that "the work of art reproduced becomes the work of art designed for repro-ducibility" (Benjamin 1969:224). This view, in which social relations are announced in the codes of aesthetic inscription, has been most strongly enunciated for music in Jacques Attali's *Noise: The Political Economy of Music,* where he argues that "repeating," the transformation from representation to reproduction in music, creates a new network for social organization:

> In this network, each spectator has a solitary relation with a material object; the consumption of music is individualized, a simulacrum of ritual sacrifice, a blind spectacle. The network is no longer a form of sociality, an opportunity for spectators to meet and communicate, but rather a tool making the individualized stockpiling of music possible on a large scale. Here again, the new network first appears in music as the herald of a new stage in the organization of capitalism, that of the repetitive mass production of all social relations. (Attali 1985:32)

Like Benjamin's "aura" or Baudrillard's "signature" (1975, 1981) in the visual mode, Attali's "repeating" (1985:87–132) and Schafer's "schizophonia" help us focus critically not just on the process of splitting but on the consequent status of the "copy" and contestation of its "authenticity" as it seeks to partake of the "legitimacy" granted to an "original." The jeopardy to primal originality posed by reproductive technologies, once more a centerpiece of high-culture critical discourses on the vulgarity of popular culture, is now more substantially situated in the discourses of cultural analysis, mediation, and commodification. Schizophonia thus needs to be imagined processually, not as a monolithic move in the history of technology, but as varied practices located in the situations, flows, phases, and circulation patterns that characterize particular cultural objects moving in and out of short and long commodity states, transforming with the experiential and material situation of producers, exchangers, and consumers (Appadurai 1986), located in historically specific national and global positions vis-à-vis late capitalism and "development" (Castoriadis 1985), cultural domination (Schiller 1976), modernity and postmodernity (Berman 1983; Harvey 1989).

In the world of popular musical traffic such issues are centrally and critically grounded in the international ascendancy of the recording industries. In "The Industrialization of Popular Music" Simon Frith's typically broad strokes help to reposition schizophonia in the larger techno-economic arena of the pop music business: "The contrast between music-as-expression and music-as-commodity defines twentieth-century pop experience and means that however much we may use and enjoy its products, we retain a sense that the music industry is a bad thing—bad for music, bad for us. Read any pop history and you'll find in outline the same sorry tale" (Frith 1988:11). Frith's own outline of the devolutionary shift from active music making to passive pop consumption (Frith 1986, 1981) sets up that straw version in order to forcefully defend both technology, arguing for the importance of rock as a mediated art form, and consumer tastes and choices, countering elitist assumptions about standardization and the passivity of pop music consumption. But Frith also retreats to a more ideologically stable bit of rock-critic turf:

> Pop is a classic case of what Marx called alienation: Something human is taken from us and returned in the form of a commodity. Songs and singers are fetishized, made magical, and we can only reclaim them through possession, via a cash transaction in the market place. In the language of rock criticism, what's at issue here is the *truth* of music—truth to the people who created it, truth to our experience. What's bad about the music industry is the layer of deceit and hype and exploitation it places between us and our creativity. (Frith 1988:12)

These defenses of technology and of the rock consumer speak to the preoccupation in cultural studies with refiguring the Adorno-Frankfurt school dogmas on production, standardization, consumption, and passivity that typified much of the earlier academic pop music literature. But to move into the world arena it is necessary to move past two general problems with this angle on the industrialization of music. Frith repeatedly uses the word "pop" when what he typically means is "rock" and, specifically, the internationally marketed American- and western European-derived rock of the last thirty-five years. Generalizations about "pop" involve additional complexities when one attempts to account for the larger *world* popular musical picture with regard to industrialization. Similarly, Frith's notion of a popular music "colonized by commerce" takes on a different range of meanings when we move beyond rock to concretely observe third- and fourth-world realities, where people and music really have been colonized and not only by commerce. What is crucial here is a view of world music industrialization that views power relations as shaping forces in the production of musical styles and icons of cultural identity.

Like Schafer's "sounds split from sources," Frith's notion of "truth to the people who created it" has particular consequences when the sounds, sources, and creators are truly exotic to the overwhelming majority of their potential consumers. This is because enormous genres of sonic otherness from the reservations beyond Western European-derived art and popular musics are unlike other mediated popular musics and specifically unlike rock in major ways. In the bush, at the outposts and edges of empire, grass-roots musical styles and distribution have long sung undulating melodies of resistance and accommodation to the hegemonic rhythms of international copyright law and the practices of record companies. Moreover, exotic world musics will always be financially and aesthetically remote from the historical loci of international recording consolidation—control and ownership of approximately ninety-three percent of the world musical sales market is now concentrated among six European–North American–Japanese companies: Time-Warner, CBS-Sony, MCA, Thorn-EMI, BMG/RCA, and Philips-Polygram. The vertical and horizontal integration of the music production and publishing industries, of technology ownership and production control, has been closely linked to the power centers of technological invention in the West and, more recently, Japan (Boyer 1988). Western art, rock, and pop stars have, in the last twenty-five years, shared in that market growth in ways that are generally unknown and almost unbelievable outside of the West, even, say, in comparison to a non-Western star of the stature of Ravi Shankar.

Jon Pareles, in his *New York Times* Pop View column (19 March 1990), considers the "larger means fewer" world of music business consolidation as concentrating power vis-à-vis promotion, investment, distribution, and overall control: "As the record business enters the 1990's it has developed a two-tiered system. Independent labels handle specialized styles and new performers—they have almost taken over scouting for talent and test marketing it—while the majors grab proven contenders." This market strategy, a good illustration of Frith's "coloniz[ation] by commerce," is particularly colonial in the realm of world music. Consolidation leads to a profit strategy based on huge single hits rather than a variety of projects or broad dissemination of myriad musics. Huge hits inevitably come from a small group of pop stars who hold major label contracts and receive industry support and promotion commensurate with their sales histories and potentials.

Schizophonia gets intensively schizoid here because of the ways the splitting of sounds from sources simultaneously implicates matters of music, money, geography, time, race, and social class. Still, many (some would argue most) researchers and writers have stressed the optimistic aspects of world musical contact and industrialization. Frith, for example, in his introduction to *World Music, Politics, and Social Change,* a collection of early-1980s conference papers from the International Association for the Study of Popular Music, writes: "The essays here celebrate, then, the richness of local music scenes, and document the remarkable skill, vigour and imagination with which local musicians and fans and entrepreneurs take over 'hegemonic' pop forms for themselves. Popular music, even in the era of Sony-CBS, MTV-Europe, and Michael Jackson as global Pepsi salesman, is still a progressive, empowering, democratic force" (1989:5). And Andrew Goodwin and Joe Gore, writing about the debate over world beat and cultural imperialism in *Socialist Review,* conclude, "Although World Beat is itself largely an effect of . . . cultural imperialism . . . the complexity of the *results* of such practices are demonstrated in . . . transculturation" (1990:77), a position curiously close to Bruno Nettl's (1985) more mainstream ethnomusicological cheer for the world of "unprecedented" musical diversity. Such perspectives, drawing on the more normative conceptualization of a world in creolization (Hannerz 1987), risk confusing the flow of musical contents and musical expansion with the flow of power relations. Even if local musicians take control in remote locales, how progressive can the world of popular music be when the practices of a transnational culture industry steadfastly reproduce the forms and forces of domination that keep outsiders outside, as "influences" and laborers in the production of pop?

The commodification of world musics in the international marketplace intensified in the 1980s. Musics once very "other" are now entirely familiar. John Szwed's 1982 review of the WOMAD *Music and Rhythm* compilation record introduced the word "ethnomusicology" to the readers of the *Village Voice,* then just as quickly dismissed its modernist purism: "Who needs a Ph.D. when there are enough record stores stocked with product in New York, Tokyo, Miami, London, and Paris to give you permanent culture shock?" In a similar vein, here's the lead-in from an *Option* magazine series on world music in 1990:

> Bored with the music you're listening to? Why not invite a Kenyan wedding band or a turbaned troupe of gypsies from the villages of the Nile into your living room? Musical treasures from the world's far-flung regions abound in record stores these days. And most of the credit for that goes to a few intrepid souls within the fringes of the pop music establishment, people who have devoted years to the thorny proposition of bringing state-of-the-art world music recordings to a mass culture. Ten years ago the international bin was populated

with high-priced French imports and muffled recordings on labels like Folkways, Nonesuch Explorer and Lyrichord—most of these licensed for a song from hungry ethnomusicologists out to cash in on their fieldwork. These releases tended to be academic, with sliced-up three minute selections, abrupt beginnings and endings, and didactic liner notes, stiff with classifications and musicological jargon. Not anymore. Aside from international pop, which has become an industry unto itself, traditional music veterans like Nonesuch Explorer and Lyrichord are forging into the CD market. But now they are being overtaken by more savvy and ambitious explorers, most notably Globestyle Records, the brainchild of restless musician and field recorder Ben Mandelson; Rykodisc's World Series, masterminded by Grateful Dead drummer Mickey Hart; and Real World Records, a project steered by Peter Gabriel in collaboration with WOMAD (World of Music Arts and Dance). These three new forces have no hangups about what is classical, traditional, folk, or pop. They are guided by a belief that the world's great music, presented right, can be commercially successful. (Eyre 1990:75)

So now, alongside international elite avant-gardes—artists such as Terry Riley, Steve Reich, Philip Glass, and the Kronos Quartet, who have promoted Asian and African musics through compositional experimentation and performance, or the prestigious New Music America Festival, which introduced Inuit throat-game vocalists and tango accordionists—we have elite pop stars setting the pace for discourses on world music, bypassing folkies, academics, and previous generations of collectors, authenticators, and promoters like Moses Asch and Alan Lomax. Folkways Records, now housed at the Smithsonian Institution, links this distant past to revitalized circulation through the Rounder distribution network. And in stores where the heading "Africa," or even "Europe," used to mark a small hodgepodge of recordings, now we find entire sections and subsections and subsubsections on the world music shelves, with multiple divisions and numerous recordings. Words like cajun, zydeco, polka, salsa, *soukous,* ska, tango, Afro-beat, *jùjú,* highlife, township, *conjunto,* and klezmer demarcate substantially diversifying and enlarging product sections mixed in with more established divisions by country and region, placed beside more familiar ethnic/regional genres like reggae or blues.

With those schizophonic notes in hand we can momentarily zoom out to the land of the Iatmul in the Middle Sepik of Papua New Guinea, where forty years before Schafer entered the fray of schizo-suffixing,

Gregory Bateson coined the term "schismogenesis" to discuss patterns of progressive differentiation through cumulative interaction and reaction (Bateson [1936] 1958:171–97, 1972:61–87, 107–27). Schismogenesis, in Bateson's more formal language, refers to "classes of regenerative or vicious circles . . . such that A's acts [are] stimuli for B's acts, which in turn [become] stimuli for more intense action on the part of A, and so on" (1972:109). Bateson identified two related patterns of schismogenesis, the second of which he called complementary schismogenesis. This pattern involves cycles "where the mutually promoting actions are essentially dissimilar but mutually appropriate, e.g., in cases of dominance-submission, succoring-dependence, exhibitionism-spectatorship and the like" (1972:109). In the complementary mode the progressive differentiation involves a mutually escalating reactivity whose continuance leads to a closer symbiotic interdependence of the parties. Simultaneously, anxiety, paranoia, and increasing distortions make the mutualism destructive and progressively impervious to forms of self-correction—unless of course the participants unite in opposition to an outside force, or mutually lessen the escalating distortions by attaining new forms of self-consciousness about their predicament. Bateson identifies three other possible end points for such cycles: fusion of the parties, elimination of one or both, or the persistence of both in a dynamic equilibrium (Bateson [1936] 1958:184). Bateson's view of the limits of stability in large-scale systems goes considerably beyond seeing cumulative, interactive escalation as a one-way path to explosive destruction; instead, he focuses on forces of self-regulation, correction, and feedback in a variety of social formations.

Juxtaposing Bateson's *schiz-* word with Schafer's may be useful in thinking about some of the material and discursive developments related to the intensified commodification and industrialization of world music. Sounds have increasingly been mediated, split from their sources, and, following the explosion of world musical products and marketing in the last ten years, we are in the throes of a major trend, where musical activities and the emergent discourse surrounding them exhibit a complementary schismogenetic pattern. The opposition or mutual differentiation scenario of this pattern rhetorically contrasts claims of "truth, "tradition," "roots," and "authenticity"—under the cover term "world music" (or, in the lingo of some zealous promoters, "real world music")—with practices of mixing, syncretic hybridization, blending, fusion, creolization, collaboration across gulfs, all under the cover term "world beat."

What "world music" signifies for many is, quite simply and innocently, musical diversity. The idea is that musics originate from all world regions, cultures, and historical formations. "World music" thus circulates broadly in a liberal, relativist field of discourse, while in a more specific way it is an academic designation, the curricular antidote to the tacit synonymy of "music" with western European art music. In this latter sense the term is explicitly oppositional, markedly more polemical and political than in the former sense, contesting Eurocentrism and opposing it with musical plurality.

But it is as a commercial marketing label that "world music" is now most commonly placed. In this context the term has come to refer to any commercially available music of non-Western origin and circulation, as well as to musics of dominated ethnic minorities within the Western world: music *of* the world to be sold *around* the world. Here the term begins to discursively overlap with "world beat," and one hears them used synonymously to refer to the best-known commercial and popular varieties of world musical styles, like reggae, blues, zydeco, *conjunto,* or salsa. Calling attention to the dialectics of isolation and hegemony, resistance and accommodation, this discursive merger of "world music" and "world beat" draws out senses of commodified otherness and of blurred boundaries between the exotic and the familiar, the local and the global in transnational popular culture.

The "world beat" label usually has more specific referents. Introduced by Austin, Texas, musician and radio personality Dan Del Santo in the 1980s and picked up rapidly by the radio and music industry, the term refers to all ethnic-pop mixings, fusion dance musics, and emerging syncretic populist musical hybrids from around the world, particularly from urban centers. What rhetorically sets world beat apart is often the assertion of a new, postmodern species of "authenticity," one constituted not in isolation or difference but in creolization proper, an authenticity precisely guaranteed by its obvious blendings, its synthesis and syncretism.

But notice the marked word: "beat." That also reminds Westerners that it is "others" who have rhythm, make music of and for the body, music for dance, for bodily pleasure. Tied to a long history of essentializing and racializing other bodies as possessing a "natural" sense of rhythm, the invention of "world beat" reproduces a Western gaze toward the exotic and erotic, often darker-skinned, dancing body. These othered "beats" thus provide the pulse and groove for Western bodies to throw their inhibitions off on the dance floor. "World beat" then is a more marked term than "world music"—critically disparaged by some as other (or just oppressed) people's party music commercially appropriated for white folks to dance to, while championed by others as a new, populist, honest, commercially viable form of dialogue or equalization between musics and musicians in different cultural spaces.

The escalating discourse of differentiation surrounding the notions of "world music" and "world beat" is located both in vernacular and academic forms. The vernacular form, popular with musicians and with journalists who like to side sympathetically with musicians, argues that market expansion, global stylistic contact, and the recognition of global musical diversity is inevitably accompanied by circulatory problems. Here commodification and promotion take a toll, graying out, vulgarizing, distorting, or maligning those who are supposedly benefiting from increased exposure. Expansion and advance in the musical style arena are thus often seen as the positive face of a process which inevitably involves contraction and mastication. The perception, common among culture producers and creators, that banality is part of the price one pays for exposure dictates that outsider musics and musicians must yield to Western pop stars and the recording industry when it comes to participating in a musical synthesis. World beat may be created from and inspired by outsider grooves, but the creators are led to understand that it is not exotic grooves that sell the music but rather the status and entrepreneurial role of pop stars and their access to the support systems of major record companies.

This anxiety is captured in the following paragraph, again from Jon Pareles's *New York Times* column (28 August 1988), titled "Pop Passports—At a Price": "When Paul Simon, Peter Gabriel and Talking Heads sell millions of records using Jamaican reggae and South African mbaqanga, their sources deserve a piece of the action. But to reach the world audience, how much will those regional musicians have to change—and for better or worse?" The piece continues in this vein, then about-faces toward a more tempered balance:

> It's not fair to simply cry "Sellout!" . . . Local and outside influences have been tangled for decades, maybe centuries. As the musicians see more of the world they're bound to incorporate the ideas and rhythms they now live with. Beyond that, most popular music means to be hospitable, and one way to make listeners feel at home is to give them something they're familiar with. . . . It would be a double standard to suggest that Paul Simon and Sting can borrow whatever they

want while their sources have to stick to local or national
styles—as if the colonies could only provide raw material for
the empire's factories.

And finally, speaking of the specific non-Western musicians involved
in world beat projects, Pareles concludes that "it will be up to them
whether they're remembered as stateless pop bands or national standard-
bearers." Pareles here both sides with and puts the heat on the musicians,
imagining that they have a degree of control that they surely don't. At the
same time he tends to ignore the larger social and economic dimensions
of the culture industries which do force musicians to "provide raw material" for the empire.

But Pareles's anxiety about "world beat" is balanced by his enthusiasm for "real world music." In a column on the "roots move," written
a few months later (6 November 1988), Pareles praises Panamanian
politician and salsero Rubén Blades and the Los Angeles–based rock
group Los Lobos (at the time enjoying fame for their recording of "La
Bamba"). Why? Because they were "telling listeners across the hemisphere that success in America is possible without cutting off roots, without jettisoning their own language and music, without assimilating and
Americanizing. While slick, mainstream American pop blankets the
world, they insist, with plinking harps and time-honored salsa rhythms,
that diversity should not be lost." That last sentence sounds to me like
the pledge of allegiance for "real world music" pop patriotism, but it
is perhaps more astonishing for the degree to which it ignores the multilayered syncretism and synthesis underlying the music of both Rubén
Blades and Los Lobos.

Moving into the academic sphere, I'll take my nervous self as a token
of anxiety about the scene. My review of the politics of Paul Simon's appropriative mixing and copyrighting practices for the album *Graceland*
(chapter 8) is perhaps more cynical and loudmouthed than Pareles's comments, but the anxiety is similar. It is an anxiety about an increasingly focused and intensified set of interactions whose consequences seem to
grow in magnitude, not just from reproduction of asymmetrical power to
control technologies, but within a space marked by a heightened symbolism of race and/or ethnicity. These discussions are situated within a
larger yet equally anxious discourse on how musical ownership and
copyright practices systematically reproduce the power imbalance between written and orally transmitted musics in the context of monetary

power and the communications industries. (On copyright, see the overviews in Frith [1987] and Schneider [1991]; Wallis and Malm [1984: 163–215] provides brief but excellent case studies of Jamaican, Cuban, and Malawian musics and the positioning of folk elites like Harry Belafonte and Pete Seeger in their ownership problems. Laing [1986] and Tomlinson [1991] locate these problems within debates on media and cultural imperialism.)

Arjun Appadurai has characterized this intensification in global interaction as follows: "The world we live in now seems rhizomic, even schizophrenic, calling for theories of rootlessness, alienation and psychological distance between individuals and groups, on the one hand, and fantasies (or nightmares) of electronic propinquity on the other. . . . The central problem of today's global interaction is the tension between cultural homogenization and cultural heterogenization" (1990:2–3, 5). Contrary to the pessimism of Jameson's vision of postmodern schizophrenia (1990)—a pastiche of detemporalized surfaces, ahistorical dispersal, decontextualized stylistic diversity, authorial erasure, and the habit of being about itself—Appadurai sees more crucial space for struggles and creative contestations marking this schizophrenic condition. Music becomes a particularly poignant locale for understanding roots versus rootlessness, homogenization versus heterogenization, because, to state the case strongly, as Attali does: "Music is prophecy. Its styles and economic organization are ahead of the rest of society because it explores, much faster than material reality can, the entire range of possibilities in a given code" (1985:11). If one finds such privileging of music suspicious, there is a more fundamental reason for music's centrality to this rhizomic moment: Music is the most highly stylized of social forms, iconically linked to the broader cultural production of local identity and indexically linked to contexts and occasions of community participation.

These journalistic and academic discourses on musical worlds versus world beats are marked by the way they sense, anticipate, or feel the presence of escalation: a progressive, cumulative, interactive, pattern differentiation from intertwined mutuality, namely, complementary schismogenesis. If schizophonia, the splitting of sounds from sources, is the antecedent to life in today's global and transnational world of music, then schismogenesis is a way of describing the resultant state of progressive mutual differentiation that is playing out in at least four ways: as (a) an escalating dominance-submission pattern of ownership among the majors and independents, paralleled by a similar relationship between

Western pop stars and non-Western musicians; (b) an escalating succoring-dependence pattern between world beat and world music; (c) an escalating exhibitionism-spectatorship pattern between third- and fourth-world creators and first-world fans; and (d) an escalating homogenization-heterogenization struggle in the realm of musical style. The practices of and discourses on world music and world beat are in an increasingly politicized, polemicized zone in which the key struggles are over questions of authenticity—the rights and means to verify what Frith called "the truth of music"—and the dynamics of appropriation, particularly the rights and means to claim musical ownership.

If authenticity and appropriation are the sites of struggle, how is complementary schismogenesis located in the current practices of producing world music and world beat? One place to look is in the construction of signs of collaboration. Defenders of "world beat" point to ways in which it is a synthetic genre and a sign of international, cooperative collaboration. Musicians like Sting, David Byrne, Peter Gabriel, and Paul Simon have said such things in interviews, and most of their fans and many critics have no trouble presenting them in a positive and politically progressive light as a result. Moreover, there can be little question that many promoters, musicians, and media people are invested in "world beat" as a politically progressive and artistically avant-garde movement. One way in which this progressive agenda is articulated is through patronage, specifically, through the promotional and curatorial involvement of pop stars with real "world music" and the careers of its makers. This process has the positive effect of validating musicians and musics that have been historically marginalized, but it simultaneously reproduces the institutions of patronage and their attendant rights of validation, as well as their connection to long-standing patterns of cultivation central to elite avant-gardism. This situation locates musical practices close to visual-graphic ones, discussed vigorously in recent analyses of how local, "primitive" "crafts" are transformed into aesthetically and commercially significant ethno- "arts" through the rhetoric, sponsorship, and connoisseurship of Western artists, dealers, academics, collectors, and museums (Clifford 1988:189–251; Myers 1991; Price 1990:23–99; Torgovnick 1990:119–37).

One pattern for establishing merit and significance, and for expressing the nature of patronage and validation in the realm of musical recording, is through historical compilation projects in which documentation of emergent traditions is mixed with promotion of contemporary musics. These are good examples of safe genre statements of authenticity; they show a concern for roots and express the desire to validate historically dynamic and evolving traditions. These practices are closely linked to the recent emergence of benign yet serious scholarly analyses of international pop genres. Good academic examples, in which professional ethnomusicologists have studied particular popular musical histories, are Christopher Waterman and Veit Erlmann's successful compilations of *jùjú* and *mbube* roots for Rounder Records, documenting the rise of major Nigerian and South African musical syntheses over the last sixty years. With these as models it is difficult to criticize the more high-toned, commercial compilations produced by major pop stars, like David Byrne's volumes of Brazilian samba classics and Cuban musics.

Likewise, who could criticize the extraordinary respect shown in the care taken to record the Gyuto Monks, Dzintars, Hamza el Din, Zakir Hussain or Babatunde Olatunji with state-of-the-art technology in Mickey Hart's Rykodisc CD series, The World? Why not join the sentiments of Kyle Kevorkian, who in a *Mother Jones* article titled "Evolution's Top Forty" (1990) says of Hart's series, "The World isn't 'world beat'—it's the real thing, unadulterated." Likewise, why be cynical about Peter Gabriel's Real World Studios and Real World Records and WOMAD Talking Book projects, projects that have produced neglected yet important recordings of recent years, like the music of Tabu Ley Rochereau and Remmy Ongala, or the extraordinary voice of Youssou N'dour, or the *qawwali* music of Nusrat Fateh Ali Khan. Why imagine that Gabriel isn't utterly sincere when he says, "We're trying to make these other artists as well-known as we are" (Cheyney 1990). And from the other side, expressing his optimism about collaborations with Gabriel, we have Nusrat Fateh Ali Khan telling interviewers that "the West should understand our music and culture, and vice-versa. With such collaboration, artistes [sic] can come closer to each other and come to know each other" (Khan 1991). Or Youssou N'dour, concluding the liner notes to his popular CD *The Lion* (1989, Virgin Records) with these words: "Special thanks to my friend Peter Gabriel for all that he has done for me and for music in general. Africa thanks him for being the biggest promoter of music without frontiers."

With the same pop stars increasingly involved in curatorial, promotional, and collaborative roles, as well as entrepreneurial and appropriative roles, it is possible to understand how, in the critical discourse surrounding the production and circulation of world beat, assertions of altruism and generosity appear as frequently as accusations of cannibalism and colonialism. But viewed more structurally, this mixing of curatorial, promotional, and appropriative roles also means that genre lines between real "world music" and "world beat" are becoming increasingly blurred. So while fans and critics debate the political intentions of the artists or the implications of stylistic fusions for "the end of tradition" or "authenticity," record companies profit substantially through market saturation and greater audience familiarity. In other words, escalating a blurred-genre market means that sales of world beat promotes sales of world music and vice versa. This leads to a situation where Peter Gabriel and Real World might make almost as much money from the soundtrack recording to *The Last Temptation of Christ* as from the *Passion Sources* compilation, which consists of extended selections from the soundtrack's source material, including Pakistani *qawwali,* Moroccan wedding music, Armenian *duduk,* Zairian *soukous,* and Cuban *son-chanqui,* with Indian, Tanzanian, and Nile pieces as well. Of course this presentational spectrum helps sell both the specific artists and the Real World network by promoting the image of artists and musics as aesthetically, politically, and commercially unified. Patterns similar to the WOMAD/Real World Studios vision could be explored with regard to Mickey Hart's *Planet Drum* CD/cassette (winner of the 1992 Grammy for World Music) and his productions for the World series; Ben Mandelson's own band, Three Mustaphas Three, and his Globestyle Records projects; or David Byrne's compilation activities in Cuba and Brazil and his *Rei Momo* project.

Such patterns have begun to extend into print media—for example, Mickey Hart's *Drumming at the Edge of Magic* (Hart and Stevens 1990) and *Planet Drum* (Hart and Lieberman 1991)—and into television. The view of Brazilian trance rituals in David Byrne's *candomblé* film *Ilé Aiyé,* made for television, provides another angle on the process of dissolving oppositional mutuality through genre blurring; arty and stylish, yet very much in the conventional mold of PBS "documentary" (syrupy narration featuring nuggets of ancient wisdom of the others, plenty of sunsets and gyrating bodies), the film predictably has no time or place for locating *candomblé* in local politics, economy, or society. Byrne the curator is so busy transporting us into a world of "purely musical being" that the question of musical control, as Amy Taubin pointed out in a typically acute *Village Voice* column (11 July 1989), only surfaces, in small print titles, at the very end: "Original score by David Byrne, performed by (long list of Brazilian musicians)."

As these varieties of homogenization-heterogenization dialectics intensify, one form of dynamic equilibrium that can emerge from the escalating complementary schismogenesis of "world music" and "world beat" takes the following form: as the discourse of authenticity becomes more militant and nativistic, more complicated, and more particularized to specific interest and taste groups, the activities of appropriation get more overt and outrageous, as well as more subtle, legally sanctioned, accepted, and taken-for-granted. By placing the same pop stars, record companies, and media conglomerates in both the curatorial roles, as keepers of "truth" and "authenticity," and the entrepreneurial roles, as keepers of ownership and appropriative means, there will be a fusion of the parties for mutual business gain and unification against competing genres and business operations. Imperial transnational adaptation, or self-regulatory anticipation, here seems to be packaged, unfortunately, with a mechanism of "cultural greyout" (Lomax 1977). But greyout, and the devolutionary assumption that anchors it, need not prevail. The promotion of "world beat" has undoubtedly led to a great interest in and concern for the promotion and circulation of "world music" than ever existed before. Greater exposure and market power has improved the prospects for survival and development of local musics in unexpected ways. Additionally, the increasing blur of "world beat," as a more and more generic ethno-pop music, can also provoke marked and highly dramatic assertions of resistance-tinged local musics. Reggae is a prime example of this tension between genericization and stylistic markedness in the international arena. Its perception by indigenous peoples outside the Caribbean as an oppositional, roots ethno-pop form has led to its local adoption by migrants and indigenes in places as diverse as Europe, Hawaii, native North America, aboriginal Australia, Papua New Guinea, South Africa, and South East Asia. At the same time, the form has come to take on generic connotations that are often nonpolitical.

To bring matters back home, the position of rap in the black-white pop music scene is an urban American example of many of these dynamics. Rap is now a genre much more marked and oppositional than soul, rhythm and blues, or other black styles long ago appropriated or crossed-over. Rap's markedness derives from the ways it disrupts assignment of the label "artistry" to only those forms which participate in a particular discourse of originality. Digital sampling, the empire's own high-technology fetish, is subversively used here to resist and refuse to participate in Euro-world conventions of authenticity, to oppose them with an oral aesthetic of citation. In particular, this interferes with practices "naturalized" by Western legal codes of copyright and ownership.

Rap thus *recovers* an oral tradition long covered by outsiders. This inversion—the reappropriation by black artists of black and white musical material through sampling and digital manipulation—talks back to a whole history of white appropriation of black musical forms and styles (see Chapple and Garofalo 1977).

If, as writers and critics as diverse as Amiri Baraka and Robert Christgau rhetorically claim, black music today still is a reverberation of the rape of African rhythm by European harmony in slavery's brothels, then Public Enemy's "Fear of a Black Planet" rap should be listened to not just as a response to the rhetoric of "race mixing," but as an allegory of musical contact as schismogenesis. In this rap, a second voice emerges in counterpoint to the dominant verbal rhyme. Speaking deliberately, almost monotonically, with all the hip smugness of high performance art, the voice calmly delivers these lines:

> black man . . . black woman . . . black baby
> white man . . . white woman . . . white baby
> white man . . . black woman . . . black baby
> black man . . . white woman . . . black baby

More than a vernacular promotional jingle for Afrocentricity, such lines confront stereotype through style, and ask:

> white music capital . . . white pop stars . . . black roots grooves . . .
> white music? . . . or . . . black music?

Rap, now routinely seen as a site of struggle or contestation involving roots and rootlessness, race and ethnicity, identity and authority, marks a particular locale of social intensification. It is a powerful local example of the same schizophonia to schismogenesis dynamic now increasingly mapping world popular musical discourses.

———

What is at stake in the struggles about the meaning of the social world is power over the classificatory schemes and systems which are the basis of the representations of groups and therefore of their mobilization and demobilization.

—Pierre Bourdieu

[Music] makes audible what is essential in the contradictions of developed societies: an anxiety-ridden quest for lost difference, following a logic from which difference is banished.

—Jacques Attali

To explore now in a more experientially specific way how these anxieties over schizophonia and the world music–world beat schismogenesis dynamic enter into the documentation and commodification practices of ethnomusicologists, I will discuss the intertwined qualities of "struggles about the meaning of the social world" and the "quest for lost difference" in *Voices of the Rainforest*, my CD/cassette recording of music and environmental sounds from Bosavi, Papua New Guinea, commercially released on the Rykodisc label in April 1991. Having turned years of research into a popular object, I now feel the ironic obligation to turn that popular commodity into an object of research. To do that is to locate the intersection of local and global forces in these new forms of cultural production, an intersection that illustrates how participation in the commodification and circulation traffic of commercial "world music" provokes a potential case of what Renato Rosaldo (1989) has termed "imperialist nostalgia," situations where highly positioned parties lament, indeed, may feel anger about the passing of what they themselves have helped to transform. In this context projects like *Voices of the Rainforest* can simultaneously encode messages that might be read as representing both ends of a moral and political spectrum.

This exercise in clarifying the nature of professional complicity in schizophonia can also be read as part of a critique of ethnomusicology's practices of making and circulating recordings and, specifically, of its representational tendencies toward the construction of transparent, authoritative, realistic samples of "traditional music." Given the centrality of recordings to the history of ethnomusicology, critical awareness of the positioned nature of representation is as important to the current state of the field as is the more politically obvious discourse on cultural ownership and repatriation. Although most of the exercises of unmasking conventions of ethnographic representation have concerned print, literary, visual, or filmic genres (e.g., Marcus and Fischer 1986; Clifford and Marcus 1986; Clifford 1988), discussions of "writing" culture or "inscribing" otherness can be readily transposed to problems of auditory "recording," "magnetizing," "ingraining," "digitizing," and "modulating."

Surely it's a mark of the contemporary moment that the collision of forces responsible for *Voices of the Rainforest* presents little surprise or sense of improbability. But substantial disjunctions are embedded in this particular cultural production. For example, there is the contrast of recording in Papua New Guinea, "the last unknown" (a phrase originated by Gavin Souter's 1963 book title and still in popular circulation), where people of the highland interior have come into contact with outsiders only in the last fifty years, and making a commercial ultra-high-tech CD with portable state-of-the-art equipment and experimental, even pioneering, field and studio recording techniques. Or, the contrast of recording the sounds of birds and music among a small group of isolated people, the Kaluli, whose rainforest environment and cultural future are now threatened by—in addition to twenty years of evangelical missionization—recent oil exploration that will yield multibillion dollar profits for American, British, Australian, and Japanese companies, as well as for the government of Papua New Guinea—a government that owns the rights to everything under the surface of the land, and hence is actively, whether or not unwittingly, creating fourth-world ghettos as it continues to provide more and more extractive riches, at the cost of civil unrest and violent protests.

Then there is the contrast of an academic anthropologist, linguist, and ethnomusicologist (me) who has studied Kaluli language, music, and culture over the course of sixteen years, working with a rock-and-roll drummer, Mickey Hart of the Grateful Dead, active in the preservation of musical diversity through educational funding, concert promotion (the Gyuto Monks tours of America), books (*Drumming at the Edge of Magic*, 1990, and *Planet Drum*, 1991), and recordings. And the contrast in the final product: my previous two LP field recordings (Feld 1981b, 1985) were published in relatively obscure academic series, while Mickey produces a successful and well-known series, The World, licensed to Rykodisc, a major independent label whose catalog ranges from popular world musics to some of the more esoteric (Frank Zappa) and more glittery (David Bowie) rock artists known today.

There are parallel contrasts in the realm of promotion too. The events that launched *Voices of the Rainforest* are extraordinary when compared to those typically surrounding the release of an academic product. The Earth Day weekend opening gala for the recording began in the Northern California Mountains at the very plush and very private high-technology screening room of George (*Star Wars*) Lucas's Skywalker Ranch, where Randy Hayes, executive director of Rainforest Action Network, and Mickey Hart spoke on the intertwined topics of rainforest survival and musical survival, and I presented a megawatt surround-sound CD preview and synchronous computerized slide show for members of the audio, radio, and record industry. The next evening the three of us presented the show again at San Francisco's Greens Restaurant and hosted a $100-a-plate fund-raiser to benefit the Bosavi People's Fund, the trust Mickey and I established to receive royalties from *Voices of the*

Rainforest, and Rainforest Action Network's campaign against logging and rainforest destruction in the Kutubu-Bosavi area of Papua New Guinea.

During the next two months I traveled across the United States with the slide-show preview to venues ranging from classrooms to zoos to nightclubs to malls. Free presentations were coordinated with radio and popular press interviews, release parties, and appearances at book and record shops; when his concert schedule permitted Mickey participated too. The coordination of these activities required constant effort from the management and technical staff of Mickey's company, 360° Productions, as well as from the marketing and publicity staff of Rykodisc. In Australia, in April 1992, Festival Records coordinated over fifty national and local radio and press interviews. The scale of these activities provides a major, indeed outrageous, contrast to both the material wealth of the few thousand Kaluli people in Bosavi and to the typical funding and promotion for most academic research and publications.

The process that resulted in *Voices of the Rainforest* originated in a powerful confrontation that highlights a number of the disjunctions mentioned above. During the course of several periods of field research between 1976 and 1984 among the Kaluli people of Bosavi, Papua New Guinea, I produced two recordings. *Music of the Kaluli* (1981b) was published in Papua New Guinea to inaugurate the record and cassette series of the Institute of Papua New Guinea Studies; *The Kaluli of Papua Niugini: Weeping and Song* (1985) was published by Bärenreiter as the third volume in the Musicaphon Music of Oceania series edited by Hans Oesch. Both series are prestigious in academic ethnomusicological terms, but distribution for each disc was minimal; each sold just a few hundred copies, and neither was reviewed in scholarly journals, much less heard over the airwaves. Most of the people who read any of my Kaluli work never heard any of these recordings.

On the other hand, a radio program titled "Voices in the Forest" that I produced for National Public Radio in 1983, featuring a twenty-four-hour soundscape of the Bosavi rainforest, was an instant popular success (Feld 1990a:264–68). More than ten million people around the world heard this program, and it has been rebroadcast on several continents, even though it wasn't formally published until 1987. As a result of these experiences, the media of popular radio and grass-roots cassettes and the audiences I could reach through them seemed to offer a much more interesting approach to the sharing of the audio riches of my Papua New Guinea research. I had no desire to make another record.

Then I met Mickey Hart. That happened in 1984, when Thomas Vennum, Jr., an ethnomusicologist at the Smithsonian Institution's Office of Folklife Programs, and Fredric Lieberman, an ethnomusicologist at the University of California at Santa Cruz, were helping Mickey assemble information for his book projects about world percussion; they suggested that he talk with me about Papua New Guinea drums. Mickey called when the Grateful Dead tour passed through Philadelphia. We talked about drums, and I invited Mickey to listen to my recently completed NPR soundscape tape. He did, occasionally interjecting amazed questions about the sources of the sounds he was hearing. When the half hour, encompassing the sounds of a whole day in a Kaluli village, was over he looked at me and said, "That's incredible, and it's much too important to be kept an academic secret." I somewhat defensively countered that this wasn't an "academic secret" but was intended for National Public Radio. He said, "Highbrow, man," and offered to play it during intermission at that night's Grateful Dead concert! If I was stunned by the offer it was mostly because Mickey was completely casual and matter-of-fact about his populist vision of a new world order of musical consumption. This created a vantage point from which I could recognize that the shift from academic records to NPR wasn't radical at all, both channels being circumscribed within securely respectable, politely bourgeois institutions and consumption locales. I gulped: "You want to play *this* at a Grateful Dead show?" Mickey smiled devilishly: "Of course! Twenty thousand Deadheads will turn into tree-climbing monkeys about two minutes after I crank up the volume." When he said that I had a strange sensation. I felt embarrassed that I hadn't thought of this music as something that could appeal to a large audience, something that many others could enjoy as I had. Part of me knew that my recordings of the Kaluli should be heard by as many people as possible. Then I felt equally embarrassed by the realization that academia punishes popularizers, that I could easily succumb to guilt over both the urge to have the music heard and the knowledge that I might be contributing to an escalation of audio voyeurism, exoticism, and crass capitalism if I really participated in the kinds of commercial productions that would make it heard.

After years of ambivalence I finally decided to do a major project with Mickey, and the decision forced me to confront how world music commodification encodes multiple significances, from the benign and noble to the suspect and crass. As the first compact disc completely devoted to indigenous music from Papua New Guinea, *Voices of the Rainforest* signifies an effort to validate a specific culture and musical region otherwise generically submerged in American record stores in a bin labeled "Pacific." While the recording would not have been possible without my research background and long-term connection to Kaluli communities, *Voices of the Rainforest* is not principally a research document (for its research background, see chapter 4 and Feld 1990a). Rather, it is an unabashedly commercial product meant to attract as large an audience as possible through the appeal of superb audio reproduction and vibrant musical and natural sounds. Press coverage, radio play, and sales of ten thousand copies during the recording's first year on the market indicate some success at this agenda.

Voices of the Rainforest evokes twenty-four hours in the life of Bosavi in one continuous hour. We begin before dawn with a section entitled "From Morning Night to Real Morning," which features the overlapping voices of birds waking up a Kaluli village. A segment of morning sago-making follows; women sing as they scrape and beat sago starch, and their voices are overlapped by those of children, some echoing the song melody with whistled imitations of the birds whose calls are heard in the distance. Another morning work activity follows: groups of men sing, whoop, and yodel in echoed polyphony as they clear trees for a banana garden; after the trees are down women clear the brush with machetes, singing as they go. These morning sections are followed by two midday tracks illustrating leisure music making, first a series of bamboo mouth harp duets with bird calls and cicada rhythms, then a woman singing at, with, and about a waterfall. A return to ambient sounds follows this section. "From Afternoon to Afternoon Darkening" chronicles the transition from afternoon bird volleys, to the dense electronic-sounding interplay of insects, to frogs of dusk. An evening rainstorm follows, with interspersed voices of frogs, insects, and bats. Next is a ceremonial sequence, first with a group of drummers and then a ritual song performance that moves an audience member to tears. The recording closes with an ambient segment, "From Night to Inside Night," in which voices of frogs, owls, kingfishers, and night insects pulse through misting winds into the hours toward dawn. In total, Bosavi is presented as a coordinated world of continuously overlapping sound clocks, of ambient rhythms and cycles intermeshed with human musical invention, performance, and spontaneous interactions.

Voices of the Rainforest departs aesthetically and structurally from the typical, commercial world music CD to take a major musical risk: the recordings, although conventionally numbered as cue bands, are fused and continuous, and they include equally the natural environmental sounds and local musical expression found in Bosavi. All of these sounds, ambient and musical, are edited together to produce one fluid sixty-minute soundscape, a metacomposition that evokes, through my technological mediation, ways Kaluli experience and express the music of nature as the nature of music. Without academic explication, the recording allows the listener to enter and subjectively experience what the Kaluli call *dulugu ganalan* "lift-up-over sounding." Kaluli invoke this idea to explain the overlapping, interlocking, alternating nature of all sounds, ambient and human, and the textural density and in-synchrony but out-of-phase organization in their vocal and instrumental genres. The vocal and instrumental tracks on the disk are inspired both sonically and textually by natural sounds, and the editing makes it possible for a listener to experience how Kaluli appropriate these sounds into their texts, melodies, and rhythms, merging with the musical ecology of their place. In work, leisure, and ceremonial contexts, Kaluli musical invention is illustrated to be of a piece with the sounds of birds or waterways or the pulses of frogs and crickets. The recording thus illuminates how "lift-up-over sounding" is the Bosavi rainforest groove, the

Jubi and Steve recording bird voices; Bosavi, Papua New Guinea, 1982. Photo Shari Robertson.

Voices of the Rainforest, cover, 1991, Rykodisc. Art by Karyl Klopp, photo courtesy of 360° Productions, Rykodisc.

Mickey Hart and Steve mixing *Voices of the Rainforest* at Studio X. Photo © John Werner, 1993.

transformative pulse that simultaneously makes nature sound so musical and their music feel so natural.

To fully evoke this rainforest groove, Mickey and I, as technological intermediaries, assembled the best field recording package we could imagine. Given the unreliability, in rainforest humidity, of current portable digital tape technology, as well as its tendency to thin out critical high frequencies that we wanted to be as warm and saturated as possible in recording birds, insects, and water sounds, we were committed to analog recording. We combined a customized Nagra tape recorder with a Bryston portable Dolby SR noise-reduction unit and an Aerco preamp, which optimized response from our phantom-powered AKG microphones. The noise-reduction unit, which had not previously been used in a remote rainforest locale, plunged the noise floor of the analog system and allowed me to record extremely soft ambient sounds with no appreciable increase in noise.

Microphones are to ears what camera lenses are to eyes, reductive technological devices that imitate human sensory apparatus by performing specific ranges of limited functions from which perceivers then recreate fuller perceptual cues. Using two cardiod capsules in an XY configuration—the ends of the microphones criss-crossed, one on top of the other to make an X—images the broadest stereo sound field in the density of the forest. But without multiple microphones and portable mixing capabilities it is impossible to simultaneously record, with full spatial dimensionality, the height and depth of the ambient rainforest environment, either alone or as musical backdrop to other sounds. Knowing that one real-time, two-track recording would not produce a full audio image, I decided to record the forest's height and depth dimensions separately and to add them back together at Mickey's studio using multitrack recording technology. This meant often mixing two or three sets of stereo tracks to re-create the full audio atmosphere of any particular time of day or musical occasion.

Obviously such a practice violates the spatial and temporal integrity of any given recorded moment or event, but in return it offers the possibility of optimizing the sense of a layered sound environment. These field and studio practices were not simply a case of *trompe l'oreille*, experimentation occasioned by a desire to transcend the technical limitations of microphones and live two-track recording. They were also stimulated by the nature of the Kaluli sound world. I had always wondered if the local idea of "lift-up-over sounding" indicated that the temporality of

sound was literally imagined by Kaluli as spatialized height arching outward. Recording component audio tracks in the field allowed me to experiment informally and attempt to further understand the "lift-up-over
sounding" aesthetic of sonic density. Playing back transfers of component tracks on two cassette recorders, I asked Kaluli assistants to adjust
volume controls on the two machines until the composite sounded good
to them. When the tracks combined musical performances and environmental surround sounds, Kaluli tended to amplify the surround tracks,
particularly of the middle and upper forest canopy. Comments made to
me on these occasions elaborated others I had heard previously, to the effect that, in the presence of musical performance, the sounds of the forest
heights are copresent and equally significant. This sort of bush premixing
studio put Kaluli in a directly dialogic editorial role in the project, extending my earlier experiments with dialogic editing (Feld 1987a). Back
at the mixing studio, where I worked for four months to edit and mix the
one-hour master from eighteen hours of original recordings, I was able
to incorporate these Kaluli ideas into the editing and mixing, pursuing
and acknowledging the socially negotiated and constructed ethnoaesthetics of the production.

Other studio practices similarly violated the basic tenets of documentary realism, creating instead a hyperrealism that I find justified by both
technoaesthetic and ethnoaesthetic ideals. In Bosavi I frequently recorded birds close-up, without parabolic reflectors, from blinds, perches,
or tree houses. By quickly playing back birds' calls I was often able to get
them to come closer and repeat their calls, and in some cases, after a few
days or weeks, I was able to record them almost as close-up as I did
Kaluli singers. To enhance our ability to reproduce the textural density
of "lift-up-over sounding," studio engineer Jeff Sterling and I digitally
sampled seventy-five bird, frog, and insect sounds from my close-up
recordings, then, using real-time guide tracks that I made in the field on
cassette, rerecorded the samples onto the multitrack master, which allowed us to locate them with greater spatial and temporal specificity in
the mix of forest height and depth. The clarity of the digital samples also
helped to optimize the lucidity of the bird and human mix, and thus to
create an ambience in which the listener experiences, as one does in the
rainforest, the strong sense of avian audio-presence in the height and
depth of the canopy. Because birds have inspired Kaluli music, are considered singers in their own right, and are also *ane mama,* "gone reflections," the spirits of dead, their presence is experientially intensified for

Kaluli in the forest. Our editing and mixing was intended to underscore this intensity by bringing the birds into the audio foreground as they are in Kaluli imagination and experience.

Apart from these considerations of *Voices of the Rainforest*'s experimental audio practices, one must scrutinize the potential for techno-aesthetics to mask technofetishism. Mass culture criticism raises the significant argument that such projects fulfill the economic and social needs of their makers, reproducing their positions of privileged access and their ability to define just what kind of adventure may be had. But it is equally important to explore the potential for technoaesthetics to create cultural respect and musical empowerment. For many years indigenous peoples have taken a second-class ride on cheap recording equipment as part of a process of "othered" record production—the dignified but masking term is "noncommercial." Minimal audio quality was often accompanied by a lack of concern for circulation and a tacit assumption that there would be no royalties to speak of, certainly none to return to the musicians or communities where the music was recorded. Such practices have been central to both the rhetorical traffic and the actual commodity circulation of musical diversity. Lack of circulation, like lack of royalties, has come to be inextricably linked to claims for authenticity; marginality in the marketplace has been the central sign or indicator of "real," "authentic," "ethno" music. Equating popularity with both vulgarity and loss of authenticity thus locates ethnomusicological projects in the elitist discourses that validate "other" musics by creating for them an imitation of the autonomous arena musicologists once created for western European art music.

But do such practices actually engender respect for musical diversity? Couldn't they as easily be interpreted as signs of the reproduction of musical colonialism, the redistribution of bounty in the form of recordings whose exotic content is indexically signaled by muffled grooves? Hart's alternative, in which I am complicit, surely has its own imperial implications. It insists that the best equipment, engineers, budgets, and distribution networks can and should be shared beyond the world of symphony orchestras and high-tech rock and roll. Mickey locates himself as an activist for the technological redistribution of wealth and musical empowerment and positions me, the Kaluli, and listeners as beneficiaries of that activism. He also positions Kaluli as principal beneficiaries of the recording's royalties. This is complicated to decode; the move simultaneously strikes back toward equity and empowerment, yet substantially reproduces the entrepreneurial and curatorial positions of the already empowered.

As liner notes I wrote an imaginary letter to Mickey from the rainforest. This device allowed me to speak in a vernacular voice and to maintain the emphasis on being there and taking the listener there. In addition to describing the contents and contexts of the recordings, the notes acknowledge the irony of the disc: just as the music receives international recognition as a volume in The World series, Kaluli songs, along with their other cultural practices, are transforming or vanishing, and the environment of the Great Papuan Plateau is being threatened by oil pipelines, roads, and logging. Drawing attention to the relationship between cultural and ecological destruction in rainforests, the notes use the term "endangered music," provoking the listener to imagine how the ravages of artistic loss suffered by indigenous people are linked to the loss of species from their local flora and fauna and the degradation of their waters and lands.

The ways these multiple dimensions of world music are figured in relation to *Voices of the Rainforest* as a commercial production are obviously connected to current debates in anthropology and other fields about the politics of cultural representation, about dimensions of control, authority, ownership, "authenticity," and power relations. Many anthropologists were once content to celebrate and embrace local intellectuals and their societies, particularly small-scale ones, for their integrity; inspired by myriad forms of inventiveness and experiential patterns that challenged their conventional senses of self and other, they celebrated diversity in idealized terms. Now, when it is widely assumed that there is much less cultural diversity or integrity left on the planet, many anthropologists have become critics of state-indigene relations, resistance cheerleaders, or cultural survival advocates, inspired to their own vision, alienation, or need to struggle, by the intensity of chaos and harm so powerfully and recklessly visited upon the others they chronicle. The politics of being an engaged and responsible researcher are now bound up with giving voice to people whose validity, indeed, whose humanity, is denied or silenced by the world's dominant cultures. Because the practices of anthropology are so firmly located within this discursive side-taking, the field's intellectual products—talk, writings, recordings, films—have been subjected to increasing scrutiny from both inside and out, by the community that undertakes the research and the community that is its subject (see Said 1989).

How then might one further scrutinize the representational politics of *Voices of the Rainforest* simultaneously as commercially avant-garde cultural production and as "world music"? One way is to acknowledge that *Voices of the Rainforest* presents a unique soundscape day in Bosavi, one without the motor sounds of tractors cutting the lawn at the mission airstrip, without the whirring rhythms of the mission station generator, washing machine, or sawmill. Without the airplanes taking off and landing, without the mission station or village church bells, Bible readings, prayers, and hymns. Without the voices of teachers and students at an airstrip English-only school, or the few local radios straining to tune in Radio Southern Highlands, or cassette players with run-down batteries grinding through well-worn tapes of string bands from Central Province or Rabaul. Without the voices of young men singing Tok Pisin songs while strumming an occasional guitar or ukulele at the local airstrip store. And without the recently intensified and almost daily overhead buzz of helicopters and light planes on runs to and from oil drilling areas ranging over thirty miles to the northeast.

Does this mean that *Voices of the Rainforest* is a falsely idealized portrait of Bosavi's current acoustic ecology, romantic at best, deceptive at worst? Certain critical viewpoints could position it that way, and an honest response could only accept why those concerns are voiced and acknowledge the currency of their politics. After all, *Voices of the Rainforest* transparently embodies the highest of postmodern ironies: it presents for us a world uncontaminated by technology, but one that is hearable only because it has been brought to us courtesy of the most high-tech audio field and studio techniques currently available. But it is also important to insist that the recording is a highly specific portrayal, one of an increasingly submerged and subverted world of the Bosavi soundscape. Clearly, it is a soundscape world that some Kaluli care little about, a world that other Kaluli momentarily choose to forget, a world that some Kaluli are increasingly nostalgic and uneasy about, a world that other Kaluli are still living and creating and listening to. It is a sound world that increasingly fewer Kaluli will actively know about and value, but one that increasingly more Kaluli will hear on cassette and sentimentally wonder about.

Lest it seem that I am hedging, let me state the stakes more bluntly and personally. I find the sound world in Bosavi to be powerful and unsettling; more importantly, it can still be heard. Because my role in *Voices of the Rainforest* is equal parts researcher and sound artist, I feel a need to amplify that world unashamedly, in the hope that hearing it might inspire and move others as it has inspired and moved me. The recording then is no illusory denial that both nature and culture in Bosavi are being drowned out by "development," the apologist's euphemism for extraction and erasure. Rather it is an affirmative "counterdrowning" of "development" noise through the aggressive assertion of a coevolved sonic ecology and aesthetics. As a celebration that is also an alarm, my representational re-erasing is motivated equally by affection and by outrage, acknowledging both the memory of florescence and the escalating sense of loss that characterizes Kaluli life today. *Voices of the Rainforest* speaks to remembrance at a moment of forgetting, talking back from my feelings of revulsion over the way mission and government rhetoric about "development" and a "better future" has meant more vulnerability, less autonomy, less culture, and diminished integrity for Bosavi people now.

The notions of "endangered music" and "endangered culture" also demand scrutiny: equating music and culture with animal and plant species may give the impression that the project is promoting protectionist purism, cultural zoos, reservations, or conservation parks. Preservationist agendas often have very conservative political slants, and invoking the notion of endangerment may dredge up fears of control, of desires to freeze time and place. There can be no doubt that the use of the "endangered" label is problematic, is potentially dangerous, and may be deeply insulting to indigenous peoples in the context of their struggles to control the terminology and imagery with which their interests and identities are represented.

On the other hand, aligning the status of certain musics and cultures with that of "endangered" species encourages a potentially important intellectual and political alliance. Every current instance of the thinning out of biological diversity is connected to the real or potential thinning out of cultural, linguistic, and artistic diversity. Environmentalists and ecologists are becoming increasingly aware of important ways in which interactions between humans and plants and animals not only shape processes of adaptation but define the very nature of regions and communities. Linking the struggles for rainforest environments with the future of the people indigenous to them is an essential aspect of promoting the integrity, indeed the survival, of people and place and of local rights. Besides, anthropologists have virtually let the environmental movement freely create the illusion that the only thing at stake in ecodestruction is cute and cuddly animals and the plants that Western pharmacy needs to cure cancer. It is critical for us to insist, to the contrary, that the struggle for these places is the struggle for the survival of people whose knowledge of the animals and plants is critical both to balanced management and future deployment for global medical betterment.

Obviously, intersecting issues such as these, the editorial politics and aesthetics of *Voices* are dense and complicated. So are the consumption concerns that extend from them. So far nobody has thoroughly confused the recording with the New Age meditation tapes whose titles, while similar, indulge and seduce with promised echoes of the audio-idyllic. But as we all know, in popular culture subordinate social formations are always the sources of fantasy and relaxation for the dominant classes or societies. *Voices of the Rainforest* hence undeniably contributes to both enhanced Western primitivist fantasy and voyeurism, allowing a listener to enjoy an hour of yuppie green politics, or audio-leisure tourism, perhaps even while feeling righteous about wealth trickle-down. "Release" from the modern world and into the "awesomeness" of nature is central to the nostalgia promulgated by the New Age movement, refashioning prior romanticisms and recreating them as quasi-spiritual experiences that connect "us" to "them." Does any of this neutralize my intentions or the potentials of the recording to work against the grain of destabilization?

Once a recording is in the marketplace one has little control over how it is consumed. Notes and contextualizing material, as well as interviews and other media interventions, may indicate one's desire to take responsibility for representation but cannot control what happens once the decision to commodify has been made. That is, significantly, also true for "merely academic" recordings (see Seeger 1991a, 1991b), even those framed by obscure jargonized notes, musical transcriptions, or specific invocations. For example, when recordings of Aboriginal Australian or Sepik (Papua New Guinea) music carry the explicit label, "Do not play this recording in the presence of any females or uninitiated male members of the [relevant] society," does this actually control who hears the music? Does discharging one's ethical duty by way of a cover sticker have any greater effect than prescribing "proper" forms of reception and consumption through notes on meaning and intention?

An additional problem in this case is that anthropological and political debate on control of and responsibility for representation is circumscribed in almost entirely realist and literalist terms. The most typical criticism of *Voices of the Rainforest* is framed in that way, as an insistence that destruction and domination be treated in more overt, "serious" terms. That critique strikes me as sincere but naive. The only response, and an old one at that, is that artistic projects are, for some of us, equally overt and serious, however much greater risk their subtleties bring to the realm of cultural politics.

Mickey and I dedicated ourselves to the hope that state-of-the-art audio techniques and a combined artistic and political vision would make the recording not only the best possible audio document but a dramatic statement of current environmental and cultural survival issues in Bosavi, an evocation of both the florescence and the loss of rainforest musical ecology. In a world where fifteen to twenty thousand species of plants and animals a year are destroyed by the logging, ranching, and mining that escalates rainforest destruction (Caufield 1984, Collins 1990), *Voices of the Rainforest* was meant as an assertion that we must be equally mindful of the precarious ecology of songs, myths, words, and ideas in these mega-diversity zones. Massive wisdom, variations on human being in the form of knowledge in and of place, is a cocasualty of the ecocatastrophe. The thinning out of ecological systems may proceed at a rate much slower than the rubbing out of cultures, but cultural rub-out is a particularly effective way to accelerate ecological thin-out. The politics of rainforest ecological and aesthetic coevolution and co-devolution are one, and Mickey's initial reaction to hearing the Bosavi rainforest was eerily appropriate in the larger political economy of musical and cultural destruction: this *is* too important to remain an academic secret.

The representational issues embodied in the recording, editing, marketing, and royalty distribution of *Voices of the Rainforest* are closely situated in the larger process I've called schizophonia to schismogenesis. Once sounds like these are split from their sources, that splitting is dynamically connected to escalating cycles of distorting mutuality, which in turn is linked to polarizing interpretations of meaning and value. "Schizophonia to schismogenesis," concretely located in the creation and circulation of "world music" for consumption, provides an example of a generalized social experience central to our historical, discursive, and cultural moment: Just as "tradition" was constructed as the nostalgia of modernity, so its vaguer cousin, "memory" is inserted as the nostalgia of postmodernity. In this context I must acknowledge that my passion for sharing what I've been privileged to experience cannot mask my complicity with institutions and practices of domination central to commodifying otherness. Hence a necessary engagement with the problematics of what Rosaldo has called "imperialist nostalgia" and the parallel necessity to explore how projects embarked upon with self-consciously progressive political and aesthetic agendas are neither innocent of nor discursively free from postcolonial critiques.

Commodified Grooves

SF: Why compare polka and blues? Is your main idea here to tease out something intrinsically significant about the similarities of those musics? Or is it to legitimate the rubric "people's music" and remind us that the "folk" idea obscures class analysis? In your pieces on style in the first part of the book, you discuss process, then texture. Now, moving into the commodified dimensions of musical experience, you position class as the driving force behind style in the mediated context. What's going on?

CK: Well, polka and blues were the two musics I had spent the most time studying here in the USA, and suddenly parallels began to emerge for me. I began to hear Walk Solek as the T-Bone Walker of polkas, Bobby Blue Bland as the Marion Lush of blues. There were so many deep parallels that I couldn't avoid the comparisions. It seems to me that just when high culture collapses, at the end of the nineteenth century and the beginning of the twentieth, and just when there is no longer any forward momentum in composing music, in the syntactic games, then the jazz, blues, and gospel processes all begin to emerge in the context of radio and records—the context of mediation, massive mediation. They are emerging in a twentieth century which has not panned out according to the Marxist vision of the proletariat becoming conscious of itself and seizing the tools of production. But all the time I was writing this piece for *Dialectical Anthropology*, Stanley Diamond's journal, I was thinking that those musical styles validated the Marxian premise that the working class is conscious, if not of its destiny, at least of its ongoing existence and its need to re-create itself weekend after weekend, vis-à-vis alienation, at a deep aesthetic, stylistic, and musical level. Despite the differences between the two styles they share a large number of common denominators. There is such a precise history of when the musics make their move, or when they emerge as powers to define identity and style, that when you see the parallels between blues and polka, like both having simple syntax but compelling grooves, it becomes persuasive that class forces are doing this, and not some ethnic essence. What else could it be?

SF: How about the record companies?

CK: Well, the media are the mediators of this class awareness. It is like putting yourself in public space via a sound or a style. Blues and polka are both acceptances of dominant culture stereotypes in the media, on radio and records. I do say in the essay that style is always and everywhere a product of class forces, but I am trying to relate it back to "lift-up-over sounding" and your whole take on style in Kaluliland. In the last chapter of *Tiv Song* I try to take Armstrong and stand him right side up; you take Armstrong and make the trope idea work for the Kaluli. So we are both saying that there is one style in a classless society that has everything to do with environment and ecology, and that when the class forces arrive is when people become unhooked from environment, ecology, and neighbors, and something else begins to shape the music. Class relations are going to shape this music. I think that is what you are going to witness during the coming years in Kaluliland, class forces grabbing hold of the Kaluli and reshaping their music.

SF: Don't you think that idealizes class, or idealizes style in relation to class, in terms of its coherence?

CK: We didn't get a proletarian revolution. I think the only thing we did get was style.

SF: So you're using style synonymously with the notion of identity here?

CK: I think that is what it's about. Style tells you who your home folks are and gives you that rock-solid reference point. Whatever the hell else is going on out there, I know that I am a polka person, a blues person, or a jazz person. The music is a deep, subconscious reference point that will confirm identity under all circumstances, and the people's response in 1927 and 1928 was to accept certain stereotypes and celebrate them rather than to disappear. I think it is a very powerful statement of just how important music is. It really does anchor people's reality in a way that nothing else can.

SF: Do you think that is happening in jazz? Last night we were watching the Louis Armstrong video and saw Louis singing "Shine" while wearing a leopard-skin suit, standing up to his ass in soap suds.

Louis Armstrong in leopard skin and soapsuds in the film *Rhapsody in Black and Blue,* 1932. Photo courtesy of Toby Byron, Avalon Archives.

And we heard Louis citing that Joe Glazer quote, that Joe turned him on to the notion that you got to be some white man's nigger; that's when Louis said, "I'm your man." It reminded me of John Lomax and Leadbelly . . .

CK: . . . or Muddy Waters and Leonard Chess, or Miles Davis and Clive Davis. I don't know how all those plantation scenarios worked themselves out . . .

SF: Are they all about accepting stereotypes in order to transcend them?

CK: I don't think that they are *all* about that, but I think you get left with a deep, deep message about the triumph of the voice and of sound over all the ugly social realities. Louis Armstrong, when he is up to his ass in soap suds, wearing a leopard skin, and singing "Shine," is nevertheless, as both Lester Bowie and Wynton Marsalis want to insist, a revolutionary figure. That is the juxtaposition made in the film. And I think it's true. Louis Armstrong is a revolutionary figure even when he is up to his ass in soap suds because the power of his voice, the power of his trumpet, and the power of his presence, his affecting presence, cut right through all that. Nothing they can do to Louis is so absurd that it will obstruct the power of his voice and his trumpet.

SF: Louis singing in his leopard skins reminded me of Leadbelly on stage in his prison stripes. That was from his time with Lomax. There is a wonderful quote from Pete Seeger that I've seen in a few places, including the *Rolling Stone* issue when Leadbelly was inducted into the rock and roll hall of fame. Seeger reminisces about being a scruffy Harvard kid wearing torn-up dungarees, T-shirts, and loafers, idolizing Leadbelly as a "true folk singer," then realizing that Leadbelly always wore a freshly laundered shirt, pressed suit, new bow tie, shined shoes; he dressed sharp and proud.

CK: This is the class issue again. The big jive played on all Americans is that they go past each other stylistically in this fashion sense of style: rich kids from the suburbs get dressed up in ripped jeans and pretend they are working class, poor, or lumpen, while poor blacks and Puerto Ricans are dressing to the teeth, going to the disco and pretending that they are part of the jet set. The equivalent of that went on throughout minstrelsy, during the whole nineteenth and into the twentieth century, in which Americans pretended to be each other, to be of different classes and regions.

SF: So is this just some massive, Bakhtinian, carnivalesque set of reversals: The suburban, upper-middle-class kids at the mall buying high-priced torn jeans, and the lower- and working-class African-Americans going to church in beautiful clothing, proud, with color, with hats, with well-polished cars?

CK: I would say that it is all testimony to the pain of class hurts on *both* sides of the class divide, the hidden and not so hidden injuries of class, being assuaged by style. But I think that in "Style and Stereotype" here, I am after something a little bit deeper in the way of style, just as you are with the "lift-up-over" thing . . .

SF: . . . the relationship between expressive ideology, identity, value . . .

CK: . . . and in some incorruptible way. I think that is why you think we're being too essentialist or putting too much of an idealized, romantic load on style here.

SF: Let me take it back to that phrase of Gregory Bateson's that I ended with in the "lift-up-over sounding" discussion of style. What does Bateson mean when he says that style is the "algorithm of the heart"? There's something there about a driving, predictable, mechanized property, but at the same time it feels like he means something like what you talk about: strong identity, feelings of community-based identity . . .

CK: . . . something so intensely collective, not planned or intended, that it is organic. I really think that style is an organic phenomenon in the sense of having seeds, growth, florescence, decay. There is something very clear in my mind about jazz fizzling as a coherent style in the late 1960s, just as classical, through-composed music fizzled in the early 1900s. You can hear styles come and go, like this whole fifties phenomenon of blues stereotypes being revived— Muddy Waters, Howlin' Wolf, and having to have those personas in the 1950s.

SF: But I want to get further into the mediation dimensions of all this and your thoughts on just how mediation is central to this change. Is it that the mediation is a rite of intensification? In other words, once people get the opportunity to put out their music on record, is there a desire, from the performers, producers, and record companies, not just to crystallize and perfect but to push further? Is that what you are talking about with these forms of getting wilder, racier at these polka parties, more drunk on style and happiness?

CK: I hint at the relationship between Apollonian recorded versions and live Dionysian versions in this article, but I think that is something to be explored in all the styles in the world that have been recorded for decades. A standard develops of what something is supposed to sound like on records, and performers then work against or with that standard in their onstage performances. I keep thinking of T-Bone Walker and Walt Solek, controlled on records and wild in person.

SF: So in the relationship between what you call the hegemonic thrust and class, can you see mediation as a series of techno-rituals of intensification whose outcome is the present discourse on authenticity? For example, once Ravi Shankar started recording live in front of American audiences, like at UCLA, he was criticized for being too jazzy, for playing to the Western audience. The authenticity of the performances was questioned by Indian music aficionados.

CK: This may be the inverse of why polkas and blues were never recorded live for forty years. In theory, there were all these opportunities to record polka live from the 1920s on. But nobody ever did it. Li'l Wally did two albums at the Club Baby Doll, and those were the only live, in-person polka recordings out of thousands and thousands of recordings. And the same thing with blues. B. B. King's, *Live at the Regal*, in '63 or whenever that came out was the first live, in-person blues recording with an audible audience responding, and all of a sudden you could hear who "Lucille" (his

B.B. King and "Lucille" working the crowd; Club Handy, Memphis, early 1950s. Photo by Ernest C. Withers, copyright © 1987 Mimosa Records Productions, Inc.

guitar) was talking to all those years. None of the Crown recordings, none of the B. B. King recordings for twenty years prior to that, none of them were live, so you never heard the audience respond to his calls. So those recordings were not an intensification, if you see what I mean. To record the music live would intensify it, would up the ante. Then the question becomes, can B. B. King do it as well live when we see him at the Regal next time? His live performances then are going to be held up against some recorded standard. So I think the polka and blues people, out of some kind of proletarian awareness, kept their recorded thing separate from their live, in-person thing. So recording is not an intensification so much as a kind of distillation, a clarification maybe, the cleanest version you can do. I think some of these styles or traditions have autonomy or authenticity in their play-place or workplace or neighborhood or locality. There they have their own integrity, and then the recorded thing is just a memory device.

SF: How do you see this in relation to live jazz recordings?

CK: Have you read that book by Roger Taylor, *Art: An Enemy of the People*? He has an analysis of jazz in there that opened my eyes. He said that by the 1920s there were already eight or nine definitions of jazz and that four or five of those definitions had to do with it being art music, or at least removed from some essence of Afro-American music. Where is the real jazz? On records? In the uptown clubs? Downtown? In after-hours sessions, when they are not playing in the club? Taylor convinced me that it was being simultaneously "artified" and commodified much earlier, that the hegemonic forces of high culture wanted jazz at some level, and the recording industry wanted jazz, and poor old jazz had to kind of walk the tightrope between commodification and artification from the git-go. These piano "professors" were playing in bordellos with impressionist paintings on the wall in 1911. It already had this exotica, erotica, artistica thing going early on.

SF: I'm still wondering about idealizing style. You pin it to Sapir's genuine culture, and for me that puts it into a whole bunch of problematic spaces about how authenticity only emerges when it is counter to forces that are trying to screw it up, transform it, dominate it, mess with it . . .

CK: If we are going to use style as the central variable and talk about it in class society or classless society, then I would say that there is a whole lot more of it in classless society. It suffuses everyday life. But style shrinks as you move to class society, where it becomes more distilled or more tenuous or may not be there at all. I think there are a whole lot of people in this world who are styleless in some fundamental way or who have to—like in the *My Music* interviews—construct an idiocultural style for themselves out of the bits and pieces of mediated stuff that they get. That is the thread that they hang onto and weave around in terms of a personal identity or a self.

SF: Don't get me wrong; I don't want style to be synonymous with
shared or undifferentiated culture. I am just saying that I know it's
tempting to make class a singular divide on the term style, because
in your stuff and Chris Waterman's, David Coplan's, and Tom
Turino's on the class/urban side, or Marina Roseman's, mine, and
Tony Seeger's on the classless/rainforest side, it's clear that style is
the place where people are working out the politics and poetics of
identity. But we haven't talked much here about how innovation
gets worked into these sort of issues, and particularly how strong
changes intensify the coherence of style . . .

CK: That's a really interesting puzzle, isn't it?

SF: . . . how does an Ulahi emerge in Bosavi? How does a woman who
has composed two hundred songs in the last twenty years emerge
in a culture where it is virtually only men who have done that sort
of thing, and why are other Kaluli, including men, singing her
songs now? . . .

CK: . . . same thing in Tivland. People are still singing Bam Gindi's
songs thirty years after he died and saying they have a special take
on what it means to be Tiv. Or Kuji Iyum's short, powerful songs
satirizing his girlfriend of fifteen years before. They were together
six weeks, and he composed songs about it which have had a phe-
nomenal staying power in the Tiv imagination. I guess that what
you are persuading me of is that there is more of a continuum here
between classless and class, or between all peoples, and that style
as a key variable is telling us different things in these different contexts. But it is also telling us the same thing: that people insist on
ordering their emotional and cognitive identity. What we are on
the planet for is to shape that identity.

SF: Well, if style is about the constructedness of identity, that is where
the politics and the poetics are fused. But why do you resist that as
a basis for thinking about processes of expression equally in class or
classless societies?

CK: When we say identity, two things are happening in my mind.
Separate identity—every signature, every dance, every person who
dances does so differently. So a different identity, a different style,
can be on the individual or idiocultural level. Then there is subcul-
tural style and so forth, all these kinds of identities. But there is also
identity in the sense of Arne Naess's deep ecology, deep identification—identification with the natural world, with natural forces,
with your totem. And that is why I see a class-classless divide. I

don't think *we* have that kind of identity. When Ulahi achieves her identity as a composer of songs in Kaluliland, it is *with* the waterfall and the natural world. The identities of most artists in the class world are not the same, are not identifications *with*. Isn't that a crucial difference? I keep wanting to extract a moral message or mission for us vis-à-vis our Western context, to say that we need more style, more of the identity *with* and participation *in* the natural forces. I think that is what your *Voices of the Rainforest* outreach is about. It's about identification, right? Getting identified with the rainforest as not just an abstract place with a lot of species, but with how it sounds and with how the Kaluli feel: here is an inkling of what Kaluli experience is like twenty-four hours a day.

SF: But when you say in your article that a vital style always has aspects competing for primacy, what drives that? And why would it be any different in classless societies? The differences between men and women, the roles of age, knowledge, and segmentation within the community—lots of forces that form dimensions of difference within a society could drive the way vital styles always have aspects competing for primacy . . .

CK: For sure in Tivland, there are men's and women's dances. Each has its own dynamic. Men are supposed to be displaying, acrobatic, and doing odd contortions. The men are angular as hell, pushing the absurd in order to keep the interest. The women play with angles in more graceful undulating ways.

SF: I keep thinking about the Kaluli men, creating that huge fuss around themselves with their ceremonies, in comparision with Kaluli women, whose funerary weeping is nowhere near as illuminated in the Kaluli spotlight. Song and weeping are central to differentiating male and female gender identities, especially in terms of this issue—the power to create an arena where performance is linked to strategic outcomes and long-ranging influence. But the distinction isn't rigid; women also compose and sing, and men also cry. Songs move men to tears and weeping moves women to sing—those dimensions embody all the tensions. Genre separation and blurring is iconic to Kaluli egalitarian tensions around gender. Their expressive economy is a very concrete locus of emergent differentiation.

CK: Deep, deep differences. In Tivland, it is intensely competitive, those dance displays in the marketplace . . .

SF: This is not as competitive, but what is so interesting is that Kaluli men and women are doing such *different* things, like ceremonial song versus ritual funerary weeping, but they do them *in the same way* stylistically. Both are "lift-up-over sounding," but one is with the costumes and the ceremonial spotlight, while in the other—people die and suddenly women are improvising sung-wept poetry. So what exactly is competing for primacy? Certainly something about the male-female struggle to establish a priority of principles: Those ways that men are charged up to put on an all-night show that can't be controlled because of the intense sadness and anger it provokes—there is a drive there to establish that as a model of action, authority, assertion. Compare that to the way women are calm, smooth, in-control when people die, the way their texted weeping turns anger into poetry, in the moment potentially inverting the whole male aesthetic which turns poetry into anger—that crying is done in the "lift-up-over sounding" way that shares in this pan-Kaluli style, but at the same time it is a somewhat oppositional model of action, control, authority.

CK: This is what is *beneath* the Apollonian-Dionysian distinction. You have to remember that Apollo and Dionysus are projections of a postclassless, postegalitarian, postanimist society. These are gods taking on what had been animist forces. What is probably represented in Apollo and Dionysus as formulations is a sublimation and projection of male and female things.

SF: As egalitarian as it might seem at certain quotidian levels, Kaluli society has numerous tensions, particularly gendered ones, which drive style. There is an echo of Kaluli female weeping within the production of male song, audible when the song turns into crying. But there is also an image of male ceremonial song within female weeping, because the weeping turns into a kind of song. The tighter, more coherent, more polished, and more powerful the weeping is, the more songlike it is, because the improvised text has more elaborate maps like the ones found in song poetry. But the more elaborate the songs are, the tighter and more powerful their maps, the greater their potential to produce crying. There is a politics of expression which is fused with this poetics, and which drives, reproduces a lot of male and female difference in this society—opposition as complementarity. It also reproduces a lot of the dominant stereotyping of male and female: that the women are more controlled, more calm, more capable of taking care of business. All *that* is evinced in their ability to do this improvised wailing under such emotionally charged circumstances, and their ability to pull it off in such a together way. Meanwhile, the guys might be flailing around out of control at the ceremonies, even though the ceremonies themselves are expressions of massive amounts of control, with all the elaborate costuming and staging. But then when the men start crying and the crying turns into anger, they want to burn somebody in response to the song; it can turn into a fight. That is how ceremonies often end; guys can't keep it together because they are so overcome by their grief. The ceremonies start out as expressions about male control, but they can turn into struggles about ritualized male chaos.

CK: Do you have the same sense I do that grief is not dealt with in our culture? I often think of how, when somebody dies among the Mbuti pygmies, they spend several weeks from dawn to dusk singing to wake up the forest. A month-long wake for one person. And here we are, dealing with the Holocaust, Biafra, southern Sudan, Kurdish kids dying on the hillsides. Massive amounts of unnecessary deaths enter our consciousness—and our consciences too, because of the injustice of it—and we should be singing dusk to dawn against all the murder and mayhem on the planet that is coming from capitalism. We aren't dealing with the grief that we all must be feeling. Things like anorexia nervosa, all the eating disorders, may be partially a function of not coping with world famines, not dealing with death, the inequality of death, or even deaths close to home.

Wakes are disappearing in the ethnic groups in America. Death has been sanitized and that is related to style. There's more style in Tiv and Kaluli because they feel more loss and feel anger over that loss. We are not angry over all this unjust death. We just let it happen. Then we struggle to find style in our own lives, but we can't invent it. Style builds up day by day; it has aura. You can't just flick a light switch. You have to build aura or patina or style with rites. I'm thinking about all-night waking, and the pun of that, waking ourselves up to style. Am I getting too poetic here? We need to learn something from the peoples who have styles that will help us create it more emphatically in our own lives . . .

SF: . . . locating style in pain, and pain in style: We're back to Louis Armstrong singing "Shine." And this is one of the things that your piece touches on which links to the Aretha correspondence too.

Isn't your notion about accepting stereotypes of the dominant culture in order to transcend them closely tied to ways of dealing with
the oppressiveness of pain?

CK: Yeah, for sure, but I have been uneasy with the term "transcendence" these past few years because it always seems to stray too
close to the wisdom-through-suffering theme, the notion that transcendent art somehow redeems all the insults and injustices. Yes,
we are agreeing on the power of the voice and the presence to
simply push through the pain. But I'd love to be able to phrase it
in terms of immanence, to say that this power is inside Louis and
his voice and his energy—coming from within, not floating above.
The term "transcendence" seems to push it out there into the Platonic stratosphere . . .

SF: One last question about "People's Music Comparatively": Don't
you think you're too blinded, too negative in your take on mass
media? I really have trouble with your view that media are such a
neutralizing, vitiating, homogenizing, culture-crushing force. Instead of analyzing what people are doing with the media, you slip
into that old mass-culture-critic view that the media just mess the
music up.

CK: I am amazed that I do as well as I do with considering mediation
in this piece, or in "Music Mediated and Live in Japan." I can be
sympathetic in analyzing what the Japanese do with media, or in
seeing what it has done for polka and blues. But bottom-line, I feel
like schizophonia, splitting sounds from their sources, is a disaster, a
crime. As you know, I have never been able to put out a record of
Tiv music.

SF: Why can't you deal with putting Tiv music out there? I've read *Tiv
Song* five times; why can't I hear Tiv music?!

CK: Well, if you ask me for a tape, I'll give you a tape! A lot of people
have read *Tiv Song,* but only a few people have asked for a tape. It
is as though, if you don't put the music out there, nobody really
wants it much . . .

SF: I don't believe that. Look at the demand for and sales of world
music in the stores . . .

CK: I started to put together a Tiv LP fifteen years ago, and I go back
to it every once in a while. I have one about ninety percent done,
but I can't bring myself to release it. I'm going to send it to the
Archives of Traditional Music at Indiana, and maybe some graduate

student will put out the notes and the album. I can't bring myself
to do it because I feel like I'm complicit in commodification and
culture-crushing . . .

SF: Come on, Charlie! Is *Tiv Song* a lesser form of culture-crushing? Is
the University of Chicago Press cleaner than any major record company on the planet?

CK: I think there is a huge difference with a written version because it
is such an abstraction away from the concrete sound. When you
put the sounds out there, they are going to get sampled and who
knows what. I feel like I am putting something out there that I can't
be responsible for.

SF: You don't think there is as much plagiarism as there is sampling?

CK: Plagiarism of words? No.

SF: Charlie, the Tiv aren't James Brown! True, as soon as you put the
stuff out there, you have no control over it. I'm not contesting that
at all. And I'm not contesting the fact that people don't even
bother to ask for permission to sample. They just use the stuff and
mulch it for their own purposes. World beat and everybody's drum
machines and samplers have completely changed the world of musical access and appropriation. But what concerns me is your politics of protectionism. It puts one more spin on this authenticity and
style problem. Is your stance that since the blues and polka records
are out there, it's OK to analyze them and talk about all those
processes? But we can't do this with Tiv because they aren't already
recorded . . .

CK: It's not a stance, as much as it is a reluctance, a refusal to associate . . .

SF: . . . but the reluctance speaks volumes in a world where *Tiv Song,* a
book about the sociology of art in a classless society, a book which
takes on Robert P. Armstrong, a book which has such a magnificent
analysis of the circles and angles, is out there. We can see the pictures. We can see the dance steps. But how many people have seen
Peggy Harper's Tiv dance film, and how many people have heard
any Tiv songs?

CK: Finally it comes down to not having the moxie, the conviction, to
want to spread that to the world. The Tiv musical dance world is
probably as rich as that in any other culture in Africa. They have a
profusion of styles, which are not tied down to castes and craft
guilds the way they are in Yorubaland. It is a profusion of creativity.
And I feel guilty now that I am not promoting that to the world in

some responsible way. But I am just sufficiently ambivalent about the whole mediation process that I have never been able to make it a priority or to take pride in doing it. For me it's always a higher priority to help children learn how to dance and sing and drum for themselves in Buffalo.

SF: Mickey Hart is the person who really turned my head around about this sort of stuff, about going high-tech in the bush. Why should Kaluli music be recorded with any less care or technological sophistication than Grateful Dead music? The symbolic statement Mickey is making is about the potential to empower silent or muted voices and cultures through the rock and roll recording and distribution mainstream.

CK: I think I agree with all of that. To me, it is an all-or-nothing situation. You should be getting your version of the other society, the classless society, to people in a persuasive, rhetorically convincing, auditorily delightful way. You really should be bringing pleasures and a sensuous feel for that culture to folks, which Colin Turnbull's *The Forest People* does as well as a book can do. And I have always thought that every anthropologist really has the obligation to try to write that way, to reach as many people as possible. I guess I have failed to see how to do that with Tiv songs. The quality of the recordings I have is not very good; and would they make that impact? If I believed I could really make that kind of impact and reach lots of people, I would not have this hesitation about doing it. But it seems that if you don't put it out there in a big way, in a popular way that really transforms consciousness for significant numbers of people, then the only people who *are* going to use it are the CIA.

SF: Believe me, Chuck, I would be gassed if the CIA tried to hack their way through "lift-up-over sounding"!

CK: No you wouldn't! And if you weren't reaching a whole lot of other people at the same time, would you be delighted?

SF: OK. I don't want to dismiss the reality of some ambivalence about putting it out there in such high quality; I'm sure drummers are out there sampling Bosavi crickets and having a lot of fun with *Voices of the Rainforest.*

CK: Why?

SF: Because it is full of sounds that percussionists get into. People will sample the birds and the crickets and the Kaluli drums. But I guess the problems with that are overshadowed by how truly delighted I am that so many people are going to get to hear this sound world almost as well as I've heard it, and almost as well as I think Kaluli are hearing it. I guess that I'm willing to trade off what people might do with the sounds in order to see Papua New Guinea and the Kaluli validated as a serious musical world to contend with.

When I walk into a great record store like Waterloo here in Austin and look at the amount of Asian, Latin, African product in the World Music section, I ask, how many languages are really being represented here? For the whole of Africa, how many languages and how many cultures are really being represented in those hundreds and hundreds of records? Twenty, thirty languages and styles, if that. It's time to scrutinize product diversity in the stores in terms of the real facts and figures of global musical and cultural diversity. There are at least eight hundred languages divided up among three and a half million people in Papua New Guinea, but *one* CD out there. That's a very, very token blow for recognizing and amplifying more of the world of musical diversity . . .

CK: . . . but any step in that direction is a good step. I think I concur. The main thing that is a global negative is that mediations split the sounds from sources: you don't have to have the musicians. In the Jayne Cortez poem—"They want the oil, but they don't want the people"—she inflects that line a hundred different ways, recites it for ten minutes and never repeats herself. It's the same deal with the music. We want the music, but we don't want the people. I think that bottom line is what has kept me from putting out a Tiv LP.

———

SF: You asked me to write a piece on Aretha for the second issue of *Echology,* which was going to put together feminism and music, feminist perspectives, and music about women, by women, addressed to women. And I copped out and laid every excuse on you that I could think of: "Chuck, I'm just a fan. . . . Chuck, I haven't done any fieldwork. . . . Chuck, I've never analyzed it," and you said, "Well, give me *that!*" which became a letter . . .

CK: . . . with some very interesting thoughts about what is at stake in the reversal of the lyrics, or the multiple layers of meaning that "Respect" can have. I have been thinking about that one for a long time, and now I may finally have some answers. I didn't answer

Aretha Franklin. Photo courtesy of Arista Records.

your letter, really; I just went off on my own autobiographical relationship to Aretha's music.

SF: When we were watching the movie last night, with Louis Armstrong singing "Shine," I was thinking of Aretha in those puffed-up
hairdos, sequined costumes . . .

CK: . . . as a waitress in that film—*The Blues Brothers,* wasn't it? She
has been exploited in a number of ways that are very similar to the
Louis travesties. Your first question to me was, "How does Aretha's

emergence on the soul scene involve the extension, ambiguation, and transformation of soul music's well-established male textual themes and male, secularized gospel performance styles?" And it certainly does involve all of that. I think you are asking, how does she *do* all that, and how do we understand the politics of her repertoire, her performance choices? My best answer is that I think she is operating by the spirit, that in some way she has not left the gospel world.

SF: When did you interview her?

CK: In 1963 or 1964 at the Regal Theater, backstage between shows, the same place as the interview with B. B. King that is in *Urban Blues*. It wasn't a very satisfying interview with Aretha. She was kind of withdrawn. I hardly remember it. I don't think I taped it. At any rate, the notion I have of how she made those performance and repertoire choices is that it was very much by feel, intuition, the way the spirit moved her to find things that resonated or felt good. So yes to the style and stereotype connections that you were making as regards accepting the dominant culture's definitions. The transformative power of her taking the Otis Redding lyric of "Respect," or "Think," or any of those anthems of the late 1960s . . .

SF: . . . subverts the lyrics so that they have not only re-resonated male-female readings, but re-resonated civil rights and conjugal rights meanings as well. Just like what Ray Charles did with "You Don't Know Me," blurring the personal "me" and creating the allegorical "us"—locating the song at a moment of intense civil rights struggle.

CK: I think that is a heightened example of something that happens in all black music—in R & B lyrics, or with B. B. King and "Lucille"— the call and the response. All of that stuff goes in two directions: First, toward the physical—the call and response as push and pull, the sexual, an even deeper body-breath-heartbeat dialectic underneath that; and there are music-lyric and sound-sentiment relationships at a parallel level to those physical, body, sexual relationships. And second, toward the public discourse of white-black implicit in every one of those blues and soul lyrics. Those lyrics play with white-black, love-hate relationships in the USA, and they become highly dramatic with the queen of soul. When Aretha does it, you really *think* about "Think . . . what *you're* trying to do to *me*"—a white "you" and a black "me." It can be made into public discourse in a moment like the late 1960s because there's a public arena for these anthemic musics to resonate in. A lot of lyrics since

then have not had a movement, a civil rights movement or a feminist movement, sufficiently mobilized and public to pick up those
songs and use them. Remember the Pointer Sisters' "We Are Family"?
The Pittsburgh Pirates used it as an anthem a while ago. It is as if
some songs have an anthem quality and can represent great big
social forces at work when there are social forces to relate them to.
Aretha's power in those lyrics is coming from social and historical
moments that the lyrics resonate into.

   This may sound crazy, but if you take this music-lyric relationship
and say it's a sexual discourse over here and a political, white-black,
civil rights discourse over there, and pull the music lyric out of that,
then the message of that music is that blacks are on top of whites
sexually, musically, and culturally. It reverses all the race and class
oppressions in the moment of the music and in the sound of the
voice.

SF: What do you mean?

CK: This comes out of the polka research in a funny way, sort of aban-
doning the role of a white man who loves black music and saying
what the hell is going on with the ethnic working class in America?
Do they have a soul music? If you don't do that, if you just stay
with the black music, resonate to jazz and blues and the power of
black music, you miss something terribly important about a distasteful projection onto black people of our own sexuality, our own
emotionality, our own musicality. We give that over to Michael
Jackson, or to Aretha, or to other black stars, and it keeps us from
getting in touch with our own emotions, warmth, and sexual power.
It's as if we have given that up as part of a trade-off: We are going
to oppress you folks racially and class wise, keeping you a permanent underclass, but we will revere you as stars of power, celebrities
of sensuality. There is something really twisted about that.

SF: But isn't that complicated here by the presence of the church in
Aretha's life and her music? Isn't your fundamental premise here
that with someone like Aretha, we are not just dealing with the
secularization of gospel music? Soul and the power of soul can't be
reduced to that.

CK: Right. I want to say that it is just the opposite, that the potential,
the utopian vision, is that popular music will be sacralized, that the
spirit in the dark will be a shining light for all human beings to be
redeemed in, that by bringing the church music into the popular
arena, you are trying to sacralize or give the spirit . . .

SF: . . . for a guy who hates the word "transcendental" . . .

CK: . . . but I don't see the sacred as transcendent. I don't think it is out there somewhere. I think it is immanent, in all human hearts to reverberate to this thing. And that is why the loss of our warmth, spirit, and sexual energy to a mediated Michael Jackson image is such a heavy loss. We are not getting the feedback that we need to vivify or vitalize our own lives if we just let our energies go into the *image* of this vital stylistic center of power. I am not quite getting this out the way that I would like.

SF: You are getting something out, and I think it has a lot to do with why Madonna appeals to me and why she appeals to Susan McClary and some other feminist analysts. Madonna is also going beyond just messing with categories, to the issue of how to make statements about control and how to package material that will make people worried, ambivalent, and concerned—material which takes on the stereotypes and works with them. It seems to me that what Aretha does so well with race and rights, Madonna—in this very powerful, working-class white way—does with Catholicism and sexuality. She is dealing with the body, with the desire to explore bodily mysteries and presences, with all this stuff about androgyny, and with the whole palette of sensual pleasure. She puts out a particular kind of statement about why it is OK to explore these things and why their exploration is necessary to overcome repressive religious forces and so forth.

CK: So the more Madonna wannabes there are, the better? If she is a liberating force, is it because she is going to help other people do this in their own lives? Or is this just a great big *substitution* for everybody's liberation? That's the problem that I have with every one of these celebrity versions or symbolic statements of liberation . . .

SF: What is your problem with Aretha's version?

CK: I have no problem as long as everybody becomes do-right men as a result. If everybody is inspired by the voice, the sound, the power, to raise their own voices and become social activists, then I have no problem at all. But if it never goes beyond vicarious, voyeuristic enjoyment of the paradoxes and the pain, then there is a problem.

SF: Well, then there is a problem! What worries me is the extent to which the most transparently stereotypical dimensions are what gets across in the era of cross-over music. I found Peter Guralnick's *Sweet Soul Music* a fantastic chronicle of what happened to Atlantic Records, and Stax, and Motown. But what then becomes so terrifically frustrating and disturbing to me is something about the cross-over. Do we know anything at all about *how* white people listened to this music? What did it reinforce? What did it change in their whole way of dealing with black America? If all of us had listened carefully to that music from the mid- and late 1960s through the early 1970s, then why isn't there more change, more inversion, or a more empowered black America? *What* crossed over? How blackened did we get from listening to all that? Why are we dealing with a rewhitened, rebrightened, more dominating version of the musical universe in the Reagan-Bush eighties when we got such a fantastic dose of cross-over in the sixties and seventies? Why didn't Aretha transform white people more? Is it just that it was too easy to read it all at the level of "That's why they call me Shine," with Louis in the soap suds? Was it easier to read the stereotypical "funky chicken" dimension and not pick up on the ambiguated, the played-with, and the reversed? Are the reversals too subtle? Are the inversions too subtle?

Maybe this is why Madonna is so powerful. Her stuff doesn't mess with subtlety *at all.* It is so heavily overt. Lying on a huge elevated bed masturbating while two male attendants, wearing deco cone bras and fondling their tits, nod as she sings "Like a Virgin": that's a kind of theater which makes the politics . . .

CK: . . . but is it? Frankly, I don't get the liberating message from Madonna. It looks to me like porn variations, testing the limits of lascivious conduct on MTV. Maybe it is a parody of Weimar Republic cabaret, but it seems to me like a cabaret writ large of what was going on in Germany just before the fascist takeover, when they were pushing every experimental button.

SF: I see it as all about Catholicism. In the two-part interview with Carrie Fisher [*Rolling Stone* 13 and 27 June, 1991], Madonna goes on about how the nuns were her heroines. She thought they were super-people. She must have spent a lot of time fantasizing about what their sexual universe was about, how they were keeping it together, what was going on inside their heads and bodies, and what kind of wild dreams of physical union with the higher spirits they were having . . .

CK: . . . so the material girl gives it all a material manifestation . . .

SF: . . . and I think all of her stuff about sex is really about the persuasive theatricality of religion, of spirit, and that is why it works so well on MTV. She *is* theatrical, a great dancer and gesturer. It is like watching somebody who has looked at countless magazine pages and has really thought about the posed body, the gendering of the body. And she has a level of talk-back toughness that is attractive across class lines.

CK: Yeah, I loved her as an interviewee on late-night television, sitting there with Arsenio Hall or whoever. There, I can see what the magic is. This woman is bold, really putting herself forward.

SF: The *Truth or Dare* film is wonderful that way. Even when you get backstage with her, she still can control everything as if it were front-stage. In fact, you never see any real backstage in that film; the film's most duplicitous move is to make you think that you are backstage with Madonna. She is always in control, always directing, always in charge of her image. The key quote in the film is when Warren Beatty says that Madonna is afraid that she has nothing to say when the cameras aren't there. But you see this extraordinarily orchestrated, controlled thing where she is doing the mother and/as/against the whore, where she's orchestrating all of these scenes in bed with all of these other guys, and she is constantly messing with all of the categories of who is gay or straight, who will reveal what about how much of their sex life to whom and when. She is going to masturbate on stage in front of her daddy and then, as the encore, bring him up on stage and hug him and make the cast sing "Happy Birthday" to him. It is control mania, but it is also extraordinary as a message about empowered women on the top.

CK: That is a long, persuasive liberatory argument, that she is all about upsetting established categories. All I can respond is that the visual message to me smells of Weimar Germany. And I can't remember the music. If you ask me to whistle a Madonna tune, I couldn't. There has never been one of them that has hooked in my consciousness. And I am easily hooked . . .

SF: I don't remember much of them either, and that's why I think it is not so much about the music as about the theatrical control of performance. The videos are magic as these extraordinary transformations of femininity and voyeurism.

CK: Earlier you were asking, with a fair amount of anger in your voice that we are not going to get onto the page here, where the hell is all the white activism that should have come from Aretha's music in the 1960s? Why didn't it mature in white minds in the 1980s? Why are we in a more racist, segregated society than we were pre-Aretha? And I guess the parallel point for Madonna should be that if her act is really liberatory, then the Madonna wannabes should be more individuated: not just copying Madonna, but making their own statements. The test is what effect it has on people's lives.

SF: Psychologists like Carol Gilligan talk about something drastic starting to happen around the sixth grade in terms of the development of self-confidence, with girls' sense of self-esteem freezing while boys' soars. The fact that Madonna appeals so much to junior high school girls is potentially cause for optimism. Where else are they being told that they can be anything they want and make people listen and watch? That controlling and caring about their appearance is normal and cool? There is something very complicated here and I would really like to see a solid ethnographic study of Madonna's youth audience, one that reads her performances not just in terms of texts and all the faddish theoretical feminist or pop culture categories, but in terms of how young girls actually engage, consume, and incorporate these possibilities into their lives.

CK: I see a thin line, though, between the sexual objectification of most pornography and our looking at Madonna's gaze. Louis's voice makes the horrible context of "Shine" small, but does Madonna's presence really reverse all the sexual objectification and the porn stereotypes in her context? Does it make her in charge of herself, and capable of inspiring every woman to take charge of herself and be proud? I'm dubious.

SF: I see the Madonna issues very much hooked up to the questions about Aretha, about James Brown, Billie Holiday, Louis Armstrong, the polka stars, about B. B. King and Muddy Waters. In each case the irony of resistance is accommodation, and the power of accommodation is the belief in resistance.

SF: In these little pieces about copyright and civilization you get into your vehement bad self. These read like little sermonettes, jabs, punches. Why do you think people would or should listen to this kind of preaching? What's the spin?

CK: The positive spin I can put on this is that I am wondering what is going to stick in people's memories. "Sieve-ilization"—I am hoping that people will remember those things, that they will stick in people's minds like hooks in a song, that they will remember the pun and keep thinking about it.

SF: Aren't you taking a really big risk when you do this?

CK: In the way of oversimplification, you mean?

SF: Yes, risking that people will think you are some reactionary court jester rather than somebody who has thought deeply and passionately about these things. Or worse, that you'll be taken as a closet elitist sniping at popular culture rather than a critic who wants to take on the way the cultural studies establishment tends to blindly elevate and defend it.

CK: I believe that condensation, not wasting people's time, is really important. Let's not waste the trees. I guess that I see what I have been doing the past seven or eight years as trying to distill my best thinking into slogans, bumper stickers, aphorisms, or poetry.

SF: Why does ethnomusicology need bumper stickers?

CK: It doesn't. But people need bumper stickers. People need slogans that give them a lift. Like "Take the toys away from the boys." If I could leave the planet knowing that I'd invented one of those, or a song lyric that people were going to sing, I would really feel good. To me that is the magical thing, to find what hooks into people's memories, and crystallizes a stance, a worldview, or a position. So it is a high-risk proposition to put these things out as a little pile of aphorisms and a couple of slogans rather than as reasoned arguments. But I figure the reasoned arguments are coming out in a lot of great places, that people can read A. B. Schmookler's *The Parable of the Tribes* or Leopold Kohr's *The Breakdown of the Nations* or other books that I wish I had written. It is my job maybe to punch that home in a song lyric or a poem, or try to get it to more people.

SF: You're talking about getting these things out to more people, but they are appearing in *Echology* or *Ethnomusicology,* which are read by a very small number of people. Even this book will be read by only a small number of people. By bringing these pieces into a world of scholarly discourse, you challenge yet one more boundary about what can count as legitimate discourse within the academy. But even that is talking to a small segment of the academy and not much of anyone else . . .

CK: I do want to stretch the boundaries of what can appear in scholarly journals and books, true. And I want to stretch it in the direction of simplification, especially in this period of infinite regression into complexity, which is what I feel constitutes a lot of postmodernism and post-Frankfurt school. There are little attacks here against

all the people who are hugging the tar baby of Western Civilization, people just as stuck to that tar baby as advanced music educators. There is a lot of reification of the reifications going on,
and I think it is important to risk being called a preacher, a moral-
izer, a philistine, a crass materialist, or any of the nasty epithets for
people who want to cut through to a Maoist sort of slogan. Everything mediated is spurious until proven genuine! Acts of creation
over acts of criticism! What are the implications of endless raps on
MTV when no black bank accounts are accumulating money from
those songs, when no money is going back into the community?
Because to me, the separation between culture, discourse, and
theory and any actual agenda of social change is getting wider.
While it gets wider, and while there is more theory about theory
and more problematization of problematization, it seems like my
role is to be as stubborn a philistine as I can be, and to ask, "Who
is getting the money?" I like "fat thoughts," as Brecht and Benjamin talked about them in relation to the Frankfurt school. We
have to hold onto some *plumpes Denken* or we can get lost in
the competing theorizations. It doesn't work, though: I have
tried it with graduate students the last couple of years, and they
look at me like I am cranky or perverse or whatever. They think
they have to master all this theory to hold their own with the
others . . .

SF: Don't they, though?

CK: I am not so sure. I survived. The way that I held onto my sanity,
my anger, my tone, and my wanting to convince people was by
holding onto those fat thoughts. I think that is part of the paradox
of being an anthropologist, folklorist, or ethnomusicologist or even
a radical popular culture person. You want to hold onto the moment, the intensity of lived experience in the present time. You
want to keep that primary and not let the theory or the insights, or
the meta-meta—the writing about it—be more important than the
stuff itself. That is probably all I am trying to say with these aphorisms: that lived experience is more important than the analysis of
it. That's all I'm insisting on.

———

CK: Planet groove. Do we want it in a musical form? Do we want
everybody grooving to the same beat at the same time?

SF: You want planetary grooves, not groove, world beats, not world beat?

CK: I think there is a need for a planetary culture, or at least a thin layer of shared values and assumptions, and some planetary muzak, if not music, that speaks to our common human condition. But even more, there is a need for planetary law and order and a minimal peacekeeping force to keep the world safe for diversity of species and cultures. I really believe that.

SF: You're lining up with Mickey Hart. A sign on his studio wall reads, "It's not World Music, it's the world's musics."

CK: That is a good way to formulate it. But, I got this whole question about legal world versus natural world from the Native American Studies people I have been working with the past twenty years in Buffalo. They make a persistent point about separating the legal world from the natural world, and the way more and more things get pulled into the legal world. That is a worldwide historical process the last few centuries. It seems to me like music could be one of the first things to be brought back into the natural world, by taking it away from copyright.

SF: How can that happen?

CK: The current technologies are feeding on themselves in such a way that people can shape their own musical samples, put together their own cassettes, dub, record concerts, trade music with each other, and use music in a thousand different ways. This technology allows people to spread music around; we don't need the big companies to do it for us anymore. The only people who profit from copyright are the huge, ever-growing companies and an ever-smaller cluster of superstars. Everybody else is getting screwed by it. Paul Simon, even with a good conscience, makes all that money off of grooves that really belong to the South Africans or the *salseros*. It is an unjust and absurd situation which can never be corrected because the grooves, the textures and the processes, are always collective and traditional, with the exception of the synthesized ones in studio dance mixes. Those are like the plastics and chemicals of our musical world.

SF: But isn't it ironic that people want to take the postmodern hybrid trajectory as a liberatory motion, where all musics can make contact, can blend, and can create some kind of groove together, where Paul Simon can sing with Miriam Makeba? This is a reprise of an old folky rainbow theme, but in newly commercialized and commodified forms, with variants ranging from ethereal New Age on the one side to politicized Pan–Third World reggae on the other.

CK: I love the impulse of privileged white males working and grooving with indigenous traditions. That's cool, and I want to see it happen more. I really mean it. But I don't want to see anyone on the white male, corporate side of the equation make a profit from it. Every time they do use those traditions, the money ought to go to the Zulu or the Puerto Rican Homeless Fund or wherever. That would be justice.

SF: But how do you respond to Joseph Shabalala when he says that without Paul Simon Ladysmith Black Mambazo would never have gotten a record contract on Warner Brothers? Now all of a sudden, they are all over the place. Ladysmith Black Mambazo was very successful, very popular, heavily recorded, internationally traveled, a known group before Paul Simon and *Graceland.* But there is no question that, quantitatively and qualitatively, the scene has changed enormously for them since 1987.

CK: I would tell Joseph to be content with Shanachie Records and world tours and making a living; nobody needs that extra margin of greatness and stardom anymore. If that is the price to pay for keeping Warner Brothers and Paul Simon from having the copyright and ownership rights to those grooves, it is worth it.

SF: Charlie, that's hopeless! I don't think you can say that to third-world musicians, period. You just can't.

CK: But the hope of copyright helping them is what has sustained this wicked exploitation for ninety years now. Everybody thinks they are going to compose a hit song, and that is why they support copyright. Muddy Waters probably went to his grave thinking that someday Leonard Chess was going to give him more than his dental bill or car payments. Everybody is hoping that they are going to make more money because of this ownership principle of music. But they never do. All the black musicians, with the exception of Michael Jackson, wind up poor. All the traditions get screwed over. That has been the case now for decades. How many more decades do we have to see before we can tell the next layer of exploited third-world musicians not to buy the dream?

SF: I don't disagree with you about the pattern of exploitation, but I am disagreeing with you about the positioning of third-world musicians within it, particularly in relationship to larger amounts of exposure, sales, and what *they* want, which is a greater cut of the

Shaka Zulu, cover, 1987. Ladysmith Black Mambazo's debut on Warner Brothers Records.

action. If their perception is that the same process that is screwing them over is the process which is eventually going to give them a larger cut, then how do you tell them to take a smaller cut?

What is so fascinating to me is the layering of contradictions in this process. How is it that moves which, from a technical, legal, political, economic, and ethical angle are entrepreneurial and cannibalizing, are at the same time moves which are being read as empowering in various third-world locations? I agree with your abhorrence of the ownership politics in all of this. But I am concerned about perceptions that these musicians have of the marketplace and about their desires. And I also have to admit being delighted to have a record by Ladysmith Black Mambazo which is better recorded and better produced; I thought a lot of the early stuff sounded crappy.

CK: I like scratchy records. All those perfection areas are totally irrelevant to me.

SF: Chuck, scratchy records won't bring about any musical equity. Can't you believe that better sound, better production, better distribution are materially and symbolically important to musicians on the planet? That this is about decolonizing the music business? That it is about the importance of producing musical products more equitably, distributing them more equitably, honoring them more equitably?

CK: Yes, but it's not as important as getting their music out of the commodity form, if that is possible.

SF: But why should groups like Ladysmith Black Mambazo settle for second-rate recording technology, engineering, and distribution? Why should it be their burden to get music out of the commodity form?

CK: Because with the high-quality recording and distribution and all the rest, ninety percent of the money winds up going to white people. Ever and always. That's why. Most of the money goes to white folks who are already in the positions of power: the gatekeepers, the copyright holders, and the distributors. Distribution is the key link, and that is where sampling, taping, home dubbing, and people trading tapes with each other becomes a bottom-up, grass-roots alternative to the distribution system that now exists. I would much rather have shitty quality tapes coming from South Africa that I could dub and give to friends, than buy them from Warner Brothers. I really resent that corporate control. It has become obscene. Three huge conglomerates are controlling the distribution of sound to people. Yet there is a high risk in abolishing copyright in order to liberate music . . .

SF: Right, namely . . .

CK: . . . that corporate control could become even greater. For a while, the people who manufacture dance music could do whatever the hell they pleased. They could sample James Brown into oblivion, with no holds barred, no threat of a lawsuit, for doing whatever the hell they wanted to do with the music. And since the big distribution centers have already accumulated the power and the pipelines, they would flood the market with whatever they wanted. They could take anything from Papua New Guinea and turn it into disco or hip-hop or whatever. It would produce an "echo-catastrophe" for a few years. My hope is that the fallout from

that strategy would be the corporations' inability to continue hyp-
ing these products by putting hundreds of thousands of dollars into
promotion, because they would no longer legally control the music
anymore. Then the risk would be that somebody else could go to
Brazil and record the same music and distribute it more cheaply.
But I am convinced that after a few years of echo-catastrophe, in
which the big powers do what they want to with the world's music,
that eventually it would find its own market level, and people
would share the music that they want to share without the hype
and corporate control. Currently, the control justifies the hype. If
you have the copyright and think it can be defended legally in
court, then you can put hundreds of thousands of dollars behind
saying that this punk rock excrescence is the one to promote this
spring. You can risk all kinds of money trying to shape people's
consciousness to like a particular music. But I trust people to go
for the music they really need . . .

SF: . . . what's with this mystification: "the music they really need"?
Who determines which music they really need?

CK: They do! At the most local and personal level, they will make their
own music. More people will make their own music in small groups
and localities, in little watershed areas. We folks around Scajaquada
Creek in Buffalo will start making our own music after the blowout
from the abolition of copyright. It would heighten the realization
that we all need our own music to be intensely personal and to
bind us to the people right around us. I don't think that is utopian.
I think it is built into us.

SF: Charlie, I think that you are mixing up two things. One is your attack on ownership, and the other is the promotion of all possible
bases of strength in the music community. If I understand your position, your key argument is that the people who will always be the
most oppressed by the ownership system are the people whose work
remains in an oral tradition. They will always have the least control
once their work is commodified. Additionally, the divide between
the musically oral and the musically literate will not become less,
but will become greater as a result of the reproduction of the power
in a copyright law system which fetishizes the written form . . .

CK: It could all be quite different. The four-tracks and eight-tracks, all
the portable studio equipment, could enable every local musical
group to make its own tapes and distribute them. The technological capacity to do away with big companies arrived a decade ago,

and is now completely available to people. You can do four-track
recording. John Collins does them with highlife bands, and they
sound wonderful on LP. You don't need a big recording studio or
a big company to make high-quality recordings anymore . . .

SF: Come on! When was the last time you were able to *get* a John
   Collins recording of West African highlife? I mean, what I'm concerned with is that your vehement politics of antiownership cuts off
   the musicians who are really struggling to get their music out there.
   And what I keep coming back to is that musicians have aspirations
   and desires to get their stuff out, to be treated with respect, and
   to make a living. Look, I would love to see a bin at Tower Records
   where there are one, two, or three hundred well-recorded CDs of
   any kind of music from Papua New Guinea, with liner notes that
   tell you what the songs are about; where you could see the people's
   pictures name-by-name so they would not be an anonymous
   bunch of bongo-bongos; where you could meet people like Ulahi,
   Gigio, Seyaka and feel like you can experience their place, their humanity, their music; where you could meet the Kalibobo Bamboo
   Band or Paramana Strangers or New Krymus or Barike and have the
   opportunity to imagine why the world sounds and feels different
   to them. That kind of presence can be developed through this
   medium, and it is powerful, a kind of presence that can't and won't
   be ignored. But you are not going to bring that about by just telling folks to be content with circulating their bushy cassettes . . .

CK: Oh no? What is going to bring that presence you want about
   more quickly? Monopoly capitalism, which can only focus on one
   star at a time? "We can only have one Sunny Adé." Do you know
   how many fantastic *jùjú* bands there are in Lagos? Besides Adé and
   Ebenezer Obey? And none of them get recording contracts. We can
   only focus on one tribe in Papua New Guinea or one star in Yorubaland. That is the tendency.

SF: Look, I agree with you: commodity capitalism, and particularly
   monopoly capitalism, promotes musical tokenism. And "world
   beat" at this juncture is deeply about musical tokenism, especially
   in the way marketing strategies oppose it to "world music"; that's
   exactly my point about how schizophonia is attached to schismogenesis . . .

CK: . . . and all in the name of racism, because "world beat" ignores the
   African foundation of so much "world" music. In the name of imperialism, because we are claiming the entire world for our Western

distribution networks. In the name of capitalism, because "world beat" is mainly a selling label. My big enemies—racism, imperialism, and capitalism—are all served by that mushy label, world beat. I even hate to see it in the title of your article or your course. It says that we have already succumbed, that this is the label that we are going to work with, or that we have accepted it.

SF: I don't buy that at all. Why is that label any worse than "jazz" or "blues" or "salsa"? Because, as a commercial gloss of syncretic hybrids, it ignores the history, strata, the real paths and roots of artistic innovation and cannibalism, the real issues about diversity and survival?

CK: It ignores all the feedback loops, the process, and the localities. Let me give you a position to think about as an alternative: a fund—and it would only take a couple of hours of American military spending to create it—to record every single one of the world's peoples on the best equipment and put all three thousand to five thousand peoples into one hell of a beautiful bin down at the record store. Every one of the world's peoples could be recorded in high-quality sound. Seventy-five million bucks would probably do it. Not a hell of a lot of money to tally the world's expressiveness in the most beautiful way, with lots of liner notes, followed by books by the people who went to each place for a few months and did the recordings. If we had the bins and a planetary UN program to make sure that the world's musical moments of the 1990s are recorded before the echo-catastrophe becomes total, before homogenization and greyout become totally sinister, I think it would be a great salvage-anthropology thing to do. I'm with Alan Lomax and anyone who thinks along those lines. Some kind of planetary insurance policy for the world's musics, coupled with the abolition of copyright, would make me a pretty happy dude.

SF: OK, that's one strategy. Tell me more about your other strategies for supporting musical diversity.

CK: I like trading tapes with people around the planet. I think that would happen more if we weren't relying on stuff to pop into the bins. If present trends continue . . .

SF: . . . the globalization of the Grateful Dead idea . . .

CK: Yeah. That is one of the nicest things about them. I would almost exempt the Grateful Dead from the "every star represents a loss for an individual" claim. I think they probably are part of that syndrome, too, as kind of a pseudo-community. But on the other hand, they are allowing everybody to tape everything.

SF: Then what do you say to Zappa, Dylan, and all those people who are talking back to the bootleggers?

CK: They are all jerks!

SF: Why?

CK: Because everyone's music belongs to everybody else. The more bootlegging, the merrier. Why should they have an extra couple of million bucks to live in Malibu? None of these guys return their money like the Grateful Dead do. What does Dylan do with his money? Have you ever heard of him buying homes for the homeless? Springsteen gives ten thousand here and ten thousand there to good things. Sting does a few good things, Phil Collins does a few good things. But I think that every one of these stars represents a rip-off of the emotions of millions of people if they don't return the buck in socially redeeming ways. I learned that in China, with Li Gu Yi, the most popular singer in China in 1980, with maybe a hundred million dedicated fans. She symbolized the hope of freedom to millions and millions of Chinese youth, and she was only paid sixty bucks a month and drove to work on a bicycle. She saw it as a privilege to be singing to so many people; it was clear that everyone involved in these songs was just honored as hell to be part of that process. And she is absolutely right, because you can't put a monetary value on being the voice of your people. It doesn't commodify or compute. But I don't think our Bob Dylans and Frank Zappas, for all their radical politics or pretensions, think that way. I don't think they have confronted the exchange of money for emotions that is represented in their royalties. And that is exactly the right word: people who get royalties think of themselves as royalty, as princes and princesses, and they don't return it. They don't think, "I got to be Bob Dylan because all these people invested in my lyrics and my emotions and it meant something to them. I should keep my tithe and the other ninety percent should go to the causes represented in my lyrics." There are a lot of places to spend money for change on this planet, and every musician with major money should have the conscience to do that.

I really think that part of our job as music critics, scholars, and analysts is to hold to the fire the feet of the people who raise consciousness but don't put bucks back into economic operations. This is where Lewis Hyde's book *The Gift* is extremely important: the gift must always circulate. Musicians have to keep moving the money around that comes out of people's emotions and their best instincts, their love vibe, their spiritual aspirations, their thirst for justice, their thirst to hear certain words expressed in a certain way. Dylan owes us. He did us a wonderful thing, and we gave him the money. Now the gift should continue to circulate.

SF: What about the way that Wallis and Malm's *Big Sounds from Small Peoples* describes money circulation in Sweden, where they created a fund that put royalties back into stimulating live musical performance? Even if the money is coming from musical homogenization, aren't there ways to put it back into heterogenization?

CK: Well, I guess this is the libertarian part of me, but I really distrust committees and subsidies to the creative, because it always involves a singling-out process. If you really believe that every single person born has their own vocal expressive destiny, that they are all musical, that they all have their own music to make and they are going to make it even better in their own local watershed, then who is to decide how to take the money from the homogenization process and use it to promote heterogenization?

SF: But there are lots of folks who are driving cabs and selling T-shirts and scuffling who need time and support to create their work, whether they are visual artists or dancers or performers or musicians. Don't think of committees as calibrating the worth of these individuals; think of how you want more music to be made, how much you want to encourage more creative spirits to be more creative. Really! You're the guy who has been making noise about more participation!

CK: All I know is that in fifty years the polka bands never got a subsidy, they were never considered folklore, they were never considered opera or symphony. Whenever money is put aside in the USA to support the arts, ninety to ninety-eight percent of it goes to the bourgeois forms, to symphonies and opera and big Bolshoi bullshit. And a little trickle, maybe five percent, goes to folklore, where you have the authenticity-purity issue, with folklorists deciding who is pure and who is a revivalist. Yech! The very person that you and I would want to see supported, which is some old-timey musician who is taking heavy metal tunes and doing them on the banjo or whatever, opening a new crack into reality, isn't going to get the money. I can't see how committees are going to anticipate new ethnogenesis, the creation of a whole new groove. A whole new groove is never going to be subsidized.

But to get back to world beat, you pivot everything on appropriation and revitalization: "The complex traffic in sounds, money, and media is rooted in the nature of revitalization through appropriation." You were saying that sometimes that doesn't happen in Papua New Guinea pop. Some folks just get appropriated from and wiped out by substitutes, by generic cover tunes. I am worried about that.

SF: Only a small number of cassettes are all cover tunes. The pattern of a lot of the string band music cassettes in Papua New Guinea is that they have just one song in Tok Pisin, the lingua franca, and the rest are in the local languages. So all these guitar bands are at some level very much celebrating their language and their locality.

CK: I can't hear enough about that. I can't hear enough about how ukuleles are being retuned. I cannot hear enough about people taking flip-flop sandals and whacking those bamboo tubes. I have to hear that to keep faith that people are reinventing themselves, their traditions, their process, their textures, and their grooves in response to new material like pipes and rubber flip-flops, putting things together, inventing themselves and their sound to keep up with the process. I need to hear that is happening, because my worry is that if it doesn't happen quickly enough, then the cassettes, headphones, and transistorized mechanisms will substitute for local creativity.

SF: It's true that a lot of music has been lost, too. But at the same time I don't doubt that some of the so-called world beat experiments or mixes yield forms of stimulation that impact musical traditions in good ways. I also don't doubt that for performers, it can be an enormous amount of fun just to have a particular kind of contact with another performer. Understand that I'm not defending world beat music here. What I am trying to do is locate as much as possible the contradictions involved in appropriation, to talk about the extent to which things which you and I like and are happy to celebrate are entwined in all the appropriating moves. I am trying to talk about how the forces that are homogenizing and those that are heterogenizing are dialectic. This is what I think is central to understanding struggles for musical diversity now: the extent to which the diversity we believe in is dependent on the forces that we more typically imagine as countering diversity.

————

SF: Your Japan piece asks heavy questions about the quality and nature of people's listening and viewing, about the social processes in which reception is embedded. By the end of the second paragraph—whamo!—you're linking mediated experience to interpretive moves, participatory practice, and consciousness . . .

CK: . . . and the social context for it, too. Usually researchers are either measuring quantities or they've got this lit-crit thing that they do with what a soap opera is really about. And they don't really go out and see what people are really doing with it. I guess Janice Radway's book *Reading the Romance* is the sort of ethnography I have in mind, except that she set up discussion groups for people: It's about how women get together in groups and interpret the bodice rippers. More books like hers would really help to bridge the gap. I think actually the experiential moment that made me rethink this whole deal was sitting in a bar in Tokyo and watching people really getting worked up singing with the microphone. They get pumped up trying to sound like Frank Sinatra or Tony Bennett. They enter in a participatory way the persona of the person they're trying to imitate. It's Kabuki or Noh theater. It's a dramatic identification. And everyone at the bar can get into the spirit of, yeah, that's our Frank Sinatra, that's our Tony Bennett, and look over there at Yoshi doing that.

SF: But in the end you move even further. It's not just personalizing, it's humanizing. And it's resistant. You end the paper stressing the importance of a sense of reclaiming the music from the record companies, arguing that that might be the underlying principle of rap and dub. That's why I don't think it is a very Luddite or cynical piece at all, despite your admissions that you treat records badly, don't think they're real music, and feel deep ambivalence about mediation. You found something pretty inspiring in rap and dub and in your experience in Japan that gave you this window for looking at mediation and its connection to participation as another site where people can, for a moment, shape and move the corporate insertion aside.

CK: I think I got as empathic as I could, given that I'm a Luddite before and a Luddite later. And I don't think the Luddism is a cynical
thing either; it's kind of like recapturing that moment when Ned
Ludd goes in there and smashes up the stocking machines or whatever. There's a crazy moment back there in the Cromwell era. I
don't have the books to cite, but there are these books about the
levelers and the ranters and diggers and all these movements
within Protestantism about people taking liberatory thoughts to
their crazy conclusions: We've got to destroy all the machines in all
the factories or we've got to . . . If Adam and Eve were naked before the fall, let's all get naked! Let's go for it! Let's level it or dig it
or rant it! Do you know about the ranters? They were out there
shouting! I mean, they really were literally ranting! Ranting and
raving! We need that shit!

SF: You're really describing a certain kind of compensation very concretely here, one that answers your question about compensating
for what's lost in the mediating process. The compensation for
schizophonia is precisely in the creative responses . . .

CK: . . . in ranting and raving? . . .

SF: . . . ranting and raving . . .

CK: . . . in leveling and digging? . . .

SF: . . . in leveling and digging and dubbing and rapping. Singing
along . . .

CK: I guess there is the spirit of that in there, isn't there?

SF: . . . getting into humanizing and personalizing mechanical
processes.

CK: Yeah. And the rappers and the dubbers are in the spirit of the diggers and the levelers and ranters and the ravers and the revelers. It's
all people getting up and acting out and saying we won't take it
anymore.

SF: So when you ask if there's any compensation for the loss caused
by schizophonia, you certainly could answer that there is an endless
struggle to reclaim . . .

CK: . . . the live moment. The present time. Right. But isn't it hard to
overestimate the power and scope of the substitutions? That is, because it's happened, because this mediated thing has happened,
it's hard to really gauge how much has been lost. We just sort of
take it for granted now that we don't make most of our music and
that live musicians don't make it within our presence, so there's a

kind of double substitution going on. We're too far removed from participation. If musical rites are primarily a response to social strains and crises and if we have massively privatized and solipsized what was once a social healing, again this raises the theme of loss. What is lost? Can you think of more examples of third worlders really getting a boost or getting something from this whole process?

SF: In straight-out material terms, I don't think we can . . .

CK: So what is gained?

SF: . . . but if you circumscribe the discussion of schizophonia only in terms of what is lost and what is gained, it casts a very dramatic negation around the process which doesn't leave all the hopeful room that I feel for the kind of creative responses that people can make.

CK: It kind of gives up the struggle before you've even struggled?

SF: Well, it gives a certain kind of sweeping, massive force and volition to these processes that puts them out of our hands rather than saying, like you do in your Japan piece, that there's really something to be looked for there in these bars, or in homes, in what people are doing with their records and what they're doing with their cassettes. Certainly there are enough examples of wonderful, vibrant emergent hybrid musics and guys beating the bamboos with their flip-flops at the outposts to inspire us.

CK: But to what extent does the mediated music represent just another addiction or drug in people's lives? In *My Music* we really identified that early on in a lot of the interviews and then we just sort of side-stepped it. Because in any one person's life it doesn't seem like a big problem, but when you look across the interviews patterns emerge in the ways that people are using music to pump themselves up and to reinforce egos and to chill themselves out before they go to the workplace—a whole bunch of ways that people would use dope. That makes me wonder if we aren't all on the wrong end of any complementary schismogenesis process in music. I keep thinking that we're on the submissive, dependent, spectator side of all those dyads.

The other question I want to raise here is about why you say rap is an example of dramatic, local resistance. What's local about it? I mean, Hammer and Tone Loc seem like national and international commodities to me. They don't seem local. Why don't rap and reggae have visible economic feedback to community channels by now, when they have all this local resistance tone about them?

SF: Well, they're resistant to the industry in a sense. There's a stylization in rap of a kind of anger and a kind of hurt that's very special
and it is local. Because it often looks like a bunch of guys in leather
jackets pointing their finger at you, and swinging their arm and
speaking in a voice which is defiant, shouting, demanding; no
matter what they're talking about or singing about, they're saying,
we've had enough of your crap. And who are they talking to?
They're talking to us and to each other, they're talking to a lot of
gender stuff, they're talking to the cops, they're talking to all the
institutions, from school to the record companies. They're saying,
we're doing this, you're making the money, controlling the scene,
so . . .

CK: . . . but they're not changing that equation. Out of all that gestur-
ing they're not changing the equation . . .

SF: . . . so they make themselves more marginal and more inaccessible
or more jive or use more words that make it impossible for anybody
to put it on the radio. And that feels like the side of it that's about
getting caught up in that cycle of anger, rather than breaking the
cycle so that the empowering part of this talking back that they're
doing can really be moved into a kind of active phase where it goes
into the communities like you're talking about.

CK: You just made it a lot clearer for me. It's like what in reevaluation
counseling we call "rehearsing," or acting out, anger. It's not the
same thing as releasing the anger or purging yourself of it. It's kind
of like . . .

SF: . . . putting it on the stage, like live wrestling on television, where
you know those guys have worked a lot of the moves out before-
hand . . .

CK: Right, like who's gonna take the fall . . .

SF: There's something about it which, particularly in the MTV version . . .

CK: . . . it's back to the Madonna point. This is dramatization before
it's music or anything else . . .

SF: Yes, rap has become such a high theater, trading on the soap
drama of street toughness, the theatricality of shouting that y'all
damn well better be afraid of us. And where it's meant to startle . . .

CK: . . . and meant to reinforce the homeboy's home turf. And that's
what you mean by "It's relentlessly local."

SF: Right, whether or not the rappers are saying, "This is our CNN,"
their representations of themselves constantly hook back to what
you say about style and stereotype in your blues and polka paper—

because rap is stylistically working within, through, and against the mainstream stereotype of the angry young black male that whitey's supposed to be scared to death about . . .

————

CK: I've got a few questions on the schizophonic side of the *Voices of the Rainforest* part of this piece. What does it mean to condense twenty-four hours into one hour? What's that condensation about? It kind of boggles my mind when I think about it, that spaced-out, real-time worlds of sound are suddenly condensed into a CD.

SF: It's not that the time is proportionally condensed in any kind of mathematical way to make that twenty-four hour day in the life into one hour. *Voices of the Rainforest* is simultaneously hyperreal and a tone poem. It's an evocation of a sound world, and it sounds like things that happen in dreams. Because space and time are simultaneously condensed and expanded. It's not just temporal condensation that frames that editing. It's that time, all these years of my time there, all of this hearing of Kaluli people and their world, and hearing them talk about this, and listening to it with them, traveling around in that place with Kaluli—all that goes into this. This is where I think Murray Schafer's insight in *The Tuning of the World* is really right on. Soundscape research really should be presented in the form of musical composition. That is one way to bend the loop back so that the research and the artistry come together and we can auditorally cross those rivers and those creeks and climb those trees and walk those paths without the academic literalism, the print mediation. So to make *Voices* I worked with a very simple idea, that things like texture, density, layers of sound are what are important to ways Kaluli hear their place and make music with it. And the technical, acoustical correlates of these things relate clearly to the height and depth and spatial-temporal cues in the rainforest . . .

CK: That's the next part of my question . . .

SF: . . . and if I could make it possible for you to hear that—I mean, what I think is really compelling is to imagine how they could possibly hear this. Of course Kaluli hear it many different ways. Just like we hear it many different ways. There are different figures emerging from grounds, different things jump out in different ways. This is not a matter of trying to give you one way of hearing it or forcing the notion that there is a singular Kaluli experience of the rainforest, but of putting it out there so that somehow you can move a little closer to their experience—not just to the experience of being there, but to the experience of imagining what kind of person a Kaluli person—a listening and sensing Kaluli person—is . . .

CK: . . . and what all that sound experience has done to shape their sensibilities . . . . Basically you're synthesizing in the studio, there with all those wide-angle or close-up recordings, different sensory experiences that you've had, or that you've had with Kaluli, or that you know Kaluli have had over and over again. And you're able to get that as vividly on the CD as possible, and you hope that your listeners will get some of the same experiential highs and wisdom from the experience.

SF: Yes, to be a translator, from a local phenomenology through a contemporary studio-based acoustical set of sounding realities, manipulating parameters and trying to feel which subtleties could be brought out a little more, which presences could be more present for uninitiated ears.

CK: I think it's going to come as news, big news for a lot of readers, that contemporary studios consciously manipulate sound in three spatial dimensions. You know, that they've got left-to-right stereo, they've got foreground and background by using all the echo effects, and then height, the vertical dimension.

SF: This hooks into the first part of the book, Charlie. There we were saying that one of the big realizations is that many musics are not syntax-based and, more important, that syntax really isn't the core of what most musical experience is about anyway. So what really is the core of musical experience? If we insist that the core has more to do with participatory discrepancies, these dimensions of process and texture and timbre, the recording has to bring alive the "lift-up-over-sounding" so that listeners can hear, can experience textural densification, can experience in-sync and out-of-phase sound with men's and women's voices in leisure, work, and ritual activities, can get that deep connection between labor and play, environmental sound and human music making. That's the acoustic ecology I want to take to your ears.

So the method of the editing for *Voices of the Rainforest* is very much oriented toward saying that this is what a nonsyntactically centered music sounds like. Here are a whole bunch of possibilities for a different listening, for one acoustic ecology, for hearing another world, for hearing another way of hearing—which should be saying to you over and over again, it's not about syntax. The melodic and rhythmic dimensions of this music are simple by some measures, but if you listen, you realize that "lift-up-over sounding" is musically anything but simple, that it is incredibly subtle, it is wonderfully nuanced. Voices are flowing like waterfalls, "lifting-up-over" one another like layers of birds duetting in the canopy, like trees arching over each other on ridges, like waterfalls flowing into pools and creekways. And when all of that synesthetic, or "sonesthetic" experience can be evoked by the juxtapositions, by these kinds of simultaneous space-time compressions and expansions, then for me there is a little bit of a possibility to move across cultures in a very . . .

CK: . . . bold . . .

SF: . . . directly feelingful way . . .

CK: . . . bold and decisive . . .

SF: . . . and bring people into the acoustical reality of Kaluli "lift-up-over sounding" . . .

CK: . . . because we can hear three spatial dimensions—things that are foreground and background, left and right, high and low—that it's real: the rainforest has three dimensions . . .

SF: . . . it has a groove, a rainforest groove—the temporality of sonic height arching upwards as outwards as onwards—"lift-up-over sounding", that's the Kaluli groove—I want you to listen and to think about the idea that some human beings hear this every day. Some human beings grow up with this version of acoustic ecology. With this ratio of ambient sounds to human sounds. This kind of interpenetration of nature and culture. Listen to that and think about what kind of human beings Kaluli might be if that's what they're grooving on . . .

CK: . . . and here, you can groove on it too . . .

Further Comments

p. 290 . . . *Stanley Diamond's journal* . . . I never had Stanley Diamond as a
teacher, but his work—the opening chapters of *In Search of the Primitive*
(New Brunswick: Transaction Books, 1974), the diligence with which he
edited *Dialectical Anthropology* for many years, and most of all his advocacy
for Biafran independence in the late 1960s—was a continuing source of
energy and encouragement for me to persevere in writing and teaching
during difficult times. For appreciations of Diamond's work by a broad
range of poets and scholars, see the recently published festschrift, Christine
Gailey, ed., *Dialectical Anthropology: Essays in Honor of Stanley Diamond*,
2 vols. (Gainesville: University Press of Florida, 1992). [CK]

p. 292 . . . *John Lomax and Leadbelly* . . . The Louis Armstrong video mentioned here is *Satchmo: Louis Armstrong,* written by Gary Giddins (Masters
of American Music series, CBS Music Video, 1989).

   Leadbelly (Huddie Ledbetter, 1889–1949)—composer, singer, and
twelve-string guitar player—is legendary for the extraordinary variety of
African and Anglo-American musical styles he sang: blues, gospel, field
hollers, prison songs, work songs, ballads, railroad songs, and cowboy
songs. He is perhaps more legendary in some quarters for singing his way
out of jail, obtaining a pardon from Texas governor Pat Neff in 1925 and,
while serving a later sentence, being recorded by John and Alan Lomax
during their 1932 Library of Congress collecting tour, which again led to
his release. He went on to a touring and recording career, performing solo
and with Big Bill Broonzy, Woody Guthrie, Sonny Terry, Josh White, and
others. In 1950, the year after Leadbelly died, a recording of his song
"Goodnight Irene" by Pete Seeger and the Weavers went to number one
on the international charts. Many of his songs were major hits during the
1950s folk song revival and have been widely recorded.

   Leadbelly's "discovery" and story is presented in John and Alan Lomax's
Negro Folksongs as Sung by Leadbelly (New York: Macmillan, 1936) and in
a new biography by Charles Wolfe and Kip Lornell, *The Life and Legend of
Leadbelly* (New York: Harper Collins, 1992). For song books see Moses Asch
and Alan Lomax, *The Leadbelly Songbook* (New York: Oak, 1962), and Julius
Lester and Pete Seeger, *The Twelve-String Guitar as Played by Leadbelly*
(New York: Oak, 1965). Ledbetter's life is also the subject of a biographical
film, *Leadbelly,* by Gordon Parks (1976); stills from the film are included
in a book by the same title featuring its songs (New York: TRO, 1976).
"The Lead Belly Letter," a newsletter edited by Sean Killeen and published
regularly since 1991, is devoted to information about Leadbelly's musical
career.

Much of the Leadbelly repertory, including his many famous songs ("Alberta," "Boll Weevil," "Bourgeois Blues," "Cotton Fields," "Go Down Ol' Hannah," "Grey Goose," "Ha Ha Thisaway," "Midnight Special," "Rock Island Line," "Goodnight Irene," "Western Plains," "Fannin Street," "John Henry," "Pick a Bale of Cotton," "Stewball," "Good Morning Blues," "Take Your Hands Off Her," "Sylvie," "Take This Hammer," "Can't You Line 'Em"), can be heard on Folkways recordings, many recently republished in digitally remastered form on the Smithsonian-Folkways label. [SF]

p. 293 . . . *Americans pretended to be each other* . . . People pretend to be of different regions, too. Country-and-western bars in the urban northeast are filled with people who are not geographically "country" or "western" but are tuned in to the ethos. Or are they? For all the scholarly interest in country-and-western over the years, I am still waiting for an ethnography, a detailed bar scene, a sense of C & W from the bottom up. [CK]

p. 293 . . . *some massive, Bakhtinian, carnivalesque set of reversals* . . . On reversal, parody, and the carnivalesque and their importance in opposing and inverting systems of domination, see M. M. Bakhtin, *Rabelais and His World* (Bloomington: Indiana University Press, 1984); Barbara Babcock, *The Reversible World: Symbolic Inversion in Art and Society* (Ithaca: Cornell University Press, 1978); and George Lipsitz, *Time Passages: Collective Memory and American Popular Culture*, chaps. 1 and 10 (Minneapolis: University of Minnesota Press, 1990). On inversions and antistructure see Victor Turner, *The Ritual Process* (Ithaca: Cornell University Press, 1969) and "Metaphors of Anti-Structure in Religious Culture," in *Dramas, Fields, and Metaphors* (Ithaca: Cornell University Press, 1974). [SF]

p. 293 . . . *class hurts on* both *sides* . . . Richard Sennett and Jonathan Cobb, *The Hidden Injuries of Class* (New York: Vintage, 1973); Anthony F. C. Wallace, *Rockdale* (New York: W. W. Norton, 1974); and Lillian Breslow Rubin, *Worlds of Pain: Life in the Working Class Family* (New York: Basic Books, 1976), which includes a large and thorough bibliography. For the fine British literature on class start with E. P. Thompson, *The Making of the English Working Class* (Harmondsworth: Penguin, 1968), and Paul Willis, *Learning to Labor: How Working Class Kids Get Working Class Jobs* (New York: Columbia University Press, 1977).

Recently, the glaring absence of class analysis in much American social science has been skillfully examined by Sherry B. Ortner, "Reading America: Preliminary Notes on Class and Culture," in *Recapturing Anthropology*, ed. Richard G. Fox, 163–89 (Santa Fe: School of American Research Press, 1991), and Benjamin DeMott, *The Imperial Middle: Why Americans Can't Think Straight about Class* (New York: William Morrow and Company, 1990). See also Penelope Eckert, *Jocks and Burnouts: Social Categories and Identity in the High School* (New York: Teachers College Press, 1989); Barbara Ehrenreich, *Fear of Falling: The Inner Life of the Middle Class* (New York: Pantheon, 1989); Margaret Ramsay Somers, "Workers of the World, Compare!"

Contemporary Sociology 17, no. 3 (1988): 325–29; Elizabeth Lapovsky Kennedy and Madeline D. Davis, *Boots of Leather, Slippers of Gold: The History of a Lesbian Community* (New York: Routledge, 1993); and Michael Frisch and Milton Rogovin, *Portraits in Steel* (Ithaca: Cornell University Press, 1993).

Little is written about the hidden injuries and mental health problems of members of the owning class, probably because a key piece of the ideology that holds everything together is the notion that people at the top are always content, adjusted, secure, and invisible, but see the novels of Louis Auchincloss and Laura Nader's classic invitation, rarely accepted, to study up, "'Up the Anthropologist'—Perspectives Gained from Studying Up," in *Reinventing Anthropology,* ed. Dell Hymes, 284–311 (New York: Random House, 1969). [CK]

p. 294 . . . *jazz fizzling as a coherent style* . . . I think I'm using "style" as shared grooves in something like the way Paul Bohannan defines culture as shared values and race as shared genes. In other words, you can draw a circle around one person, say Thelonious Monk, or a few people, the beboppers at Minton's, or four generations of jazz improvisers, or the whole stream of unwritten music in the world and speak of an improvised "style."

As to whether or not jazz lost its stylistic coherence and continuity some time in the 1960s, opinions vary, but to my ears the feeling of necessary organic development, branches filling out and flowering and fruit maturing, began to disappear after the Coleman and Coltrane quartets peaked and free jazz blew itself into little corners. The steady flow of funk-fusion after Miles Davis, Weather Report, and Mahavishnu Orchestra feels good, reconnects in important ways to African-American dance continuities, and is still improvised, but it doesn't grow or flow necessarily out of Coleman, Coltrane, the Aylers, and Cecil Taylor; it's something else. [CK]

p. 296 . . . *Sapir's genuine culture* . . . Edward Sapir (1884–1939) was a brilliant exponent of the Boasian vision of the centrality of language to the implementation of culture, displayed in his analyses of Navajo, Yana, Nootka, Chinook, Southern Paiute, and other North American languages, as well as studies of Germanic and Indo-European languages. He was also a humanist who wrote literary and critical works. His book *Language: An Introduction to the Study of Speech* (1921; New York: Harcourt, 1949) is still widely read, as are his papers, of which many of the best known are collected in *Culture, Language and Personality: Selected Essays by Edward Sapir,* ed. David G. Mandelbaum (1949; Berkeley: University of California Press, 1985). Assessments of Sapir's impact during his time at the University of Chicago (1925–31) and Yale University (1931–39) can be found in the short biographical articles on his contributions to anthropology and linguistics by David Mandelbaum and Zelig Harris in *International Encyclopedia of Social Sciences,* ed. David Sills (New York: Macmillan/Free Press, 1968), and, more substantially, in Regna Darnell's study, *Edward Sapir: Linguist, Anthropologist, and Humanist* (Berkeley: University of California Press, 1990). Sapir's complete writings are currently being assembled and published; thus far volume 5, writings on American Indian languages has appeared, edited by William Bright (Berlin and New York: Mouton de Gruyter, 1990). [SF]

I return to Sapir's essay "Culture: Genuine and Spurious" ([1949] 1985:308–31) over and over again. I usually think about participation from the point of view of individual action (swingwrights crafting grooves) or as a means of promoting spiritual/political reform (how can we create a little ritual space and/or an effective demonstration with lots of music and drama?) whereas Sapir theorizes participation from the cultural theory side—what are the characteristics of a culture that encourage participation and how have industrial civilization and social science alienated us?

In his early attempts to define "genuine culture," Sapir tried to fuse the concept of "national character" ("the specific manifestations of civilization that give a particular people its distinctive place in the world") with the concept of "high culture" ("the conventional ideal of individual refinement" in the arts and letters sanctioned by a dominant class). These notions are dangerous taken singly, potentially deadly in combination, and often genocidal when backed by delusions of empire. As a student of Native American cultures Sapir knew this, yet he desperately wanted to salvage a qualitative definition of culture from the threat of mass-mediated homogenization, on the one hand, and the scientific values of ethnographic neutrality and relativism, on the other, either of which can blindly reinforce the truism that everyone is equally cultured. An open-eyed awareness of this truth is, of course, a prerequisite for working effectively with people from different cultures, who are often labeled with racist epithets like "deprived," "disadvantaged," "underdeveloped" as if people who don't share our supposedly universal values are naturally prefixable as de-, dis-, under-, sub-, and so forth. Sapir tried to guard against these dangerous nationalist and elitist sources synthesized as "genuine" by insisting that "genuine culture is not of necessity either high or low; it is merely inherently harmonious, balanced, self-satisfactory . . . a culture in which nothing is spiritually meaningless. . . . The genuine culture is internal, it works from the individual to ends." For further discussion along these lines see my "Culture, Music and Collaborative Learning" in *Dialectical Anthropology: Essays in Honor of Stanley Diamond*, vol. 2, *The Politics of Culture and Creativity: A Critique of Civilization*, ed. Christine Ward Gailey, 327–33 (Gainesville: University Press of Florida, 1992). [CK]

p. 296 . . . *the* My Music *interviews* . . . Susan Crafts, Daniel Cavicchi, and Charles Keil, eds., *My Music* (Middletown: Wesleyan University Press, 1993). The book consists of forty-one interviews clustered in six groups according to age, from children to elders, in which people talk about music in their lives. The puzzle for readers is that each person seems so unique, not conforming to the Billboard chart categories at all, pulling together diverse musical resources to shape a personal identity, and yet one gets a sense of underlying negative common denominators—mediated music replacing music making as people get older, varying kinds of isolation that music soothes with a substitute feeling of togetherness, music as memories of life, music as just another drug or coping mechanism. [CK]

p. 297 . . . *the politics and poetics of identity.* The music ethnographies I have in mind are Christopher Waterman's work on Yoruba *jùjú,* reported in *Jùjú: A Social History and Ethnography of a West African Popular Music* (Chicago: University of Chicago Press, 1990) and "Jùjú History: Toward a Theory of Sociomusical Practice," in *Ethnomusicology and Modern Music History,* ed. S. Blum, P. Bohlman, and D. Neuman, 49–67 (Urbana: University of Illinois Press, 1991); David Coplan's work on South African pop and worker's music, reported in *In Township Tonight! South Africa's Black City Music and Theatre* (New York: Longman, 1985) and "Eloquent Knowledge: Lesotho Migrants' Songs and the Anthropology of Experience," *American Ethnologist* 14, no. 3 (1987):413–33; Thomas Turino's work on Andean urban and rural musical contacts and identity formations, reported in "The Coherence of Social Style and Musical Creation among the Aymara in Southern Peru," *Ethnomusicology* 33, no. 1 (1989):1–30, and *Moving Away from Silence: Music of the Peruvian Altiplano and the Experience of Urban Migration* (Chicago: University of Chicago Press, 1993); Marina Roseman's work with the Temiar of Peninsular Malaysia, reported in "The Social Structuring of Sound," *Ethnomusicology* 28, no. 3 (1984):411–45, and *Healing Sounds from the Malaysian Rainforest: Temiar Music and Medicine* (Berkeley: University of California Press, 1991); and Anthony Seeger's work on the Suyá, reported in *Why Suyá Sing: A Musical Anthropology of an Amazonian People* (Cambridge: Cambridge University Press, 1987) and "When Music Makes History," in *Ethnomusicology and Modern Music History,* ed. S. Blum, P. Bohlman, and D. Neuman, 23–34 (Urbana: University of Illinois Press, 1991). [SF]

p. 297 . . . *Arne Naess's deep ecology, deep identification . . .* See p. 189, comments following dialogue 2, at the reference to p. 168. Other deep ecology classics are Elisabet Sahtouris, *Gaia: The Human Journey from Chaos to Cosmos* (New York: Pocket Books, 1989); Bill Devall, *Simple Means, Rich in Ends: Practicing Deep Ecology* (Salt Lake City: Peregrine Smith Books, 1988); and Bill Devall and George Sessions, *Deep Ecology: Living as if Nature Mattered* (Salt Lake City, Peregrine Smith Books, 1985). *The Trumpeter: Journal of Ecosophy* is a good current source of deep ecology thinking (available from LightStar, P. O. Box 5853, Station B, Victoria, British Columbia V8R 6SB, Canada). [CK]

p. 299 . . . *Apollo and Dionysus . . .* On Dionysian blown and beaten outdoor music in relation to indoor singing with strings, see my "Applied Ethnomusicology and a Rebirth of Music from the Spirit of Tragedy," *Ethnomusicology* 26, no. 3 (1982):407–11. Friedrich Nietzsche's *Birth of Tragedy from the Spirit of Music* (New York: Doubleday, 1956) and Jane Ellen Harrison's books—*Themis: A Study of the Social Origins of Greek Religion* (1912; Cleveland: Meridian Books, 1962) and *Prolegomena to the Study of Greek Religion* (1903; Princeton: Princeton University Press, 1991)—are the classic resources for understanding the struggle between Apollo and Dionysus in the transition from animism to polytheism, from matricentric classless society to class society and patriarchal law in ancient Greece. [CK]

p. 300 . . . *struggles about ritualized male chaos.* On gender, emotion, and crying see my "Wept Thoughts: The Voicing of Kaluli Memories," *Oral Tradition* 5, nos. 2–3 (1990):241–66; Jerome Neu, "'A Tear is an Intellectual Thing,'" *Representations* 19 (1987):35–61; and C. Nadia Seremetakis, *The Last Word* (Chicago: University of Chicago Press, 1991). Good reviews of important issues can be found in June Crawford, Susan Lippax, Jenny Onyx, Una Gault, and Pam Benton, *Emotion and Gender: Constructing Meaning from Memory* (Newbury Park: Sage, 1992). On the anthropology of emotions see Catherine Lutz, *Unnatural Emotions* (Chicago: University of Chicago Press, 1990) and "Emotion, Thought and Estrangement: Emotion as a Cultural Category," *Cultural Anthropology* 1, no. 3 (1986):287–309; Catherine Lutz and Geoffrey White, "The Anthropology of Emotions," *Annual Review of Anthropology* 15 (1986):405–36; John Kirkpatrick and Geoffrey White, eds., *Person, Self and Experience* (Berkeley: University of California Press, 1985); Michelle Rosaldo, "Toward an Anthropology of Self and Feeling," 137–57, Robert Levy, "Emotion, Knowing, and Culture," 214–37, and Robert Solomon, "Getting Angry: The Jamesian Theory of Emotion in Anthropology," 238–54, in *Culture Theory: Essays on Mind, Self, and Emotion,* ed. Richard Shweder and Robert LeVine (New York: Cambridge University Press, 1984); Renato Rosaldo, "Grief and a Headhunter's Rage: On the Cultural Force of Emotions," in *Text, Play and Story: The Construction and Reconstruction of Self and Society,* ed. Edward Bruner, 178–95 (Washington, D.C.: American Ethnological Society, 1984). [SF]

p. 302 . . . *how many people have heard any Tiv songs?* I don't know what has happened to the dance film, *Tiv Women: The Icough Dance,* by Francis Speed, Peggy Harper, and Akwe Doma, that I reviewed in *American Anthropologist* 70 (1969):1234, but it was part of a very valuable series documenting dance traditions in Nigeria. Tiv songs are available on *Rise Up Africa* by the Benues (World Record Series, W W Communications, 112 a & b Westbourne Grove, London W2 5RU, England). [CK]

p. 303 . . . *dance and sing and drum for themselves* . . . Musicians United for Superior Education, Inc. (81 Crescent Avenue, Buffalo, New York 14214), is a nonprofit organization dedicated to incorporating the muses into the lives of primary school children. We teach African, African-American, Afro-Latin, and Native American drumming, singing, and dancing traditions to children in primary schools and after-school programs. [CK]

p. 304 *It's the same deal with the music.* Mainstream Afro-Pop and Planet Groove dance parties on the air do a great job of celebrating the existence of Africa and the diaspora's musical products but never say anything about the wars, the assaults, the people, the hunger, the AIDS, the ecological and biological and cultural devastation and destabilization of Africa. In the context of increasing culture crushing, it is hard to be completely positive about this kind of airwave representation when the price is the total depoliticization and decontextualization of the music. Lack of interviews, historical commentary, documentary responsibility, seem to be a particular problem in the current commercialization of Afro-Pop, of which National Public Radio's widely syndicated show "Afropop Worldwide," hosted by "Josh Colonial," is the slickest, most apolitical and acultural version. [SF and CK]

p. 307 *. . . the ethnic working class in America?* One reason we had so much trouble getting our polka work published was that we wanted to do a large book for both polka people and an academic audience. Editors advised us that if we tried to cross the great class divide we would lose both audiences; "Scholars won't read a popular book with pictures and polka people don't want to hear about theory," was the word. Another reason was that we wanted to compare black and white stylistic developments; this desire comes up against a kind of left-liberal orthodoxy that considers comparing polkas to blues or jazz as an insult to African-Americans or a denigration of "American Improvised Music," jazz as art.

There is finally (from 1844 to 1975 no scholar was interested) an emerging body of research (see p. 189, comments following dialogue 2, at the reference to page 169) on the six main styles of polka in the United States (Slovenian-American, Polish-American, German-American, Czech-American, Native American, and Mexican-American), but the only work that is sophisticated in terms of class analysis is Manuel Peña, *The Texas-Mexican Conjunto: History of a Working Class Music* (Austin: University of Texas Press, 1985), and José Limon, "Representation, Ethnicity, and the Precursory Ethnography: Notes of A Native Anthropologist," in *Recapturing Anthropology,* ed. Richard G. Fox, 115–35 (Santa Fe: School of American Research Press, 1991). [CK]

p. 308 *. . . why she appeals to Susan McClary . . .* Susan McClary's essay on Madonna is in her collection, *Feminine Endings: Music, Gender, and Sexuality* (Minneapolis: University of Minnesota Press, 1991). The Carrie Fisher–Madonna interviews appear in *Rolling Stone,* nos. 606 and 607, 13 and 27 June 1991. On Madonna and sexual alternatives see Lisa Henderson, "Justify Our Love: Madonna and the Politics of Queer Sex," in *The Madonna Connection,* ed. Cathy Schwichtenberg, 107–28 (Boulder: Westview Press, 1993). For a counterview, arguing that academics have merely appropriated Madonna in the service of their own theoretical positions, hence rewriting popular culture in and as elite discourse, see Daniel Harris, "Make My Rainy Day," *The Nation,* 8 June 1992, 790–93. Other provocative pieces of Madonnology suggested by Lisa Henderson include Susan Bordo, "Material Girl and the Effacements of Post-Modernism," *Michigan Quarterly,* Fall, 1990; John Fiske, *Reading the Popular* (Boston: Unwin-Hyman, 1988), which includes a chapter on Madonna; and Jane Brown and Laurie Schulze, "The Effects of Race, Gender, and Fandom on Audience Interpretations of Madonna's Music Videos," *Journal of Communication* 10 (1990):88–102.

Nine months later: Now that Madonna's new book, *Sex,* and recording, *Erotica,* are out and delighting, angering, and enriching (in all senses) various parties, I feel all the more strongly that her subversive and liberatory tendencies need to be debated and analyzed, in the context of late-80s–early-90s homophobia, censorship, and intolerance, and subjected specifically to ethnographic scrutiny. A good recent polemic can be found in the articles by Mim Udovitch, Vince Aletti, and Simon Frith, under the heading "In Defense of 'Sex'" *Village Voice,* 24 November 1992, 25–31. [SF]

p. 308 . . . *Atlantic Records, and Stax, and Motown.* Soul music may not have transformed the lives of white people en masse but numerous authors have heard the messages and interpreted them with great skill; see Peter Guralnick, *Sweet Soul Music: Rhythm and Blues and the Southern Dream of Freedom* (New York: Harper and Row, 1986); Gerri Hirshey, *Nowhere to Run: The Story of Soul Music* (New York: Times Books, 1984); Christopher Small, *Music of the Common Tongue: Survival and Celebration in Afro-American Music* (London: John Calder, 1987); David Ritz, *Divided Soul: The Life of Marvin Gaye* (New York: McGraw Hill, 1985). The failure of white people to listen and learn from soul music was perhaps paralleled by the failure of black people to hold on to what they had and earn from it. See Nelson George's astute *The Death of Rhythm and Blues* (New York: Pantheon Books, 1988) and *Where Did Our Love Go? The Rise and Fall of Motown Sound* (New York: St. Martin's Press, 1985). [CK]

p. 311 . . . *girls' . . . self-esteem freezing while boys' soars.* On gender differences in socialization, see Carol Gilligan, *In a Different Voice: Psychological Theory and Women's Development* (Cambridge: Harvard University Press, 1982), and Carol Gilligan, Nona Lyons, and Trudy Hammer, eds., *Making Connections: The Relational Worlds of Adolescent Girls at Emma Willard School* (Cambridge: Harvard University Press, 1990). "Confident at 11, Confused at 16" (*New York Times Magazine,* 7 January 1990) is a recent popular distillation of the implications of Gilligan's work on socialization. [SF]

For a well-argued anti-Gilligan view, see Katha Pollitt, "Are Women Morally Superior to Men?" *The Nation,* 28 December 1992. On gender socialization and the sources of misogyny in the modern world, the key texts for me have been Marilyn French's *Beyond Power* (New York: Summit Books, 1985) and Dorothy Dinnerstein's *The Mermaid and the Minotaur* (New York: Harper/Colophon, 1976). Read in conjunction with Marshall

Sahlins' *Stone Age Economics* (Chicago: Aldine, 1972) and the growing literature on the "two-hour workday" and the larger amounts of leisure time
once available in classless, preagricultural, preindustrial societies, Dinnerstein's main psychoanalytic argument (put very simply, that newborns
receive insufficient intimacy and nurturance from fathers and thus grow up
to scapegoat women as the source of all good and evil) gathers greater
force with every civilized step toward longer workdays, ever busier busi-
nessmen, ever more absent fathers, ever more nurturant and therefore
scapegoatable mothers and feminine others. [CK]

p. 312 . . . *books that I wish I had written.* Andrew Bard Schmookler, *The Parable
of the Tribes: The Problem of Power in Social Evolution* (Boston: Houghton
Mifflin, 1984), and Leopold Kohr, *The Breakdown of Nations* (New York:
E. P. Dutton, 1978). [CK]

p. 313 . . . *"fat thoughts"* . . . *Brecht and Benjamin talked about* . . . See Walter
Benjamin, "Coarse Thinking" (on Brecht), in *Reflections,* 199–200 (New
York: Harcourt Brace Jovanovich, 1978), and *Illuminations,* trans. Hannah
Arendt (New York: Schocken, 1969); *Brecht on Theatre,* ed. and trans. John
Willett (New York: Hill and Wang, 1964); and Russell Jacoby, *Social Amne-
sia: A Critique of Conformist Psychology from Adler to Laing* (Boston: Beacon
Press, 1975), which also has good references to the Frankfurt school fusion
of Marx and Freud. [CK]

p. 314 . . . *things get pulled into the legal world.* For a few summers in the early
1980s I performed a lot of street music with a variety of musician friends.
People were always surprised and glad to see us, and returns in the hat
were almost always proportional to the number of people playing; three
people made thirty dollars at lunch hour in the plaza downtown, five
people made fifty dollars. And no problems with the police. Then a lawyer
came along and introduced a piece of "busking legislation" with over a
dozen provisions and a ten-dollar-per-musician license fee—supposedly
in the interest of protecting and empowering musicians. Just a local example of the legal world defining natural matters that did not need to be
defined. [CK]

p. 318 . . . *without the hype and corporate control.* On the music business and
the development of the popular music and communications industries
after 1900, see volume 3 of Russell Sanjek's monumental study, *American
Popular Music and Its Business: The First Four Hundred Years* (New York:
Oxford University Press, 1988). See also his *From Print to Plastic: Promoting
America's Popular Music 1900–1980* (Brooklyn: Institute of Studies in American Music, 1983). Other significant studies in the vast literature on music,
technology, and society include Steve Chapple and Reebee Garofalo, *Rock
and Roll is Here to Pay: The History and Politics of the Music Industry* (Chicago:
Nelson-Hall, 1977); Wayne O. Coon, *Some Problems with Musical Public-
Domain Material under United States Copyright Law as Illustrated Mainly*

by the Recent Folk-Song Revival (New York: Columbia University Press, 1971); R. Serge Denisoff, *Solid Gold: The Popular Recording Industry* (Brunswick, N.J.: Transaction Books, 1975); Simon Frith, *Music for Pleasure* (London: Routledge, 1988); Reebee Garofalo, *Rockin' the Boat: Mass Music and Mass Movements* (Boston: South End Press, 1992); Charlie Gillett, *Making Tracks: Atlantic Records and the Growth of a Multi-Billion Dollar Industry* (New York: Dutton, 1974); Pekka Gronow, "The Record Industry: The Growth of a Mass Medium," *Popular Music* 3 (1983):53–75, and "Sound Recording," in *International Encyclopedia of Communications,* ed. Erik Barnouw, 4:112–21, (New York: Oxford University Press, 1989); Steve Jones, *Rock Formation: Music, Technology and Mass Communication* (Newbury Park: Sage, 1992); Paul Hirsch, *The Structure of the Popular Music Industry* (Ann Arbor: Institute for Social Research, University of Michigan, 1970); George Lipsitz, *Time Passages* (Minneapolis: University of Minnesota Press, 1990); James Lull, ed., *Popular Music and Communication,* 2d ed. (Newbury Park: Sage, 1992); Peter Manuel, *Cassette Culture* (Chicago: University of Chicago Press, 1993); Graham Murdock, "Large Corporations and the Control of the Communications Industries," in *Culture, Society and the Media,* ed. M. Gurevich et. al., 118–50 (London: Methuen, 1982); Deanna Campbell Robinson, Elizabeth B. Buck, and Marlene Cuthbert, *Music at the Margins: Popular Music and Global Cultural Diversity* (Newbury Park: Sage, 1991); and Roger Wallis and Krister Malm, *Big Sounds from Small Peoples: The Music Industry in Small Countries* (New York: Pendragon Press, 1984). The journal *Popular Music* (Cambridge University Press) often carries incisive essays about pop and since 1981 has been the single best indicator of the range and variety of viewpoints and concerns that exist under the umbrella of popular music studies. [SF]

p. 320 *I'm with Alan Lomax . . .* Alan Lomax's "Appeal for Cultural Equity," *Journal of Communication* 27, no. 2 (1977):125–39, introduced the notions of "cultural pollution" and "cultural greyout" and argued vehemently that monopoly funding and support of dominant, high-culture forms produces false consciousness by presenting the American cultural heritage as generic. Lomax currently directs the Association for Cultural Equity at Hunter College, and his work of the last thirty years on the evolution and diversification of human musical and movement styles, mostly published under the headings cantometrics and choreometrics and now integrated on CD-ROM as Global Jukebox, is being promoted as an attempt to share, reinvigorate, and stimulate musical diversity and equity worldwide. On the discursive and political relation of Lomax's views to issues of anthropological interventions for human rights, see Robin Wright, "Anthropological Presuppositions of Indigenous Advocacy," *Annual Review of Anthropology* 17 (1988):365–90.

For a perspective on cultural loss among the Kaluli, see Edward L. Schieffelin, "The End of Traditional Music, Dance, and Body Decoration in

Bosavi, Papua New Guinea," in *The Plight of Indigenous Peoples in Papua New Guinea,* vol. 1, *The Inland Situation,* ed. Robert Gordon, 1–22 (Cambridge, Mass.: Cultural Survival, Occasional Paper no. 7, 1981). This piece was originally written to outline Schieffelin's views on cultural greyout in Bosavi in 1975–77, following up the situation he encountered during his initial research in 1966–68; it was first published in 1978 as a discussion paper by the Institute of Papua New Guinea Studies. [SF]

p. 322 . . . *the gift must always circulate.* On gift giving and the circulation and exchange of commodities and sentiments, see Lewis Hyde, *The Gift: Imagination and the Erotic Life of Property* (New York: Random House, 1979), and the classic by Marcel Mauss, *The Gift* (1925; New York: Norton, 1976). For an update on the famous Kula ring exchange of the Trobriand Islands, see Jerry W. Leach and Edmund Leach, eds., *The Kula: New Perspectives on Massim Exchange* (Cambridge: Cambridge University Press, 1983). For another kind of Papua New Guinea perspective, from Bosavi, see Edward L. Schieffelin, "Reciprocity and the Construction of Reality," *Man* 15 (1980): 502–17, and Bambi B. Schieffelin, *The Give and Take of Everyday Life: Language Socialization of Kaluli Children,* esp. chap. 6, "Socializing Reciprocity and Creating Relationships" (Cambridge: Cambridge University Press, 1990). [SF]

p. 323 . . . *new groove is never going to be subsidized.* For as long as music departments remain dedicated to Old White Men's music and mass-mediated music continues steadily to displace live music, we will have to make common cause with folklorists. They represent one source of strategies for keeping traditions going that might otherwise fade or disappear faster. But one wonders if it isn't time to change the focus from "folk" and "folklore" to people, everyday life, and strategies for reemergent cultural and biological diversity; see my debate with Richard Dorson in the *Journal of the Folklore Institute:* Keil, "Who Needs 'the Folk'?" 15 (1978):263–66; Dorson, "We All Need the Folk" (editor's comment), 15 (1978):267–69; and Keil, "The Concept of 'the Folk'" (comment), 16 (1979):209–10. [CK]

p. 323 . . . *celebrating their language and their locality.* On the vitality of Papua New Guinea pop bands see Don Niles, *Commercial Recordings of Papua New Guinea Music 1949–1983* (Boroko: Institute of Papua New Guinea Studies, 1984), with subsequent annual supplements. These catalogs give a good sense of the level of activities and the varieties of Papua New Guinea pop recording, although they include no figures on sales and circulation or on radio play. Michael Webb and Don Niles's *Riwain: Papua New Guinea Pop Songs* (booklet and cassette tapes; Boroko: Institute of Papua New Guinea Studies, 1986) is an anthology of lyrics and guitar chords for fifty well-known tunes from the 1970s and early 1980s. Michael Webb's "Lingua Franca Songs and Identity in Papua New Guinea" (M.M. thesis, Department of Music, Wesleyan University, 1991) is the first thorough academic review of Papua New Guinea pop; it will appear shortly in revised form as volume 3 of the series *Apwitihire: Studies in Papua New Guinea Musics,* from the Cultural Studies Divison of the National Research Institute, Papua New Guinea. The only commercial recordings to bring something of the Papua New Guinea string band pop sound to the attention of a world pop audience are *Tabaran,* a collaboration between the Australian rock group Not Drowning, Waving, and Telek and musicians of Rabaul, Papua New Guinea (WEA, 1990), and two short pieces on the soundtrack to David Fanshawe's self-promotional adventure-television compilation, *Musical Mariner—Pacific Journey* (Mercury, 1989). [SF]

p. 325 *Ranting and raving!* See Norman Cohn, *The Pursuit of the Millennium: Revolutionary Millenarians and Mystical Anarchists of the Middle Ages* (1957; New York: Oxford University Press, 1970). [CK]

p. 328 *Soundscape research . . . in the form of musical composition.* Canadian composer, author, and researcher R. Murray Schafer was founder and director of the World Soundscape project at Simon Fraser University and inventor of the notions of soundscape and acoustic ecology. His major statement of the principles of soundscape research, design, and composition is *The Tuning of the World* (New York: Knopf, 1977). Other important Schafer books include *The Vancouver Soundscape* (Vancouver: World Soundscape Project, 1978), *Five Village Soundscapes* (Vancouver: World Soundscape Project, 1977), *European Sound Diary* (Vancouver: World Soundscape Project, 1977), *The New Soundscape* (Toronto: Clark and Cruickshank, 1969), and *The Book of Noise* (Wellington: Price Milburn, 1970). [SF]

Sources and Acknowledgments

Chapter 1 originally appeared in slightly different form in the *Journal of Aesthetics and Art Criticism* 24 (1966):337–49. Many thanks to Leonard Meyer, Roswell Rudd, Louis Feldhammer, and Angeliki Keil for the comments which helped me revise this paper. [CK]

Chapter 2 is revised from the version that appeared in the *Yearbook for Traditional Music* 16 (1984):1–18. Thanks to the students at the Annenberg School of Communications in the early 1980s who took my classes on sound, especially Barry Dornfeld, Ira Greenberg, Lisa Henderson, Jane Hulting, Marsha Siefert, Scott Sinkler, Nilita Vachani, and Mike Willmorth, for many stimulating discussions about communications, sound, and music. [SF]

Chapter 3 is slightly revised from the version that appeared in *Cultural Anthropology* 2, no. 3 (1987):275–83. The negative aspects of participatory consciousness are given fuller description thanks to Robert Dentan's critical reading of an earlier draft of this article. Thanks also to John Shepherd, Steve Feld, Larry Chisolm, Joe Blum, Mike Frisch, Mark Dickey, and all the family, friends, and musicians who have participated in and precipitated my thinking on this subject. Comments and questions from people at the University of Pennsylvania, the University of Texas at Austin, and Columbia University, where versions of this paper were presented, helped me to reshape it. [CK]

Chapter 4 is revised from the version that appeared in the *Yearbook for Traditional Music* 20 (1988):74–113. Numerous aspects of this paper were stimulated by and formulated in response to two of my favorite groovesters, Robert Plant Armstrong (uptown) and Charles Keil (downtown). Research support for fieldwork with the Kaluli 1976–77, 1982, 1984, 1990, and 1992 was generously provided by the Institute of Papua New Guinea Studies, the National Endowment for the Arts, the National Science Foundation, the Wenner-Gren Foundation for Anthropological Research, the American Philosophical Society, 360° Productions, Rykodisc, and the John D. and Catherine T.

MacArthur Foundation. Audiences at the University of Texas Semiotics Colloquium, Rice University Circle, Columbia University Center for Ethnomusicology, American Anthropological Association annual meetings, New York University Anthropology Department, and Carleton University Conference on Alternative Musicology were generous in their responses as the paper was in process, as were my collaborators and kinsmen, nado Babi (Bambi B. Schieffelin) and nabas Bage (Edward L. Schieffelin). Jubi, Kulu, Gigio, Ho:nowo:, Ayasilo, and many other Kaluli shared ideas as well as song, talk, food, and trail. Helpful "lift-up-over" comments from Dieter Christensen, John Miller Chernoff, Charlie Keil, Gail Kligman, Don Niles, and Greg Urban also made a big difference. Thanks too to Shari Robertson for some of her photographs. [SF]

Chapter 5 originally appeared in slightly different form in *Dialectical Anthropology* 10 (1985):119–30. Thanks to the people who gave these ideas full discussion after presentations at Yale University in 1981, the American Anthropological Association annual meetings in 1982, and the Annenberg School of Communications in 1983. This paper took a while to evolve and I'm sure that all eight arguments are a product of years of discussion with Angeliki Keil as we pursued polka happiness together in the 1970s. [CK]

Chapter 6 originally appeared in slightly different form in *Echology* 2 (1988):89–94. Portions of the Feld letter are derived from "Sock It to Me: Sex and Politics in Soul Music," presented orally at the 1987 annual meetings of the American Ethnological Society. [SF and CK]

Chapter 7 draws from thoughts that originally appeared in *Buckethead*, no. 2 (1988):19; *The Society for Ethnomusicology Newsletter* 18, no. 3 (1984); and *Echology* 1 (1987):28. [CK]

Chapter 8 is revised from the version that originally appeared in *Public Culture* 1, no. 1 (1988):31–37. Thanks to Carol Breckenridge and Arjun Appadurai, for requesting a little piece to help inaugurate their journal, and to graduate students in my first University of Texas classes on Popular Musics and Mass Media in 1986, especially Venise Berry, Barbara Burton, Louise Meintjes, Tom Porcello, and Tom Solomon, for spirited discussion of appropriation issues. [SF]

Chapter 9 originally appeared in *Ethnomusicology* 28, no. 1 (1984): 91–96. Thanks to David Hughes for showing me around Tokyo and sharing so much of his knowledge and research-in-progress with me, to Yo Numata for hosting me at his favorite karaoke bar, and to Hiro Nakamura Shigeo for patiently making every possible arrangement for me to experience a variety of musical scenes during a short period of time. [CK]

Chapter 10's first section, in part published in *Working Papers and Proceedings of the Center for Psychosocial Studies,* no. 53 (1992), was originally presented orally at the 1990 meetings of the Society for Cultural Anthropology, where Chris Waterman's pithy comments started me off on the revision process. The paper later developed with help from audiences at the Center for Ethnomusicology at Columbia University, the departments of Performance Studies and Anthropology at New York University, the Music Department at the University of Sydney, the Anthropology and Music departments of LaTrobe University, and the Anthropology Department and the Research School of Pacific Studies at the Australian National University. Parts of the essay's second section are drawn from "Voices of the Rainforest," *Public Culture* 4, no. 1 (1991): 131–40; "Ethnoaesthetics and High-Tech Recording: The Making of *Voices of the Rainforest,*" presented orally at the 1991 meetings of the Society for Ethnomusicology; and "Voices of the Rainforest: 'Imperialist Nostalgia' and the Politics of Music," *Arena* 99/100 (1992):164–77. The material was helped along by discussions following presentations at the Department of Music at Vassar College, the Music, Anthropology, and Sociology departments of Monash University, and the Music Department of the University of Sydney, where Allan Marett's comments were particularly helpful for teasing out the issues. [SF]

Academic and musical influences are mentioned in numerous places in the book but in no place did I get around to acknowledging some good musician friends in New Mexico and Texas with whom I've made, listened to, and talked about a lot of music over the last twenty years. When it comes to grooves, Pete Amahl, Alex Coke, Tom Guralnick, Mark "Kaz" Kazanoff, Jack Loeffler, David Moir, Zimbabwe Nkenya, Jay Peck, and Jefferson Voorhees have been as persuasive as the books, articles, and records cited. [SF]

Recently my fellow groovers in Buffalo are in the 12/8 Path Band (Kilissa McGoldrick, Ringo Brill, Wayne Swanson, Greg Horn, Gilberto Rivera, Jim Whitefield, Marlowe Wright, Spencer Bolden, Junko Kanamura, Cyndi Cox, Debbie Stein), the Biocentrics (Ed Handman, Lou Mang, Mark Dickey, Charlie Izzo, Martin Dalmasi), and Papa Eclectic

(Andrew Case, Jim Capik, Synyer Hanesworth, John Allen, Emille Latimer, M'baye Diagne, Vince Fossit), but I'd like to thank the many members of the Outer Circle Orchestra over two decades (Mark Dickey, Synyer Hanesworth, Bill Nowak, Elliot Sharp, Wanda Edwards, Alex Meyer, Andy Byron, Carl Keil, Spencer Bolden, Rick McCrae, Nick Brabson, Susan Slack, Herb Tillman, John Allen, and Oren Hollasch, among many others) for keeping the flame lit and the Inner Circle Orchestra (John Allen, Kilissa McGoldrick, Martin Dalmasi, Mark Dickey, Bobby Rodriquez) for letting me hear a three flutes and finger piano blend better than I had ever imagined it. Kilissa McGoldrick, in addition to spilling over with catchy melodies, is the person who keeps the MUSE Incorporated dream coming true in the primary schools and a lot of people are thankful for that. [CK]

References

The essays in which a work is cited are identified in brackets at the end of each entry by chapter number (1–10) or dialogue number (D1–D3).

Abbate, Carolyn. 1991. *Unsung Voices: Opera and Musical Narrative in the Nineteenth Century.* Princeton University Press. [D2]

Ackerman, James. 1962. A Theory of Style. *Journal of Aesthetics* 20:227–37. [4]

Adams, Richard N. 1975. *Energy and Structure: A Theory of Social Power.* Austin: University of Texas Press. [4, D1]

Alén Rodriguez, Olavo. 1986. *La Música de las Sociedades de Tumba Francesa.* Havana: Casa de las Americas. [D2]

American Heritage Publishing. 1969. *American Heritage Dictionary of the English Language.* New York. [3]

Appadurai, Arjun. 1986. Introduction. Commodities and the Politics of Value. In *The Social Life of Things: Commodities in Cultural Perspective,* ed. Arjun Appadurai, 3–63. New York: Cambridge University Press. [10]

———. 1990. Disjuncture and Difference in the Global Culture Economy. *Public Culture* 2(2):1–24. [10]

Apter, Andrew. 1992. *Black Critics and Kings: The Hermeneutics of Power in Yoruba Society.* Chicago: University of Chicago Press. [D1]

Armstrong, Louis. [1954] 1986. *Satchmo: My Life in New Orleans.* New York: Da Capo. [D1]

Armstrong, Robert Plant. 1971. *The Affecting Presence: An Essay in Humanistic Anthropology.* Urbana: University of Illinois Press. [3, 4, D1]

———. 1975. *Wellspring: On the Myth and Source of Culture.* Berkeley: University of California Press. [4, D1]

———. 1981. *The Powers of Presence: Consciousness, Myth, and the Affecting Presence.* Philadelphia: University of Pennsylvania Press. [4, D1]

Asch, Moses, and Alan Lomax. 1962. *The Leadbelly Songbook.* New York: Oak. [D3]

Attali, Jacques. 1985. *Noise: The Political Economy of Music.* Minneapolis: University of Minnesota Press. [10, D2]

Babcock, Barbara. 1978. *The Reversible World: Symbolic Inversion in Art and Society.* Ithaca: Cornell University Press. [D3]

Baily, John. 1990. Obituary for John Blacking. *Yearbook for Traditional Music* 22:xii–xxi.[D1]

Bakhtin, Mikhail M. 1973. *Problems of Dostoevsky's Poetics*. Ann Arbor: Ardis.
    [D1]
——. [1934–35] 1981. Discourse in the Novel. In *The Dialogic Imagi-
    nation,* ed. Michael Holquist, 259–422. Austin: University of Texas
    Press. [4]
——. 1981. *The Dialogic Imagination*. Austin: University of Texas Press. [D1]
——. 1984. *Rabelais and His World*. Bloomington: Indiana University Press.
    [D1, D3]
——. 1986. *Speech Genres and Other Late Essays*. Austin: University of Texas
    Press. [D1]
Ballantine, Christopher. 1984. *Music and Its Social Meanings*. New York: Gor-
    don and Breach. [D2]
Barber, Karin. 1991. *I Could Speak Until Tomorrow: Oriki, Women and the Past
    in a Yoruba Town*. Edinburgh: Edinburgh University Press. [D1]
Barfield, Owen. 1965. *Saving the Appearances: A Study in Idolatry*. New York:
    Harcourt Brace Jovanovich. [3, D1]
——. [1928] 1973. *Poetic Diction: A Study in Meaning*. Middletown: Wes-
    leyan University Press. [4]
——. 1984. *Speaker's Meaning*. Middletown: Wesleyan University Press. [3]
Barnouw, Erik, ed. 1989. *Encyclopedia of Communications*. 4 vols. New York:
    Oxford University Press. [D2]
Barthes, Roland. 1968. *Elements of Semiology*. London: Cape. [D2]
Basso, Keith. 1990. *Western Apache Language and Culture*. Tucson: University
    of Arizona Press. [4]
Basso, Keith, and Henry Selby, eds. 1976. *Meaning in Anthropology*. Albu-
    querque: University of New Mexico Press. [D1]
Bastide, Roger. 1978. *The African Religions of Brazil: Toward a Sociology of the
    Interpenetration of Civilizations*. Baltimore: Johns Hopkins University
    Press. [D1]
Bateson, Gregory. [1936] 1958. *Naven*. Stanford: Stanford University Press. [10]
——. 1972. *Steps to an Ecology of Mind*. New York: Ballantine. [2, 4, 10, D1]
——. 1979. *Mind and Nature: A Necessary Unity*. New York: Dutton. [D1]
——. 1991. *A Sacred Unity: Further Steps to an Ecology of Mind*. New York:
    Cornelia & Michael Bessie Books. [D1]
Bateson, Gregory, and Margaret Mead. 1942. *Balinese Character*. New York:
    New York Academy of Sciences. [D1]
Baudrillard, Jean. 1975. *The Mirror of Production*. Saint Louis: Telos Press. [10]
——. *For a Critique of the Political Economy of the Sign*. Saint Louis: Telos
    Press. [2, 10]
Bauman, Richard. 1977. *Verbal Art as Performance*. Prospect Heights, Ill.:
    Waveland Press. [4]
Beatles. 1969. Come Together. *Abbey Road*. Capitol C11H-46446. [4]
Becker, Alton. 1979. Text-Building, Epistemology, and Aesthetics in Javanese
    Shadow Theatre. In *The Imagination of Reality,* ed. A. L. Becker and
    Aram Yengoyan, 211–43. Norwood: Ablex. [4]
Becker, Howard. 1974a. Art as Collective Action. *American Sociological Review*
    39(6):767–76. [4]

———. 1974b. Photography and Sociology. *Studies in the Anthropology of Visual Communication* 1(1):3–26. [D1]

———. 1978. Do Photographs Tell the Truth? *Afterimage* 5 February, 9–13. [D1]

Becker, Judith. 1968. Is Western Art Music Superior? *Musical Quarterly* 72(3):341–59. [D2]

———. 1979. Time and Tune in Java. In *The Imagination of Reality,* ed. A. L. Becker and Aram Yengoyan, 197–210. Norwood: Ablex. [4]

Becker, Judith, and Alton Becker. 1981. A Musical Icon: Power and Meaning in Javanese Gamelan Music. In *The Sign in Music and Literature,* ed. Wendy Steiner, 203–15. Austin: University of Texas Press. [2, 4]

Bego, Mark. 1989. *Aretha Franklin: The Queen of Soul.* New York: St. Martins Press. [D1]

Benedict, Ruth. [1947] 1967. *The Chrysanthemum and the Sword.* New York: Meridian Books. [9]

Benjamin, Walter. 1969. *Illuminations.* Ed. Hannah Arendt. New York: Schocken. [3, 10, D3]

———. 1978. Coarse Thinking. In *Reflections,* 199–200. New York: Harcourt Brace Jovanovich. [D3]

Bennett, Lerone. 1964. *The Negro Mood.* New York: Ballantine. [3]

Benues. 1987. *Rise Up Africa.* LP. World Record Series, WWC-D007, London: Wallbank-Warwick Communications. [D3]

Berger, Peter, and Thomas Luckman. 1967. *The Social Construction of Reality.* New York: Anchor Doubleday. [2, D1, D2]

Bergson, Henri. 1914. *Dreams.* London: T. Fisher Unwin. [D1]

———. 1980. *Introduction to Metaphysics: The Creative Mind.* Indianapolis: Bobbs-Merrill. [D1]

———. 1988. *Matter and Memory.* New York: Zone Books. [D1]

Berman, Marshall. 1983. *All That is Solid Melts into Air: The Experience of Modernity.* London: Verso. [10]

Berman, Morris. *The Reenchantment of the World.* New York: Bantam. [D1, D2]

Birdwhistell, Ray L. 1952. *Introduction to Kinesics.* Louisville, Ky.: University of Louisville Press. [1]

Blacking, John. 1955. Some Notes on a Theory of African Rhythm Advanced by Erich von Hornbostel. *African Music* 1(2):12–20. [1]

———. 1967. *Venda Children's Songs: A Study in Ethnomusicological Analysis.* Johannesburg: Witwatersrand University Press. [D1]

———. 1971. The Value of Music in Human Experience. *Yearbook of the International Folk Music Council* 1:33–71. [D1]

———. 1973. *How Musical is Man?* Seattle: University of Washington Press. [D1]

———. 1977. *The Anthropology of the Body.* London: Academic Press. [D1]

———. 1979. Some Problems of Theory and Method in the Study of Musical Change. *Yearbook of the International Folk Music Council* 9:1–26. [D1]

———. 1980. Political and Musical Freedom in the Music of Some Black South African Churches. In *The Structure of Folk Models,* ed. L. Holy and M. Struchlik, 35–62. London: Academic Press. [D1]

———. 1981a. Making Artistic Popular Music: The Goal of True Folk. *Popular Music* 1:9–14. [D1]

———. 1981b. The Problem of Ethnic Perceptions in the Semiotics of Music. In *The Sign in Music and Literature,* ed. Wendy Steiner, 184–94. Austin: University of Texas Press. [2, D1, D2]

———. 1987. *"A Common-Sense View of all Music": Reflections on Percy Grainger's Writings on Ethnomusicology and Music Education.* Cambridge: Cambridge University Press. [D1]

———. 1992. The Biology of Music-Making. In *Ethnomusicology: An Introduction,* ed. H. Myers, 301–14. New York: W. W. Norton. [D1]

Bley, Carla. 1978. *The Carla Bley Band: European Tour 1977.* LP. Watt Records 8. [2]

Bley, Paul. 1965. Interviewed by Don Heckman. *Downbeat,* March 12, 16–17. [1]

Boas, Franz. [1927] 1955. *Primitive Art.* New York: Dover. [4]

Boilès, Charles. 1982. Processes of Musical Semiosis. *Yearbook for Traditional Music* 14:24–44. [2, D2]

Boon, James. 1982. *Other Tribes, Other Scribes.* New York: Cambridge University Press. [D1]

Bordo, Susan. 1990. Material Girl and the Effacements of Post-Modernism. *Michigan Quarterly,* Fall. [D3]

Born, Georgina. 1989. The Ethnography of a Computer Music Research Institute: Modernism, Post-modernism, and New Technology in Contemporary Music Culture. Unpublished Ph.D. dissertation; Department of Anthropology, University of London. [D2]

Bourdieu, Pierre. 1977. *Outline of a Theory of Practice.* New York: Cambridge University Press. [D1]

———. 1984. *Distinction: A Social Critique of the Judgement of Taste.* Cambridge, Mass.: Harvard University Press. [10]

Bouwsma, O. K. [1954] 1970. The Expression Theory of Art. In *Aesthetics and Language,* ed. William Elton, 73–99. Oxford: Basil Blackwell. [4]

Boyer, Peter. 1988. What a Romance! Sony and CBS Records. *New York Times Magazine,* September 18, 34–49. [10]

Brecht, Berthold. 1964. *Brecht on Theatre.* Ed. and trans. John Willett. New York: Hill and Wang. [D3]

Bregman, Albert. 1990. *Auditory Scene Analysis.* Cambridge, Mass.: MIT Press. [D2]

Brenneis, Donald. 1985. Passion and Performance in Fiji Indian Vernacular Song. *Ethnomusicology* 29(3):397–408. [D1]

———. 1986. Shared Territory: Audience, Indirection, and Meaning. *Text* 6(3): 339–47. [4]

Brown, James. 1966. *Ain't That a Groove.* LP. King Records K 6025. [4]

———. 1984a. *Ain't That a Groove—The James Brown Story 1966–69.* LP. Polydor 422-821231-1. [D1]

———. 1984b. *Doing It to Death—The James Brown Story 1970–73.* LP. Polydor 422-821232-1. [D1]

———. 1984c. *Roots of Revolution, Soul Classics.* LP. 2 vols. Polydor 817304-
    1. [D1]

———. 1985. *Dead on the Heavy Funk—1974–76.* LP. Polydor 422-827439-1.
    [D1]

———. [1962] 1986. *Live at the Apollo.* 2 vols. Rhino RNLP-217, 218. [D1]

———. 1988. *Motherlode.* CD. Polydor 837126-2. [D1]

———. 1991. *Startime.* 4 CD set. Polydor 849108-2. [D1]

Brown, James, and Bruce Tucker. *James Brown: The Godfather of Soul.* New
    York: MacMillan. [D1]

Brown, Jane, and Laurie Schulze. 1990. The Effects of Race, Gender, and Fan-
    dom on Audience Interpretations of Madonna's Music Videos. *Journal
    of Communication* 10:88–102. [D3]

Brown, Norman O. 1959. *Life Against Death: The Psychoanalytic Meaning of
    History.* New York: Vintage. [1, D2]

———. 1968. *Love's Body.* New York: Vintage. [D2]

———. 1974. *Closing Time.* New York: Vintage. [D2]

Bunzel, Ruth. 1938. Art. In *General Anthropology,* ed. Franz Boas, 535–88.
    New York: D. C. Heath. [4]

Burgess, Anthony. 1982. *This Man and Music.* New York: Avon. [4]

Burke, Kenneth. 1945. *A Grammar of Motives.* Englewood, N.J.: Prentice-Hall. [2]

———. 1968. *Language as Symbolic Action.* Berkeley: University of California
    Press. [D1]

———. [1950] 1969. *A Rhetoric of Motives.* Berkeley: University of California
    Press. [4]

Byers, Paul. 1966. Cameras Don't Take Pictures. *Columbia University Forum*
    9(1):28–32. [D1]

Canetti, Elias. 1963. *Crowds and Power.* New York: Viking Press. [4]

Card, Caroline, and Carl Rahkonen. 1982. Alan P. Merriam: Bibliography and
    Discography. *Ethnomusicology* 26(1):107–20. [D1]

Carpenter, Edmund. 1969a. Comments. In *Tradition and Creativity in Tribal
    Art,* ed. Daniel Biebuyck, 203–13. Berkeley: University of California
    Press. [D1]

———. 1969b. If Wittgenstein Had Been an Eskimo. *Varsity Graduate* (Univer-
    sity of Toronto) 12(3):50–66. [D1]

———. 1971. The Eskimo Artist. In *Anthropology and Art: Readings in Cross-
    Cultural Aesthetics,* ed. Charlotte Otten. Garden City: Natural History
    Press. [D1]

———. 1972. *Oh, What a Blow That Phantom Gave Me!* New York: Holt,
    Rinehart Winston. [D1]

———. 1973. *Eskimo Realities.* New York: Holt, Rinehart Winston. [D1]

———. 1980. If Wittgenstein Had Been an Eskimo. *Natural History* 89(2):
    72–77. [D1]

Carpenter, Edmund, and Ken Heyman. 1970. *They Became What They Beheld,*
    New York: Weidenfeld. [D1]

Carpenter, Edmund, and Marshall McLuhan, eds. 1960. *Explorations in Com-
    munication.* Boston: Beacon. [D1]

Carpenter, Edmund, D. Varley, and R. Flaherty. 1959. *Eskimo*. Toronto: University of Toronto Press. [D1]

Cash, Alice. 1991. Feminist Theory and Music: Toward a Common Language (conference report). *Journal of Musicology* 9(4):521–32. [D2]

Cassirer, Ernst. [1923] 1955. *The Philosophy of Symbolic Forms*. New Haven: Yale University Press. [D1]

Castoriadis, Cornelius. 1985. Reflections on "Rationality" and "Development." *Thesis Eleven* 10/11:18–36. [10]

Caton, Steven. 1987. Contributions of Roman Jakobson. *Annual Review of Anthropology* 16:223–60. [D2]

Caufield, Catherine. 1984. *In the Rainforest: Report from a Strange, Beautiful, Imperiled World*. Chicago: University of Chicago Press. [10]

Cavanaugh, Beverly. 1981. Obituary for Mieczyslaw Kolinski. *Ethnomusicology* 25(2):285–86. [D2]

Cervantes, Linda Levalley. 1992. Going West: Poetry, Poetics, and Anthropology. In *Dialectical Anthropology: Essays in Honor of Stanley Diamond*. Vol. 2, *The Politics of Culture and Creativity: A Critique of Civilization*, ed. Christine Gailey, 249–80. Gainesville: University Press of Florida. [D1]

Chanan, Michael. 1981. The Trajectory of Western Music; or, As Mahler Said, The Music is Not in the Notes. *Media, Culture, and Society* 3:219–41. [D2]

Chapple, Steve, and Reebee Garofalo. *Rock and Roll is Here to Pay: The History and Politics of the Music Industry*. Chicago: Nelson-Hall. [10, D3]

Chester, Andrew. 1970a. For a Rock Aesthetic. *New Left Review* 59:83–87. [D2]

———. 1970b. Second Thoughts on a Rock Aesthetic: The Band. *New Left Review* 62:75–82. Reprinted in *On Record*, ed. Simon Frith and Andrew Goodwin (New York: Pantheon, 1990). [D2]

Cheyney, Tom. 1990. The Real World of Peter Gabriel. *The Beat* 9(2):22–25. [10]

Chilton, John. 1989. *Billie's Blues: The Billie Holiday Story 1933–1959*. New York: DaCapo. [D1]

Citron, Marcia. 1990. Gender, Professionalism, and the Musical Canon. *Journal of Musicology* 8(1):102–17. [D2]

Clarke, Kenny. 1955. *Bohemia after Dark*. LP. Savoy 12017. [1]

Cleary, David. 1990. *Anatomy of the Amazon Gold Rush*. Oxford: Basingstoke. [D2]

Clément, Catherine. 1988. *Opera; or, The Undoing of Women*. Minneapolis: University of Minnesota Press. [D2]

Clifford, James. 1988. *The Predicament of Culture*. Cambridge, Mass.: Harvard University Press. [10, D1]

Clifford, James, and George Marcus, eds. 1986. *Writing Culture*. Berkeley: University of California Press. [10]

Clynes, Manfred, ed. 1982. *Music, Mind and Brain*. New York: Plenum. [D2]

Cohn, Norman. [1957] 1970. *The Pursuit of the Millennium: Revolutionary Millenarians and Mystical Anarchists of the Middle Ages*. New York: Oxford University Press. [D3]

Colby, Benjamin, James Fernandez, and David Kronenfeld. 1981. Toward a Convergence of Cognitive and Symbolic Anthropology. *American Ethnologist* 8(3):422–50. [D1]

Collier, James Lincoln. 1985. *Louis Armstrong: An American Success Story.* New York: Macmillan. [D1]

Collier, John. 1967. *Visual Anthropology: Photography as a Research Method.* New York: Holt, Rinehart, Winston. [D1]

Collins, Harold R. 1969. *Amos Tutuola.* New York: Twayne Publishers. [D1]

Collins, Mark, ed. 1990. *The Last Rainforests: A World Conservation Atlas.* New York: Oxford University Press. [10]

Collins, Richard, ed. 1986. *Media, Culture and Society: A Critical Reader.* Beverly Hills: Sage Publications. [D2]

Coltrane, John (John Coltrane Quartet). 1959. *Giant Steps.* LP. Atlantic 1311. [D1]

———. 1959–60. *Coltrane Jazz.* LP. Atlantic 1354. [D1]

———. 1960. *My Favorite Things.* LP. Atlantic 1361. [D1]

———. 1961a. *Africa/Brass.* LP. Impulse 6. [D1]

———. 1961b. *Live at the Village Vanguard.* LP. Impulse 10. [D1]

———. 1962a. *Ballads.* LP. Impulse 32. [D1]

———. 1962b. *Coltrane.* LP. Impulse 21. [1]

———. 1963a. *Impressions.* LP. Impulse 42. [D1]

———. 1963b. *Live at Birdland.* LP. Impulse 50. [D1]

———. 1964a. *Crescent.* LP. Impulse 66. [D1]

———. 1964b. *A Love Supreme.* LP. Impulse 77. [D1]

———. 1965. *Ascension.* LP. Impulse 95. [D1]

Connell, John, and Richard Howitt, eds. 1992. *Mining and Indigenous Peoples in Australasia.* Sydney: University of Sydney Press. [D2]

Coon, Wayne O. 1971. *Some Problems with Musical Public-Domain Material under United States Copyright Law as Illustrated Mainly by the Recent Folk-Song Revival.* New York: Columbia University Press. [D3]

Coplan, David. 1985. *In Township Tonight! South Africa's Black City Music and Theatre.* New York: Longman. [D3]

———. 1987. Eloquent Knowledge: Lesotho Migrants' Songs and the Anthropology of Experience. *American Ethnologist* 14(3):413–33. [D3]

Cousins, D., and J. Niuewenhuysen. 1984. *Aboriginals and the Mining Industry.* Sydney: Allen and Unwin. [D2]

Cowell, Adrian. 1990. *The Decade of Destruction: The Crusade to Save the Amazon Rainforest.* New York: Holt. [D2]

Crafts, Susan, Daniel Cavicchi, and Charles Keil, eds. 1993. *My Music.* Middletown: Wesleyan University Press. [2, D1–D3]

Crawford, June, Susan Lippax, Jenny Onyx, Una Gault, and Pam Benton. 1992. *Emotion and Gender: Constructing Meaning from Memory.* Newbury Park: Sage. [D3]

Crawford, Peter, and David Turton, eds. 1992. *Film as Ethnography.* Manchester: Manchester University Press. [D1]

Critchley, MacDonald, and R. A. Henson, eds. 1977. *Music and the Brain.* London: William Heinemann Medical Books Ltd. [D2]

Culler, Jonathan. 1976. *Saussure*. London: Fontana. [D2]

Darnell, Regna. 1990. *Edward Sapir: Linguist, Anthropologist, and Humanist.* Berkeley: University of California Press. [D3]

Dauer, A. M. 1969. Research Films in Ethnomusicology. *Yearbook of the International Folk Music Council* 1:226–31. [D1]

Davies, John Booth. 1978. *The Psychology of Music*. London: Hutchison. [D2]

Davis, Miles (Miles Davis All Stars). 1954. *Walkin'*. Prestige 7076. [D1]

Davis, Miles (Miles Davis Quintet). 1956. *Round about Midnight*. Columbia 949. [1]

Davis, Miles. 1967. *Nefertiti*. Columbia CL 2794. [4]

DeMott, Benjamin. 1990. *The Imperial Middle: Why Americans Can't Think Straight about Class*. New York: William Morrow and Company. [D3]

Denisoff, R. Serge. 1975. *Solid Gold: The Popular Recording Industry*. Brunswick, N.J.: Transaction Books. [D3]

Deren, Maya. 1953. *Divine Horsemen: Living Gods of Haiti*. New York: Thames and Hudson. [D1]

Deutsch, Diana, ed. 1982. *Psychology of Music*. New York: Academic Press. [D2]

Devall, Bill, and George Sessions. 1985. *Deep Ecology: Living as if Nature Mattered*. Salt Lake City: Peregrine Smith Books. [D3]

Devall, Bill. 1988. *Simple Means, Rich in Ends: Practicing Deep Ecology*. Salt Lake City: Peregrine Smith Books. [D3]

DeVeaux, Alexis. *Don't Explain: A Song of Billie Holiday*. New York: Harper and Row. [D1]

Diamond, Stanley. 1974. *In Search of the Primitive*. New Brunswick: Transaction. [5, 7, D3]

Dickenson, G. S. 1965. *A Handbook of Style in Music*. Poughkeepsie: Vassar College. [4]

Dinnerstein, Dorothy. 1976. *The Mermaid and the Minotaur: Sexual Arrangements and Human Malaise*. New York: Harper Colophon. [D2, D3]

Dixon, R. A., and M. C. Dillon, eds. 1990. *Aborigines and Diamond Mining*. Perth: University of Western Australia Press. [D2]

Dolgan, Robert. 1977. *The Polka King: The Life of Frankie Yankovic*. Cleveland: Dillon/Liederbach. [D2]

Dolgin, Janet, David Kemnitzer, and David M. Schneider, eds. 1977. *Symbolic Anthropology*. New York: Columbia University Press. [D1]

Dorney, Sean. 1990. *Papua New Guinea: People, Politics, and History Since 1975*. Sydney: Random House Australia. [D2]

Dorson, Richard M. 1978. We All Need the Folk. Editor's comment. *Journal of the Folklore Institute* 15:267–69. [5, D3]

Douglas, Mary. 1971. *Natural Symbols: Explorations in Cosmology*. New York: Pantheon. [D1]

Douglas, Mary, ed. 1973. *Rules and Meanings: The Anthropology of Everyday Knowledge*. Hammondsworth: Penguin. [D1]

Dowling, W. Jay, and Dane Harwood. 1986. *Music Cognition*. New York: Academic Press. [D2]

Drewal, Henry, and Margaret Drewal. 1983. *Gelede: Art and Female Power Among the Yoruba*. Bloomington: Indiana University Press. [D1]

Duranti, Alessandro. 1986. The Audience as Co-author. *Text* 6(3):239–47. [4]

Durkheim, Emile. [1905] 1961. *The Elementary Forms of the Religious Life*. New York: Collier. [D1]

Dynatones. 1982. *Live Wire*. WAM Records LP4067. [5]

Eckert, Penelope. 1989. *Jocks and Burnouts: Social Categories and Identity in the High School*. New York: Teachers College Press. [D3]

Eco, Umberto. 1979. *A Theory of Semiotics*. Bloomington: Indiana University Press. [D2]

Ehrenreich, Barbara. 1989. *Fear of Falling: The Inner Life of the Middle Class*. New York: Pantheon. [D3]

Emmons, Charles Frank. 1971. Economic and Political Leadership in Chicago's Polonia: Sources of Ethnic Persistence and Mobility. Unpublished Ph.D. dissertation, University of Illinois at Chicago Circle. [D2]

Erickson, Robert. 1975. *Sound Structure in Music*. Berkeley: University of California Press. [4]

Erlmann, Veit. 1989. A Conversation with Joseph Shabalala of Ladysmith Black Mambazo: Aspects of African Performers' Lifestories. *World of Music* 31(1):31–58. [8]

———. 1990. Migration and Performance: Zulu Migrant Workers' *Isicathamiya* Performance in South Africa, 1890–1950. *Ethnomusicology* 34(2): 199–220. [8]

———. 1991. *African Stars: Studies in Black South African Performance*. Chicago: University of Chicago Press. [8]

Evans, Bill. 1950. Improvisation of Jazz. Liner notes to Miles Davis, *Kind of Blue*. Columbia LP-1355. [1]

Eyre, Banning. 1990. Bringing it all Back Home: Three Takes on Producing World Music. *Option,* November, 75–81. [10]

Fairley, Jan. 1990. Obituary for John Blacking. *Popular Music* 10(2):115–19. [D1]

———. 1991. Interview with John Blacking. *Ethnomusicology* 35(1):55–76. [D1]

Falk, Robert, and Timothy Rice, eds. 1982. *Cross-Cultural Perspectives on Music*. Toronto: University of Toronto Press.[D2]

Fanshawe, David. 1989. *Musical Mariner—Pacific Journey*. CD. Mercury 426 185-2. [D3]

Farrell, Barry. 1964. The Loneliest Monk. *Time,* February 28, 84–88. [1]

Featherstone, Mike, ed. 1990. *Global Culture: Nationalism, Globalization and Modernity*. Newbury Park: Sage. [10]

Feher, Ferenc. 1992. Weber and the Rationalization of Music. In *Dialectical Anthropology: Essays in Honor of Stanley Diamond,* ed. Christine Gailey, 309–26. Gainesville: University Press of Florida. [D2]

Feld, Steven. 1976. Ethnomusicology and Visual Communication. *Ethnomusicology* 20(2):293–325. [D1]

———. 1981a. "Flow like a Waterfall": the Metaphors of Kaluli Musical Theory. *Yearbook for Traditional Music* 13:22–47. [2]

———. 1981b. *Music of the Kaluli*. LP. Institute of Papua New Guinea Studies IPNGS 001. [4, 10, D1]

———. 1983a. Sound as a Symbolic System: The Kaluli Drum. *Bikmaus* 4(3):78–89. [2, 4]

———. 1983b. *Voices in the Forest*. Recording. National Public Radio. [10, D1]

———. 1984. Sound Structure as Social Structure. *Ethnomusicology* 28(3): 383–409. [2, 4, D1]

———. 1985. *The Kaluli of Papua Niugini: Weeping and Song*. LP. Bärenreiter Musicaphon/Music of Oceania BM 30 SL 2702. [4, 10, D1]

———. 1986. Orality and Consciousness. In *The Oral and Literate in Music*, ed. Y. Tokumaru and O. Yamaguti, 18–28. Tokyo: Academia Music. [D1]

———. 1987a. Dialogic Editing: Interpreting How Kaluli Read Sound and Sentiment. *Cultural Anthropology* 2(2):190–210. [2, 4, 10]

———. 1987b. *Voices in the Forest*. Cassette. Wafe Sambo! 001. [4, 10]

———. 1989. Themes in the Cinema of Jean Rouch. *Visual Anthropology* 2:223–47. [D1]

———. 1990a. *Sound and Sentiment: Birds, Weeping, Poetics and Song in Kaluli Expression*. 2d ed. Philadelphia: University of Pennsylvania Press. [2, 4, 10, D1, D2]

———. 1990b. Wept Thoughts: The Voicing of Kaluli Memories. *Oral Tradition* 5(2–3):241–66. [D3]

———. 1991. *Voices of the Rainforest*. CD. Rykodisc RCD 10173. [4, 10, D1]

Feld, Steven, and Carroll Williams. 1974. Toward a Researchable Film Language. *Studies in the Anthropology of Visual Communication* 2(1): 25–32. [D1]

Fernandez, James. 1986a. The Argument of Images and the Experience of Returning to the Whole. In *The Anthropology of Experience*, ed. Victor Turner and Edward Bruner, 159–87. Urbana: University of Illinois Press. [4]

———. 1986b. *Persuasions and Performances*. Bloomington: Indiana University Press. [D1]

Fernandez, James, ed. 1991. *Beyond Metaphor: The Theory of Tropes in Anthropology*. Stanford: Stanford University Press. [D1]

Filer, Colin. 1990. The Bougainville Rebellion, the Mining Industry, and the Process of Social Disintegration in Papua New Guinea. *Canberra Anthropologist* 13:1–40. [D2]

Fisher, Carrie. 1991. Interview with Madonna. *Rolling Stone*, nos. 606 and 607, 13 and 27 June. [D3]

Fiske, John. 1988. *Reading the Popular*. Boston: Unwin Hyman. [D3]

———. 1989a. *Television Culture*. London: Routledge. [D2]

———. 1989b. *Understanding Popular Culture*. Cambridge, Mass.: Unwin Hyman. [10]

———. 1990. *Introduction to Communication Studies*. 2d ed. New York: Routledge. [D2]

Foucault, Michel. 1981. The Order of Discourse. In *Untying the Text*, ed. R. Young, 48–78. London: Routledge Kegan Paul. [10]

Fox, James. 1977. Roman Jakobson and the Comparative Study of Parallelism. In *Roman Jakobson: Echoes of His Scholarship,* ed. D. Armstrong and C. H. van Schooneveld, 59–90. Lisse: Peter de Ridder. [D2]

Franklin, Aretha. 1967a. *Aretha Arrives.* LP. Atlantic SD 8150. [D1]

———. 1967b. *I Never Loved a Man the Way I Love You.* LP. Atlantic 8139. [4, D1]

———. 1968a. *Aretha Now.* LP. Atlantic SD 8186. [D1]

———. 1968b. *Lady Soul.* LP. Atlantic SD 8176. [D1]

———. 1971. *Live at the Fillmore.* LP. Atlantic SD 7205. [D1]

———. 1972. *Amazing Grace.* LP. Atlantic SD 906. [D1]

———. 1985a. *Thirty Greatest Hits.* LP. Atlantic 81668. [D1]

———. 1985b. *Who's Zoomin Who?* LP. Arista 8286. [D1]

———. 1986. *Aretha.* LP. Arista SD 8556. [D1]

———. 1987. *One Lord, One Faith, One Baptism.* LP. Arista 2CD 8497. [D1]

Freidrich, Paul. 1986. *The Language Parallax.* Austin: University of Texas Press. [4]

French, Marilyn. 1985. *Beyond Power.* New York: Summit Books. [D3]

Freud, Sigmund. 1930. *Civilization and Its Discontents.* London: Hogarth Press. [1]

Frisch, Michael, and Milton Rogovin. 1993. *Portraits in Steel.* Ithaca: Cornell University Press. [D3]

Frith, Simon. 1981. *Sound Effects.* New York: Pantheon. [8, 10]

———. 1986. Art vs. Technology: The Strange Case of Popular Music. *Media, Culture and Society* 8:263–79. [10]

———. 1987. Copyright and the Music Business. *Popular Music* 7(1):57–75. [10]

———. 1988. *Music for Pleasure.* London: Routledge. [10, D3]

Frith, Simon, ed. 1989. *World Music, Politics, and Social Change.* Manchester: Manchester University Press. [10]

Gabriel, Peter. 1986. *So.* CD. Geffen 24088. [8]

Gadamer, Hans-Georg. 1986. The Play of Art. In *The Relevance of the Beautiful and Other Essays,* ed. Robert Bernasconi, 123–30. New York: Cambridge University Press. [4]

Gailey, Christine, ed. 1992. *Dialectical Anthropology: Essays in Honor of Stanley Diamond.* 2 vols. Gainesville: University Press of Florida. [D3]

Garnier, Philippe. 1984. *Goodis: La vie en noir et blanc.* Paris: Seuil. [D1]

Garofalo, Reebee. 1992. *Rockin' the Boat: Mass Music and Mass Movements.* Boston: South End Press. [D3]

Garvin, Paul, ed. 1964. *A Prague School Reader on Esthetics.* Washington, D.C.: Georgetown University Press. [D2]

Geertz, Clifford. 1973. *The Interpretation of Cultures.* New York: Basic Books. [D1]

———. 1983. *Local Knowledge: Further Essays in Interpretive Anthropology.* esp. Art as a Cultural System, 94–120. New York: Basic Books. [2, 4, D1]

Gennep, Arnold van. [1909] 1960. *The Rites of Passage.* London: Routledge and Kegan Paul. [D1]

George, Nelson. 1985. *Where Did Our Love Go? The Rise and Fall of Motown Sound.* New York: St. Martin's Press. [D3]

——. 1988. *The Death of Rhythm and Blues.* New York: Pantheon. [D3]

Gerbrands, Adrian. 1969. The Concept of Style in Non-Western Art. In *Tradition and Creativity in Tribal Art,* ed. Daniel Biebuyck, 58–70. Berkeley: University of California Press. [4]

Giddens, Anthony. 1979. *Central Problems in Social Theory.* Berkeley: University of California Press. [D1]

——. 1984. *The Constitution of Society.* Berkeley: University of California Press. [D1]

Giddins, Gary. 1988. *Satchmo.* New York: Doubleday. [D1]

——. 1989. *Satchmo: Louis Armstrong.* Masters of American Music series. CBS Music Video. [D3]

Gillett, Charlie. 1974. *Making Tracks: Atlantic Records and the Growth of a Multi-Billion Dollar Industry.* New York: Dutton. [D3]

Gilligan, Carol. 1982. *In a Different Voice: Psychological Theory and Women's Development.* Cambridge, Mass.: Harvard University Press. [D3]

Gilligan, Carol, Nona Lyons, and Trudy Hammer, eds. 1990. *Making Connections: The Relational Worlds of Adolescent Girls at Emma Willard School.* Cambridge, Mass.: Harvard University Press. [D3]

Gillis, Frank. 1980. Alan P. Merriam, 1923–1980. *Ethnomusicology* 24(3): v–vii. [D1]

Godoy, R. 1985. Mining: Anthropological Perspectives. *Annual Review of Anthropology* 14:199–217. [D2]

Goffman, Erving. 1959. *The Presentation of the Self in Everyday Life.* Garden City: Doubleday. [D2]

——. 1963. *Stigma: Notes on the Management of Spoiled Identity.* Englewood Cliffs: Prentice Hall. [D2]

——. 1967. *Interaction Ritual: Essays on Face-to-Face Behavior.* New York: Doubleday. [D2]

——. 1970. *Strategic Interaction.* Oxford: Blackwell. [D2]

——. 1971. *Relations in Public.* New York: Harper and Row. [D2]

——. 1974. *Frame Analysis: An Essay on the Organization of Experience.* Cambridge, Mass.: Harvard University Press. [2, D2]

——. 1979. *Gender Advertisements.* New York: Macmillan. [D2]

——. 1981. *Forms of Talk.* Philadelphia: University of Pennsylvania Press. [D2]

——. 1983. The Interaction Order. *American Sociological Review* 48:1–17 [2]

Gonzalez, Jerry. 1989. *Rumba Para Monk.* CD. Sunnyside 1036D. [D1]

Gonzalez-Crussi, F. 1989. *The Five Senses.* New York: Vintage. [D2]

Goodis, David. 1946. *Dark Passage.* New York: Messner. [D1]

——. 1956. *Down There.* New York: Gold Medal. Reissued as *Shoot the Piano Player* (New York: Grove, 1962; New York: Vintage, 1990). [D1]

——. [1947] 1987. *Night Fall.* New York: Creative Arts. [D1]

——. [1951] 1988. *Cassidy's Girl.* New York: Creative Arts. [D1]

——. [1955] 1988. *Street of No Return.* New York: Creative Arts. [D1]

——. [1953] 1989. *Burglar.* New York: Creative Arts. [D1]

——. [1960] 1989. *Night Squad.* New York: Creative Arts. [D1]

———. [1954] 1990. *Black Friday*. New York: Vintage. [D1]

Goodman, Nelson. 1975. The Status of Style. *Critical Inquiry* 1:799–811. [4]

———. [1968] 1976. *Languages of Art*. 2d ed. Indianapolis: Hackett Publishing. [4]

Goodwin, Andrew, and Joe Gore. World Beat and the Cultural Imperialism Debate. *Socialist Review* 20(3):63–80. [10]

Gourlay, Ken. 1978. The Role of the Ethnomusicologist in Research. *Ethnomusicology* 22(1):1–36. [D1]

Grainger, Percy. 1915. The Impress of Personality in Unwritten Music. *Musical Quarterly* 1:416–35. [4]

Green, Victor. 1992. *A Passion for Polka*. Berkeley: University of California Press. [D2]

Grimshaw, Allen, ed. 1982. *Sociological Methods and Research* (special issue on sound-image records in social-interaction research) 11(2). [D1]

Gronow, Pekka. 1983. The Record Industry: The Growth of a Mass Medium. *Popular Music* 3:53–75. [D3]

———. 1989. Sound Recording. In *International Encyclopedia of Communications,* ed. Erik Barnouw, 4:112–21. New York: Oxford University Press. [D3]

Guiraud, Pierre. 1975. *Semiology*. London: Routledge, Kegan Paul. [D2]

Guralnick, Peter. 1986. *Sweet Soul Music: Rhythm and Blues and the Southern Dream of Freedom*. New York: Harper Colophon. [6, D3]

Gurevitch, Michael, et. al., eds. 1982. *Culture, Society and the Media*. London: Methuen. [D2]

Hall, Edward T. 1959. *The Silent Language*. New York: Doubleday. [1, D2]

———. 1963. A System for the Notation of Proxemic Behavior. *American Anthropologist* 65(5):1024–26. [1]

———. 1966. *The Hidden Dimension*. New York: Doubleday. [D2]

———. 1976. *Beyond Culture*. New York: Doubleday. [D2]

———. 1983. *The Dance of Life*. New York: Doubleday. [D2]

———. 1992. *An Anthropology of Everyday Life*. New York: Doubleday. [D2]

Hall, Stuart, et al., eds. 1980. *Culture, Media, Language: Working Papers in Cultural Studies, 1972–1979*. London: Hutchinson. [D1]

Hamm, Charles. 1988. *Afro-American Music, South Africa, and Apartheid*. Brooklyn: Institute for Studies of American Music [8]

———. 1989. Graceland Revisited. *Popular Music* 8(3):299–304. [8]

Hannerz, Ulf. 1987. The World in Creolisation. *Africa* 57(4):546–59. [10]

———. 1989. Notes on the Global Ecumene. *Public Culture* 1(2): 66–75. [10]

Harrah-Conforth, Bruce. 1984. Laughin' Just to Keep From Cryin': Afro-American Folksong and the Field Recordings of Lawrence Gellert. M.A. thesis, Indiana University. [5]

Harris, Daniel. 1992. Make My Rainy Day. *The Nation,* 8 June, 790–93. [D3]

Harrison, Jane Ellen. [1912] 1962. *Themis: A Study of the Social Origins of Greek Religion*. Cleveland: Meridian Books. [D3]

———. [1903] 1991. *Prolegomena to the Study of Greek Religion*. Princeton: Princeton University Press. [D3]

Hart, Mickey, and Fredric Lieberman. 1991. *Planet Drum*. San Francisco: Harper Collins. [10]

Hart, Mickey, and Jay Stevens. 1990. *Drumming at the Edge of Magic.* San Francisco: Harper Collins. [10]

Harvey, David. 1989. *The Condition of Postmodernity.* Oxford: Basil Blackwell. [10]

Harwood, Dane. 1976. Universals in Music: A Perspective from Cognitive Psychology. *Ethnomusicology* 20(3):521–33. [D2]

Hatten, Robert S. 1982. Toward a Semiotic Model of Style in Music. Unpublished Ph.D. dissertation. School of Music, Indiana University. [4]

Hawkes, T. 1977. *Structuralism and Semiotics.* London: Methuen. [D2]

Hebb, D. O. 1949. *The Organization of Behavior.* New York: Wiley. [1]

Hebdige, Dick. 1979. *Subculture: The Meaning of Style.* London and New York: Methuen. [4]

Hecht, Susanna, and Alexander Cockburn. 1989. *The Fate of the Forest: Developers, Defenders and Destroyers of the Amazon.* London: Verso. [D2]

Heidegger, Martin. 1971. *Poetry, Language, Thought.* New York: Harper and Row. [D1]

———. 1974. *Identity and Difference.* New York: Harper and Row. [D1]

Held, Richard, and Danford Freedman. 1963. Plasticity in Human Sensorimotor Control. *Science* 142(3591):455–62. [1]

Henderson, Lisa. 1993. Justify Our Love: Madonna and the Politics of Queer Sex. In *The Madonna Connection,* ed. Cathy Schwichtenberg, 107–28. Boulder: Westview Press. [D3]

Hentoff, Nat. 1972. The Real Lady Day. *New York Times Magazine,* 24 December. [D1]

Herndon, Marcia. 1974. Analysis: The Herding of Sacred Cows? *Ethnomusicology* 18(2):219–62. [D2]

———. 1976. Reply to Kolinski: *Taurus Omicida. Ethnomusicology* 20(2):217–31. [D2]

Hershey, Gerri. 1985. *Nowhere to Run.* New York: Penguin. [6]

Herzog, George. 1928. The Yuman Musical Style. *Journal of American Folklore* 41(160):183–231. [D2]

———. 1934. Speech Melody and Primitive Music. *Musical Quarterly* 20:452–66. [D2]

———. 1936. A Comparison of Pueblo and Pima Musical Styles. *Journal of American Folklore* 49(194):284–417. [D2]

———. 1945. Drum Signalling in a West African Tribe. *Word* 1:217–38. Reprinted in *Language in Culture and Society,* ed. Dell Hymes, 312–29 (New York: Harper and Row, 1964). [D2]

———. 1950. Song. In *Standard Dictionary of Folklore, Mythology and Legend,* ed. Maria Leach, 2:1032–50, New York: Funk and Wagnalls. [D2]

Heusch, Luc de. [1960] 1988. *Cinema and Social Science.* Paris: UNESCO. Reprinted in *Visual Anthropology* 1(2):99–156. [D1]

Hirsch, Paul. 1970. *The Structure of the Popular Music Industry.* Ann Arbor: Institute for Social Research, University of Michigan. [D3]

Hirshey, Gerri. 1984. *Nowhere to Run: The Story of Soul Music.* New York: Times Books. [D3]

Hockings, Paul, ed. 1975. *Principles of Visual Anthropology.* The Hague: Mouton. [D1]

Hockings, Paul, and Yasuhiro Omori, eds. 1988. *Cinematographic Theory and New Dimensions in Ethnographic Film.* Senri Ethnological Studies, no. 24. Osaka: National Museum of Ethnology. [D1]

Hodeir, André. 1956. *Jazz: Its Evolution and Essence.* New York: Grove. [1]

Hodge, Robert, and Gunther Kress. 1988. *Social Semiotics.* Cambridge: Polity Press. [D2]

Holiday, Billie, and William Dufty. [1956] 1984. *Lady Sings the Blues.* Hammondsworth: Penguin. [D1]

Holquist, Michael. 1990. *Dialogism: Bakhtin and His World.* London: Routledge. [D1]

Holquist, Michael, and Katerina Clark. 1984. *Mikhail Bakhtin.* Cambridge, Mass.: Harvard University Press. [D1]

Hood, Mantle. 1957. Training and Research Methods in Ethnomusicology. *Ethnomusicology Newsletter* 11:2–8. [D2]

———. 1960. The Challenge of "Bi-Musicality." *Ethnomusicology* 4(1):55–59. [D2]

———. 1963a. Musical Significance. *Ethnomusicology* 7(3):187–92. [D2]

———. 1963b. Music the Unknown. In *Musicology,* ed. F. Harrison, C. Palisca, and M. Hood, 215–326. Englewood Cliffs: Prentice-Hall. [D2]

———. 1969. Ethnomusicology. In *Harvard Dictionary of Music,* ed. Willi Apel, 298–300. 2d. ed. Cambridge, Mass.: Harvard University Press. [D2]

———. 1977. Universal Attributes of Music. *World of Music* 19(1/2): 63–69. [D2]

———. [1971] 1981. *The Ethnomusicologist.* New York: Macmillan; Kent, Ohio: Kent State University Press. [D2]

Horkheimer, Max. 1972. The Culture Industry: Enlightenment as Mass Deception. In *Dialectic of Enlightenment,* 120–67. New York: Seabury Press. [D1]

Hornbostel, Erich M. von. 1927. The Unity of the Senses. *Psyche* 7 (April): 83–89. [4]

———. 1928. African Negro Music. *Africa* 1:30–62. [1]

Howard, M. 1988. *The Impact of the International Mining Industry on Native Peoples.* Sydney: University of Sydney, Transnational Corporations Research Project. [D2]

Howell, P., I. Cross, and R. West, eds. 1985. *Musical Structure and Cognition.* New York: Academic Press. [D2]

Howes, David, ed. 1991. *The Varieties of Sensory Experience: A Reader in the Anthropology of the Senses.* Toronto: University of Toronto Press. [D1]

Hyde, Lewis. 1979. *The Gift: Imagination and the Erotic Life of Property.* New York: Random House. [D3]

Hymes, Dell. 1974. *Foundations in Sociolinguistics: An Ethnographic Approach.* Philadelphia: University of Pennsylvania Press. [D2]

Hymes, Dell, ed. 1972. *Reinventing Anthropology.* New York: Random House/ Viking. [D1]

Hyndeman, David. 1987. Mining, Modernization, and Movements of Social Protest in Papua New Guinea. *Social Analysis* 21(3):33–41. [D2]

———. 1988. Melanesian Resistance to Ecocide and Ethnocide: Transnational Mining Projects and the Fourth World on the Island of New Guinea. In *Tribal Peoples and Development Issues: A Global Overview,* ed. John H. Bodley, 281–98. Mountain View, Calif.: Mayfield. [D2]

Ibrahim, Abdullah. 1989. *African River.* CD. Enja RZ 79617. [D2]

Ichioka, Yasuko. 1986. *Gisaro: The Sorrow and the Burning.* Japanese public television film. Tokyo: NAV. [D2]

Jackson, Richard. 1982. *Ok Tedi: The Pot of Gold.* Port Moresby: World Publishing. [D2]

Jacoby, Russell. 1975. *Social Amnesia: A Critique of Conformist Psychology from Adler to Laing.* Beacon Press. [D3]

Jahn, Janheinz. 1961. *Muntu: An Outline of the New African Culture.* New York: Grove Press. [D1]

Jakobson, Roman. 1960. Linguistics and Poetics. In *Style in Language,* ed. T. A. Sebeok, 350–77. Cambridge, Mass.: MIT Press. [2, 4]

———. 1962–87. *Selected Writings.* Vol. 5, *On Verse, Its Masters and Explorers* (1979). Vol. 3, *Poetry of Grammar and Grammar of Poetry* (1981). The Hague: Mouton. [D2]

Jameson, Fredric. 1990. Postmodernism and Consumer Society. In *Postmodernism and its Discontents: Theories, Practices,* ed. A. Kaplan, 13–29. New York: Verso. [10]

Jolly, Margaret, and Nicholas Thomas, eds. 1992. The Politics of Tradition in the Pacific. *Oceania* 62(4). [4]

Jones, A. M. 1959. *Studies in African Music.* London: Oxford University Press. [1]

Jones, Leroi [Amiri Baraka]. 1963. *Blues People.* New York. William Morrow. [D1]

———. 1970. *Black Music.* New York: William Morrow. [D1]

Jones, Max, and John Chilton. 1971. *Louis: The Louis Armstrong Story.* New York: Little Brown. [D1]

Jones, Steve. 1992. *Rock Formation: Music, Technology and Mass Communication.* Newbury Park: Sage. [D3]

Jung, Carl G. 1964. *Man and His Symbols.* Garden City: Doubleday. [D2]

———. 1966. *The Spirit in Man, Art and Literature.* New York: Bollingen Foundation. [D2]

———. 1983. *The Essential Jung.* Ed. Anthony Storr. Princeton: Princeton University Press. [D2]

Kaemmer, John. 1989. Social Power and Music Change among Shona. *Ethnomusicology* 33(1):31–45. [D1]

Kaeppler, Adrienne L. 1978. Melody, Drone and Decoration: Underlying Structures and Surface Manifestation in Tongan Art and Society. In *Art in Society,* ed. Michael Greenhalgh and Vincent Megaw, 261–74. London: Duckworth. [4]

Keesing, Roger. 1974. Theories of Culture. *Annual Review of Anthropology* 3:74–98. [D1]

Keesing, Roger, and Robert Tonkinson, eds. 1982. Reinventing Traditional Culture: The Politics of Kastom in Island Melanesia. *Mankind* 13(4). [4]

Keil, Charles. 1969. Review of *Tiv Women: The Icough Dance* (film by Francis Speed, Peggy Harper, and Akwe Doma.) *American Anthropologist* 70:1234. [D3]

———. 1978. Who Needs "the Folk"? Comment. *Journal of the Folklore Institute* 15:263–66. [5, D3]

———. 1979a. The Concept of "the Folk." Comment. *Journal of the Folklore Institute* 16:209–10. [5, D3]

———. 1979b. *Tiv Song: The Sociology of Art in a Classless Society.* Chicago: University of Chicago Press. [3–5, D1]

———. 1982a. Applied Ethnomusicology and a Rebirth of Music from the Spirit of Tragedy. *Ethnomusicology* 26(3):407–11. [D1, D3]

———. 1982b. Slovenian Style in Milwaukee. In *Folk Music and Modern Sound,* ed. W. Ferris and M. Hart, 32–59. Jackson: University Press of Mississippi. [5]

———. 1985. Paideia con Salsa: Ancient Greek Education for Active Citizenship and the Role of Latin Dance-Music in Our Schools. In *Becoming Human through Music,* ed. David McAllester. Reston, Va.: Music Educators National Conference. [D1]

———. [1966] 1991. *Urban Blues.* Chicago: University of Chicago Press. [3–5, 8, D1]

———. 1992. Culture, Music and Collaborative Learning. In *Dialectical Anthropology: Essays in Honor of Stanley Diamond,* vol. 2, *The Politics of Culture and Creativity: A Critique of Civilization,* ed. Christine Ward Gailey, 327–33. Gainesville: University Press of Florida. [D1, D3]

Keil, Charles, and Angeliki Keil. 1977. In Pursuit of Polka Happiness. *Cultural Correspondence* 5:5–11, 74. Reprinted in *Popular Culture in America,* ed. Paul Buhle, 75–87. Minneapolis: University of Minnesota Press, 1987. [5]

Keil, Charles, Angeliki Keil, and Dick Blau. 1992. *Polka Happiness.* Philadelphia: Temple University Press. [3, D1, D2]

———. Forthcoming. *Polka Perspectives.* Chicago: University of Chicago Press. [D1]

Kennedy, Elizabeth Lapovsky, and Madeline D. Davis. 1993. *Boots of Leather, Slippers of Gold: The History of a Lesbian Community.* New York: Routledge. [D3]

Kessler, Edward, Christa Hansen, and Roger Shepard. 1984. Tonal Schemata in the Perception of Music in Bali and the West. *Music Perception* 2(2):131–65. [D2]

Kevorkian, Kyle. 1990. Evolution's Top Forty. *Mother Jones,* April–May. [10]

Khan, Zeman. 1991. "Classical Music Is Not against Islam": An Interview with Nusrat Fateh Ali Khan. *The Herald* (Karachi, Pakistan), March, 117–20. [10]

King, B. B. 1965. B. B. *King Live at the Regal.* LP. ABC-Paramount 509. [5]

Kingsbury, Henry. 1988. *Music, Talent, and Performance: A Conservatory Cultural System.* Philadelphia: Temple University Press. [D2]

Kippen, James. 1987. An Ethnomusicological Approach to the Analysis of Musical Cognition. *Music Perception* 5(2):173–96. [D2]

———. 1990. Obituary for John Blacking. *Ethnomusicology* 34(2):263–70. [D1]

Kirkpatrick, John, and Geoffrey White, eds. 1985. *Person, Self and Experience.* Berkeley: University of California Press. [D3]

Kivnick, Helen Q. 1990. *Where is the Way: Song and Struggle in South Africa.* New York: Penguin. [8]

Kleeman, Janice Ellen. 1982. The Origins and Stylistic Development of Polish-American Polka Music. Unpublished Ph.D. dissertation, Department of Music, University of California at Berkeley. [5, D2]

Knight, Roderic. 1991. Vibrato Octaves: Tunings and Modes of the Mande Balo and Kora. *Progress Reports in Ethnomusicology* 3(4):1–49. [D2]

Kochman, Thomas, ed. 1972. *Rappin' and Stylin' Out: Communication in Urban Black America.* Urbana: University of Illinois Press. [D2]

Kohr, Leopold. 1978. *The Breakdown of Nations.* New York: E. P. Dutton. [D3]

Kolinski, Mieczyslaw. 1959. The Evaluation of Tempo. *Ethnomusicology* 3:45–57. [D2]

———. 1962. Consonance and Dissonance. *Ethnomusicology* 6:66–74. [D2]

———. 1965. The Structure of Melodic Movement: A New Method of Analysis. In *Studies in Ethnomusicology,* ed. M. Kolinski, 95–120. New York: Oak Publications. [D2]

———. 1967. Recent Trends in Ethnomusicology. *Ethnomusicology* 11:1–24. [D2]

———. 1968–69. Barbara Allen: Tonal vs. Melodic Structure. *Ethnomusicology* 12(2):208–18, 13(1):1–73. [D2]

———. 1970. Review of *Ethnomusicology of The Flathead Indians* by Alan P. Merriam. *Ethnomusicology* 14(1):77–99. [D2]

———. 1973. A Cross-Cultural Approach to Metro-Rhythmic Patterns. *Ethnomusicology* 17(3):494–506. [D2]

———. 1976. Herndon's Verdict on Analysis: *Tabula Rasa. Ethnomusicology* 20(1):1–22. [D2]

———. 1977. Final Reply to Herndon. *Ethnomusicology* 21(1):75–83. [D2]

Kroeber, A. L. 1963. *Style and Civilizations.* Berkeley: University of California Press. [4]

Krumhansl, Carol. 1990. *The Cognitive Foundations of Music Pitch.* New York: Oxford University Press. [D2]

Lacy, Steve. 1958. *Reflections.* LP. Prestige NJ 8206. [D1]

———. 1983. *Regeneration.* LP. Soul Note SN 1054. [D1]

———. 1985. *Only Monk.* LP. Soul Note SN 1160. [D1]

Lacy, Steve, Roswell Rudd, Henry Grimes, and Dennis Charles. 1975. *School Days.* LP. Emanem 3316. [D1]

Laing, Dave. 1986. The Music Industry and the "Cultural Imperialism" Thesis. *Media, Culture and Society* 8:331–41. [10]

———. 1990. Call and Response. *Popular Music* 9(1):137–38. [8]

Laing, R. D. 1967. The Politics of Experience. New York: Pantheon. [D2]

LaRue, Jan. 1970. *Guidelines for Style Analysis.* New York: W. W. Norton. [4]

Leach, Edmund. 1974. *Lévi-Strauss.* London: Fontana. [D2]
——. 1976. *Culture and Communication: The Logic by which Symbols are Connected.* Cambridge: Cambridge University Press. [D1]
Leach, Jerry W., and Edmund Leach, eds. 1983. *The Kula: New Perspectives on Massim Exchange.* Cambridge: Cambridge University Press. [D3]
Leadbelly. 1976. New York: TRO. [D3]
Leary, James. 1991. *Polka Music, Ethnic Music: A Report on Wisconsin's Polka Traditions.* Wisconsin Folk Museum, bulletin 1. [D2]
Leary, James P., and Richard March. 1991. Dutchman Bands: Genre, Ethnicity, and Pluralism in the Upper Midwest. In *Creative Ethnicity,* ed. Stephen Stern and John Allan Cicala, 21–43. Logan: Utah State University Press. [D2]
Leenhardt, Maurice. [1947] 1979. *Do Kamo: Person and Myth in the Melanesian World.* Chicago: University of Chicago Press. [D1]
Leppert, Richard. 1988. *Music and Image: Domesticity, Ideology and Socio-Cultural Formation in Eighteenth-century England.* Cambridge: Cambridge University Press. [D2]
——. 1989. Music, Representation, and Social Order in Early-Modern Europe. *Cultural Critique* 12:25–55. [D2]
Leppert, Richard, and Susan McClary, eds. 1987. *Music and Society: The Politics of Composition and Performance.* New York: Cambridge University Press. [D2]
Lerdahl, Fred, and Ray Jackendoff. 1983. *A Generative Grammar of Tonal Music.* Cambridge, Mass.: MIT Press. [D2]
Lester, Julius, and Pete Seeger. 1965. *The Twelve-String Guitar as Played By Leadbelly.* New York: Oak. [D3]
Levine, Lawrence. 1988. *Highbrow-Lowbrow: The Emergence of Cultural Hierarchy in America.* Cambridge, Mass.: Harvard University Press. [D2]
Lévi-Strauss, Claude. 1962. *The Savage Mind.* Chicago: University of Chicago Press. [D1]
——. 1963. The Effectiveness of Symbols. In *Structural Anthropology,* New York: Basic Books. [D1]
Levy, Robert. 1984. Emotion, Knowing, and Culture. In *Culture Theory: Essays on Mind, Self, and Emotion,* ed. Richard Shweder and Robert LeVine, 214–37. New York: Cambridge University Press. [D3]
Lévy-Bruhl, Lucien. 1923. *Primitive Mentality.* New York: MacMillan. [D1]
——. 1928. *The "Soul" of the Primitive.* New York: MacMillan. [D1]
——. [1910] 1966. *How Natives Think.* New York: Washington Square Press. [3, 5, D1]
Libby, T. 1989. *Hawke's Law: The Politics of Mining and Aboriginal Land Rights in Australia.* Perth: University of Western Australia Press. [D2]
Lidov, David. 1977. Nattiez's Semiotics of Music. *Canadian Journal of Research in Semiotics* 5(2):13–54. [2, D2]
——. 1980. Musical and Verbal Semantics. *Semiotica* 31(3/4):369–91. [2]
Limon, José. 1991. Representation, Ethnicity, and the Precursory Ethnography: Notes of A Native Anthropologist. In *Recapturing Anthropology,* ed.

Richard G. Fox, 115–35. Santa Fe: School of American Research Press. [D3]

Lipsitz, George. 1990. *Time Passages: Collective Memory and American Popular Culture.* Minneapolis: University of Minnesota Press. [D1–D3]

Lomax, Alan. 1971. Choreometrics and Ethnographic Filmmaking. *Filmmaker's Newsletter* 4(4):22–30. [D1]

———. 1976. *Cantometrics: An Approach to the Anthropology of Music.* Berkeley: University of California Extension Media Center. Book and cassettes. [4]

———. 1977. Appeal for Cultural Equity. *Journal of Communication* 27(2): 125–39. [10, D3]

Lomax, John, and Alan Lomax. 1936. *Negro Folksongs as Sung by Leadbelly.* New York: MacMillan. [D3]

Lull, James, ed. 1992. *Popular Music and Communication,* 2d. ed. Newbury Park: Sage. [D3]

Lutz, Catherine. 1986. Emotion, Thought and Estrangement: Emotion as a Cultural Category. *Cultural Anthropology* 1(3):287–09. [D3]

———. 1990. *Unnatural Emotions.* Chicago: University of Chicago Press. [D3]

Lutz, Catherine, and Geoffrey White. 1986. The Anthropology of Emotions. *Annual Review of Anthropology* 15:405–36. [D3]

Lydon, Michael, and Ellen Mandel. 1974. *Boogie Lightning.* New York: Dial Press. [3]

Manuel, Peter. 1993. *Cassette Culture.* Chicago: University of Chicago Press. [D3]

Maranhão, Tulio, ed. 1990. *The Interpretation of Dialogue.* Chicago: University of Chicago Press. [D1]

Marcus, George, and Michael Fischer. 1986. *Anthropology as Cultural Critique.* Chicago: University of Chicago Press. [10, D1]

Matejka, Ladislav, and Irwin Titunik. 1976. *Semiotics of Art.* Cambridge, Mass.: MIT Press. [D2]

Mauss, Marcel. [1925] 1976. *The Gift.* New York: Norton. [D1, D3]

May, R. J., and Matthew Spriggs, eds. 1990. *The Bougainville Crisis.* Bathurst: Crawford House Press. [D2]

McAllester, David P. 1949. *Peyote Music.* Viking Fund Publications in Anthropology, no. 13. [D2]

———. 1954. *Enemy Way Music: A Study of Social and Esthetic Values as Seen in Navaho Music.* Cambridge, Mass.: Peabody Museum; Papers of the Peabody Museum of American Archeology and Ethnology, Harvard University, vol. 41, no. 3, Reports of the Rimrock Project Values Series, 3. [D2]

———. 1985. George Herzog: In Memoriam. *Ethnomusicology* 29(1): 86–87. [D2]

McClary, Susan. 1991. *Feminine Endings: Music, Gender, and Sexuality.* Minneapolis: University of Minnesota Press. [10, D2, D3]

McClary, Susan, and Robert Walser. 1990. Start Making Sense: Musicology Wrestles with Rock. In *On Record,* ed. Simon Frith and Andrew Goodwin, 277–92. New York: Pantheon. [D2]

McGuire, William, and R. F. C. Hull, eds. 1986. *C. G. Jung Speaking: Interviews and Encounters.* Princeton: Princeton University Press. [D2]

McLuhan, Marshall, ed. 1967. *Verbi-Voco-Visual Explorations.* New York: Something Else Press. [D1]

Meintjes, Louise. 1990. Paul Simon's *Graceland,* South Africa, and the Mediation of Musical Meaning. *Ethnomusicology* 34(1):37–73. [8]

Merleau-Ponty, Maurice. 1962. *The Phenomenology of Perception.* London: Routledge and Kegan Paul. [D1]

———. 1964a. *The Primacy of Perception and Other Essays.* Evanston: Northwestern University Press. [D1]

———. 1964b. *Sense and Non-Sense.* Evanston: Northwestern University Press. [D1]

———. 1974. *Phenomenology, Language and Sociology: Selected Essays.* London: Heineman. [D1]

Merriam, Alan P. 1960a. *Congo: Background to Conflict.* Evanston: Northwestern University Press. [D1]

———. 1960b. Ethnomusicology: Discussion and Definition of the Field. *Ethnomusicology* 4:107–14. [D1]

———. 1963. The Purposes of Ethnomusicology: An Anthropological View. *Ethnomusicology* 7:206–13. [D1]

———. 1964. *The Anthropology of Music.* Evanston: Northwestern University Press. [4, D1]

———. 1967. *Ethnomusicology of the Flathead Indians.* Chicago: Aldine. [D1, D2]

———. 1968. Ethnomusicology. In *International Encyclopedia of the Social Sciences,* ed. David Sills, 10:562–66. New York: Macmillan. [D1]

———. 1969. Ethnomusicology Revisited. *Ethnomusicology* 13(2):213–29. [D1]

———. 1970. *African Music on LP.* Evanston: Northwestern University Press. [D1]

———. 1974. *An African World.* Bloomington: Indiana University Press. [D1]

———. 1975. Ethnomusicology Today. *Current Musicology,* no. 20, 50–66. [D1]

———. 1977. Definitions of "Comparative Musicology" and "Ethnomusicology": An Historical-Theoretical Perspective. *Ethnomusicology* 21(2):189–204. [D1]

———. 1982. On Objections to Comparison in Ethnomusicology. In *Cross-ultural Perspectives on Music,* ed. Robert Falk and Timothy Rice, 174–89. Toronto: University of Toronto Press. [D2]

Mertz, Elizabeth, and Richard Parmentier, eds. 1985. *Semiotic Mediation: Sociocultural and Psychological Perspectives.* New York: Academic Press. [D2]

Meyer, Leonard. 1956. *Emotion and Meaning in Music.* Chicago: University of Chicago Press. [1–4, 9, D1]

———. 1967. *Music, the Arts, and Ideas.* Chicago: University of Chicago Press. [1, 4, D1]

———. 1973. *Explaining Music.* Chicago: University of Chicago Press. [2, D1]

———. 1987. Toward a Theory of Style. In *The Concept of Style,* ed. Berel Lang, 21–71. 2d ed., rev. Ithaca: Cornell University Press. [4]

———. 1989. *Style and Music*. Philadelphia: University of Pennsylvania Press. [2, 4, D1]

Meyer, Leonard B., and Bertram Rosner. 1982. Melodic Processes and the Perception of Music. In *The Psychology of Music*, ed. Diana Deutsch, 316–41. New York: Academic Press. [D2]

Mihalic, F., S.V.D. 1971. *The Jacaranda Dictionary and Grammar of Melanesian Pidgin*. Queensland: Jacaranda Press. [4]

Mills, C. Wright. 1959. *The Sociological Imagination*. New York: Oxford University Press. [D1]

Mingus, Charles. 1960. *Mingus Presents Mingus*. LP. Candid 8005. [1]

———. 1964. *Mingus Mingus Mingus Mingus Mingus*. LP. Impulse 54. [D2]

Molino, Jean. 1975. Fait musicale et sémiologie de la musique. *Musique en jeu* 17:37–62. [2]

Monbiot, George. 1989. *Poisoned Arrows*. London: Sphere. [D2]

Monk, Thelonious. 1957a. *Brilliant Corners*. LP. Riverside RLP 12-226. [D1]

———. 1957b. *Monk and Coltrane*. LP. Riverside Jazzland 946. [D1]

———. 1959. *Alone in San Francisco*. LP. Riverside RLP 12-312. [D1]

———. 1960. *Live at Town Hall*. LP. Riverside 300. [D1]

———. 1962. *Monk's Dream*. LP. Columbia CS 8765. [1, D1]

———. 1963. *Criss-Cross*. LP. Columbia CS 8838. [D1]

———. 1964a. *Misterioso*. LP. Columbia CS 9216. [D1]

———. 1964b. *Monk's Music*. LP. Riverside RLP 242. [D1]

———. 1964c. *Monk's Time*. LP. Columbia CS 8984. [D1]

———. 1965. *Solo Monk*. LP. Columbia CS 9149. [D1]

———. 1971. *The Complete Black Lion and Vogue Recordings*. 2 LP set. Mosaic MR4-112. [D1]

———. [1958] 1977. *Live at the Five Spot*. LP. Milestone M47043. [D1]

———. 1983. *The Complete Blue Note Recordings*. 4 LP set. Mosaic MR4-101. [D1]

———. [1957] 1987. *Thelonious Himself*. CD. Riverside 254-2. [D2]

Moreno, J. L. 1946. *Psychodrama*. Beacon, N.Y.: Beacon House. [1]

Morson, Gary Saul, and Caryl Emerson, eds. 1989. *Rethinking Bakhtin: Extensions and Challenges*. Evanston: Northwestern University Press. [D1]

Murdock, Graham. 1982. Large Corporations and the Control of the Communications Industries. In *Culture, Society and the Media*, ed. M. Gurevich et al., 118–50. London: Methuen, 1982. [D3]

Myers, Fred. 1991. Representing Culture: The Production of Discourse(s) for Aboriginal Acrylic Paintings. *Cultural Anthropology* 6(1):26–62. [10]

Nader, Laura. 1969. "Up the Anthropologist"—Perspectives Gained from Studying Up. In *Reinventing Anthropology*, ed. Dell Hymes, 284–311. New York: Random House. [D3]

Naess, Arne. 1989. *Ecology, Community and Lifestyle: Outline of an Ecosophy*. Trans. David Rothenberg. Cambridge: Cambridge University Press. [D2]

Nash, June. 1979. *We Eat the Mines and the Mines Eat Us*. New York: Columbia University Press. [D2]

Nattiez, Jean-Jacques. 1975. *Fondements d'une sémiologie de la musique*. Paris: Union Générale des Éditions. [2]

———. 1977. The Contribution of Musical Semiotics to the Semiotic Discussion in General. In *A Perfusion of Signs*, ed. T. A. Sebeok, 121–42. Bloomington: Indiana University Press. [D2]

———. 1990. *Music and Discourse: Toward a Semiology of Music*. Princeton: Princeton University Press. [2, D2]

Nelson, Hank. 1976. *Black, White and Gold: Goldmining in Papua New Guinea 1878–1930*. Canberra: Australian National University Press. [D2]

Nettl, Bruno. 1956. *Music in Primitive Culture*. Cambridge, Mass.: Harvard University Press. [D2]

———. 1964. *Theory and Method in Ethnomusicology*. New York: Free Press. [D2]

———. 1981. George Herzog: An Eightieth Birthday Appreciation. *Ethnomusicology* 25(3):499–500. [D2]

———. 1982. Alan P. Merriam: Scholar and Leader. *Ethnomusicology* 26(1): 99–105. [D1]

———. 1985. *The Western Impact on World Music: Change, Adaptation, and Survival*. New York: Shirmer Books. [10]

Neu, Jerome. 1987. "A Tear is an Intellectual Thing." *Representations* 19: 35–61. [D3]

New Krymus. 1978. *Krymus Rua*. Cassette. Papua New Guinea NBC B19. [4]

New York Times Magazine. 1990. Confident at 11, Confused at 16. 7 January. [D3]

Nietschmann, Bernard. 1987. Militarization and Indigenous Peoples: The Third World War. *Cultural Survival Quarterly* 11(3):1–16. [D2]

Nietzsche, Friedrich. [1872] 1967. *The Birth of Tragedy out of the Spirit of Music*. New York: Vintage Books. [5, D3]

Niles, Don. 1984, with annual supplements. *Commercial Recordings of Papua New Guinea Music 1949–1983*. Boroko: Institute of Papua New Guinea Studies. [D3]

Norris, Christopher, ed. 1989. *Music and the Politics of Culture*. New York: St. Martins Press. [D2]

Not Drowning, Waving, and the musicians of Rabaul, Papua New Guinea featuring Telek. 1990. *Tabaran*. CD. WEA 903172999.2. [D3]

Noth, Winfried. 1990. *Handbook of Semiotics*. Bloomington: Indiana University Press. [D2]

O'Faircheallaigh, C. 1984. *Mining and Development*. London: Croon Helm. [D2]

O'Meally, Robert. 1991. *Lady Day: The Many Faces of Billie Holiday*. New York: Arcade.

Ortner, Sherry B. 1984. Theory in Anthropology since the Sixties. *Comparative Studies in Society and History* 26(1):126–66. [D1]

———. 1991. Reading America: Preliminary Notes on Class and Culture. In *Recapturing Anthropology*, ed. Richard G. Fox, 163–89. Santa Fe: School of American Research Press. [D3]

Ortner, Sherry, and Harriet Whitehead, eds. 1981. *Sexual Meanings: The Cultural Construction of Gender and Sexuality*. New York: Cambridge University Press. [D1]

Palmer, Robert. 1981. *Deep Blues*. New York: Viking Press. [5]

Panassié, Hughes. [1969] 1979. *Louis Armstrong.* New York: Da Capo. [D1]

Pareles, Jon. 1988a. Pop Passports—At a Price. *New York Times,* August 28. [10]

———. 1988b. Cross Over and Cross Back: You Can Go Home Again. *New York Times,* November 6. [10]

———. 1990. When the Business of Music Becomes Even Bigger. *New York Times,* March 19. [10]

Parks, Gordon. 1976. *Leadbelly.* Film. Paramount Pictures. [D3]

Peirce, Charles Sanders. 1931–58. *Collected Papers.* Cambridge, Mass.: Harvard University Press. [D2]

———. [1893–1902] 1955. *Philosophical Writings.* Ed. J. Buchler. New York: Dover. [4]

Peña, Manuel. 1985. *The Texas-Mexican Conjunto: History of a Working Class Music.* Austin: University of Texas Press. [D3]

Penfield, Wilder, and Lamar Roberts. 1959. *Speech and Brain Mechanisms.* Princeton: Princeton University Press. [1]

Penley, Constance, and Andrew Ross, eds. 1991. *Technoculture.* Minneapolis: University of Minnesota Press. [D2]

Pleasant, Henry. 1969. *Serious Music—And All That Jazz.* London: Victor Gollancz. [D1]

Pollitt, Katha. 1992. Are Women Morally Superior to Men? *The Nation,* 28 December. [D3]

Price, Sally. 1990. *Primitive Art in Civilized Places.* Chicago: University of Chicago Press. [10]

Rabinow, Paul, and William Sullivan, eds. 1987. *Interpretive Social Science: A Reader.* 2d ed. Berkeley: University of California Press. [D1]

Radway, Janice. 1984. *Reading the Romance: Women, Patriarchy, and Popular Literature.* Chapel Hill: University of North Carolina Press. [D3]

Rappaport, Roy. 1979. *Ecology, Meaning and Religion.* Berkeley: North Atlantic Books. [D1]

Rice, Tim. 1987. Toward the Remodeling of Ethnomusicology. With responses by Kay Shelemay, Anthony Seeger, Ellen Koskoff, Dane Harwood, and Richard Crawford. *Ethnomusicology* 31(3). [D1]

Rico (Rico Rodriquez). 1982. What You Talkin' Bout. *On Music and Rhythm.* PVC Records 201. [4]

Ricoeur, Paul. 1978. The Metaphorical Process as Cognition, Imagination, and Feeling. In *On Metaphor,* ed. Sheldon Sacks, 141–57. Chicago: University of Chicago Press. [4]

———. 1979. *The Rule of Metaphor.* Toronto: University of Toronto Press. [D1]

———. 1981. *Hermeneutics and Human Sciences.* New York: Cambridge University Press. [D1]

Ritz, David. 1985. *Divided Soul: The Life of Marvin Gaye.* New York: McGraw Hill. [D3]

Robinson, Deanna Campbell, Elizabeth B. Buck, and Marlene Cuthbert. *Music at the Margins: Popular Music and Global Cultural Diversity.* Newbury Park: Sage. [D3]

Roffler, S. K., and R. A. Butler. 1968. Localization of Tonal Stimuli in the Vertical Plane. *Journal of the Acoustical Society of America* 43(6):1260–66. [4]

Rollwagen, Jack, ed. 1988. *Anthropological Filmmaking*. New York: Harwood. [D1]

Rosaldo, Michelle. 1984. Toward an Anthropology of Self and Feeling. In *Culture Theory: Essays on Mind, Self, and Emotion*, ed. Richard Shweder and Robert LeVine, 137–57. New York: Cambridge University Press. [D3]

Rosaldo, Renato. 1984. Grief and a Headhunter's Rage: On the Cultural Force of Emotions. In *Text, Play and Story: The Construction and Reconstruction of Self and Society*, ed. Edward Bruner, 178–95. Washington, D.C.: American Ethnological Society. [D3]

———. 1989. Imperialist Nostalgia. *Representations* 26:107–22. [10]

Roseman, Marina. 1984. The Social Structuring of Sound: The Temiar of Peninsular Malaysia. *Ethnomusicology* 28(3):411–45. [D1, D3]

———. 1987. Inversion and Conjuncture: Male and Female Performance among the Temiar of Peninsular Malaysia. In *Women and Music in Cross-Cultural Perspective*, ed. Ellen Koskoff, 131–49. Westport: Greenwood Press. [D1]

———. 1988. The Pragmatics of Aesthetics: The Performance of Healing among Senoi Temiar. *Social Science and Medicine* 27(8):811–18. [D1]

———. 1990. Head, Heart, Odor and Shadow: The Structure of the Self, the Emotional World, and Ritual Performance among Senoi Temiar. *Ethos* 18(3):227–50. [D1]

———. 1991. *Healing Sounds from the Malaysian Rainforest: Temiar Music and Medicine*. Berkeley: University of California Press. [D1, D3]

Rosner, Bertram, and Leonard B. Meyer. 1986. The Perceptual Roles of Melodic Process, Contour and Form. *Music Perception* 4:1–39. [D2]

Ross, Andrew. 1989. *No Respect: Intellectuals and Popular Culture*. New York: Routledge.

Rothenberg, David. 1993. *Is it Painful to Think? Conversations with Arne Naess*. Minneapolis: University of Minnesota Press. [D2]

Rouch, Jean. 1974. The Camera and Man. Trans. Steven Feld. *Studies in the Anthropology of Visual Communication* 1(1):37–44. [D1]

———. 1975. The Situation and Tendencies of the Cinema in Africa. Trans. Steven Feld. *Studies in the Anthropology of Visual Communication* 2(1):51–58, 2(2):112–21. [D1]

———. 1978. On the Vicissitudes of the Self: The Possessed Dancer, the Magician, the Sorcerer, the Filmmaker and the Ethnographer. Trans. Steven Feld and Shari Robertson. *Studies in the Anthropology of Visual Communication* 5(1):2–8. [D1]

———. 1989. Conversation between Jean Rouch and Enrico Fulchignoni. Trans. Steven Feld and Anny Ewing. *Visual Anthropology* 2:265–300. [D1]

Rouch, Jean, and Edgar Morin. 1985. Chronicle of a Summer. Trans. Steven Feld and Anny Ewing. *Studies in Visual Communication* 11(1):2–78. [D1]

Rubin, Alton, Sr. 1977. *Rockin' Dopsie and the Twisters*. LP. Rounder Records 6012. [8]

Rubin, Lillian Breslow. 1976. *Worlds of Pain: Life in the Working Class Family*. New York: Basic Books. [D3]

Ruby, Jay. 1982. Ethnography as Trompe l'Oeil: Film and Anthropology. In *A Crack in the Mirror: Reflexive Perspectives in Anthropology*, ed. Jay Ruby and Barbara Myerhoff, 121–31. Philadelphia: University of Pennsylvania Press. [D1]

Ryan, Peter. 1991. *Black Bonanza: A Landslide of Gold*. Melbourne: Hyland House. [D2]

Sahlins, Marshall. 1972. *Stone Age Economics*. Chicago: Aldine. [D3]

———. 1976. *Culture and Practical Reason*. Chicago: University of Chicago Press. [D1]

———. 1985. *Islands of History*. Chicago: University of Chicago Press. [D1]

Sahtouris, Elisabet. 1989. *Gaia: The Human Journey from Chaos to Cosmos*. New York: Pocket Books. [D3]

Said, Edward. 1989. Representing the Colonized: Anthropology's Interlocutors. *Critical Inquiry* 15:205–25. [10]

Sanjek, Russell. 1983. *From Print to Plastic: Promoting America's Popular Music 1900–1980*. Brooklyn: Institute of Studies in American Music. [D3]

———. 1988. *American Popular Music and Its Business: The First Four Hundred Years*. New York: Oxford University Press. [D3]

Santoro, Gene. 1991. James Brown. *The Nation*, 3 June, 748–52. [D1]

Sapir, Edward. 1924. Culture, Genuine and Spurious. *American Journal of Sociology* 29:401–29. [5, 7]

———. 1925. Sound Patterns in Language. *Language* 1:37–51. [4]

———. [1921] 1949. *Language: An Introduction to the Study of Speech*. New York: Harcourt. [D3]

———. [1949] 1985. *Culture, Language and Personality: Selected Essays by Edward Sapir*. Ed. David G. Mandelbaum. Berkeley: University of California Press. [7, D3]

———. 1990. *American Indian Languages*. Ed. William Bright. Berlin and New York: Mouton De Gruyter. [D3]

Sapir, J. David, and Christopher Crocker, eds. 1977. *The Social Use of Metaphor*. Philadelphia: University of Pennsylvania Press. [D1]

Saussure, Ferdinand de. [1916] 1959. *Course in General Linguistics*. New York: Philosophical Library. [D2]

Schafer, R. Murray. 1969. *The New Soundscape*. Toronto: Clark and Cruickshank. [D3]

———. 1970. *The Book of Noise*. Wellington: Price Milburn. [D3]

———. 1977a. *European Sound Diary*. Vancouver: World Soundscape Project. [D3]

———. 1977b. *Five Village Soundscapes*. Vancouver: World Soundscape Project. [D3]

———. 1977c. *The Tuning of the World*. New York: Alfred A. Knopf. [4, 5, 9, 10, D3]

————. 1978. *The Vancouver Soundscape*. Vancouver: World Soundscape Project. [D3]

Schapiro, Meyer. 1953. Style. In *Anthropology Today*, ed. A. L. Kroeber, 287–312. Chicago: University of Chicago Press. [4]

Schieffelin, Bambi B. 1983. Talking Like Birds: Sound Play in a Cultural Perspective. In *Acquiring Conversational Competence*, by E. Ochs and B. B. Schieffelin, 177–84. London: Routledge and Kegan Paul. [4]

————. 1986. Teasing and Shaming in Kaluli Children's Interactions. In *Language Socialization Across Cultures*, ed. B. B. Schieffelin and E. Ochs, 165–81. New York: Cambridge University Press. [4]

————. 1990. *The Give and Take of Everyday Life: Language Socialization of Kaluli Children*. New York: Cambridge University Press. [4, D1–D3]

Schieffelin, Edward L. 1976. *The Sorrow of the Lonely and the Burning of the Dancers*. New York: St. Martins Press. [4, D1, D2]

————. 1980. Reciprocity and the Construction of Reality. *Man* 15:502–17. [D3]

————. 1985a. Anger, Grief and Shame: Towards a Kaluli Ethnopsychology. In *Person, Self, and Experience: Exploring Pacific Ethnopsychologies*, ed. Geoffrey White and J. Kirkpatrick, 168–82. Berkeley: University of California Press. [4, D2]

————. 1985b. Performance and the Cultural Construction of Reality. *American Ethnologist* 12(4):707–24. [4]

————. 1981. The End of Traditional Music, Dance, and Body Decoration in Bosavi, Papua New Guinea. In *The Plight of Indigenous Peoples in Papua New Guinea*, vol. 1, *The Inland Situation*, ed. Robert Gordon, 1–22. Cambridge, Mass.: Cultural Survival, Occasional Paper no. 7. [D3]

Schieffelin, Edward L., and Robert Crittenden. 1991. *Like People You See in a Dream: First Contact in Six Papuan Societies*. Stanford University Press. [D1]

Schiller, Herbert. 1976. *Communication and Cultural Domination*. New York: M. E. Sharpe. [10]

Schmookler, Andrew Bard. 1984. *The Parable of the Tribes: The Problem of Power in Social Evolution*. Boston: Houghton Mifflin. [D3]

Schneider, Albrecht. 1991. Traditional Music, Pop, and the Problem of Copyright Protection. In *Music in the Dialogue of Cultures: Traditional Music and Cultural Policy*, ed. Max Peter Bauman, 302–16. International Music Studies, no. 2. Berlin: International Institute for Comparative Music Studies and Documentation. [10]

Schouten, J. F. 1968. The Perception of Timbre. In *Reports of the Sixth International Congress on Acoustics*. GP-6-2:35–44, 90. Tokyo. [4]

Schuller, Gunther. 1968. *Early Jazz*. New York: Oxford University Press. [D1]

Schweder, Richard, and Robert Levine, eds. 1984. *Culture Theory: Essays on Mind, Self, and Emotion*. Cambridge University Press. [D1]

Sebeok, Thomas A. 1975. *The Tell-Tale Sign: A Survey of Semiotics*. Lisse: Peter de Ridder. [D2]

———. 1991. *Semiotics in the United States*. Bloomington: Indiana University Press. [D2]

———. ed. 1977. *A Perfusion of Signs*. Bloomington: Indiana University Press. [D2]

———. 1978. *Sight, Sound and Sense*. Bloomington: Indiana University Press. [D2]

———. 1986. *Encyclopedic Dictionary of Semiotics*. 3 vols. Berlin: Mouton de Gruyter. [D2]

Seeger, Anthony. 1987. *Why Suyá Sing: A Musical Anthropology of an Amazonian People*. Cambridge: Cambridge University Press. [D3]

———. 1991a. Creating and Confronting Cultures: Issues of Editing and Selection in Records and Videotapes of Musical Performances. In *Music in the Dialogue of Cultures: Traditional Music and Cultural Policy*, ed. Max Peter Bauman, 290–301. International Music Studies, no. 2. Berlin: International Institute for Comparative Music Studies and Documentation. [10]

———. 1991b. Singing Other People's Songs. *Cultural Survival Quarterly* 15(3): 36–39. [10]

———. 1991c. When Music Makes History. In *Ethnomusicology and Modern Music History*, ed. S. Blum, P. Bohlman, and D. Neuman, 23–34. Urbana: University of Illinois Press. [D3]

Seeger, Charles. 1977. *Studies in Musicology 1935–1975*. Berkeley: University of California Press. [2, D2]

Sennett, Richard, and Jonathan Cobb. 1973. *The Hidden Injuries of Class*. New York: Vintage. [D3]

Serafine, Mary Louise. 1988. *Music as Cognition*. New York: Columbia University Press. [D3]

Serematakis, C. Nadia. 1991. *The Last Word*. Chicago: University of Chicago Press. [D3]

Shepherd, John. 1977a. The "Meaning" of Music. In *Whose Music? A Sociology of Musical Languages*, by John Shepherd et al., 53–68. New Brunswick: Transaction. [4]

———. 1977b. Media, Social Process, and Music. In *Whose Music? A Sociology of Musical Languages*, by John Shepherd et al., 7–52. New Brunswick: Transaction. [2]

———. 1982. A Theoretical Model for the Sociomusicological Analysis of Popular Musics. *Popular Music* 2:145–77. [2, 5]

———. 1991. *Music as Social Text*. London: Polity Press. [D2]

Shepherd, John, Phil Virden, Graham Vulliamy, and Trevor Wishart. 1977. *Whose Music? A Sociology of Musical Languages*. New Brunswick: Transaction. [D2]

Schutz, Alfred. 1967. *The Phenomenology of the Social World*. Evanston: Northwestern University Press. [D1]

———. 1970a. *Collected Papers*. 2 vols. The Hague: Nijhoff. [D1]

———. 1970b. *On Phenomenology and Social Relations: Selected Writings*. Chicago: University of Chicago Press. [D1]

———. [1951] 1977. Making Music Together: A Study in Social Relationship. *Social Research* 18(1):76–97. Reprinted in *Symbolic Anthropology,* ed. Janet Dolgin, David Kemnitzer, and David M. Schneider, 106–9. New York: Columbia University Press. [2, 4, D1]

Shweder, Richard, and Robert LeVine, eds. 1984. *Culture Theory: Essays on Mind, Self, and Emotion.* New York: Cambridge University Press. [D3]

Sills, David, ed. 1968. *International Encyclopedia of Social Sciences.* New York: Macmillan/Free Press. [D3]

Silverstein, Michael. 1976. Shifters, Linguistic Categories, and Cultural Description. In *Meaning in Anthropology,* ed. Keith Basso and Henry Selby, 11–55. Albuquerque: University of New Mexico Press. [D2]

———. 1984. On the Pragmatic Poetry of Prose: Parallelism, Repetition, and Cohesive Structure in the Time Course of Dyadic Conversation. In *Meaning, Form and Use in Context: Linguistic Applications,* ed. Deborah Schiffrin, 181–99. Washington, D.C.: Georgetown University Press. [D2]

Simon, Paul. 1986. *Graceland.* CD. Warner Brothers 25447. [8, D3]

Slawson, Wayne. 1985. *Sound Color.* Berkeley: University of California Press. [D2]

Sloboda, John. 1985. *The Musical Mind: The Cognitive Science of Music.* New York: Oxford University Press. [D2]

Sloboda, John, ed. 1988. *Generative Processes in Music: The Psychology of Performance, Improvisation and Composition.* New York: Oxford University Press. [D2]

Small, Christopher. 1977. *Music-Society-Education.* London: John Calder. [D1, D2]

———. 1987. *Music of the Common Tongue: Survival and Celebration in Afro-American Music.* London: John Calder. [D1, D3]

Snell, Bruno. 1953. *The Discovery of Mind: The Greek Origins of European Thought.* Cambridge, Mass.: Harvard University Press. [D1]

Solie, Ruth. 1991. What Do Feminists Want? A Reply to Peter van den Toorn. *Journal of Musicology* 9(4):399–411. [D2]

Solomon, Maynard, ed. 1974. *Marxism and Art: Essays Classic and Contemporary.* New York: Vintage Books. [D1]

Solomon, Robert C. [1976] 1983. *The Passions: The Myth and Nature of Human Emotion.* Notre Dame: University of Notre Dame Press. [4]

———. 1984. Getting Angry: The Jamesian Theory of Emotion in Anthropology. In *Culture Theory: Essays on Mind, Self, and Emotion,* ed. Richard Shweder and Robert LeVine, 238–54. New York: Cambridge University Press. [D3]

Somers, Margaret Ramsay. 1988. Workers of the World, Compare! *Contemporary Sociology* 17(3):325–29. [D3]

Souter, Gavin. 1963. *New Guinea: The Last Unknown.* Sydney: Angus and Robertson. [10]

Spaulding, Mary. 1986. The Irene Olszewski Orchestra: A Connecticut Band. Unpublished M.M. thesis, Department of Music, Wesleyan University. [D2]

Stearns, Marshall W. 1956. *The Story of Jazz*. New York: Oxford University Press. [1]

Steiner, Wendy, ed. 1981. *The Sign in Music and Literature*. Austin: University of Texas Press. [D2]

Stewart, Susan. 1983. Shouts on the Street: Bakhtin's Anti-Linguistics. *Critical Inquiry* 10:265–81. [D1]

Stoller, Paul. 1992. *The Cinematic Griot*. Chicago: University of Chicago Press. [D1]

Stone, Ruth, and Verlon Stone. 1981. Event, Feedback, and Analysis: Research Media in the Study of Music Events. *Ethnomusicology* 25(2):215–25. [D1]

Subotnick, Rose. 1991. *Developing Variations: Style and Ideology in Western Music*. Minneapolis: University of Minnesota Press. [D2]

Szwed, John. 1982. The Sun Never Sets on Music and Rhythm. *Village Voice*, September 7. [10]

Tagg, Philip. 1982. Analysing Popular Music: Theory, Method, and Practice. *Popular Music* 2:37–68. [2]

Talking Heads. 1980. *Remain in Light*. LP. Sire SRK 6095. [8]

———. 1988. *Naked*. CD. Fly/Sire 25654. [8]

Taruskin, Richard. 1988. The Pastness of the Present and the Presence of the Past. In *Authenticity and Early Music*. ed. N. Kenyon, 137–210. London: Oxford University Press. [D2]

Taubin, Amy. 1989. Songs of Innocence and Experience. *Village Voice*, July 11. [10]

Taussig, Michael. 1980. *The Devil and Commodity Fetishism in South America*. Chapel Hill: University of North Carolina Press. [D2]

Taylor, Rogan P. 1985. *The Death and Resurrection Show: From Shaman to Superstar*. London: Anthony Blond. [D1]

Taylor, Roger. 1978. *Art, an Enemy of the People*. Hassocks, U.K.: Harvester Press. [D1, D3]

Tedlock, Barbara. 1984. The Beautiful and the Dangerous: Zuni Ritual and Cosmology as an Aesthetic System. *Conjunctions* 6:246–65. [4]

———. 1986. Crossing the Sensory Domains in Native American Aesthetics. In *Explorations in Ethnomusicology in Honor of David P. McAllester*, ed. Charlotte Frisbie, 187–98. Detroit Monographs in Musicology, no. 9. Detroit: Information Coordinators. [4]

Tedlock, Dennis. 1979. The Analogical Tradition and the Emergence of a Dialogical Anthropology. *Journal of Anthropological Research* 35(4):387–400. [D1]

———. 1983. *The Spoken Word and the Work of Interpretation*. Philadelphia: University of Pennsylvania Press. [D1]

———. 1987. Questions Concerning Dialogical Anthropology. *Journal of Anthropological Research* 43(4):325–37. [D1]

Tejera, Victorio. 1988. *Semiotics from Peirce to Barthes: A Conceptual Introduction*. New York: E. J. Brill. [D2]

Tempels, Reverend Placide. [1945] 1959. *Bantu Philosophy*. Elizabethville, Congo: Lovania; Paris: Collection Présence Africaine. [D1]

Thompson, E. P. 1968. *The Making of the English Working Class*. Harmondsworth: Penguin. [D3]

Thompson, Robert Farris. 1971. *Black Gods and Kings: Yoruba Art at UCLA*. Los Angeles: University of California, Museum and Laboratories of Ethnic Arts and Technology. [D1]

———. 1974. *African Art in Motion: Icon and Act*. Los Angeles: University of California Press. [D1]

———. 1983. *Flash of the Spirit: African and Afro-American Art and Philosophy*. New York: Random House. [D1]

Time. 1983. Closet Carusos: Japan Reinvents the Sing-along. February 28, 47. [9]

Todorov, Tzvetan. 1984. *Mikhail Bakhtin: The Dialogical Principle*. Minneapolis: University of Minnesota Press. [D1]

Tomlinson, Gary. 1982. The Web of Culture: A Context for Musicology. *Nineteenth Century Music* 7:350–62. [D2]

———. 1988. The Historian, the Performer, and Aesthetic Meaning in Music. In *Authenticity and Early Music*, ed. N. Kenyon, 115–36. London: Oxford University Press. [D2]

———. 1993. *Music in Renaissance Magic*. Chicago: University of Chicago Press. [D2]

Tomlinson, John. 1991. *Cultural Imperialism*. Baltimore: John Hopkins Press. [10]

Toorn, Peter van den. 1991. Politics, Feminism, and Contemporary Music Theory. *Journal of Musicology* 9(3):275–99. [D2]

Torgovnick, Marianna. 1990. *Gone Primitive: Savage Intellects, Modern Lives*. Chicago: University of Chicago Press. [10]

Treitler, Leo. 1989a. *Music and the Historical Imagination*. Cambridge, Mass.: Harvard University Press. [D2]

———. 1989b. The Power of Positivist Thinking. *Journal of the American Musicological Society* 42:375–402. [D2]

Turino, Thomas. 1989. The Coherence of Social Style and Musical Creation among the Aymara in Southern Peru. *Ethnomusicology* 33(1):1–30. [D1, D3]

———. 1993. *Moving Away from Silence: Music of the Peruvian Altiplano and the Experience of Urban Migration*. Chicago: University of Chicago Press. [D3]

Turner, Victor. 1967. *The Forest of Symbols*. Ithaca: Cornell University Press. [D1]

———. 1969. *The Ritual Process*. Ithaca: Cornell University Press. [D1, D3]

———. 1974a. *Dramas, Fields, and Metaphors: Symbolic Action in Human Society*. Ithaca: Cornell University Press. [D1]

———. 1974b. Metaphors of Anti-Structure in Religious Culture. In *Dramas, Fields, and Metaphors*. Ithaca: Cornell University Press. [D3]

———. 1975. Symbolic Studies. *Annual Review of Anthropology* 4:145–61. [D1]

Turner, Victor, and Edward Bruner, eds. 1986. *The Anthropology of Experience*. Urbana: University of Illinois Press. [D1]

Tutuola, Amos. 1953. *The Palm Wine Drinkard*. New York: Grove. [D1]

———. 1954. *My Life in the Bush of Ghosts*. London: Faber and Faber. [D1]

———. 1962. *Feather Woman of the Jungle*. London: Faber and Faber. [D1]

Udovitch, Mim, Vince Aletti, and Simon Frith. 1992. In Defense of "Sex." *Village Voice*, 24 November, 25–31. [D3]

Urban, Greg. 1985. The Semiotics of Two Speech Styles in Shokleng. In *Semiotic Mediation*, ed. Elizabeth Mertz and Richard Parmentier, 311–29. New York: Academic Press. [4]

———. 1991a. *A Discourse-centered Approach to Culture*. Austin: University of Texas Press. [4, D2]

———. 1991b. Semiotics and Anthropological Linguistics. *International Encyclopedia of Linguistics*, 3:406–7. New York: Oxford University Press. [D2]

Van Pragg, Joost. 1936. Étude sur la musique de jazz. *Jazz-Hot* 6, January. [1]

Voloshinov, V. N. 1986. *Marxism and the Philosophy of Language*. Cambridge, Mass.: Harvard University Press. [D1]

Wachsmann, Klaus. 1982. The Changeability of Musical Experience. *Ethnomusicology* 26(2):197–216. [2]

Wagner, Jon, ed. 1979. *Images of Information: Still Photography in the Social Sciences*. Beverly Hills: Sage. [D1]

Wagner, Roy. 1981. *The Invention of Culture*. Chicago: University of Chicago Press. [D1]

———. 1986. *Symbols that Stand for Themselves*. Chicago: University of Chicago Press. [4, D1]

Wallace, Anthony F. C. 1974. *Rockdale*. New York: W. W. Norton. [D3]

Wallis, Roger, and Krister Malm. 1984. *Big Sounds from Small Peoples: The Music Industry in Small Countries*. New York: Pendragon. [10, D3]

Walser, Robert. 1990. The Polish-American Polka Mass: Music of Postmodern Ethnicity. Paper presented at the Sonneck Society sixteenth annual conference, Toronto. [D2]

Waterman, Christopher. 1990. *Jùjú: A Social History and Ethnography of a West African Popular Music*. Chicago: University of Chicago Press. [D1, D3]

———. 1991. Jùjú History: Toward a Theory of Sociomusical Practice. In *Ethnomusicology and Modern History*, ed. S. Blum, P. Bohlman, and D. Neuman, 49–67. Urbana: University of Illinois Press. [D3]

Waterman, Richard. 1952. African Influence on the Music of the Americas. In *Acculturation in the Americas*, ed. Sol Tax, 207–18. Proceedings of the Twenty-ninth International Congress of Americanists, vol. 2. Chicago. [1]

Webb, Michael. 1991. Lingua Franca Song and Identity in Papua New Guinea. M.M. thesis, Department of Music, Wesleyan University. Forthcoming, as vol. 3 of the series *Apwitihire: Studies in Papua New Guinea Musics*. Cultural Studies Division of the National Research Institute, Papua New Guinea. [D3]

Webb, Michael, and Don Niles. 1986. *Riwain: Papua New Guinea Pop Songs*. Booklet and 2 cassette tapes. Boroko: Institute of Papua New Guinea Studies. [D3]

Weber, Max. 1958. *The Rational and Social Foundations of Music*. Carbondale: Southern Illinois University Press. [3, D2]

Weiner, Jon. 1991. *Professors, Politics and Pop.* New York: Verso. [D2]

Wickwire, Wendy. 1985. Theories of Ethnomusicology and the North American Indian: Retrospective and Critique. *Canadian University Music Review* 6:186–221. [D1]

Wild, Stephen. 1982. Alan P. Merriam: Professor. *Ethnomusicology* 26(1):91–98. [D1]

Williams, Raymond. 1958. *Society and Culture 1780–1950.* New York: Harper and Row. [D1]

———. 1973a. Base and Superstructure in Marxist Cultural Theory. *New Left Review,* no. 82. Reprinted in *Problems in Materialism and Culture.* London: Verso, 1980. [7]

———. 1973b. *The Country and the City.* New York: Oxford University Press. [D1]

———. 1977. *Marxism and Literature.* New York: Oxford University Press. [4]

———. 1980. *Problems in Materialism and Culture.* London: Verso. [D1]

———. 1981. *The Sociology of Culture.* New York: Schocken Books. [D1]

———. 1989a. *Raymond Williams on Television: Selected Writings.* London: Routledge. [D1]

———. 1989b. *Resources of Hope: Culture, Democracy and Socialism.* London: Verso. [D1]

Willis, Paul. 1977. *Learning to Labor: How Working Class Kids Get Working Class Jobs.* New York: Columbia University Press. [D3]

———. 1978. *Profane Culture.* London: Routledge and Kegan Paul. [4]

Witherspoon, Gary. 1977. *Language and Art in the Navajo Universe.* Ann Arbor: University of Michigan Press. [4]

Wolfe, Charles, and Kip Lornell. 1992. *The Life and Legend of Leadbelly.* New York: Harper Collins. [D3]

Woollacott, J. 1977. *Messages and Meanings.* Milton Keynes: Open University Press. [D2]

Worth, Sol. 1981. *Studying Visual Communication.* Philadelphia: University of Pennsylvania Press. [D1]

Worth, Sol, and Larry Gross. 1974. Symbolic Strategies. *Journal of Communication* 24(4):27–39. [2]

Wright, Robin. 1988. Anthropological Presuppositions of Indigenous Advocacy. *Annual Review of Anthropology* 17:365–90. [D3]

Zemp, Hugo. 1979. Aspects of 'Are 'are Musical Theory. *Ethnomusicology* 23(1):6–48. [2]

———. 1986. *Yootz and Yodel.* Film. [D2]

———. 1988. Filming Music and Looking at Music Films. *Ethnomusicology* 32(3):393–427. [D1]

Zuckerkandl, Victor. 1956. *Sound and Symbol: Music and the External World.* Princeton: Princeton University Press. [4]

Index

References to illustrations are printed in *italics;* references in **boldface** type are to the color photograph section, numbering the photos C1–C8